HELL'S BEND

A MOMENT FROM ETERNITY

BY
ANGIE CAMP
AND
BARRY WESTMORELAND

To Sweet Ali Grace ... &
Always hope ...
Psalm 46:5

9-20-2017

Reviews

"*Hell's Bend* is a gripping, fast-paced story with clever plot twists and some surprising outcomes that entertain and challenge both teen and adult readers." —Tim Wildmon, President, American Family Association

"In this debut novel, Angie Camp crafts a fast-paced, engaging novel with characters who illustrate the best and the worst of Christ-followers. With its surprising plot twists, engaging characters and too-real conflicts, it will keep the reader up late and challenge any serious reader to take inventory of his own faith." —Randall Murphree, Editor, *AFA Journal*, American Family Association

"I love this story. It reminds me that in our mistakes or running from God, He is forever waiting on us. God isn't just sitting there, though; He is continually casting out bait, waiting for us to taste and see The Lord is good! This book will encourage Christians to always love and pursue the lost. Somebody's 'No' today, could be their 'Yes' tomorrow! Great read for the lost and for seekers—especially teen-agers." —Mark Boren, Fellowship of Christian Athletes D1 Rep

"I believe the book *Hell's Bend* will have a tremendous effect on the lives of many young people. The choices they make today can greatly affect their entire lives. To read this book and hear the words come alive from a teenager's experience will be a very powerful tool. I am convinced it will have a profound impact on many lives." —Jim H. Johnson, Sheriff, Lee County, MS

"What an extraordinary book! The captivating plot serves as such an incredible example of how one person's poor decision can affect an entire community. I was reminded of John 10:10 (NLT)— 'The thief's purpose is to steal, and kill, and destroy. My purpose is to give them a rich and satisfying life.' Author Angie Camp communicated so effectively the truth that, though our actions have consequences, the grace of God offers hope and strength to face another day. I cannot comprehend the impact that *Hell's Bend: A Moment From Eternity* will have on readers." —Crystal C. Russell, CPA, business manager, Comedic Storyteller

"To mourn is to know God and His deepest wounds for His Son who bore our infirmities and our sorrows. This intimate, honest, and unforgettable story of tragedy and triumph takes you on a journey, as despair is conquered and the wounded are made whole again." — Merle Temple, *The Redeemed*

"God's grace and mercy is something many of us hold on to as we navigate life. The unexpected ups and downs, the decisions we make and the people's lives we touch and are touched by, help define who we are. *Hell's Bend* is a story that shows all of this to be true. I had intended to read *Hell's Bend* over a week of traveling, but God had another plan. Once I started it, I could not put it down until I was finished! I was riveted by the stories of each person and the twists and turns they each encountered. God has a plan. You're in it. How will you handle the bend in your life?" —Stephen Tybor III, President, Eight Days of Hope/Hope Reigns

"A young man's arrogance and pride—with a spoonful of boyish lust for a classic muscle car—is a formula for disaster. And yet, this is a story of redemption and grace. A novel of pain, brokenness, and second chances…*Hell's Bend* has it all.' —Chad McMahan, Senator, Mississippi Senate District 6

ARe you Choosing God's Best for you?

Acknowledgements

Writing *Hell's Bend* has been an incredible journey, to say the least. It has certainly been a journey which I did not travel alone. Although it was a daunting task at times, my path was filled with encouragers, providers, and supporters. Over the course of the past two years, many have offered their gifts, talents, and experiences in helping get *Hell's Bend* to its finished product. I'd like to publicly thank them for their investment in this God-ordained project that will, without a doubt, enlarge His Kingdom. May you each be abundantly blessed for giving of yourself…all for the glory of God.

Thanks to…

My business partner and friend, Barry Westmoreland, for locking arms with me at the very beginning and financially carrying this assignment from start to finish, along with your prayers and trust in my giftedness. And to your precious wife, Donna, whom God blessed us with in the midst of our journey. She saw the vision, sowed seeds in faith, and served as an incredible prayer warrior along the way.

Editor Caroline Pugh, who turned many of my words into sheer poetry. You are incredibly gifted. Thank you for showing me much grace in my areas of lack.

Editor Jennifer Nanney, who has an incredible eye for dotting every *i* and crossing every *t*. Your sweet spirit and diligence are so refreshing.

My pastor, David Ball of The Anchor Church, who, under the anointing of the Holy Spirit, taught an incredible lesson on hell, then helped to orchestrate the sermon portraying hell in truth, according to God's word. The reality of hell is brought to life and will lead many into the fold, saving their souls from an eternity apart from God. Your passion for the lost creates a hunger in those around you. You walked with my family through the fire and have been a friend who sticks closer than a brother.

Scooter Noland, pastor at Hope Church, who first stepped into my family's life as our youth pastor, leading my boys during difficult times. Your sermon, "God's Guardrails Against Hell," is powerful and was ordained for this book...no doubt. The impact it will have on our young readers will help reveal how important their choices are, not just for themselves, but for many others around them. Thank you for your time and effort in aiding this story's sense of urgency. You have truly been a source of strength to me.

Sheriff Jim H. Johnson, Sergeant Mike Mayhew, and his team of deputies at the Lee County Sheriff's Department, Lee County Coroner Carolyn Green, 911 administrator Paul Harkins, 911 dispatcher Jason Nichols, D.A.R.E. director Sheri Hall, and various medical professionals who aided me in the writing process, ensuring its authenticity. Not only have you helped professionally, you have become life-long friends.

Those who have read, written reviews, and are recommending this work to others on my behalf. You have encouraged me with words of validation and critiqued me with words of wisdom. Bless you for making me better.

Precious family members and friends, some of whom helped to create and shape the personalities of most of the characters in the

ELLS BEND
MOMENT
ERNITY
HELLS BEND
A MOMENT FROM ETERNITY
ANGIE CAMP
ISTIAN
N
5/9/2017

9-20-17

story, along with supporting me through your prayers and encouraging me to press on. You are beautiful and cherished.

Dedication

This book is dedicated to the One True Living God, who took this very broken and imperfect human being and used her to pen His work. Barry and I are still dazed at the thought that God, in His great mercy, would choose to use us for such a task. We delight in Him and pray that He will use this book to redeem the lost, lift the fallen, give hope to the weary, and heal the brokenhearted. The step of faith that we took in accepting His call to complete this work is far less a step of faith than the one He took by entrusting it to us. Of course, He had an advantage. For in His great sovereignty, He knew that by His grace, we would see it through. We are amazed at how God Almighty surely works all things for good and brings beauty from ashes. There is always a purpose in our pain.

To my five biggest blessings…Bryant, Chase, Zeke, Landon, and Millie. God has seen us through. It's time for the harvest. May He find us faithful. Love, Mom.

Chapter 1

Every twelve-year-old boy has a best bud. For me, it's Ross Kelly. We've been best friends since kindergarten. I even remember the first time I saw him. It was our first day of school. He wore denim shorts, sandals, and a red shirt. A not-so-scary dinosaur was plastered across the front. I remember thinking to myself, "Why would that kid wear sandals to school? How does he expect to play ball with those 'sissy shoes' on his feet?"

I also remember noticing the girls huddling and whispering, looking at Ross, then giggling. Ross was kinda shy and didn't have a clue. I guess I'd have to say he was a good-looking guy – golden-brown hair and big, brown, puppy-dog eyes. For some reason, his looks were more appealing to the girls than my blue-eyed, tow-headed self. If I'd been a silly ol' girl, I probably would've liked him, too. My first words to Ross were in the form of the most important question a kindergarten boy could ever say to another kindergarten boy. I walked up to him and asked, "What's your favorite team?" Immediately, Ross responded, "Alabama. What's yours?" That sealed the friendship deal! We hit it off right out of the gate and have been inseparable ever since.

We are both the only children in our families. Having each other has helped fill that emptiness of not having a brother or sister to play with like most kids. To tell you the truth, I don't think we could be any closer if we were actual brothers. For six years we've done every-thing together – Little League baseball, flag football, park-and-rec basketball. You name it, we've done it...together.

Ross is a little awkward and lacks coordination and confidence when it comes to sports, though. Now, that's quite the opposite of *this* guy. I guess that's why our friendship works so well. I do most of the talking and decision-making, and Ross usually follows my lead. I like that – being in control, I mean. It's funny. It doesn't seem to bother him, either.

So here we are. The end days of summer. For almost three months, we've played hoops, hung out, spent the night with each other, and gotten into mischief. Now, what I call mischief is nothing too dangerous, just adventurous fun. Although there was that one time my mom had to call 911...but I won't go there. For the past two years, I have had one adventure weighing heavily on my mind, but even I, THE Jake Adams, have been too afraid to attempt it. Today, after thinking about it constantly, I will conquer my fear! It's time! After all, I'm not a little kid anymore. I am practically a man. I will enter that barn with courage and fulfill a dream that I've had for a long time.

It's a sizzling summer day. The heat reflects off my concrete driveway into our faces and onto our arms and bodies, causing a sweaty mess. But we're twelve, so we don't care. In fact, it makes us feel more like real men. Ross has fouled me on a goal, so I get one free shot. But first, I must complete my ritual. As I prepare to shoot, I align the ball so the large red "J" is on top, facing me, before each bounce. That "J" is important. My dad had drawn it on the ball when he gave it to me. I intently bounce three dribbles. I stop, my eyes returning to the goal. I aim the ball. Three more dribbles. Stop. Eyes on the goal. Aim the ball. Swivel my left foot twice, bend and shoot. Normally, it's a super easy shot, but I find myself strangely distracted by my view of the barn, which sits adjacent to our driveway. When I'm facing the goal, it's in plain view. Man, do I want inside that barn. I must put it out of my mind – I have a game to win at the moment. The barn will have to wait. I refocus, repeat my ritual and shoot.

Nothin' but net! The "J" is kind of like my banner flying on the inside of my head, spurring me on to victory. Ross rebounds the ball and takes it out. We are eye-to-eye. He's thinking too hard about what his next move is gonna be. And I know the move that's comin'; I can read him like a book. Finally, he shifts the ball from his right hand to his left and darts toward the goal. I'm ready for it! You see, Ross is a lefty. Because of his lack of coordination, he has to dribble with his left hand to advance toward the goal. It's a dead give-away every time. Bam! I steal! I turn and shoot and…swoosh!

"Three points, bro!"

"Three points?" Ross yells, his voice cracking. He's twelve. Enough said.

"Yeah, it's three!" I quickly reply with bold confidence. I say it in a deeper tone to try to intimidate him and because I want to make sure that my voice doesn't crack like his did.

Ross recovers the ball and bounces it as hard as he can on the concrete, keeping perfect rhythm with the words he exclaims with indignation, "There's no way that was a three!"

He stands there, staring a hole through me with sweat rolling off his beet-red face and breathing so hard that his chest looks like his lungs are going to explode. I'm beginning to notice that Ross isn't as much of a pushover as he used to be, and I'm not sure how I feel about that. I sternly walk over to him and grab the ball, trying to regain the upper hand. I stand inches from his face and, without looking, point my finger behind me toward the landscaping on the side of the house.

"We both agreed the third bush is our line for the three-point shot!" I nearly scream.

"Oh, no, we didn't!" he replies just as loudly. "You made that up in your own mind! Stop changing the rules as we go along!" he yells, his voice cracking again.

Ross's rant only pushes me to stand my ground even more. "We made that rule three years ago and it hasn't changed!"

We are now in a stand-off, staring each other down, breathing breaths of fury but saying nothing. The racing of my heart is so loud in my head, I'm sure I would not have heard myself if I had chosen to speak. I remind myself, I'm not giving in to him. I just won't do it.

After a pause that seems to last an eternity, Ross finally retreats. "Fine! Just give me the ball!"

I knew he would give in. I hoped he would give in. Ross hates confrontation. I, however, eat it up! It gives me quite an adrenaline rush.

I start to dribble again, coaxing Ross back into the game. Even though I don't mind confrontation, I'm uncomfortable when we argue, and I sure don't like our unfinished game getting off track. Ross slowly begins to come around and returns to his defensive stance. Then…

"Who's thirsty?" a familiar female voice gently yells. And there she is, right on time. My mom, Grace, can always sense our thirst. I'm sure our arguing prompted her. She's always listening. I've come to realize the timing of her entrance isn't a coincidence like I used to think it was.

"Ice-cold Gatorade!" Mom calls enthusiastically. Ross shoots the ball randomly as we run quickly to the cold drinks.

"He scores!" Ross shouts as he throws his arms up in the air, then emits a raspy, throaty sound as he imitates a crowd erupting in enormous applause and cheers after his game-winning shot.

"Too bad that one doesn't count," I repugnantly respond. We each grab a drink and guzzle it, and even that becomes a competition. We stare at each other over our drink bottles, oblivious to the liquid running down our mouths, gulping furiously to finish first. Suddenly Ross's hand shoots into the air with the empty bottle.

"Done! Beatcha!" Ross yells as he tries to catch his breath. He had beaten me! This really ticks me off.

"I wasn't racing," I reply calmly, trying to appear untouched emotionally by his small victory. Although I know it's a given that we were racing, I deny that I was participating in it.

"You boys get along," Mom says gently but firmly. "Life's too short to spend it arguing. Use encouraging words and stop talking smack."

Ross and I look at each other, our brows furrowed. We're thinking the same thing: "Did she really just say the words 'talking smack'?"

"Remember," she continues. "Do unto others."

My mom is a peacemaker. She always tries to point us to the positive. It sounds lame, though, to a twelve-year-old. She really is a good person and very religious. I bet she's the kindest person on planet Earth. Most mornings, she's up before the sun studying her Bible and praying. Once I got up to go to the bathroom, and I heard her talking. I couldn't imagine who in the world she would be talking to at that hour of the morning. I heard her say my name, so I walked quietly down the hallway to hear what she was saying about me. As I drew closer and could hear better, I realized she wasn't on the phone. She was praying! She was praying for me! She was talking to God about me. It felt weird at first, but when I lay back down in my bed, I couldn't stop thinking about what she had said in her prayers for me. The more I thought of her comforting words of thanks and requests of the Lord for my protection, the less weird they seemed. Hearing them actually kinda made me feel good inside. Peaceful like.

Mom likes to go to church a lot. I go sometimes, mainly just to see a really cute girl, Chloe. She doesn't go to my school, so the only way I can get a glimpse of her and try to impress her is to go to Sunday school. Usually, rejection is about all I get from Chloe, but a guy's gotta try, right?

Sometimes I just sleep in on Sunday mornings like my dad. He knows it's important to Mom, but he says church just ain't his thing. Mom asks him sometimes if he wants to go with her, but he always very politely declines. Except on special occasions, like Easter Sunday and Christmas, to hear Mom singing in the pageant…

Sorry! I kinda got distracted. It's a twelve-year-old boy thing, I guess.

So, back to the Gatorade and basketball. Ross and I stand in the driveway, our thirsts quenched and our bodies resting a bit and enjoying a cool-down. I start to zone out as Mom and Ross chit chat.

"Ross, did you enjoy the D.A.R.E. Camp last week?" Mom asks.

"Oh, yes, ma'am," Ross says.

"Well, good! So what did you enjoy the most?"

"Sergeant Mayhew showing me some really cool hockey moves. Even though we don't have a hockey team, it was still cool. He used to be a professional hockey player. He played for the T-Rex. He's a really nice guy."

"I've heard Mitch talk about him. I believe he's from Canada, right?"

"Yes, ma'am." He begins to laugh. "He spent more time in the penalty box than he did on the ice."

"Why is that?" Mom asks. She doesn't understand how the game of hockey works.

"He liked to brawl quite a bit," Ross says.

"Oh, I see…Kind of like a time-out for hockey players?"

Ross laughs, realizing she doesn't quite understand how accurate she is. "Yes, ma'am. I guess you could call it that."

"Well, I'm going back inside and leave you boys to your game," Mom says.

She notices my silence because it's quite unusual. I'm never at a loss for words or comments, especially when I get the opportunity to be sarcastic.

Mom waves her hand in front of my face while snapping her fingers. "Earth to Jake," she says. Ross's laughter, along with the snaps of Mom's fingers, grabs my attention.

"What's so funny?" I ask, feeling paranoid and fearing I was the object of his laughter, because I wasn't sure what I might have done while my mind drifted.

"Your mom," Ross replies, shaking his head. "She's a hoot!"

"I was just asking Ross about D.A.R.E. Camp," Mom says.

"I thought it was pretty lame…little kid stuff. I got stuck with Deputy Daniels. He's such a little dweeb."

"Well, I thought it was cool," Ross says, defending the program.

"I thought it was a wonderful opportunity for you guys," Mom says, messing up my hair.

"You always side with Ross," I complain.

Mom looks at Ross and winks. She collects our empty Gatorade bottles and gives us each another one.

"OK. Carry on. Oh, and Ross, come inside before you leave. I've got some freshly-baked banana nut bread for you to take home to Kate." Mom returns inside the house.

"Yes, ma'am," Ross replies.

We stand there sipping on the extra drinks. Our guts feel like they are going to burst. The cool-down doesn't last long standing in the blazing sun. My thoughts shift again to the barn. Even while I'm resting, I'm thinking of it. You know, I've been waiting for two years to get inside that barn, and I'm not waiting any longer. Today is the day! I look to make sure Mom has completely disappeared. With a slight nod that I'm sure was invisible to Ross, I make the decision. I'm goin' in. I'm slightly surprised at myself, but the time seems right. "It's time to put up or shut up," I whisper under my breath, as if to give myself a pep talk.

"Hey, Ross, come here," I hear myself say in a voice somewhere between a whisper and a low mumble. "I wanna show you something."

I'm sure from the sound of my voice, Ross knows immediately it's something we shouldn't do, but it doesn't stop him from joining me.

"What now?" he asks with one part dread and two parts curiosity.

"Quick, before Mom sees us! Follow me!" I whisper as loudly as I can, taking off in a run toward the barn. I can see that Ross is hesitant and keep motioning for him to join me. I stop at the barn door and wait for Ross to catch up, but I can tell he's unsure. He's having mixed feelings about it, I'm sure, yet I know his curiosity will win out, as well as his pride. He is taking forever!

"Christmas is gonna get to me before you do!" I complain. Ross sticks with his same steady pace, never looking up. My rushing him isn't helping at all. Anxiousness was about to get the best of me. I feel a frustrated scream work its way up my throat but try to suppress it, because I know my mom would hear. It wasn't necessary, thank goodness, because Ross had finally reached me.

Stopping and staring at the ground for a moment, Ross seems like he's thinking, then he slowly lifts his eyes toward me. "What is it?"

He sounds as if he's afraid of my answer. I step up to Ross very closely. His puppy-dog eyes stare at me intently. I stare right back at him for a moment, and then, with all seriousness, I say, "What I'm about to show you, you cannot ever share with anyone. Understand?"

With his eyes still fixed on mine, Ross slowly nods his head to say yes.

"If my dad knew we were doing this, he would kill us!" I inform him, reinforcing the importance of keeping quiet.

"Then why are we doing it?" Ross asks, confused.

I look at him with a big grin and reply, "Because...I want to. Come on – help me get this two-by-four off here so we can open the doors. Be careful not to get a splinter."

Using our fists, we pound that board up from the wood blocks that hold it tightly in place. I didn't think it would be this hard to open. We keep at it. The longer we work at it, the more the anticipation grows. How desperately we need inside now! Finally, with bloody fists and sweat once again running down our faces, it breaks loose!

"Thank goodness!" Ross exclaims. "I didn't think we would ever get that off!"

"Where there's a Jake, there's a way," I say, relieved.

We toss the board over to the side and slowly begin to open the doors. We had worked so hard getting that two-by-four free, but now the reality of getting inside causes a little bit of fear to surface. For Ross, it's fear of the unknown. For me, it is fear of getting my bottom worn out if this goes wrong.

"These doors are heavier than they look!" Ross comments as he strains to pull the doors open.

"Hang on," I said. "I've got an idea. Let's just pull one door open at a time together."

"Yeah, that's a great idea, Jake."

Finally, after several minutes of tugging and pulling and moaning and groaning, we conquer! We're already nervous as house cats, then all of a sudden, a bird flies up to the rafters and we about jump out of our skins! Our nerves must be playing tricks on us, because the fluttering of that bird's wings sounds like machine guns going off, and I don't know how we manage not to yell out loud except for the fact that we are in such shock. Nothing comes out of our mouths, although I'm sure they are wide open. My knees shake as if I'm in the middle of Antarctica. As we stand there regaining our composure, I begin looking around at the old place. It has been over two years since I have been allowed to come in here. It was made off limits to me, and I had forgotten how it looks on the inside…and how it smells. Immediately, I notice my grandfather's old saddle sitting on the "half door," as I used to call it, which leads to the stall that belonged to his favorite horse, Crimson Rose.

I loved to help brush her down after an evening run. She was a very gentle horse. I still hate thinking about the day they had to put her down. Grandfather never got another horse after her. And there's her bridle hanging on a nail. I don't remember us having to ever really use that thing. Crimson Rose seemed almost human. I think she understood English. We could just tell her what to do and she'd obey.

In the corner is the bucket I used to feed her oats. It's sitting on the hay bale I sat on to watch Grandfather clean the poop out of her stall. I don't know why I sat there to watch that, or to smell it.

Now, the barn has been transformed into a shop where my dad houses his project. I've heard him talk about it many times, but I've never seen it, except in pictures before Dad started restoring it. I've spent countless nights lying in bed wondering what it must look like. Today, I won't have to wonder anymore.

The barn seemed to be a lot bigger before. With this huge object in the middle of it, there's hardly enough room to breathe.

"It's so dusty in here," Ross complains. "Look at all those spider webs!"

"I'm sure cleaning is the last thing on my dad's mind while he's working," I say. *How can Ross worry about spider webs at a time like this?*

At last, we focus our attention on the huge article in the middle of the barn. Ross had stood silently as I took that short trip down memory lane, but now that I'm obviously focused on the object, he asks the question he's been holding inside for several minutes, which I'm sure felt like an eternity to him.

"Jake, what is that big thing?" he blurts out.

I can tell he has been holding that in.

"Shhh! Would you be quiet? Help me take off the tarp," I order in my harsh, whispery voice.

"Are you sure?" Ross asks nervously.

"Just do it, all right? You grab the back and I'll grab the front."

We begin to pull off the tarp. Dust fills the air. It's been sitting here a while. I start coughing. Dust covers us, in our mouths and in our eyes. We have to let our tears flush out the dust particles so we can see again.

"That's nasty!" Ross exclaims.

"Just keep at it. We're almost there." I didn't think about it being this hard and taking so long. It went a whole lot faster in my mind. *Next time, I'll have to remember that*, I think to myself.

The tarp is off, and now we stand there in awe of what sits before us.

"Oh, wow! Jake!"

"Would you hush already? Get in!"

"What?"

"I said get in."

We very carefully and quietly open the doors. I am on the driver's side, of course.

"Wow! Where did your dad get this car?" Ross asks.

"He's had it for years and years."

"I haven't ever seen one like this."

"It's a 1979 Trans-Am. My grandparents gave it to him for his high school graduation. My dad loves this car. He said it was one of the coolest cars back in the day."

"It's still cool!" Ross exclaims.

"Dad said it used to be gold metallic, but the paint started to fade and peel. He's spent the past two years restoring it."

"I can't believe it! Why did he change the colors to red and white?"

"That's the colors of the Alabama Crimson Tide, baby!"

"Oh, yeah! Duh!" Ross replies, realizing the obvious.

We do our "cool" handshake for which only Ross and I know the combination. We made it up ourselves. Then we end it by calling out our nickname for each other in rhythm. "Bama Bros!"

"Wanna take her for a spin?" I ask.

"Huh?" Ross asks, puzzled.

"Just for pretend."

"You bet!" Ross replies, eyes wide open.

I pretend to start the car by using the proper motor noises with my mouth. "Brummmm."

Ross gives me his approval with a thumbs-up. Our imaginations begin to kick in. We are now teenagers cruising down the main strip where all the cool people hang out on the weekend. I start some dialogue with all the girls who are fine and want to be mine.

"Hey, Chloe girl!" I shout to a five-foot-high stack of hay bales. "How you doin'? Oh, you like me now, huh?"

Chloe doesn't even acknowledge me at church. So I'm just gonna ignore her and move on.

"Oh, yeah...hey, baby! Like the ride?" Ross chimes in.

"That's right. It's Ross Daddy in the Trans-Am. Call me!" Ross says, holding his hand to his ear as if it is a phone. He then turns to inspect the interior. "Jake, man, she purrs like a kitten."

"Like a lion," I correct him.

Our attention span usually lasts only about five minutes. Today, we are overcome with curiosity and begin to explore all the car's gadgets. Ross runs his hands over the dashboard area.

"What's this thing?" Ross inquires.

"I'm not sure what it's called," I reply, "but my dad said it's something they used to play music on. Weird-lookin', huh?"

"I've never seen a CD player shaped like that before," Ross says.

27

Well, he's on the right track; after all, it is an eight-track *player*. We both continue to check out the interior of the car until Ross looks up and sees something that absolutely freaks him out.

"You gotta be kidding me!" he exclaims. "Windows on the ceiling?"

"Yeah, and you can take them out, too!" I explain.

That would be the T-tops.

"Where would you keep 'em?" Ross questions.

"I dunno…Stick 'em in the trunk, I guess."

Ross sits there for a minute trying to figure out how in the world those things would come out and fit in the trunk.

"Oh, well, back to Fantasy Land!" I say. "Whammmmm …whammmmm!"

"What are you doing?" Ross chuckles.

"I'm pretending to be in a race going around a dangerous, curvy road," I explain.

I whip the steering wheel to the left, then quickly whip it to the right.

"I'm winning a race at Hell's Bend!" I say excitedly. "Don't distract me! Hold on to your seat!"

"Hey, you better slow down!" Ross warns. "You don't want to hurt this baby!"

"Don't worry – this car was built for speed!"

I pretend to turn on the radio. We begin to sing the lyrics to a song that is very fitting for the occasion – a song about fast cars and death-defying stunts.

We may not live through it, but the thrill is worth it!

"Hey, Ross, from now on, that will be our theme song!"

"You got it!" Ross agrees. "Boy, do we sound awful!"

We both burst out laughing – laughing at ourselves and each other. Man, how I wish in this moment that time would fast-forward to the day when I'm no longer pretending to drive this awesome car, getting all the girls and winning all the races, but when it is a reality!

"Ross, one day, I'm gonna drive this car." I reposition myself and look straight ahead.

"Floor it, Jake!" Ross yells.

"You got it, Bama Bro! Whammmmm! Hold on, Ross!"

"Woo-hoo! Watch that curve, Jake!"

I spin the wheel to the left, and we lean to the right, entering our imaginary curve.

"Here comes another one!" I warn, quickly steering right. We instinctively lean to the left.

"How fast are you going?" Ross asks.

"Whammmm…Whammmm…"

Whammmm…

The sound of the engine is no longer from my overly-animated pre-teen mouth, but from the actual engine of that 1979 Trans-Am. It seems like only yesterday I was dreaming about being in the driver's seat, but here I am, an eighteen-year-old high school senior, sporting a blue letterman jacket while trying once again to prove I'm number one.

"Jake, how fast are you going?" asks a frantic Ross Kelly, also a senior wearing an identical blue letterman jacket. Again he's my passenger, but this time, he sees that his co-captain, teammate and best friend since kindergarten is out of control.

"Man, what are you doing?" he asks. "Are you crazy?"

I focus intently at the dark highway before me and completely disregard Ross's questions.

"Jake, please slow down! You're gonna kill us!"

I continue to ignore Ross. It's as if I don't even hear him. My pride has really gotten the best of me tonight, and everything rational that Ross has been saying to me has fallen on deaf ears. My face is cocked straight ahead, and my white-knuckled hands tightly grip the steering wheel. Six years have passed since we had pretended to race this car. The only scary thing about it then was that my dad might catch us. Now, though, the fear is much greater, and so is the risk. Due to my selfish, short-sighted, teenage choices, I would soon learn how tragic consequences could be – so much that it would shake our community to its core. Ultimately, I would be the one responsible for it all.

Chapter 2

In hindsight, I realize it had been so easy to see — so clear. I look back to as recently as a few months earlier and can see how God had been showing us an escape. He was trying to intervene through the prayers of my mom, but I had remained steadfastly cocky and obnoxiously self-absorbed.

Music blared through white earbuds tucked tightly inside Ross's ears. The methodical, driving beat of the drums and the squealing guitar riffs mixed randomly to create a din that had wound its way into every nook and cranny of his head. Taped on the wall with no attention to uniformity were edgy posters displaying tattooed bodies and overly-moussed hair. There was no denying that Ross was a fan of heavy metal.

In what could be described as a bit of irony, the well-planned lyrics took refuge underneath the noise of the instruments, never to be heard by even the sharpest-eared teenager. One could only assume this to be a good thing, considering the questionable message being conveyed. And the wonder in all of it was the fact that Ross remained sound asleep.

Sunday morning had arrived. Kate Kelly – the beautiful, tall and slender, brown-eyed brunette and mother of the head-banging music lover – stood at his bedroom door knocking, earnestly trying to wake him. She quickly glanced at her white-gold watch, a wedding gift from her husband, Lance, nearly 21 years ago. Who knew then, while they dated and consequently fell in love, that one day they would sound like their parents, shunning their children's music. She smiled to herself and shook her head. This wasn't the first time she had experienced difficulty waking Ross. But she took comfort in the fact that these teenage years and the troubles they brought would fade with college looming ahead, and Ross would metamorphose into a productive, responsible young man who could actually wake himself up for class and church.

Kate snapped back into the present and realized church would start soon. Her mild raps on the door had not proven productive, and she now resorted to forceful blows with her fists.

"Ross, it's time to get dressed for church! Can you hear me? You need to get up right now and get in the shower or you'll be late!"

She waited a few moments for a response. Nothing.

"Come on, son, you're going to make us late. You told me to wake you up, so here I am!"

Kate stood silently for a moment and again listened for a response. Now she heard the extremely faint, tinny sound of heavy metal from the tiny headphones.

There is no way on God's green earth it's possible for Ross to sleep through that, she thought.

A few miles away, Lauren dialed Ross's cell phone. He had asked her to call him that morning to make sure he was up in time for church. She wondered to herself why his mother couldn't do it, but she suspected it was a slick way to get them to talk.

The two had struck up quite a friendship. The sweet affection between them was quite noticeable to Lauren's friends, who had started asking questions and seemed to support her, as she had not dated anyone seriously in a while.

So she sat on the edge of her bed, dressed, face made up and ready to go, but no sign of a response from Ross. Twice she had dialed and let it ring until his voicemail picked up. Determined, she continued the process, hoping to eventually get an answer.

"Lauren, breakfast is ready!" announced her mother from the kitchen. Margaret McKay was a beautiful, fair-skinned Irish woman with big blue eyes and blonde, mid-length, layered hair. Funny thing, she was born on St. Patrick's Day. It was apparent why she referred to Lauren as her "mini me." Margaret, often called Meg by her closest friends, was a single mom of two: Lauren and her freckle-faced, strawberry-blonde brother, Luke. According to Lauren, her brother was a goofy, middle-school-aged boy who spent half of his time bragging about being the man **of** the house and the other half complaining about being the only man **in** the house. Tragedy five years earlier had left Margaret in the place of being Mother and Father. She consistently made her faith part of her children's lives and took care of their needs as well as she knew how – physically, mentally, emotionally and spiritually.

Lauren continued to blow up Ross's phone with calls as she paced the floor, chewing her fingernails as she often did when frustrated and anxious.

"Don't bite those nails," Lauren heard Margaret rebuke playfully. She looked up to find her mother at the door. Lauren sat on the edge of her bed, rocking back and forth with nervous energy. "Come on in," she said.

Margaret had been watchful yet silent over the past few weeks as she observed Lauren's behavior while with Ross. Lauren's feelings for him were obvious. While endearing in one sense, it was bothersome in another. Margaret had real concerns about the condition of Ross's soul. She and Ross's mother, Kate, had been friends since grade school. They cheered together for varsity football, served in youth choir and were bridesmaids in each other's weddings. She had tremendous respect for Ross's parents. They truly walked out their faith. Yet, in Ross, although he was very respectful, kind-hearted and good-natured, she'd never seen nor heard anything of his own personal salvation experience. Margaret felt a conversation needed to take place, but she wanted to be careful in handling it, knowing Lauren's reaction would depend on her approach – when the time was right.

But for the moment, Lauren sat quietly, contemplating her next move. This girl didn't give up easily. Lauren's looks were deceiving. She may have been a petite, fair-skinned, blue-eyed blonde, but on the inside, she possessed the heart of a lioness. She was relentless in her efforts to rehabilitate Ross. Failure was incomprehensible to Lauren. She was an honor student and student body president, had leading roles in the school musicals, was president of the Bible club, ran circles around the guys when it came to computers, and was now a self-proclaimed missionary to Ross Kelly. The word "over-achiever" certainly fit. Lauren was quite the go-getter, and rejection didn't intimidate her at all. She simply used it to fuel her motivation. Jake Adams had met his match with her. In a lot of ways, Lauren was the female version of him, which explained a lot of their clashing.

The two stayed in a constant tug-of-war, and Ross was the rope. Lauren was the angel on Ross's right shoulder, and Jake was the devil on his left.

Finally, it dawned on her. *Airplane mode*, she said to herself. *His phone's in airplane mode.*

This wasn't uncommon for Ross to do. He loved his music and was notorious for blocking texts and calls on his iPhone while listening to it. He often slept with it that way, which was odd to most of his friends who would rather not eat than to miss a call or a text.

Lauren decided to make another call, but this time to someone who hopefully could get Ross to respond.

———————————

Kate Kelly had retreated from the battle of waking Ross and resumed her Sunday morning duties in the kitchen. As she mixed the batter for pancakes, the back door opened and caught her attention. Just as she expected, it was her husband, Lance. His dark hair with gray filtering in through his sideburns accentuated his deep-set blue eyes. He was a little above average in height with a medium-built but well-maintained body. His Sunday morning had started early with Brotherhood Breakfast at church.

"How was it?" Kate asked, giving Lance a peck on the check.

"Very good," he replied. "Our guest speaker was JJ Jasper, the national Christian radio host. Very encouraging and inspiring." He returned Kate's affection with a hug.

"I love listening to him on AFR," Kate said. "Funny guy."

"Yep. That's the one. Powerful message. He shared his testimony about the loss of their only son, and how the Lord had helped them to grieve. I bought his book," he said, handing Kate a brightly-colored hardback book.

The title read *Losing Cooper, Finding Hope to Grieve Well*. Kate stared at the book's cover – the blond-haired little boy sporting a royal blue baseball t-shirt against a field of grass. She traced her finger around the outline of his sweet face.

"Oh, bless them," Kate said sympathetically. "I've heard his wife share their story. I think her name is Melanie? How do you ever get over something like that?" she asked rhetorically.

"I don't think you do," Lance said as he stared over Kate's shoulder at the face of the deceased child. The thought was unnerving for him.

"Changing the subject, is Ross up yet?"

"No. I've tried but failed," Kate said.

"Let me give it a shot," Lance said.

Kate's cell phone lit up as it rang. The caller ID read *Lauren calling*.

"That won't be necessary," Kate said. She turned her phone around so Lance could read the display. "Here's our cavalry now," Kate said.

Lance grinned. "Uh-oh."

"Hello, Lauren," Kate answered.

"Good morning, Mrs. Kelly. I've been trying to call Ross, but he's not answering. I think his phone may be on—"

"Airplane mode?" Kate interjected.

"Yes, ma'am," Lauren giggled.

"I've had no luck, either. I could make out some music from those earphones. If he's wearing them, he wouldn't hear a tornado ripping through his room. Although it probably looks like one has touched down in there."

Lauren laughed. Kate was so easy to talk to. "My brother's room is the same way," she replied empathetically. "Ross had asked me to call him to make sure he's up for church on time. I hope that's OK."

"Absolutely! I'm glad he has someone to hold him accountable. I've been trying to wake up that boy for half an hour. I need some reinforcement. You are right on time, girl! Let me take him the phone. That is, if I can wake him."

"OK, thanks!"

As Kate walked to Ross's room to hand him the phone, Lauren felt a little giddy. In the meantime, she saw her mother at the door again – a reminder about breakfast. Trying to avoid being short with her but not wanting to risk missing a conversation with Ross, she held up an index finger, smiled, and winked, indicating she needed just a moment.

Kate rapped on the door once more and yelled, "Lauren's on the phone for you!"

Within seconds, the music was silenced and the door opened. *Could it be that the magic word was "Lauren"?* Kate thought to herself. Ross quickly took the phone from his persistent mother.

"Hey, let me call you back on my phone," Ross said.

Ross handed Kate's phone back to her. Lance and Kate stood at his door with ear-to-ear grins. Ross carefully avoided eye contact as he stepped back into his room and shut the door. Kate and Lance remained at the door, waiting for an opportunity to playfully tease their son. Leaning into the door, they tried to eavesdrop.

On the other side, Ross lay back down on his bed and tried hard to speak in a way that made him sound as if he had been up for a while. Although their conversation was brief, it was invigorating to him. He continued to lie in bed for a minute, trying to get his bearings. As his mind returned to the present, he looked at his phone to check the time. Realizing how late it was, he leaped out of bed, grabbed some clothes, swung open the door and was startled to find his parents still standing there. Their smiles were a dead give-away that they knew what had transpired behind that closed door. Ross attempted to calmly pass them, hoping there would be no dialogue, but apparently it was too good an opportunity for them to pass up.

"Wow! I had no idea that cute little blond-headed, blue-eyed thing had the power to raise the dead," Kate declared sarcastically but light-heartedly. Ross immediately threw his hands up in the air and shouted, "It's a miracle – hallelujah!" then cut his eyes toward his father and winked. Kate and Lance could not contain themselves and burst out laughing.

"Good cover, son!" Lance said and returned the wink.

Trying to regain her composure, Kate followed up with a reminder for Ross to hurry.

———————————

Lauren sat in a trance-like state. She couldn't help but giggle as she mulled over her conversation with Ross. How funny it was listening to him trying to sound wide awake, knowing he was dead asleep only seconds before. Her mother's voice broke the spell.

"Well, any progress?" Margaret asked, her head peeping in Lauren's doorframe.

"Mission accomplished," Lauren replied confidently, as if there was any question she would triumph.

"Good," her mother responded. "Now let's eat."

"Yes, ma'am," Lauren said with a salute. "By the way, where is Luke? I haven't seen him all morning," she remarked with surprise as they made their way to the kitchen table.

"He's picking up his room. After church today, his Sunday school class is going out to eat and then bowling. I told him he couldn't go anywhere until his room was spotless."

"Spotless? Don't you think that's a little unrealistic?"

"Of course, but I figure by telling him spotless, it will get it to a level of tolerable."

"Smart," Lauren commented. "I'd say judging by the smell, there is probably something growing in there."

"I've had the same thought," her mother said. "You think the Biology teacher at school might want it for an experiment for lab class?"

"That's quite possible," Lauren chuckled. "I'd just be too embarrassed for him to know it came from a room in my house."

"You're right. We probably need to just keep that under wraps."

The two continued to snicker over the thought. Their laughter could be heard all over the house, stirring Luke's curiosity. He desperately wanted to know what the chuckles were about, but at the same time he had a strong feeling that he was probably the punch line.

"What are you two cackling about?" he asked with disdain, walking into the nook of their cozy kitchen. His hair was in disarray, only one foot was covered with a sock, and his pajama shirt covered only one shoulder.

Ignoring his question, Margaret asked, "How's that room looking?"

"It looks OK," Luke replied.

"OK enough to persuade me to allow you to go with your Sunday school class after church?"

Luke immediately became defensive. "Mom, why don't you hammer Lauren about her room the way you do me?"

"I don't have to 'hammer' her," Margaret replied, making air quotes around the word *hammer*. "She keeps her room neat and organized."

"Yeah, bro," Lauren added. "Let's face it. You are a slob."

"And you are so adopted!" Luke shouted in aggravation. "Mom, are you going to allow her to talk to your boy like that?"

Undermining his indignation, Margaret redirected the conversation.

"Back to my original question…"

Realizing he was fighting a losing battle, Luke retreated to his demolition area as the females in the house continued their conversation over breakfast. As their chuckles simmered down, Margaret's demeanor quickly changed to a more serious mode, a move Lauren noticed and found almost frightening if there had been the slightest chance she had done something wrong, which she proudly knew she hadn't.

"Lauren, I want to talk to you about Ross for a minute."

"OK, shoot."

"Honey, you know I like Ross. He's very polite and sweet and comes from a fine Christian family. But from what I know about him and based on what you have shared with me, I'm not convinced that he is a believer."

Lauren shifted in her seat.

Her mother continued. "I know your feelings for him are stronger than friendship, and I just want you to be careful. You need to consider God's word on this. In 2 Corinthians 6:14, it says that we are not to be unevenly yoked to unbelievers. We see good fruit in the lives of his parents, which makes it obvious they are believers. I just don't believe Ross has made their faith his own. Honestly, Lauren, you should never allow your feelings for someone to grow if you wouldn't consider marrying him."

Caught off guard with her mother's comments, Lauren immediately felt the need to defend herself and Ross. Although Margaret had pegged her perfectly, she refused to admit her feelings for him.

"I know that, Mom. Don't worry. We're only friends, and I wouldn't allow myself to become serious about anyone unless he was a believer. I just want to be there to influence Ross in the right direction – toward the cross. Regardless of my feelings, he needs to come to know Christ."

Lauren felt her response sounded as if it were scripted and rehearsed in the event that someone should ever call her out on her feelings for Ross. But the person who had called her out on it was the very one who knew her best...her mother.

Margaret indulged her. "I agree. But remember, you are not the Holy Spirit. I am glad that you're being a good friend to him. I do think a lot of him and his parents. I just want you to keep your relationship with Ross in line with God's word. In the meantime, we can continue to pray for him."

The use of the pronoun *we* stood out vividly to Lauren, which showed that her mom was truly on her side. As she leaned over to give Margaret a hug, she said, "Thanks, Mom."

"For what?" Margaret asked.

"For loving me so much."

"I **do** love you so much."

Returning to the kitchen, Luke walked in just in time to see the embrace between his mother and sister. Pretending to be repulsed, he teased them. "Now, that's a Facebook profile pic if I ever saw one. You want me to grab your phone and snap it for you?"

"How 'bout that room of yours?" Margaret interjected to bring him down a few notches. "I'm sure it's not 'picture perfect.' "

"Ha-ha-ha, Mom! Well, you can walk in there now…and breathe." Understanding that he stood alone, he had resorted to making fun of himself.

"OK, well, you sit down and eat, and I'll go inspect your room," Margaret said. "Now, where is my gas mask?"

Caught off guard by her mom's quick wit, Lauren began laughing with a mouthful of milk. Unable to swallow, she spewed it all over the table…and Luke. The look on his face was priceless. Margaret and Lauren began to snicker uncontrollably.

"That's it! It's on now!" Luke yelled in disbelief. His immediate reaction was to do what any normal middle-school-aged boy would do. He leaned over, grabbed Lauren in a headlock and gave her a noogie.

"Stop! You're messing up my hair!" Lauren screamed.

"Looks better now!" Luke yelled.

"OK, you two, that's enough," Margaret refereed. "Let's get done so we can go."

Luke was incensed and refused to just let it go. "You know, it's really hard having to live with two women. Actually, it's torture! I need a man cave!"

The shock of his outburst brought silence. Then, out of nowhere, the two women again erupted in laughter – the two women from whom Luke needed to escape!

"Aw…come here, Mommy's baby boy," Margaret mocked, trying to change his mood and get a grin out of him before having to enter the doors of God's house. It wasn't working. Luke had reached the point of no return.

Only one thing could repair the damage inflicted by the traumatic teasing at the hands of the two females Luke was forced to endure. Only one remedy had proven itself consistent in bringing him back to a place of solace, even under the direst circumstances. Margaret made sure to keep it on hand at all times. The cure…Rocky Road.

"Mom, you check Luke's room," Lauren said, "and I'll get the ice cream."

Chapter 3

Sunday mornings at my humble abode, 1137 Orchid Circle, were the best. I got to sleep in. My nose was always my alarm clock on those sleep-in mornings. I'd wake up to the scrumptious smells of fresh coffee brewing and applewood-smoked bacon frying and would know how long I could stay in my comfortable bed until called to breakfast.

I loved listening to Dad update Mom on the latest sports news. I always got a kick out of listening to her pretending to be interested and trying to have a conversation about it. I'm sure Dad appreciated her effort.

This particular morning proved to be different. My mom was always a "morning person," usually rising before the sun. "Early in the morning will I rise up and seek Thee," was her response whenever I asked her why she never slept in on Sundays. But this particular Sunday, Mom wasn't up early. She made it to church on time, but she was definitely off her routine.

Along with the smell of coffee, silence filled the kitchen of the Adams home, with the exception of an occasional ruffling of paper as Mitch turned the pages of the *Daily Journal*'s Sunday morning sports section. Now he stared intently at one headline in particular:

AP Chooses Alabama as Number One Pre-Season Pick

"Now that's what I'm talking about," he whispered under his breath, almost bursting with pride. The silence was soon broken by the clomping of high heels stepping quickly up the hallway and toward the kitchen. Mitch loved that sound. It set up his favorite moment on Sunday morning, the moment he got to check out his bride of twenty years. To him, Grace was always a ravishing beauty, from the flawless makeup that accentuated her blue eyes to her perfectly-styled blonde hair. Her wardrobe was always conservative and sophisticated yet very stunning.

However, out of all of her attire, his favorite thing she wore was her beautiful smile. Expecting to see *his* total package round the corner, Mitch pulled down the newspaper and called out enthusiastically, "Good morning, Sunshine!"

His broad smile quickly turned into a look of confusion when her appearance lacked its usual glamour. Straying hair, half-applied makeup, and a very downcast countenance – it wasn't at all what he expected. This was not normal. Now his excitement in sharing with her the sports headlines had waned.

"Grace, honey, what's wrong?"

"Good morning, sweetie. I'm so sorry you had to fix your own coffee. You want some breakfast?"

"That's no big deal," Mitch replied. "I'm fine. I grabbed a bagel out of the pantry. What's wrong? You look like you don't feel good. Can I get you something?"

"No...I just need my caffeine fix," she joked, trying to brush off being out of sorts. "I'll be fine."

"Here, let me fix it for you."

"No, that's OK. I'm good."

"Are you sure?"

"Yeah, I am."

Grace mixed her ritualistic Sunday morning concoction – regular coffee with two teaspoons of sugar, along with two splashes of hazelnut coffee creamer. She loved hugging her favorite mug with both hands as she stood for a moment with her eyes closed, smelling the sweet aroma of her blessed morning brew. She remained silent, staring out the kitchen window above the farmhouse sink.

Mitch felt uncomfortable with the silence. After a few moments, he jumped up from the table and walked toward Grace with the sports section in hand. Understanding that she was only indulging him, he began to share the headline with her in hopes it would bring her around.

"Guess who came in as AP's number one pre-season pick?" Mitch asked in a whimsical tone.

"Well, judging by the grin on your face, I'd say it's got to be...Auburn," she said with a wink, trying to change her demeanor.

"Ha-ha," he responded playfully. "How'd you guess?" Mitch embraced her. "That's my girl. You had me worried there for a minute."

"I'll be fine," Grace said.

Mitch was not convinced. "Are you sure you're OK?"

"I will be. I just haven't had much sleep," Grace said as she laid her head on Mitch's chest. "I had a terrible dream last night about Jake."

"What about?" he asked, caressing her hair.

"Well...I dreamed he was in a terrible accident. A lot of people were crying, and there was a charred vehicle. I don't know...I don't remember all of it, just bits and pieces. I woke up and couldn't shake it. It was so vivid – like it was happening right then. I was expecting someone to ring our doorbell at any second to drive us to the hospital. I stayed up and prayed until five this morning. I'm just not rested."

"Why didn't you wake me up?" Mitch said. "I hate you went through that all alone."

"Now, what good would it have done for both of us to have had no sleep?"

"Why don't you just go back to bed and get some rest?"

"No. I need to go to church," Grace said. "I know I'll feel better once I get in God's house."

"Are you sure?" Mitch asked.

"Very." Grace hesitated for a moment. "You know, you could go with me."

His mind raced, searching for an excuse. Finally, Mitch gently responded, "I appreciate it, but I think I'm just gonna catch up on some things around the house that I don't get to take care of during the week."

"Sure?" she asked, hoping for a change of mind.

"Yeah, I'm sure," he said with a smile.

To escape the awkwardness of the moment, Mitch changed the subject. He had something he wanted to talk to Grace about. He was hesitant because he lacked confidence that she would see it his way. He desired her blessing, and the way it came out of his mouth could make all the difference in her response.

"Honey, I have something I wanted to talk to you about," Mitch said.

"OK. What is it?"

"Now just hear me out."

"Oh, here comes the sales pitch," Grace said.

"I know we were planning to give the car to Jake on graduation day, but I would really love to give it to him now."

Puzzled, Grace asked, "What? Why?"

"Hang on. Now, I know that wasn't the plan. I understand that traditionally, graduates receive their gifts on graduation day, but when my parents gave me that car on my graduation day, I was grateful, but always wished they had given it to me at the beginning of my senior year instead of the end. I want Jake to enjoy it his senior year."

Still dazed from a lack of sleep and lacking the energy to debate it, Grace agreed.

"Well...I do see your point. I guess it doesn't really matter."

Mitch tried to contain his excitement and responded calmly, although his insides were about to implode. "Thanks, sweetie, for your blessing. Jake is going to be so excited!"

"Oh, Jake will be?" Grace laughed. "I bet he falls short in the overjoyed department compared to you."

"You think?" Mitch responded with a huge grin.

"I just hope this isn't a bad idea. I'm still not sure about Jake driving a fast car like that, especially with his high-strung personality."

"He will be fine. We'll have some rules and a curfew. That should help keep him in line."

"I hope you're right." She pointed a finger at Mitch. "You'll have to enforce those rules, you know."

"Of course. Not a problem," he reassured her.

Grace stopped for a moment. Mitch became a little uneasy. He wasn't quite sure what the pause meant.

"I tell ya what," Grace said.

Mitch felt a sinking feeling inside. A compromise was coming. Agreeing that quickly and easily was too good to be true.

Grace looked into Mitch's eyes. "This is very important to you, isn't it?" she asked.

"You have no idea," Mitch answered anxiously.

"For years, you've worked so hard at keeping that car in top notch condition and restoring it to perfection so that you could give it to your son one day. Before you had a son, you had that dream," she affirmed, holding his face in her soft, well-manicured hand.

Tears began to well in Mitch's eyes. He *had* invested countless hours of hard work preserving the Trans-Am. Now he was moments away from the very reason for it all. And now, hearing Grace acknowledge that was glorious.

"I think that this should be a 'father-son' moment," Grace said.

"You mean just Jake and me?" Mitch asked.

"Well, yeah. You're the father. Jake is the son," Grace said.

"And you are amazing!" Mitch boasted with intense gratitude. He placed his hand on the back of Grace's head, pulled it toward him and gently kissed her forehead.

Grace closed her eyes and smiled, then glanced at her phone to check the time.

"Oh, and I'm also late. I can forget Sunday School," Grace said.

"There goes your gold star," Mitch teased.

"Yeah, I know, right? And I had perfect attendance until now!" Grace said sarcastically.

Mitch chuckled at her cute sense of humor. Grabbing her purse, keys and Bible, Grace headed toward the door. She stopped and turned back for a moment. Looking intently at Mitch, she smirked, "Enjoy your 'guy' moment." She flashed an animated wink and her big, contagious smile. Mitch couldn't help but smile back.

"I will. Thank you, sweetheart," Mitch said, blowing her a kiss good-bye.

As soon as Grace made her exit, Mitch immediately began to put his plan into action. He had thought about this moment a million times. Walking to a drawer that was designated as a "catch-all" for tools, bread ties, coupons and other miscellaneous items, he reached toward the back and pulled out a set of keys. Attached to them was a keychain with a red "J." Mitch looked around, trying to find the perfect spot for it. He set it on the bar where Jake would see it right away. The red "J" stood out well against the chocolate-brown swirl design of the granite countertop.

Mitch returned to his sports article and read it for the fifth time while he anxiously waited for Jake to join him in the kitchen. A few minutes later, Jake shuffled in – ratty-haired, wearing boxers and a t-shirt, stretching and yawning like a cat.

"Was that Mom leaving?" Jake asked, rubbing his belly underneath his shirt.

"Yep," Mitch replied shortly.

Jake walked to the coffee maker, grabbed his favorite coffee mug out of the cabinet and poured his coffee. He looked around the kitchen.

"No bacon this morning?" Jake asked in disappointment.

"Nope. Not this morning. Your mom wasn't feeling very good. Didn't get much sleep last night. Bad dreams kept her up."

"That's not good," Jake said sympathetically.

"It must have been pretty bad. She was really shaken by it. You know something's wrong when she's not up and at it."

"That's for sure," Jake said.

As Jake sipped the coffee, he read the headlines on the front page of the newspaper as Mitch held it up and read details on the inside.

"So today's the day we've been waiting for, right, Dad?"

"You know it!" Mitch replied with excitement.

"Where did Bama show up in the poll?" Jake asked.

"Number one!" Mitch cheered.

"Oh, yeah, baby!" Jake exclaimed, stepping toward Mitch to give him a high five.

Jake turned a chair around and straddled it as he continued drinking his hot brew.

"So...you think it might be a national championship year?" Jake asked.

"With Alabama, that's always a possibility."

"What other SEC teams made it in the top twenty-five?"

"Oh, the usual," Mitch said. "LSU, Auburn, Georgia. Ole Miss and Mississippi State even made it in there."

"Wow! So what are they saying about our quarterback situation?" Jake asked.

"Well, here, let me just read it to you," Mitch said.

As Mitch began to read the article concerning his alma mater, Jake listened to the high marks given to their favorite team. He was one of the many readers who trusted the sports writers as if their words were biblical. Suddenly, the red object on the bar caught his attention. As Mitch continued to read, Jake slowly got up from his chair and walked toward the gleaming object. He picked it up and turned around quickly, facing his dad.

Interrupting Mitch's reading of the article on Alabama, Jake asked abruptly, "What is this?"

"What's what?" Mitch asked, pretending to be oblivious.

"This! This key ring!" Jake said impatiently, pointing to it as it dangled in the air.

Mitch laid the paper on the table. He made his way quietly to the bar and took the keychain from Jake's hand and held it up as if he were examining it. Jake was almost dancing with anxiousness.

"Well?!" Jake said, demanding an answer.

"Well, whoever it belongs to has a name that begins with the letter 'J,' " Mitch said.

"The only person in this house whose name begins with a 'J' is me!" Jake said.

Mitch shifted his eyes from the keychain to his overly-anxious son and handed the keys back to him. A huge grin appeared across Mitch's face. "Then I suppose they belong to you."

Jake stood quietly as his mind processed what this meant. After a moment, he looked at Mitch and asked, "The Trans-Am?"

"The Trans-Am," Mitch delightfully confirmed.

"No way! For me?"

"Who else?"

"No way!"

Impulsively, Jake darted out the back door and ran straight to the car, Mitch close behind him.

"Are you kidding me! Whoo-hoo!" Jake cheered. He hopped around the car several times in total disbelief. Mitch stood still with his arms folded, shaking his head and laughing at Jake's delirious behavior. Having released enough energy to finally sit still, Jake climbed into the car to check out the inside.

"Come on, Dad! Get in!"

Continuing to laugh at him, Mitch joined him on the passenger's side.

"I didn't see this coming!" Jake said. "Why today? My senior year just started."

"I talked your mom into letting me give it to you early. It wasn't a hard sell. It was her idea that I make it a 'guy moment,' as she called it."

"I'm certainly not complaining, but what made you decide to do it so early?"

"Well, I got this car on graduation day. I was so thankful and excited to have it, but soon after, I left for college and didn't really get to enjoy it with my friends...or rub it in the faces of my enemies," Mitch joked.

They both erupted in laughter. Jake fully understood where his dad was coming from.

Jake continued to sit behind the wheel in disbelief. As he looked, Mitch began to point out some specifics.

"Look, it's still got the eight-track player in it," Mitch said.

"It's incredible!" Jake responded. "It's totally restored, but you kept it true to its original design! I gotta call Ross! He is going to freak out!"

Mitch chuckled at Jake's animated behavior.

"Now, listen. There are a couple of issues under the hood I'm working out, so be sure to take it easy driving it until I take care of everything, OK?"

"Gotcha!" Jake agreed.

"OK. You call Ross. I'm going back inside and read that article a couple of more times. This has shaped up to be a great day early, hasn't it, son?"

"The greatest!"

"I'll see you inside."

Chapter 4

What a dream come true! A dream I never expected to see fulfilled at the beginning of my senior year! Seeing that red "J" keychain on the counter is a sight I'll never forget. It will be forever etched in my mind. That keychain signified freedom for me. Freedom to come and go as I please. It would also require responsibility. That's the part I would hate and – regretfully – ignore.

"**C**ome on, answer."

After three rings, there was a familiar voice.

"Hi..." Ross said.

"Ross, you will never—"

"This is Ross. If you're hearing this message then I must be busy."

Oh, come on! Of all the times I need you to answer, and I get your voice mail!

Typical of Jake's controlling personality, he became relentless. He was determined to call as many times as it took until Ross answered.

Why are you not answering? he asked the phone, as if it knew.

Ross sat on a tightly-packed pew beside Lauren, feeling annoyed at Jake. This was the fifth time he had felt his phone vibrate. Ross was able to check it during the first call without Lauren's noticing. When he saw it was Jake calling, he slipped it back into his pocket. Now it buzzed and buzzed again, and Lauren was certain to hear.

Ross felt a nudge. She had heard it. He turned to her and knew she was growing upset – a medley of emotions radiated from her face. It was a mixture of disbelief and embarrassment with a hint of disgust. Ross was even feeling a little embarrassed himself. He quickly reached into his pocket, and without looking, silenced it, then returned his gaze to Lauren, as if to say, *It wasn't my fault.*

Ross refocused his attention to Pastor David Glenn. Just when he had gotten past feeling three inches tall from Lauren's glare, the vibrations began again. Ross grabbed his phone through his pocket and again tried to stop the vibration. Slowly he removed the phone from his pocket, trying not to alert Lauren.

Where are you, Bama Bro?

Ross knew the texts wouldn't stop until he replied. Very carefully, not to attract attention, Ross tried texting a reply with one hand.

Church. Where do you think?

Ross hoped that would deter Jake from continuing the texting. It was obvious to Lauren what was going on. Once again he could feel her stare. Had Lauren's eyes been lasers, Ross would have been toast. He stared straight ahead, continuing to avoid eye contact.

Another buzz. He cut his eyes toward his phone to read Jake's response.

How lame.

What a hit to Ross's ego. He hated this emotional tug-of-war. He slowly turned the phone to silent mode; now only an amber light would alert him to a new message.

Another text.

Meet me out front when church is over, Jake ordered.

Ross was thankful that a simple response of "K" was sufficient. Slowly he looked back at Lauren. She was obviously frustrated, her arms crossed and her eyes in a dead stare toward the preacher. Ross leaned in close.

"Sorry," he whispered.

"Don't tell me. Tell Pastor Glenn," Lauren whispered.

With that, the choir began singing an altar call. The congregation rose to its feet and joined in the anthem. Still in a state of disdain, Lauren stood silently.

Using his sad, brown eyes as a weapon of mass affection, Ross leaned in toward Lauren and whispered.

"I said I'm sorry."

Lauren hesitated for a moment, thinking about her next move. Finally, she swung her hair around in a dramatic move, looked him square in the eyes and said very bluntly, "Altar's open." Ross stood stunned as she slung her head back to her initial position. His puppy-dog eyes didn't work! His only hope of getting back in Lauren's good graces had failed miserably.

After a prayer of blessing over the congregation, the pastor dismissed them. To emphasize her disappointment in Ross, Lauren turned her back to him and disappeared into a flock of teenage girls exiting the west side of the sanctuary.

"Wow," Ross smirked, shaking off Lauren's brush-off. To avoid further confrontation, he decided to join the more populated east side, making its exit all at once.

Ross looked for a place to step into the line of people leaving. His parents, Lance and Kate, and his number-two mom, Grace, were congregated together.

"Oh, I almost forgot," Grace said abruptly as she dug deep into her purse. She pulled out a neatly wrapped box topped with a colorful bow and handed it to Kate.

Surprised, Kate looked at it for a moment and asked, "What's this?"

"Just a little happy for you," Grace replied.

Kate smiled as her hands tore into the wrapping surrounding the unexpected gift. She uncovered two boxes, each containing a set of DVDs. The cover read *Wednesdays with Beth.* The picture on the front was that of renowned author and Bible study teacher Beth Moore. The upper left corner of the cover read *Life Today with James and Betty Robison.*

Kate quickly recognized it. "Oh, my! I love her!" she exclaimed as she stared at the author's face on the packaging.

"I know, silly," Grace said playfully.

"That's so sweet of you!" Kate said as she hugged Grace.

"Kate, you've been such a good friend and a huge help at the flower shop during my busiest seasons. I just wanted to say thank you," Grace said humbly. "I know what a Beth Moore-ite you are."

"Yes, I am," Kate confirmed, continuing to look through the many lesson titles. "Hey, there are two sets here," Kate said, holding one in each hand up in the air. "Why don't you take one set and watch it and I'll keep the other and when we are done, we can swap?"

"Kate, I got them for you, not me," Grace said.

"I know, but I can't watch them both at the same time. Here, pick one," Kate said, offering them for Grace to choose. "You might as well get something out of your investment."

"OK, then," Grace agreed.

Grace randomly chose one DVD set.

"That's a perfect gift for her, Grace," Lance said. "You're making me look bad on my gift-picking!"

"Oh, honey, you do great on picking out my gifts," Kate encouraged as she pointed out the white-gold watch she wore on her left wrist.

Lance smiled. Directing the conversation toward Grace, he said, "You know, I invited Mitch to Brotherhood this morning. I hoped he would come."

"I know," Grace said. "Thank you for always thinking of ways to try and get him involved. I don't know why he's so uninterested." She frowned and looked down, avoiding her friends' faces. "It scares me to think what it may take to bring him around."

"Well, we'll just have to keep trying," Lance said.

Grace noticed Ross standing alone between two nearby pews. She waved to get his attention, then motioned for him to join them in line.

Ross begrudgingly joined them. In his mind, it wasn't cool standing by his parents in public, but the urgency he felt to get outside to Jake's mystery superseded his need to look cool. Being the polite young man he was, Ross thanked Grace for letting him cut line.

"Where did Lauren go?" Kate asked.

"She's hanging out over there with her friends," Ross said nonchalantly, as if nothing had happened.

He turned to face the exit and realized he was positioned behind Ms. Mary Whit and Ms. Alice Faye. He had known these two ladies since his birth. Both widowed, these geriatric besties with beehive-style hairdos were full of personality, had boisterous laughs and could cook like nobody's business. As sweet as they were, getting stuck behind them in line waiting to tell the pastor good-bye was not a good thing. They were notorious for starting a conversation about

Pastor Glenn's sermon. It was as if they were trying to have Sunday school all over again.

This is going to take all day, Ross thought to himself. He tried to figure out a way to get around them without appearing rude, but it wasn't possible. The ladies were standing in such a way that the entire entry was blocked. Scooting around them would be a very bad move on his part, especially with his parents standing right behind him. His only choice was to wait it out.

Ross fidgeted while waiting, popping his knuckles and adjusting his shirt, trying to stifle his anxiousness. Finally, he was next in line to speak to Pastor Glenn, and then he was home free. Then…it happened. Ms. Mary and Ms. Alice had a question for Pastor Glenn about his sermon. They simply didn't agree with a particular point he had made, and they felt the need to straighten him out on it ASAP.

"Hello, ladies," Pastor Glenn said respectfully, but with reservation. Ross could see in his face the minister hoped he'd get out of this conversation easily.

Ms. Alice wasted no time getting straight to her point. "Now, Pastor, you know we enjoy your preachin'," she assured him while patting his hand, "but we have a question about something you said halfway through the sermon."

With wavy, graying hair and blue eyes, the preacher looked like a 255-pound overgrown teddy bear. He stood there with a smile on his face while his mind raced through his sermon notes in his head, evidently trying to remember the halfway point of his sermon.

Although being stuck in line behind these two fixtures had Ross agitated, he was enjoying the show. He watched as Pastor Glenn tried to gracefully and adequately answer their concerns yet quickly end the conversation. Ross couldn't help getting tickled. The longer he watched, the funnier the situation became. He then looked away in fear the pastor would catch him laughing. It was too late. Ross was "busted."

Pastor David Glenn looked at Ross sternly. Ross cringed. This was the third time in only a matter of hours Ross had felt embarrassed. First, at home that morning with his parents concerning the phone call from Lauren. Later, with Lauren's admonishments over Jake's texts, and now, the preacher, for heaven's sake! He got the feeling it wasn't going to end soon.

Somehow, Pastor Glenn was able to quickly smooth things over with the elderly ladies. Ross stepped up.

"Ladies, look behind you," the pastor instructed as they started to walk away.

Ross was suddenly nervous. He knew Pastor Glenn's capabilities of humiliation. There was no telling what he would say.

Ms. Alice and Ms. Mary followed the pastor's instruction and turned toward Ross.

The preacher continued. "Now, is that not the sweetest face you have ever seen?" he asked as if talking about a baby in a stroller.

Ross's face turned three shades of red.

Ms. Alice reached for Ross's face. "It IS the sweetest face I've ever seen!" she said with a big smile as she pinched his right cheek.

Ms. Mary joined in the conversation. "I've always thought Ross Kelly was the cutest little thing! I remember changing that boy's diapers in the nursery when he was a baby!" she reminisced, patting him on the back. "You got me real good one time, sweet boy!"

Ross stood in disbelief at the extreme lengths his pastor was willing to go to exact revenge on him.

By this time, Ross's parents and Grace had caught on to the joke. They couldn't help but join in.

"Oh, thank you, sweet ladies," Kate said. "You know, he's always been Momma's little pride and joy!"

"Well, it's very understandable," Pastor Glenn said sarcastically.

"Oh, yes!" Grace added. "That baby face just sucks me in every time. As a matter of fact, Jake has always accused me of loving Ross more than him."

Suddenly, a rumble erupted from the pastor's throat. It was laughter. All of the other adults surrounding Ross joined him. As Ms. Alice and Ms. Mary waved good-bye and made their way down the steps, Ross looked at each of his hecklers with disgust and said, "That's just wrong."

This created even more hilarity among the group.

"Aw...come on, son," Lance said. "We're just having a little fun."

"Well, not all of us are having fun here," Ross said brashly.

"Well, the important ones are," Pastor Glenn said, wiping tears from his eyes.

"Oh, OK then," Ross said, letting it go.

He reached out to shake Pastor Glenn's hand. The preacher smiled and accepted. Just before their two hands met, Ross jerked away his hand and smoothed it over his head.

The quick-witted pastor asked, "Oh, are you 'dissing' me, sweetheart? Is that what you're doing?" he said, patronizing him.

Ross shook his head and gave up the fight. The rest of the hecklers continued to joke and giggle at their pastor's mischief.

Suddenly their laughs were interrupted by the sound of squealing tires, a revving engine and a car horn playing the Alabama Fight Song. The conversations and fellowship taking place throughout the churchyard came to a screeching halt. All heads swung toward the '79 crimson-and-white Trans-Am with the T-tops removed.

Realizing it was Jake, Grace was immediately overcome with humiliation. This was a perfect example of why she feared Jake getting the car so soon. Pastor Glenn patted her on the back in consolation. The multiple gasps and whispering lips only fueled the heat wave of embarrassment that overcame her.

Ross made a mad dash to the car. "You gotta be kidding me!" he declared.

Lance debated whether or not to stop him but decided to let him go, concerned it would create a bigger scene.

Jake raised himself through the open roof. Realizing he had captured the attention of the remaining congregation, he tried to maintain as cool an appearance as possible. Sliding his shades down his nose and scanning his accidental audience, Jake fixed his eyes on Ross and very confidently said, "I told you one day I was gonna drive this car."

Lauren broke her way through her circle of friends who were hurrying toward the Trans-Am. With a look of utter disgust, she watched the girls as they made a fuss over the car.

"Whatcha think, ladies?" Jake asked.

"Oh, my gosh, Jake! It's incredible!" one girl yelled.

"It looks awesome!" Ross exclaimed.

"Hop in, Bama Bro, and we'll take her for a spin," Jake said.

Lauren grabbed Ross's arm and stopped him from getting into the car.

"You are supposed to have lunch at my house and then study for a chemistry test, remember?" she reminded him as she glared at Jake.

In retaliation, Jake made a goofy face and with every ounce of sarcasm he could muster said, "Aw, Ross...how dull."

Feeling torn once again between the girl he liked and his long-time best friend, and wanting to go for a ride so badly, Ross tried to gently work his way into the car as he assured Lauren it wouldn't take long.

"It'll just be a few minutes, I promise."

"Yeah, Lauren. Just a few minutes," Jake chimed in with a patronizing wink.

"I'll have Jake drop me off at your house in just a bit. OK?"

"Ross, we need to study!" Lauren said, exasperated.

"I know! And we will, I promise."

Knowing she had lost this battle, Lauren relented. "Fine."

Jake mocked her by poking out his bottom lip. Lauren continued glaring at Jake.

"I'll see you in a few," Ross reassured her.

Jake revved the engine once again, causing the curious teens in the churchyard to step away from the car and ensuring he left a lasting impression.

"Woo-hoo!" Ross howled as they sped away.

The boys pulled into the parking lot of the popular lunch spot Johnny's Drive-In. Adored for its 1960's atmosphere, their burgers were a town favorite. Apparently today, the local rich kid, Eric Williams, and his buddies had chosen to eat lunch here as well.

The parking spot to the right of Eric's Challenger was vacant. Jake couldn't resist the opportunity to pull in beside him so spectators would mentally compare the two rides.

Jake and Eric were known nemeses at school. Jealousy was an obvious factor, but no one could exactly pinpoint what started the rivalry. The rusty-red-headed, brown-eyed teen was small for his age and often exhibited "Napoleon Syndrome" because of it, particularly against athletes. He also seemed to have a chip on his shoulder more often than not, and it didn't take much to set him off. Eric's family was wealthy and, as a result, one of the most prominent families in the area. He was the "black sheep," though, avoiding church and barely attending school. Except for the last name, no one would suspect he was one of "the" Williamses.

He did, however, use his wealth to always drive the coolest car on campus, the one object he clung to and dangled over Jake and the rest of the athletes like a piece of meat – enticing them, provoking them at every opportunity.

Once Jake had parked, Eric looked at him and gave his new ride a once-over, clearly growing angry at the sight of the classic muscle car.

As Jake ordered food for Ross and himself, he noticed Eric staring at him with a look of absolute hatred. Seeing his arch-rival simmer in such jealousy was a pleasure. Jake enjoyed this feeling, though it almost frightened him a little.

Jake smirked, and instantly Eric began talking trash. The deafening noise from the two idling cars drowned out most of Eric's diatribe, but Jake clearly heard his name in the mix, and it stirred something inside – an emotion from deep within that seemed to erupt only when Eric Williams was in the picture.

"Eric, what's your problem?" he blurted out.

"You are! You think your Matchbox car is all that? I can prove it's not! My car would smear your Trans-Am!"

"Oh really, now?" Jake asked sarcastically.

"Really!" Eric replied. "You wouldn't stand a chance in Daddy's do-over car!"

Jake had been challenged, and his insides burned with anger. "And when do you expect to prove it?"

"I can prove it right now," Eric stated confidently.

"You wanna go?" Jake asked. "Let's go! Just name the place and time!"

"OK, County Line Road. *Now!*" Eric said.

"You got it!" Jake said.

Eric threw his car into reverse and sped away. Not to be outdone, Jake did the same.

"Hey, where are we going?" Ross yelled, frustrated. "We haven't even gotten our food!"

"We've got something to settle," Jake said calmly. "The food will have to wait."

"But I'm starving!"

"Just give it a few minutes. My friend, the adrenaline rush you're about to experience will cause your hunger to disappear. Trust me."

There was no question where on County Line Road they were supposed to be. The straight-away near Ephraim Farms was a favorite spot for drag racing, and in five minutes Jake and Ross were there, pulling in next to Eric, who had just arrived.

Eric's friend Blake bailed out of the Challenger to line up the cars and start the race. No time was to be wasted; the two super-egos wanted to get this done. Blake's hands went up. Hearts were racing and adrena-line was pumping. The few seconds it took for Blake to signal the start seemed to last forever. Finally, his hands dropped with a shout of the command, "Go!"

Both drivers gunned their accelerators. After the initial spin-out, Eric and Jake were well on their way to a full-force race. Each took turns taking the lead on the asphalt. Jake's knuckles turned white from his tight grip on the steering wheel. Ross was nervous. Hunger pangs would have been more comfortable than the needles he now felt in his stomach.

"How fast are you going, Jake?"

Jake remained silent, concentrating on the road, the dashboard, then the road again, then the location of Eric's car. Ross leaned over toward the driver's side to view the speedometer. It read 98 mph. The '79 Trans-Am began to shake.

"That's it! That's all she has!" Ross exclaimed in hopes Jake would back off.

Jake's eyes were trained on the black Challenger that was pulling away from them. Suddenly, smoke erupted from the hood of the Trans-Am, clouding the view for Jake and Ross.

"Ah!" Jake growled. "No way is this happening!"

Jake was in disbelief – his new car had failed him. Frustrated, he stomped on the brakes. A cloud of dust rolled around them.

"No way!" Jake ranted, punching the steering wheel repeatedly with his fist. The car honked short beeps with each strike.

Ross sat back in the seat and tried to catch his breath. Relief rolled over him like a wave of cool water.

Both boys sat silently for a moment as smoke continued to waft from the engine. They heard the rumbling sound of a muffler, and soon another car appeared beside them. Eric had returned to gloat in his victory.

Smirking, Eric asked, "Need a ride, Dale Earnhardt?"

"I'd rather walk!" Jake replied.

"Suit yourself." Eric peeled out, his tires leaving billows of smoke in their place.

"Jerk," Ross said. "Our time is coming."

Unimpressed by Ross's intended pep talk, Jake became infuriated. He quickly got out to see what had happened to the engine. Ross joined him.

Jake slowly raised the hood. Smoke overpowered them.

"What do you think is wrong with it?" Ross asked.

"It's the top radiator hose," Jake whined, frustrated more than Ross had ever seen. "The car's overheated. Man! How could this happen?"

Ross was at a loss. "So what do we do now?"

"I'm gonna call my dad and see what I need to do. He's not going to be happy about this."

While Jake waited for Mitch to answer, a patrol car pulled up beside them. Immediately Jake hung up the phone. The driver stepped out of the vehicle and removed his sunglasses as he walked toward the boys.

It was Ross's mentor from the sheriff's department. Mike Mayhew, a former hockey player, was a beast: 6'3" and 255 pounds in stature, his body showed signs of the fierce sport from years ago. His naturally bald head he laughingly blamed on the five concussions received during his time on the ice. On his temple and cheeks were old war wounds that had required stitches.

"Oh, Mayhew," Ross said with a sigh of relief.

"What's going on, guys?" the sergeant asked.

"My car broke down. That's all," Jake said.

"Just like that, huh?" Mayhew asked.

"Yep, just like that," Jake said.

"You really think I believe that?" Mayhew asked.

Jake and Ross didn't answer.

"You were racing, weren't ya?" Mayhew asked.

The boys still offered no response. Mayhew stepped closer to Ross. Ross looked at him but said nothing.

"Weren't ya?" Mayhew repeated, not raising his voice.

"Yes, sir," Ross quietly responded.

"Way to go, genius," Jake whispered to Ross.

Mayhew calmly stepped over to Jake. "Walk with me," he ordered, wishing to speak to Jake without embarrassing him in front of Ross.

Reluctantly, Jake followed. They stopped just a few yards away.

"Look, I don't like being lied to. I don't like your attitude, and I certainly don't like the influence you are on Ross," Mayhew said sternly. "Ross is a good kid. You're taking him in the wrong direction."

Not the least bit intimidated, Jake glared at him. "You're not Ross's dad, Mayhew."

"Maybe not. But I care about him like he's my son. I care about you too, Jake. I want you to make good choices, but today..." He paused and shook his head. "You didn't do that."

The sound of tires hitting gravel interrupted their conversation. Another patrol vehicle pulled up next to Mayhew's. Deputy Galen Daniels appeared from the driver's side. This officer stood 5'7" and weighed about 170 pounds. His boyish looks with brown hair and sparkling blue eyes made him the butt of "pretty boy" jokes around the sheriff's office. Often referred to as "The Golden Child," Daniels was meek and rarely got upset, even when dealing with hard-to-control suspects. He got out of the SUV and walked over to Mayhew.

"Great," Jake said. "Let's just get the whole force out here."

"What's going on?" Daniels asked.

"Oh, these boys decided to do a little Sunday afternoon racing and she ran hot on 'em," Mayhew explained.

"Jake, you know better," Daniels said.

Daniels, too, was a part of the D.A.R.E. mentor program. He had been assigned to Jake. Blessed wasn't at all how he would describe his feeling about that, however. No matter how much he tried to reach out to Jake, Daniels received nothing but disrespect and a contemptuous attitude in return.

"Oh, come on, Lil' Mayhew," Jake said, mocking Daniels. "It wasn't nothin'."

"Your dad's gonna blow a gasket," Daniels said. "No pun intended."

Daniels's humor amused Mayhew but infuriated Jake all the more.

"I'm gonna call my dad," Jake said. He dialed Mitch's number.

———————

Mitch sat in his favorite recliner watching the Sunday afternoon NFL pre-season game. Grace cleaned the kitchen after serving lunch. She could think of nothing but her embarrassment at Jake's behavior only an hour earlier at church. After the scene he created by arriving and leaving in a cloud of dust, she quickly left her friends and returned home, not mentioning the incident to Mitch. Jake had had the car only a couple of hours; surely this would be an isolated incident. If she started complaining already, would Mitch take her concerns seriously?

Mitch's phone rang. He knew without looking at the ID it was Jake because of the *Sweet Home Alabama* ring tone.

"Hey, son. What's up?"

"Hey, Dad. Whatcha doin'?" Jake asked.

"Just sitting here, watching the game," Mitch said. "Where are you? You missed lunch."

"Yeah, Dad. Sorry about that. Listen, I've had a little incident."

Mitch could easily tell that Jake was trying to sound nonchalant, but it didn't help. Mitch leaped out of his chair.

"Have you been in a wreck?" Mitch asked.

"No, Dad. It's nothing like that. The car overheated – that's all. I just need you to come get me."

"I'm about to walk out the door," Mitch said. "Where are you?"

Jake hesitated. He knew as soon as he told Mitch where he was, it would be obvious what he had been doing. Not having a choice in the matter, he swallowed hard and spit the words out of his mouth.

"County Line Road."

Mitch stopped in his tracks. "County Line Road?" Mitch asked. "Jake, were you racing?"

"Oh, my word," Grace whispered under her breath, with her face in her hand. She could be silent no longer. "This was exactly what I was worried would happen if you gave Jake that car."

Ignoring her statement, Mitch continued, "Answer me, son. Were you racing?"

Finally, Jake broke the silence. "Dad, it wasn't my fault! It was Eric's. He challenged me! I couldn't walk away from that. How would that make me look to everyone?"

"Jake, I told you to take it easy, that the car still needed work. Why didn't you listen?"

"I'm sorry, Dad. I'm really sorry."

"Well, we'll talk about all that later. Right now let's just get you and that car home. I'm about to leave. I'll call Vic while I'm headed that way and get his car hauler over there. Are you alone?"

"No...Ross is here...and so are Sergeant Mayhew and Deputy Daniels," Jake replied.

"What are Mayhew and Daniels doing there?" Mitch asked.

"They drove up after the car got overheated. They were just checking on us. That's all," Jake said.

"Yeah, I'll bet," Mitch said. "The last thing we need is the law involved in this."

"Everything's OK, Dad. Just chill out," Jake said.

"Don't tell me to chill out!" Mitch scolded. "Do you know how many hours I've invested in that car?"

Realizing he was getting too upset, Mitch stopped and took a deep breath, then calmly spoke. "I'll be there as soon as I can."

As Mitch grabbed his keys, Grace grabbed his arm.

"Mitch, I think that giving him that car wasn't a good idea. He's had it for less than three hours and he's already broken the one rule you gave him...and now it's not even drivable."

Mitch understood Grace's concern but empathized with Jake. He remembered how it felt to have his manhood challenged. He couldn't expect her to understand. It was a "guy" thing. Mitch tried to downplay the situation.

"Grace, come on, honey. It's really not that big a deal. He's a teenage guy. The Williams boy challenged him. You know how Jake is. He's not going to back down from that. I probably wouldn't have either. Look, I'll reinforce what I said. Besides, I really haven't had the chance to go over rules and stuff. He was in such a hurry to show off the car, I didn't have time to deal with that. I'll take care of it. OK?"

Mitch's speech wasn't very convincing to Grace. "The rules should have been established before he was ever handed the keys."

Mitch was taken aback. It wasn't typical for Grace to react in such a firm way. He didn't know how to respond.

"I better go. Jake is waiting on me."

As Mitch pulled out of the driveway, Grace made her way to what she referred to as her "prayer closet." It was her special place she retreated to when she felt she needed to be alone with God. In actuality, it was a space in her closet where she went to seek the Lord's counsel. She knew she had quite a battle on her hands, and she needed to know how to deal with it – not only from her position as a wife, but also as a prayer warrior standing in the gap for family.

While Grace was on her knees fervently praying, Jake and Ross stood on County Line Road waiting for Mitch and Spears Towing. Jake fumed about his loss to Eric. Ross leaned against the car in silence as Jake ranted.

Finally, Ross had heard enough of Jake's complaining and thought about Lauren. He had not been true to what he told Lauren he would do, and that bothered him.

"Hey, man, I'm gonna head out," Ross said. "Lauren is waiting on me. I promised her I'd be there to study. I'm gonna keep that promise."

Mayhew overheard him. "Ross, you want me to give you a ride to her house?"

"Yeah, that'd be great," Ross said.

Jake was shocked. "Seriously? You're gonna just leave me here?" he asked.

Mayhew looked at Daniels. "You got this?"

"Yeah, we're good," Daniels said.

As Ross climbed into Sergeant Mayhew's SUV, Jake grasped at his last effort to keep Ross from leaving.

"Go ahead, Ross. Just leave me here! Better hurry so you won't be in too much trouble with Saint Lauren!"

Ross said nothing.

"Man, you are so whipped!" Jake yelled. "I'd be embarrassed if I *ever* let a girl run my life like that!"

Ross ignored Jake's efforts to intimidate him. He seemed to be immune to it, especially when it concerned Lauren.

Just miles away, Mitch drove above the speed limit trying to reach Jake and the Trans-Am as quickly as possible. His heart felt as if it were beating in his throat. He had spent years restoring that car so that he could give it to Jake for graduation.

Daniels waited with Jake. For five years, he had tried to be a good influence on Jake. Of all the guys who went through D.A.R.E. Camp, he was stuck with the one kid who refused to be receptive.

"You don't have to babysit me, you know," Jake said.

"Yeah...I know," Daniels replied.

Jake continued his rant, blaming Eric for his car overheating and complaining about Ross choosing Lauren over him.

"Jake, just calm down," Daniels said.

"Look, Barney Fife. I haven't listened to you in the past five years. You think I'm gonna start listening to you now?" Jake said.

The gentle Daniels simply looked at the ground, shaking his head.

The Trans-Am appeared ahead. Mitch's heart sank. The joy of that special moment just a few hours earlier was now overshadowed by the sight of smoke rolling out from underneath the hood. The look of defeat and humiliation on his son's face was difficult for Mitch to see. He pulled up beside the car and motioned for Jake as he rolled down the window.

"You OK, son?"

"Yeah, I'm fine. Just mad as all get out. I don't understand. How could Eric beat me like that?"

"Son, I told you the car still needs work and to take it easy."

"I know, Dad, but you don't understand."

Daniels approached them. "Hey, Mitch."

"Hey, Daniels. I appreciate you staying here with Jake until I could get here," Mitch said.

"Not a problem. You know I think a lot of him," Daniels said. He paused for a moment, then said, "You do know Jake was racing, right?"

Mitch became defensive. "Yeah, Jake told me. Look, Daniels. I appreciate your concern, but I believe this is a family matter. I'll discuss it with my son at home, if that's OK with you."

"I'm not trying to get in your business, Mitch. I just—"

"Then don't," Mitch said firmly.

Before their conversation could go any further, a wrecker pulled up beside the car. An older gentleman with thinning hair and a heart-warming grin dismounted from the driver's side.

Mitch stepped out of his truck to greet him. "Hey, Vic! How's it going?"

"Afternoon, Mitch!" he replied cheerfully. "Hey, Deputy! What you up to?"

"Hey, Vic! I'm headed out. My job's done here," Daniels said as he climbed in his patrol vehicle. He waved and left.

Quickly turning his attention to the car, Vic looked under the hood, moving a few of the parts around with his hands as he muttered under his breath. Mitch and Jake stood silently and watched Vic in action, snickering under their breath. They got a big kick out of his method of assessing the car.

After a few minutes of investigating the situation, Vic leaned against the Trans-Am, looked straight at Jake and asked, "Boy, what did you do?"

"That's a very good question, sir," Jake replied.

"That's a mighty fine ride you got there. Your dad has put a lot of work into it over the years. I'd hate to see it done in vain."

Jake was stunned by the man's reprimand. The moment was awkward for Mitch as well as for Jake.

"Do you need our help getting it loaded?" Mitch asked, trying to change the subject.

"Nope. I've got my system down pat. You want me to haul it to the barn?"

"Yeah, that'd be great," Mitch said.

"Alrighty then. I'll have her there in just a little while."

"Fantastic! I'll have a check waiting for you, along with a piece of Grace's coconut cake," he said.

"Now you're talking!" Vic said, smiling.

Mitch and Jake headed home. A few minutes into the ride Jake asked, "Does Mom know?"

"Yep, she knows. But I talked to her a little before I left. She's probably had time to settle down by now. Just let me deal with her."

Riding to the house, Jake was filled with anxiety. Although his dad offered to handle the situation, he knew his mom was not going to take this well. The thing he dreaded most was the sermon about his stupid decision that he knew awaited him. Grace was sure to impose some form of punishment. He hoped his dad going to bat for him would be enough.

Grace returned to the kitchen after praying over today's events and the dissonance it had caused. As the only female, she felt like she stood alone in that household most of the time. She and Mitch often didn't see eye-to-eye on parenting Jake. The guys always sided against her in these kinds of situations. This time, righteous anger had her ready to take a firm stand. She knew she was right, and she wasn't going down without a fight.

Soon she heard the front door open and hurried to meet Mitch and Jake. Immediately, her motherly instinct kicked in.

"Are you OK?" she asked, looking him over for injuries.

"Yeah, Mom. I'm OK," he said, pushing her away from him. "But the car isn't."

"I'm going to be honest with you, son," she said. "I didn't really have a peace about your dad giving you that car this soon, but I complied anyway. I'm seeing that my judgment was accurate. Having a car like that comes with responsibility. Today's events have proven that you can't handle that responsibility."

Mitch interrupted her. "Hold on, honey. I think you're overreacting a bit."

Grace was indignant. "Overreacting? You gave him one rule and he didn't follow it. You didn't witness what I witnessed after the church service today!" Incensed by his apathy and poor judgment, she let it all out.

"I couldn't believe my eyes!" Grace exclaimed. "And neither could anyone else! He showed no restraint!" Grace had never felt so outraged, and her voice began to quiver. It was a warning buzzer to Mitch and Jake.

"He's not just a danger to himself, but to others as well!" she yelled, pointing her finger at Jake. "I cannot in good conscience allow him to drive like that, and I'm very bothered that you don't see it."

Mitch and Jake stood silently, staring at the floor, completely still. They dared not make eye contact with her, nor each other.

Grace grew quiet. Cautiously, Mitch interceded.

"Look, honey, please calm down. I can fix the car. His other car still hasn't sold. He can drive it until I get the Trans-Am going again," Mitch suggested.

Jake broke into the conversation. "But Dad, that old thing doesn't crank half the time! Do you know how aggravating it is not knowing if it's going to run or not?"

Mitch thought for a moment. "OK, Jake, you can drive my truck to school, and I'll drive your car."

"Absolutely not!" Grace exclaimed. "We are not going to be put out with our vehicles to accommodate his disobedience and irresponsible behavior!"

"Well, then, what's he supposed to do, huh?" Mitch asked in frustration.

She turned her gaze to Jake. Jake was afraid now. He had never seen his mother so angry before.

"I will take him to school on my way to the shop until he can make better choices."

It was worse than Jake could have imagined.

"What?" Jake asked in disbelief. "Not the floral shop van! Do you know how humiliating that will be?"

Grace moved close to Jake and spoke barely above a whisper as tears welled in her eyes.

"Do you have any idea how humiliating your behavior in front of the church was for *me*?"

Jake's expression dropped. He had not given a thought to how his behavior had affected his mom. Her feelings had never entered his mind.

Grace walked away as she wiped the tears that trickled down her face.

Jake's feelings of guilt lasted only moments, though, as he thought of his peers seeing him dropped off at school in that multi-colored, floral van.

Instead of offering his mother an apology, Jake turned to Mitch, his eyes pleading.

"Dad, please. Talk to her. Don't make me ride in that ridiculous van! It's bad enough that I lost that race today. How much more humiliation should I have to endure?"

Still emotionally paralyzed by Grace's outburst, Mitch stood silent. He knew a line had been crossed with her, and he wasn't about to make things worse. Although he was unwilling to admit she was right, he looked at Jake. "You will do what your mother said. I'm treading lightly here. We need to sit still on this one and let some time pass."

"Are you serious?" Jake declared in disbelief. His dad always had his back. Until now. Jake wasn't used to this.

Mitch put his hand on his boy's shoulder.

"Let's just ride this out. She'll come around."

"Dad, if I have to ride to school in that florist van tomorrow, I'll be committing *social suicide.*"

Mitch patted Jake on the back, took a deep breath and said, "Well, if it makes you feel any better, I'll sing at your funeral."

Chapter 5

Unbelievable. In less than two hours, I had already damaged my car and lost privilege to it as well. Everything my dad had said just moments earlier went through one ear and out the other. It's amazing how blinding pride can be. It landed me in a place of utter humiliation. But this was only the beginning.

As the weekend came to a close, the shift of deputies led by Sergeant Mayhew assembled for their evening meal at the fish-and-steak hot spot, The Driskills'. The country-style, down-home restaurant with humble décor was quite cozy and welcoming. This "mom and pop" establishment was not a luxurious restaurant by any means, but it felt like home to many of its regular patrons. And the steaks, fried catfish and buffet items were outstanding.

The sheriff's office deputies ate there so often, the restaurant staff had the guys' shift schedule memorized, knew without asking what they wanted, and had their drinks waiting at their favorite tables just before they arrived. The employees also could bring speeding tickets to the co-owner, Mal, who in turn would give them to Mayhew to see about having them dropped.

Today the men met in the restaurant parking lot, preparing for their daily briefing over a good dinner. As they walked in, they were greeted by Hannah, a petite young brunette wearing a red t-shirt, jeans and a black waist apron filled with straws. She had worked at The Driskills' since she was old enough to be hired and was now in her freshman year of college. Hannah had a beautiful voice and was going to school on a music scholarship. The deputies had literally watched Hannah grow up while working there.

"Hey, guys," Hannah said as she looked at each one, mentally assessing the group. She quickly realized someone was missing.

"Where's Hollis?" she asked.

"Oh, he'll be here," Ramon said with a grin. The others snickered.

"What have y'all done to that poor fella now?" Hannah asked.

"Oh, nothing major," Mike Mayhew said. "It just may be a little bit before he joins us."

"Did y'all hide his patrol car again?" Hannah asked.

Galen Daniels spoke up defensively. "Hey, he had it coming," he said, holding up his hand, revealing a black stain.

"What in the world?" Hannah asked.

"That would be black shoe polish," Mayhew informed her. "Juicy – I mean, Hollis – put it on Daniels's door handle the other day, and he still hasn't been able to get it off."

"OK – suddenly I don't feel so sorry for Juicy anymore," Hannah commented.

"As you shouldn't," Mayhew said.

Hannah laughed. "Well, enjoy your meal. I'll be back there to check on y'all in a few minutes." Checking on them wasn't her job; it was an excuse to talk to them.

As the men made their way through the restaurant, they were immediately greeted by guests as they passed. These law enforcement officers were well-known and respected. They cared about the people they served, and the community knew it.

The banquet room where they loved to eat had a large table by a front window under the flat-screen television mounted on the wall. Strategic? Perhaps. But it didn't matter. Between the waitress taking their orders, visitors starting conversations and dispatchers talking over their radios, the men rarely got to watch the TV. They didn't mind, though. They adored interacting with the people they served, and with each other.

"Hey, fellas!" Stella appeared, one of their favorite waitresses. "What can I get you boys to drink?" She really didn't have to ask, because she knew the answer.

As the guys gave her their drink order, Mal walked to the table and patted Mayhew on the back. "Evening, guys," he said, a piece of paper in his hand.

"Whatcha got there?" Mayhew asked, taking the paper from Mal.

Mal didn't beat around the bush about it. "Well, Pattie got a speeding ticket the other day. It's questionable, if you ask me. Wanted to see if you might could check into it to help her out," Mal said.

"Sure, let me take a look at it," Mike said. He looked for the name of the officer who had written the ticket. "Oh, yeah, I know him well. He's a pretty good guy. If it's questionable and he knows her situation, he'll work with us."

Mike took out his iPhone and snapped a shot of the ticket, then returned it to Mal. "I'll see what I can do."

"I appreciate that," Mal said. "She's a single mom with no help, working two jobs. A speeding ticket really affects her, ya know?"

"I know," Mike sympathized. "I'll do the best I can to help her out."

"I know you will," Mal said. "I appreciate it."

About that time, Deputy Hollis walked in with a less-than-joyful look on his face.

The rest of the guys struggled to suppress their laughs.

"Where ya been, Juicy?" Mayhew asked.

"Don't act like you don't know, Mayhew," Hollis said firmly. He looked around the table at his fellow officers. "OK, who did it this time?" he asked.

"Who did what?" Ramon asked.

"You know what," Hollis said. "You know how long I had to look for my ride? Too long!" he said angrily. "And y'all over here ordering your food and I'm the one starving to death!"

"Aw, Juicy, you always starving to death," Daniels said. "You're in the middle of breakfast and you start asking what's for lunch."

The guys laughed.

"I can't help it, y'all!" Hollis exclaimed. "Ever since I started doing CrossFit, my appetite has gotten bigger."

The guys laughed even harder.

"Man, how long have you been doing CrossFit?" Ramon asked.

"Couple of months," Hollis replied.

"And you've lost how much?" Ramon asked.

Hollis stood silent for a moment. "Well, nothing yet, but I've been turning fat into muscle and muscle weighs more that fat. You oughta know that!" Hollis said, referring to Ramon's obsession with health and fitness.

Hollis sat down beside Daniels. "I know it was you," Hollis said to him.

Daniels held up his shoe-polish-stained hand. "And what makes you think I'd do something like that?"

Hannah had waited as long as she could stand it and suddenly appeared at their table.

"So you boys look like you're having a slow night."

"Hey, Hannah, we heard you got you a tattoo on your foot. Is that true?" Daniels asked.

Hannah grinned. "Yes, sir, I did," she replied, slipping off her sandal to show it to them. The men leaned down to see three words in deep red, outlined in navy blue – *Walk by faith.*

Noticing the reference to scripture, Ramon said, "Now, that's all right."

"Yeah, well, I bet your granddaddy about beat you, didn't he?" Hollis asked.

"Naw," Hannah said. "Of course, he ain't seen it, either."

Glancing at the front entrance, Hannah eyed a couple waiting to pay for their meal.

"Gotta git." She slipped her sandal back on.

The waitress returned to take Hollis's drink order. "What can I get you, Juicy?"

"I'll have water, Stella," Hollis said. Then, looking at Daniels, he added, "...with lemon."

Daniels shook his head and grinned.

"While I'm here, let me just go ahead and take your food order, if y'all are ready," Stella suggested.

Mayhew ordered first. "I'll take my usual – patty melt with a side of extra-crispy fries – not crispy...**extra** crispy," he said.

"Gotcha," Stella said, acknowledging she understood the difference.

"And give me a side of gravy to help keep my arteries from clogging," Mayhew added.

"You got it," Stella replied. "And what can I get for you, Daniels?"

"Oh, just give me a cheeseburger with a side of crispy fries, and I'll get one of those chocolate molten cakes a little later," Daniels said.

"OK, Ramon?" she asked.

"I'll take two fish, grilled," Ramon said.

Stella nodded. She looked at Hollis. "And, Juicy?"

Now self-conscious, Hollis thought for a minute. He could feel all the guys watching him, waiting to hear his order, but he could also feel his stomach rumbling. The hunger pangs won out over his pride. He didn't care what they thought. He was hungry and was going to enjoy his food. Looking over the menu, he answered, "I'll have a steak and fries, and add four fried shrimp on the side…to assist my cholesterol," he said with a grin. His friends were staring. Clearing his throat, he said, "And the salad bar."

"Good grief, Juicy!" Mayhew exclaimed. "No wonder you can't lose weight!"

About that time, Sheriff Howell walked up. "Hey, fellas."

"Evening, Sheriff," Mayhew said along with the others.

Sheriff Howell was well-respected by all the guys who served under him. Tall and thin, his looks were not intimidating by any means, but he commanded respect nevertheless. Howell had many years of experience in all areas of the sheriff's office and was now serving in his third term as sheriff. While tough on crime, he had a heart for the criminal. His ultimate goal was to see everyone rehabilitated, and he worked with other local agencies and ministries to try his best to make that happen. Howell loved his job, but he was a family man as well, able to balance both. He knew the divorce rate among law enforcement officers, and he was determined not to be a statistic.

Sheriff Howell pulled up a seat where he could see everyone at the table but looked specifically at Mayhew. "So, I hear y'all had a little run-in with the Adams boy today."

"Yeah, a little. Daniels and I came across him and Ross Kelly broken down on County Line Road," Mayhew replied. "Apparently, Mitch gave Jake the Trans-Am, and he couldn't wait to test it out."

"Great...One more renegade on the road to deal with," Howell said.

"Yeah," Daniels interjected. "Mitch was more worried about that car than he was Jake's immature behavior."

"I could have told you that," Howell said.

"I tried to talk to Mitch, but he shut me down real quick," Daniels said. "Based on the smoke pouring out from under that hood, I don't think the boy'll be driving it for a while."

"He's right about that," Mayhew commented. "I gave Ross a ride and talked to him on the way. Said they were racing against Eric Williams and a couple of his buddies."

"There's another spoiled one," Howell said. "What is it with these parents who let their kids have free rein? No rules...no boundaries. Drives me crazy."

"I hate seeing Ross get tied up in that," Mayhew said. "He's a good kid."

"Yeah, but Ross Kelly and Jake Adams have been best friends since birth just about," Sheriff Howell said. "You're not gonna get Ross away from him."

The waitress returned with their drink order.

"Well, hey there, Sheriff. I didn't see you come in. What can I get you?" she asked.

"Oh, I just slipped in. Give me the biggest steak you got with a side of fries and sweet tea."

"You got it!" she said. "Ramon, you and Hollis can go get your salad."

"Juicy got a salad?" Sheriff Howell questioned. "I'm impressed!"

Hollis winked at him as he got up from the table. After he was out of hearing range, Daniels said, "Don't be."

"Yeah, wait 'til you see the rest of his order," Mayhew added.

"That figures," the sheriff said. "Well, back to the Adams boy, let's just keep an eye on him."

Shortly after, Hollis returned with a salad bowl piled high with green leaf lettuce, accompanied by every vegetable and topping from The Driskills' salad bar, doused with Thousand Island dressing.

As Hollis sat down and dug into it, Sheriff Howell looked at the pile of food. "Juicy, don't you think that's kinda defeatin' the purpose?"

"Oh, naw, Sheriff. I got all kinds of healthy stuff in here," Hollis replied.

As Hollis ate his salad, he started another conversation with Daniels.

"So, Daniels, you look at the house plans I gave ya?" he asked.

"Yep," Daniels replied.

"Well, what ya think you could build it for?" Hollis asked.

"Oh, probably around a hundred forty grand," Daniels said.

Hollis choked on his salad. "What? Why you wanna take advantage of me like that? You trying to retire off my house?" he asked sharply.

"No, Juicy," Daniels replied. "I put a pen to it and that's what I came up with. You don't have to go with it. It won't hurt my feelings."

Chomping on his salad, Hollis replied, "Well, it seems like you're shooting it high to me. I think I can do better than that."

"That's fine. Just let me know," Daniels said.

Chapter 6

Stupid…stupid…stupid. That's the only way I know how to describe my choice to race that car. It's all about choices. At that point in time, I would say that was the most humiliating week of my life – losing a race to Eric Williams, then having my mother take me to school in her floral shop van. "Pride goeth before a fall" were the words of my wise mother following my little escapade. I don't think I had ever seen her that upset until that day. It was earth-shaking. I chose not to debate it with her anymore and simply suffered through it in fear that lightning might strike me dead. This event was an incredible opportunity to change. It's heartbreaking to think about it now. Had I chosen to learn from it, things could have been very different.

Monday morning came. Jake dressed for school, but he felt like he was dressing for a funeral. His mind raced, trying to devise a plan to get to school without being seen by anyone in that ridiculous-looking van. He stalled his morning routine to ensure he'd arrive after the tardy bell, when the students were sure to be inside.

"Hurry up, Jake! You're going to be late, which will make *me* late!" Grace exclaimed.

Jake continued taking his time. Grace left the house and sat in the van, waiting for Jake. Her frustration grew, suspecting his tardiness was intentional. Finally, she laid down on the horn until she saw him coming out the door.

The trip to school was a quiet one. The only sounds were uplifting praise music from the radio and the dry humor of the disc jockeys on *JJ and Ron in the Morning*. Grace and Jake found themselves chuckling at the DJs' quick wit, and the tension between them began to dissipate. A few minutes later Grace parked her flower-decaled minivan in the Lee County Academy parking lot near the window of Mr. Anders's creative writing class. Inside sat Ross, Lauren, Eric, and fifteen other students.

"Writing is a process," the tall, thin, 50-something teacher explained. "We would like to think that people are just born with the ability to write. And though some may be more inclined to..." Mr. Anders was interrupted by the sound of students shuffling to the window. Outside, a white van wildly decorated with colorful, larger-than-life flowers had pulled into a space with a screeching halt. The *Flowers of Grace* van was a welcome distraction for the students, already tired of the teacher's dull, lifeless monologue. Everyone recognized the vehicle that represented the town's most popular florist. Inside the van, Jake reclined his seat, desperately hoping to go unnoticed.

"Would you please pull around to the back?" Jake pleaded. "I don't want anyone to see that I'm being carpooled by my mom!"

"Jake, I don't have time for this. I have arrangements to deliver."

"Great," Jake muttered.

"Do you need me to pick you up after school?"

"I'll walk."

Seeing Jake's agitation, she couldn't resist the opportunity to needle him.

"Not my baby!" she cried sarcastically.

Jake tried to open the door, but Grace had pressed the van's power locks, preventing him from getting out. She quickly leaned over and planted a kiss on his cheek.

"Mmmmwaaa…"

Jake grimaced, struggling to unlock the door, and hurried out. As he rushed into the building, Grace rolled down the passenger-side window. "Don't you wipe that off!"

Jake continued into the school without acknowledging his mother's goofy affection. As Grace watched him enter, she couldn't help but break into laughter.

"Oh, one of the joys of motherhood – embarrassing your child," she mumbled under her breath.

———————

The commotion outside the window had drawn a crowd. Ross was embarrassed for Jake, while Lauren and Eric were having a ball.

"This is too good," Eric said to Lauren.

"I know, right?" she agreed. "How humiliating."

Realizing he had lost his audience's attention, Mr. Anders cleared his throat, hoping to regain control of his class.

"…to creative thinking, good writing still requires study and hard effort."

Jake entered the classroom and offered Mr. Anders a salute.

"Sorry I'm late."

"Good to see you, Mr. Adams," Mr. Anders said.

Jake made his way to his seat, avoiding eye contact with anyone, but he could surely feel their stares. In his peripheral view he noticed a smirk on Eric's face. Jake wasn't about to look at him. Instead, he laid his backpack on the desk and plopped down, staring straight ahead and ignoring the barely audible laughs coming from Eric's direction.

Relieved that he had now regained control of his students, Mr. Anders continued.

"All good writing requires structure. The trick is to make the reader think the story came out of thin air – to make him or her feel like the idea just *happened*."

Occasionally, Jake caught Eric looking at him, in which case Jake would quickly avoid the glance. Jake sighed as he looked over his shoulder and watched Lauren talk to Ross using only facial gestures. Jake shook his head. Mr. Anders finally wrapped up his uninteresting recitation on creative writing.

"OK, so we are going to do some brainstorming," Mr. Anders said, changing directions. "I want you to take out a blank sheet of paper and break into groups."

Before the words left his mouth, bored students spun their desks around, now excited about the break in the monotony. Wood and metal slammed together across the room. Jake and Lauren simultaneously turned their desks to partner with Ross. The three desks gently collided, and Lauren smiled an obnoxious grin at Jake. He returned one to her.

Mr. Anders continued with his instruction.

"Now, I want you to pick a basic storyline. It can be as simple as *A Dragon Pursues Its Prey*."

Now face-to-face with Ross, Jake smiled, ready to start the project and forget his less-than-stellar entrance into school. Apparently, though, Ross wasn't going to let him off easily. He chuckled and formed the letter "L" with his thumb and forefinger and held it to his forehead.

Jake mouthed, "Watch it."

Lauren rolled her eyes.

"So, in the center of your paper, draw a circle," Mr. Anders instructed as he demonstrated on the whiteboard. Lauren followed his example and drew a circle in the center of her paper. Jake had still not opened his backpack. Lauren offered him a pen, but he waved her off.

Mr. Anders continued his demonstration by writing *A Dragon Pursues Its Prey* inside his circle.

Ross grabbed Lauren's paper and scribbled something that Jake could not make out. Lauren read it, then giggled. Ross smiled at Jake as he passed the paper to him. Ross's writing in the middle of the roughly drawn circle read: *Loser Needs Car*. Jake loudly crumpled the paper and threw it at Ross, striking him on the forehead.

Lauren produced a new sheet of paper and gave Jake an annoyed look for his childish behavior. Drawing another circle in the center of the fresh sheet of paper, she thought for a moment, then penned: *Girl Surrounded by Idiots*. Proud of herself, she grinned. Jake shrugged in agreement. Ross playfully stuck his tongue out at her. She erased the words from the circle.

Mr. Anders continued his demonstration.

"Now that we have a premise, begin brainstorming. Write down whatever comes to mind about your main character or plot. Notate it around your primary circle. There are no wrong ideas at this point."

The students snickered.

"Within reason," he added, apparently realizing he had given them perhaps too much freedom.

Sighs of disappointment rang through the classroom.

"Begin. Quietly. I do realize that's an oxymoron," he jested.

Lauren wrote a new topic, then shared it with the boys. It read: *Woman Seeks Revenge.* Ross raised his eyebrows and checked Jake for his reaction. Jake responded with the first brainstorming idea: *A woman scorned.*

"Wow," Ross commented, surprised. Impressed, he nodded affirmatively. Jake winked.

Lauren began brainstorming verbally instead of on paper. "Cheating husband."

Jake turned to her, stunned. "Nagging wife," he retorted.

Lauren and Jake began addressing each other directly.

"Anger," she continued.

Jake shrugged. "Doesn't care."

Ross observed the ping-pong of insults between the two.

"Reaching out."

"Still doesn't care."

"Exactly!"

Lauren and Jake stared intently at each other.

"What are we talking about here?" Ross asked with a confused look on his face.

While writing, Lauren began to speak without looking up. "So, we're basically talking about a woman who is in pain," she explained.

At that moment, Jake noticed a commotion outside the classroom door. A pretty brunette stood in the hall with a couple he assumed to be her parents along with the principal, Dr. Sharp. The young lady looked inside the classroom toward Jake, making eye contact for a brief moment, then quickly looked away.

"...and a jerk husband who doesn't care," Lauren concluded.

Jake kicked Ross under the table to get his attention, but Ross was too into Lauren at the moment.

"Couldn't we pick something else?" Ross suggested.

Jake kicked him again.

"Dude! What's up with that?" Ross questioned, obviously growing agitated.

Lauren cut her eyes to Jake, cocked her head and said to Ross as if it were obvious, "He wants you to look at that girl," she said, motioning toward the hallway.

Jake smiled at Lauren. "Thank you."

Ross looked toward the door and studied the brunette for a moment. Bewildered, he said, "That's Morgan Pierce." His head snapped toward Jake. "Is she transferring?"

"Please, God," Jake said prayerfully.

Miffed by their attention toward the new girl, Lauren cocked her head to the side and addressed Jake. "You're in luck. She'll date almost anybody...if you know what I'm saying."

Perturbed, Jake said, "Nice, Lauren."

Morgan was a beautiful brunette with hazel eyes. This tall, lean, ballerina figure with long flowing hair had no problem getting any guy she wanted. Her natural beauty was accompanied by seductive behavior and a provocative sense of fashion.

Dr. Sharp escorted Morgan into the room and introduced her to Mr. Anders, who offered her a seat with Eric's study group. She sat down and introduced herself to Eric, who shook her hand. Eric looked thrilled to have her join their group. Jake shook his head in disbelief.

Could it really get any worse? He sighed under his breath pitifully.

"Irony," Ross softly noted.

Lauren smiled with satisfaction, then refocused on their brainstorming activity.

"Um...So, why doesn't this husband care about his wife anymore?"

The bell rang. With that, Mr. Anders' project was abandoned. The class emptied in no time into the hall. Students began pouring out of other classrooms, slinging backpacks over their shoulders and bumping into each other as they noisily filled the hallways. Jake watched Morgan make her way through the jumble of people. As he approached his locker, he noticed Morgan walking toward him holding a piece of paper and looking at the rows of lockers. It was obvious she was trying to find the one assigned to her. Jake kept his eye on her, hoping she would continue to come closer to him. He knew the locker beside his was vacant. *Could it be possible that she is looking for that one?* he thought. Finally, Morgan stopped at the locker next to his. Looking upward, Jake clasped his hands and mouthed the words *Thank you*.

Jake pretended to look for items in his locker as he continually glanced over at Morgan, waiting on the perfect opportunity to strike up a conversation.

Morgan opened her purse and began to pull out cosmetic items, along with a hairbrush and magnetic mirror, which she mounted on the inside of her locker door. Within just a couple of minutes, she had set up house in her new locker. She gazed in her newly mounted mirror and brushed through her long brown hair. Jake extended his hand to her.

"Jake Adams."

"I know," she replied as she continued to primp.

"Didn't we...we had D.A.R.E. Camp together, right?"

"Yeah," Morgan responded, smiling.

"Morgan, right?"

She nodded as she put away the book she had just acquired from her first class.

"What are you doing here?" he asked.

Morgan thought for a moment as she fumbled with the lock for her locker door. "My parents," she answered while adding a combination to the lock.

Jake stood awestruck by Morgan's beauty. He was having a hard time feeling confident, a highly unusual predicament for him. For some reason, Jake found Morgan somewhat intimidating. He gathered courage to ask her what had been on his mind since seeing her first thing this morning.

"You going to the game this weekend?" he asked.

"I hadn't really planned on it. I'm not too into football." She smiled again. Jake was smitten but very confused. Her positive smile didn't match her negative words.

"Me, either," he said with sarcasm.

Morgan looked him over. "Right. You're the quarterback, huh?"

"You're good," he admitted.

Morgan grinned as she shut the locker door. "Well, if I do make it, you better not let me down," she warned, walking away.

"Let you down?" Jake asked.

"Yeah, as in lose," Morgan clarified.

"Oh, I won't!"

Morgan turned to walk to her next class. She stopped and turned back to Jake.

"I know a party happening later Friday night. Wanna go?" she asked.

Jake was caught off guard but was elated.

"Sure! Where is it?" Jake asked anxiously.

"It's close to my old school. Give me your number and I'll text you the address."

The two pulled out their phones and swapped numbers.

"OK, then. I'll text you," Morgan said with a wink. Jake was surprised at how forward she was.

"I'll be looking for it," Jake said with a smile, waving his phone in the air.

As Morgan merged into the sea of students making their way to class, Jake's smile soon turned into a frown as he had a crippling thought... *What if I have to drive that clunker of a car?*

Suddenly Eric appeared at Jake's locker, placing his hand on Jake's shoulder.

"Bummer," Eric said, pretending to show sympathy.

Eric had overheard the conversation and apparently had the same thought.

Jake jerked his shoulder from under Eric's hand.

"No one asked for your input," he said and stomped off.

Lauren passed Eric in the hall and noticed a pleased look on his face as Jake walked away. She straightened the stack of fliers in her hands and stopped beside Eric.

"Hey, Eric. Youth Explosion's coming up." She handed him a flier.

Eric continued to grin as he stared at Jake walking away.

"What have you done now, Eric Williams?" she inquired.

"Oh, nothing. Just bringing Jake back to reality."

He stood there silently for a few more seconds, savoring the moment. Snapping out of it, he noticed the fliers in Lauren's hands.

"What's that you got?"

"I just told you. Youth Explosion in a couple of weeks. Our school Bible group, FISH, is sponsoring it. Wanna come?"

"I don't know…I'm not big on those things," Eric confessed.

"Well, this year is going to be the best ever. We've got some awesome, well-known people leading it."

"Like who?" Eric inquired.

"A really hot new Christian band is leading the worship, and the evangelist is George Preston!" she said with excitement.

"Never heard of him," Eric replied.

His statement deflated her.

"Are you kidding me? Have you never been to any church camps or youth rallies?"

"Nope."

Lauren looked at him as if he had three heads.

"Well, surely you heard about Youth Explosion last year. Almost every church in the area brought their youth groups, and it was publicized for months on every radio station in town. I even hung posters all over the mall, at convenience stores and restaurants, and in every hallway at this school. Even if you didn't go, you must have heard about it!"

Eric shook his head and said, "Sorry."

Exasperated, she continued down the hall, passing out more fliers to more students. She paused once more to double-check that she had heard Eric correctly.

"Never?"

Eric shrugged.

The tardy bell rang. The halls grew quiet. Two more classes started, then ended. Now was the next opportunity to socialize. Lunch time. Each student had his or her own table of friends. Just like most high schools in America, lunchtime identified the cliques. Everyone knew their place.

Jake made his way through the cafeteria line. The food choices weren't very appealing. He snarled as he looked at the limited menu. The lunch room ladies, adorned in their hairnets and aprons, were used to Jake's derogatory comments and facial expressions. They also had a motto for him: *If you don't like it, move on.* They were, by no means, impressed by his jock status.

After picking out a couple of items he thought would upset his stomach the least, he headed straight to *his* table. Lauren sat to the right of Ross, looking over one of the fliers she had passed out to students earlier that morning. A football teammate, Marcus Riley, sat to Ross's left. Marcus was an African-American young man with a buff, athletic physique. He had a vibrant personality and was very bold in his faith. His high standard of work ethic was paying off for him. With a 4.0 grade point average, as well as self-discipline on the football field and in the weight room, he was highly sought after by universities. He was also very blunt. If you didn't want to hear the truth, you needn't ask Marcus.

He and Ross drilled each other on routes in their play book while scarfing down their lunch. Jake came along, always needing to make a scene, even when sitting down at the table. He held his tray a few inches above the table, then let it fall, causing a loud crashing noise, startling everyone in the cafeteria. Simultaneously, they looked at Jake in annoyance. He got a charge out of their reaction. Jake opened a carton of milk and gulped it dry within seconds. Then, turning his face toward Lauren, he let out a very loud belch. As she waved her hand back and forth in front of her face, Lauren went into a mini-rant about Jake's rude behavior and bad manners. Jake could almost finish her sentences for her, considering he heard the same sermon almost every day.

"Would you guys please not start in on each other today?" Ross requested.

Jake and Lauren turned quickly to Ross. He sounded like a father reprimanding his unruly children.

"Anyone sitting here?" a voice asked softly. Jake looked up to find Morgan standing there. Shocked, but certainly not wanting to miss the opportunity, he quickly said, "You are!" and patted his hand in the empty chair.

A little startled by his bold response, she gently sat down beside him. Morgan's approach boosted his confidence ten-fold. In turn, he became somewhat flirtatious. Once Morgan was situated, Jake leaned in to her, putting his mouth close to her ear, and asked, "Miss me?"

Morgan replied, "I can't miss someone I don't really know."

Jake had no idea how to respond and was silent for a moment, then bursts of laughter erupted from those at the table.

"Well, then, we'll just have to do something about that, won't we?" Jake recovered.

"You're just full of charm, aren't you?" Morgan stated facetiously.

"He's full of something, all right," Marcus joked.

"You just missed his show of charm with a milk carton," Lauren sarcastically remarked.

Morgan looked confused.

Marcus changed the subject. "So, bro, what's the story behind your ride?"

"The Trans-Am?" Jake asked.

"No, the Fred Flintstone car," Marcus said sarcastically. "Of course I mean the Trans-Am!"

Marcus was loud. When he mentioned "Trans-Am," it caught the attention of Eric Williams, who sat at the table next to them. Eric began to eavesdrop on the conversation.

"Not much to tell," Jake answered. "It was my dad's graduation gift from his parents. He's kept it in our barn for years. Ross and I used to sneak out there and pretend to drive it. My dad's spent years restoring it so he could give it to me someday for my graduation. He always wished he'd had it at the beginning of his senior year instead of the end. So with that in mind, he gave it to me now so I can enjoy it my whole senior year."

"So what happened to it?" asked Marcus.

"Allow me," Ross interrupted. "Mr. Adams told him to take it easy, but Jake's ego got in the way."

"It was all Eric's fault. He challenged me," Jake said.

"He raced the car and it overheated," Ross explained. "He's lucky it didn't do more damage than it did."

"So how long 'til it's fixed?" Marcus asked.

"Probably in a few days. My dad's been working hard on it. My mom's overheated about it, so Dad wants me to chill for a while."

Lauren had sat quietly, a big accomplishment for her, especially where Jake was concerned. Finally, she broke. "In other words, Marcus, he's grounded."

The guys at the table began to rag Jake. It was obvious by the expression on Eric's face he was enjoying the conversation.

"You're a senior and you're grounded?" Marcus asked. "You drove that car how many hours?"

"Way to try and smooth it over, Jake," Ross complimented sarcastically.

Eric was having too much fun with all of this. He jumped up from his seat to return his lunch tray. He wasn't about to miss the opportunity to pour salt in Jake's wounds, especially in front of Morgan.

"Hey, Jake. How's your Matchbox car?" Eric smarted off.

"It's just fine, Eric. Not that it's any of your concern."

Eric laughed. "You know, Jake, I don't know why you were so surprised when it ran hot like that. I mean, after all, your dad drove it during the Stone Age."

"What's your problem, Eric?" Jake asked in frustration.

"*You're* my problem!" Eric assured him. "You really think you have a cool car?"

"I know I do," Jake said confidently.

"It's junk," Eric said.

Jake ignored Eric's comment and tried to return to the conversation with his friends.

"Did you hear me, boy?" Eric asked in a challenging tone.

Jake slammed his hands on the table and stood up. "Boy?" Jake asked. "If you've got a problem with me, then just spit it out!"

"I have a big problem with your bragging!" Eric admitted.

"Well, keep your ears at your own table, and it shouldn't bother you anymore," Jake brashly suggested.

"I'm pretty sure I proved yesterday what a joke your car is," Eric taunted.

Jake had heard enough of Eric's trash talk. He jumped up and moved in extremely close to Eric, inches from his face.

"Well, apparently yesterday wasn't enough to convince you, because you're still standing here talking about it. You wanna go again, we'll go again. You just tell me when and where."

Eric looked around at the audience they had acquired. He didn't realize how loud the heated argument had grown. He looked at Jake for a moment, then his temper began to cool.

"We're not done here," Eric assured Jake.

"Agreed. Round two...let me know when and where, and I'll be there."

Without another word, Eric walked away. Jake sat back down in his seat. His anger still stirred like a passing storm.

"Do you two always act like that toward one another?" Morgan asked.

"That's how Jake's relationship is with most people," Lauren replied.

The last thing Jake needed was Lauren's opinion.

Still fuming from his confrontation with Eric, Jake snapped, "Nobody asked you, Lauren!"

"Come on, Jake. You're mad at Eric," Ross said. "Don't take it out on her."

"She needs to keep her comments to herself," Jake complained. "She's always running her mouth about me!"

"You both need to shut it down!" Ross said firmly. "I'm sick of listening to you two!"

The table was silent. The bell rang, alerting students that lunch was over. The friends at Jake's table parted ways without speaking a word. Once again, the halls began to fill with teens exchanging books in their lockers, enjoying casual conversation. The heated moment passed, and the confrontations were momentarily pacified.

The school day drew to a close. For Jake and Ross it meant one thing…time for football practice. The players lived for this part of the day. For these young men, going to class was the necessary evil in order to play football.

Oddly, they loved the smell of the locker room. The odors that repelled most were sweet aromas to them, for they were smells of blood, sweat and tears spilled for the joy of victory week after week… season after season. They were the smells of tremendous effort and persistence poured out on that football field. This was where Jake shined. He was a beast on the field. It was his stage where he performed, and he did it well, too. Several athletes on the Eagles team were worthy of college scholarships because of their athletic ability. Most of them would have to take whatever was offered to them. But for Jake, he could go to the university of his choice. There was no need for consideration, however. He knew where he was headed. Jake and his dad had it all planned out.

Football practice had been productive that day. Still early in the season, the afternoon temperatures soared. Practice in the heat of the day was tough, and hydration was a major concern. The Eagles pressed on, however, giving it their all. The team's work ethic was admirable, but there were major character flaws.

The captain of the team was self-centered and suffered from an inflated ego. He was obnoxious and conceited, but his peers learned to live with it. On the field, however, he was a dynamic leader. His teammates trusted his judgment in making calls and had no problem following his lead.

Jake had a somewhat violent temper and an appalling attitude. He was belittling to everyone, even his best friend, Ross. He saw everyone as "beneath" him. One of those in particular was a player on the team named "Hamm," which was actually his last name: Bartholomew Fitzpatrick Hamm III, in its full form. However, because of his size and eating habits, they just called him Hamm. Did it bother him? Probably so, but the 6-foot, 300-pound boy with a buzz cut had a meek spirit. Hamm endured a lot of humiliation from the team, mostly instigated by Jake, yet he remained loyal to them.

The locker room reeked of male body odor – a foul blend of sweat, stinky tennis shoes, oily hair and gym bags that more than likely had not been cleaned out since the practice season began.

The red, white and blue walls of the locker room were adorned with championship banners and posters bearing motivational quotes. The temperature was kept quite cool to ensure the boys an immediate cool-down when practice was over.

The guys took turns running through the showers for a quick clean-up. As Hamm gathered his things for his turn, Jake walked past him and smirked. Hamm gave him a quick look out of the corner of his eye. He never knew what to expect with Jake.

"'Sup...Hamm," Jake said with a devious grin.

"Jake," Hamm acknowledged.

As Jake continued past him, he glanced next at Marcus, the team's best running back and co-captain, and gave him "the look."

"Are you serious?" Marcus mouthed.

"Yes, I'm serious," he whispered.

Jake motioned to Marcus with his head, reiterating his plan.

Marcus walked over to Jake and stood close to him so that Hamm wouldn't pick up on the plot.

"You just need to leave that poor boy alone, man," he rebuked.

"Naw...You don't understand," Jake said. "You see, he would be terribly disappointed if I didn't mess with him. That's how I show my affection for him. He knows that."

"Man, you're just cruel."

Jake brushed off Marcus's comment. Sadly, it had no effect on his conscience.

"Who makes the calls on the field?" Jake asked.

"You do," Marcus answered. Understanding that Jake had some control over how many passes he was thrown, which determined how good his stats looked on paper, Marcus caved. "Fine. I'll do it," he begrudgingly complied.

Jake would use any tactic to manipulate people into doing what he wanted them to do. He made his way back to the locker to pack his things. Suddenly he heard a pop and felt a burning sensation on the back of his leg. He immediately turned to the players who encircled him. They laughed uncontrollably. Jake was enraged. His face flushed with anger and embarrassment.

"Whatcha gonna do, boy?" one of the team's skill players asked.

"Drew Collins, you wait," Jake warned.

Drew, a dark-headed, golden-eyed, tall and slender senior, was known for his impulsive behavior. Diagnosed with ADHD in first grade, Drew had taken medication throughout his school life to help with his impulses and emotional outbursts. This made him a target for ridicule at times, but still, he brought a lot of it on himself.

Marcus stepped up. "The boy can dish it out, but he can't take it."

"I'll take you," Jake retaliated.

"All right, guys," Ross intervened. "Stop it. You got your thrill."

"Aw, come on, y'all!" a voice cried out from the shower room.

It was Hamm. Once again, after showering, he realized he was stranded without his clothes.

"Man, you are sorry," Ross pointed out.

"He'll be OK," Jake responded with a wink. As he opened his locker, an envelope fell out and onto the floor.

"What's that?" Ross asked.

Jake picked it up and looked at the return address. "Oh, it's just another scholarship application from another no-name school that I won't be attending."

"Man, how many offers you got?" Drew asked. "I'll bet your list is about a mile long."

"It's been pretty wild," Jake said. "I can probably go anywhere I want to go."

"Do I even need to ask what your pick's gonna be?" Drew asked.

"Alabama, of course. I'm going to Tuscaloosa in October for Recruiting Day."

"Alabama vs. Tennessee, baby!" Ross cheered, giving Jake a high five.

"There are supposed to be three schools here scouting me out at the next home game," Jake added.

"Jake's gonna be more famous around here than Elvis," Ross joked.

Pointing at Ross, Jake said, "Thank you. Thank you very much."

His teammates responded to his cheesy humor by throwing their towels at him.

"So, Drew, have you had any offers?" Ross asked.

"I've had a couple," Drew replied. "Of course, the scholarship offers aren't to the schools I want."

"Hang in there, man," Ross said. "It's early in the season."

"I know. I'm not worried," Drew assured him. "I still have academic scholarships for the school I really want. Then I'll just walk on and try to earn a football scholarship that way."

"Sounds like a plan," Ross confirmed.

"Come on, guys! Somebody bring me my stuff!" Hamm continued to plead. The poor guy was merely background noise, like elevator music. This was such a normal occurrence, no one really noticed it.

"What about you, Ross?"

"Are you kidding me?" Jake interrupted. "This guy's goin' with me. Right, Bama Bro?"

"Yep!" Ross replied. "Jake and I have been making plans to room together at the University of Alabama since kindergarten, basically."

"What if you don't get a scholarship offer there?" Marcus asked.

"I'll walk on," Ross said. "I love football, but I'd rather be at Alabama and not get to play than be playing somewhere that isn't Alabama."

"I hear ya," Marcus replied.

"Besides," Ross said, "I'm more concerned about doing well with my studies. I'm very passionate about what I want to do."

"Which is what?" Drew asked.

"Law enforcement," Ross said.

"Yeah, Ross wants to be like Mike," Jake mocked.

"Don't start, Jake," Ross said.

"Man, I just don't understand you following that guy around all the time," Jake said.

"He's a cool guy. Besides, I've learned a lot from him," Ross said, defending his mentor.

"I feel ya, Ross," Marcus said. "If it wasn't for Deputy Ramon, I probably would have dropped out of school by now."

"I've heard Juicy call him Blambo. I don't get it," Drew said.

"You ever heard of Rambo?" Marcus asked.

"Yeah, from the movie, right?" Drew asked.

"Right," Marcus said. "Well, Deputy Ramon is black like me. So, Blambo...black and Rambo."

"Is that not offensive to him?" Ross asked.

"Naw," Marcus replied. "He ain't like that. In fact, he eats it up."

"Oh!" Drew replied. "Now it makes sense."

"The guys call Deputy Hollis 'Juicy,' " Drew said.

"Because?" Marcus asked.

"Because he's so plump!" Drew said, laughing.

The guys began to laugh.

"Hey...in Juicy's defense, he has been working out," Drew said.

"It's not gonna do him any good when he's got a weight in one hand and a burger in the other," Jake said sarcastically.

"If he'd do it the Blambo way, he'd shape up in a heartbeat," Marcus said. "That guy's got it going on."

"Hey, Marcus, tell the story again about how you met him," Drew said.

"Oh, not again," Jake complained.

"I'd love to," Marcus said dramatically, eyeing Jake. "When I was in fifth grade, I didn't want to go to school. I gave my momma fits about it. She couldn't make me go either. Finally, she called the sheriff's department and asked Sheriff Howell if he'd come talk to me. He did. Deputy Ramon came with him. They asked me why I refused to go to school. I told them it was because the kids made fun of me... the way I dressed. You see, my momma had to get whatever she could find me to wear. Not only were they not in style or name brand, they usually didn't fit me right, either."

The guys stood silent, listening to every word, even the ones who had heard him share it several times.

"Deputy Ramon put me in his patrol car, took me to his house and picked me out some clothes and shoes. Man, I was stylin'!" he said with a big smile. His teammates laughed. "That summer, he invited me to the D.A.R.E. Camp. I've been hangin' out with him ever since. Thanks to him stepping into my life, not only do I have a bright future with football, I came to know Christ. Now, that's life-changing."

"Preach!" Drew said, giving Marcus a high five. "I'm thankful for Deputy Hollis, too. It's tough growing up without a dad. I'm glad the Lord put Juicy in my life."

"Jake, you were at the same camp and had the same opportunity we did," Marcus said.

"Yeah, well, I got stuck with Galen Daniels. That dude is a moron," Jake said.

"He has several nicknames, by the way," Ross said.

"I guess one for each personality," Jake mocked.

"I've heard Mayhew call him a couple of them," Ross said.

"Me, too," Marcus said. "Where did he get them?"

"I have no idea," Jake said. "I've never cared to ask."

"I know," Ross said. "He got the nickname '4.2' because he once told the guys that in high school, he could run a forty-yard dash in 4.2 seconds."

"If he could do that, he would have gone to the NFL," Jake said. The other players laughed.

"Exactly," Ross said.

"What about the other names?" Marcus asked out of curiosity.

"The Golden Child and Mini Mayhew," Ross replied.

"Yeah, Juicy said because he's Mayhew's pet," Drew said.

"So, why don't you like Daniels, Jake?" Marcus asked.

"Primarily because he gets on my nerves with all of his 'encouragement' and 'motivation,' " Jake said.

"Jake, you've never given him a chance," Ross said.

"Well, I ain't got time for dat," Jake said.

He looked at the time on his phone. "It's gettin' late. Ross, you ready?"

"Yeah, I guess," Ross replied.

"Come on, Bama Bro. Let's roll," Jake said.

"Later, guys," Ross said.

Jake and Ross grabbed their bags to leave. Just before they walked out the door, Jake's ears caught the cries of Hamm still echoing from the shower stall.

"Man, I almost forgot about him," Jake said. "Hey, Marcus. Give Hamm his stuff, will ya?"

"Yeah, man," Marcus said.

"Jake, you are gonna traumatize that boy," Ross said.

"Oh, it'll make a man out of him," Jake said.

Ross listened to Hamm wail as they walked outside. "Well, he doesn't sound like a man."

Chapter 7

I was enjoying a great start to my senior year: serving as co-cap-tain with my best friend, receiving my dream car as an early gradua-tion present and watching scholarship offers pour in from across the country. Although Alabama was my choice, knowing so many other schools wanted me still was a big ego boost...as if I needed that. The new girl in school had her eye on me. She could be a distraction if I wasn't careful, but who could resist her? The even bigger question in my mind was how could she resist me? Wow...how arrogant! I must have seemed like a clown to so many. My frustration grew over the never-ending feuds with that "pathetic" Eric Williams and the "overbearing, self-righteous" Lauren. I am amazed to this day at my ability to blame and find fault in others. Looking back, I realize I brought a lot of the frustration on myself. They were two individuals I could not control. But, of course, there were other things I couldn't control either, such as my temper, my future...my dad. Had I focused on controlling the things that were within my power, life would be very different today.

Friday night had finally arrived, and Eagle Stadium was packed. Football was a big deal at this school. Although game time was 7:30 p.m., the temperature was still sweltering, even this early in the season. The aroma of charcoal-grilled hamburgers floated across the bleachers, enticing spectators to the concession stand. Lee County Academy's cheerleaders danced to their nationally-ranked marching band. The loud crash of helmets echoed across Eagle Stadium as the opposing team's defense tackled a running back.

Grace and Kate sat together as they had for the past five years, watching their boys play. Margaret and Lauren sat on the bleacher just below them.

"Marcus Riley on the carry for a gain of seven yards," the announcer commentated. "Eagle quarterback Jake Adams called a reverse at the last second there. Adams is eight for eight on pass completions at the beginning of the second half."

Mitch Adams stood close to the sideline and cupped his hands around his mouth. "Let him throw it!" he demanded.

Lance Kelly and Mike Mayhew stood close by. Although Mitch's behavior was embarrassing, they remained silent, knowing it did no good to say anything.

Head varsity football coach J.C. Scott heard Mitch but ignored him. The hefty bald fellow was in his mid-forties and had coached long enough to be immune to parents' comments. The players settled into offensive stances as Jake moved fluidly behind them. In the stands, Grace leaned forward on her elbows, always a bundle of nerves during his games.

Jake stood at the line of scrimmage, ready for the hand-off. "Down! Set...Hut! Hut!" he called out.

He rolled backward as bulky linemen collided in an explosion of plastic and padding. Linebackers rushed through a small gap in the offensive line and forced Jake to run toward the outside of the line.

"Get out of there!" Mitch yelled.

Back on the field, Jake spotted Ross, an open receiver, and tossed a short pass toward him. Ross caught it just as defensive players tackled him.

"Yes! Way to go, son!" Lance cheered. Mayhew clapped along.

Kate stood with hands cupped over her mouth. No matter how many hits Ross took, she still was unnerved watching. Seeing that he was up and running back into position, she sat down in intense relief. Grace patted her knee in empathy.

Jake pointed a cocked finger at his best friend and receiver and pretended to shoot him. The crowd went wild! Suddenly Jake spied Morgan in the crowd. She watched him but played it cool. Jake found this frustrating yet attractive.

"That's nine for nine," the announcer exclaimed. "Adams is on fire!"

As the Eagle huddle formed, Ross joined in. "Could you make it any tighter?" Ross said sarcastically.

"Next time, I'll make sure you're wide open!" Jake assured him, slapping his helmet.

"They're running scared!" Marcus said.

"And we're going to stay on them!" Jake warned. "Keep up or get left behind!"

He looked to Coach Scott for a series of signals, then ducked back into the huddle.

Jake called the play. "Forty-two gap on one!"

With each player's hands on the next player's shoulder pads, they chanted in unison, "Break!"

The team separated and returned to the line. Mitch grew agitated as he saw that Jake was settling into a running formation. He looked into the stands and located a University of Alabama scout who wore a crimson-colored ball cap with the script *A* logo. The scout made a note on his clipboard. Unclear of what that meant, Mitch turned his attention back to the field.

Jake set up the next play. "Down! Set! Hut!"

Jake stepped back and handed off the football to a large running back, who crashed through the line and ran the remaining twenty yards for a touchdown. The crowd went wild as the scoreboard changed to Eagles 20, Wolves 6.

With that score, the Eagles' momentum soared. Every play was perfectly executed. Jake jumped and weaved in and out of the masses of defenders, an obvious but hard-to-peg target for the opposition. He was untouchable, firing the ball over the tops of leaping defensive linemen and hitting his open men over and over. Jake's rope-like calf muscles flexed as he quickly and nimbly changed direction each time a defender suddenly appeared. Linebackers rushed him, forcing him to run the ball. His powerful legs propelled him upward as he jumped over falling defensive players.

Grace watched with nerves on end. Jake ran the ball into the end zone, bringing the home crowd to its feet. They erupted with cheers as the band performed the fight song and the cheer squad danced. Play after play, Jake ruled the game as the fans rewarded him with deafening chants. Mitch paced on the sideline. Morgan tracked Jake's moves, her interest in him increasing with every successful play. The score was now Eagles 28, Wolves 13. The clock was frozen at eleven seconds when Coach Scott called a timeout. Realizing they had the game in hand, Coach Scott turned to his assistant and instructed him to sub in a few rookie players. His strategy was clear: give the young players some experience and save his starters from possible injury.

The assistant coach motioned for sophomore player Hamm. "Left guard! Go!" he ordered. Hamm hustled onto the field. Coach Scott motioned for Jake, who quickly trotted to the sideline to receive instruction.

"Stop the clock," Coach Scott instructed him as he patted his helmet.

Out of breath, Jake responded, "Yes, sir."

From the sideline, Mitch motioned for Jake. Jake pushed his way through the sideline toward his father. Mitch grabbed Jake's face mask and pulled him close to his face. Coach Scott watched, trying to figure out what Mitch was doing.

"Pass it," Mitch said to Jake calmly.

Jake questioned him with his eyes. Mitch noticed Coach Scott watching. Turning back to Jake, his facial expression quickly changed to stone.

Again, he said, "Pass it."

Confused by his father's orders, Jake studied Mitch's eyes. He turned his attention to the scout clad in Crimson Tide attire, an obvious stand-out in the sea of Eagles blue.

"You don't play for an SEC school because you can hit a ten-yard toss," Mitch said. "There are things at stake here bigger than you can understand."

Jake hesitated for a moment, then nodded in agreement. He turned and rushed onto the field into the huddle. Looking to the sideline at his coach, then at his dad, Jake knew he had a decision to make and a split second in which to make it... *Who do I obey?*

Jake returned to the huddle. He had made his decision. "Bootleg pass...all the way. Marcus...burn him."

Ross looked at Jake. "Coach said to down it," he said firmly.

Jake was committed. He double-checked the sideline. There was his mother with her face nervously perched in her hands. Jake then studied Mitch. The scout continued to make notations on his clipboard. A different Jake leaned back into the huddle, his face resolute with the same stone-like expression as his dad's.

"This is the part where you keep up or get left behind," Jake said.

Jake swept the huddle with his eyes and noticed the rookie players who had been substituted in the game, specifically Hamm.

"Hamm, they've been coming hard on the left. You're going to have to step up."

Hamm nodded nervously in agreement.

"Ready, on two!" Jake dictated.

"Break!" the team chanted as they took their positions.

Ross eyed Jake. Jake turned from Ross and focused on the field. Hamm assumed his stance and zoned in on the large Wolf before him. Lacking confidence in his ability, he sucked back his mouthpiece that kept escaping. Jake placed his hands under the player at center and inhaled a calming breath.

"Down! Set! Hut hut!"

The lines collided. Jake rolled out.

"What are you doing?" Coach Scott yelled in total confusion.

Jake ran back as his linemen fought to hold steady. Marcus pulled away from his coverage and headed down the sideline. The defensive player whom Hamm was blocking easily ran around him and toward Jake.

"Hamm!" Jake called out through his mouthpiece. He pointed at the defensive player. Hamm chased him but couldn't keep up. The defensive player drove Jake deeper into the backfield toward his own end zone. Marcus was wide open.

Coach Scott could see the play forming and could tell it wasn't going to be successful.

"No!" he cried out as he threw his hat on the ground.

Jake cocked his arm, lining up the pass to Marcus. Out of nowhere a Wolf grabbed him. Jake spun away from the defender just as Hamm's player approached him. Jake regained his footing and fired the ball. The crowd stood to their feet. Mitch ran down the sideline to follow the action. The ball sailed through the air the length of the football field and floated perfectly into the hands of the opposing team's safety.

"Ah!!!!" Jake exclaimed, pulling at his face mask.

Marcus lunged toward the safety in a desperate attempt to stop him, but stumbled and fell to the ground in a discouraged heap. The safety turned and ran. A collective "Nooo!" came from the crowd as the agile defender ran the ball back through the line of scrambling offensive players. The Wolves quickly rallied and blocked for their runner. An unstoppable wall ran downfield. Confused, Hamm quickly stood and watched. Jake chased the safety and dived at him in a last-ditch effort to stop him from scoring. Jake's impact spun the player, who crashed just inside the end zone. The Wolves' section went crazy over their unexpected score.

The announcer updated the spectators on the action while questioning Jake's decision to throw the ball instead of downing it. "That's going to be a touchdown Wolves. What was Adams thinking? The Wolves are excited, but it really doesn't matter. Eagles win it twenty-eight to nineteen."

Even though the Eagles had still won the game, the atmosphere was tense on the home side. The crowd emptied the bleachers with little noise. On the other side of the field, although the Wolves did not win, they continued to celebrate the final play of the game. Infuriated, Jake threw down his helmet and pointed to Hamm, his face filled with blame toward the sophomore.

The Eagles and the coaching staff slowly and silently made their way to the locker room. Jake stood near the entrance, waiting, and as soon as Hamm entered, Jake slammed him violently against a row of lockers. Immediately Ross and three other players grabbed Jake, who struggled against them. Marcus jumped in front of Hamm, protecting him while taking on Jake himself.

"Like you ain't never messed up!" Marcus yelled, pushing Jake away.

Ross also stepped in front of Jake, shoving his hands against Jake's chest. Jake's breathing was deep and heavy.

"You need to calm down right now!" Ross said. "You are way out of line!"

The sound of a heavy metal door slammed shut and echoed throughout the locker room. The players froze.

"Jake!" The yell was completely recognizable; the young men had heard this tone of extreme anger, but this time, the scream seemed a bit more ominous.

The players' heads snapped toward the sound to find Coach Scott standing in the doorway of his office. He scanned each player thoroughly, looking for the player who had directly defied his play call.

"Come see me...now!" Coach Scott ordered, his eyes finally resting on Jake.

The players released Jake, whose muscles had somewhat relaxed. They watched Jake as he walked toward the coach's office, each internally glad not to be Jake at that moment.

Coach Scott sat on the edge of his messy desk as a guilty Jake Adams entered the room. The coach stared at him for an awkward moment.

"What was that?" he asked angrily, motioning his head toward the football field.

Jake tensed. Once again, the stone-like look appeared on his face. "It's called a pass," he replied obnoxiously.

Coach Scott walked to the teenager, his face now inches from Jake's. Jake could see the pupil in each eye and for the first time noticed that Coach had one blue eye and one green eye.

"It's called disobedience," he corrected him.

Jake stood quietly and looked away.

"It's called putting yourself before the team," the man added. Coach Scott had dealt with egos before and knew how to deal with this one. "You think you're a superstar? Try playing without someone to catch your passes..."

Coach retreated a few inches. Jake relaxed a little.

"...or block for you so the defense doesn't cram the ball down your throat." He paused. "We don't play for scouts. Understand?"

Jake struggled to nod.

"This is more than a game," Coach Scott continued. "You're making decisions that'll define your life."

Coach Scott nodded toward the locker room. "Hit the showers."

Jake left the office without rebuttal. As he walked away, Coach Scott continued to study him, concern on his face; this boy seemed to have no remorse.

Only a few cars remained in the school parking lot. Halogen lights flickered above. Jake exited the field house with a duffle bag slung over his shoulder and his head down. Mitch had waited for him outside to make sure he was OK. He could tell by the look on Jake's face that he felt defeated.

"Hey," Mitch called to him.

Jake turned around, surprised to see him.

"What happened?" Mitch asked.

Jake chose his words carefully. "We won." Jake continued walk-ing away.

"That was quite a pass!" Mitch said, trying to encourage his son. Jake kept walking.

"...Wasn't your fault!" Mitch reinforced. Apparently Jake was going to ignore him. Mitch shook his head and walked to the field house, a conversation with J.C. Scott on his mind.

———

Jake ignored his father and walked toward his old Honda. He had been given permission to drive it home after the game. In the distance, he noticed a group of students gathered around a couple of sports cars. One of the vehicles was a black Challenger, and in the dim light, he could barely make out Eric's form standing next to it. *Perfect*, Jake thought sarcastically.

He stared for a moment. "No way," he whispered under his breath, recognizing one of the female figures as Morgan. Jake could tell by the way she was behaving with Eric that Morgan didn't realize he was there. *I just don't know where I stand with that girl*, he thought to himself.

Jake continued to his car and remotely unlocked it. The three short but loud beeps caught the teens' attention. Jake raised the lid to the trunk, tossed in his duffle bag, then slid into the driver's seat, wanting nothing else but to get home. As he turned the key, the starter struggled to respond.

"No," Jake whispered, commanding his car not to stall.

He tried again, only to hear a loud metallic clank in the engine. He turned the key again. This time, he heard nothing. Tightly gripping the steering wheel, he closed his eyes and released a breath through pursed lips.

A peck on his driver's side window startled him. Morgan was leaning over, looking into the car with a sympathetic grin. Relieved it was not Eric, Jake rolled down the window.

"That was some game," Morgan commented.

Unsure of how to respond, Jake said, "Could've been better."

Morgan shrugged. Jake inhaled. "Look, I'm not going to be able to give you a ride to the aft—"

Morgan interrupted, "That's cool. I'll catch a ride with Eric." She studied Jake as he attempted to hide a grimace.

"That's probably a good idea," Jake confirmed.

"See ya Monday?" Morgan asked.

"Yeah," Jake said, deflated. His mind was blown away by how quickly the day had turned sour. Only hours earlier, the night had looked so promising. Jake had expected an overwhelming win followed by an exciting night with a gorgeous girl on his arm. The win felt like a loss, and the girl was walking away from him toward a boy Jake hated with an intensity he had never before felt. He watched Eric meet Morgan halfway, placing his hand on her back. Then, as if to add insult to injury, Eric looked back at Jake with a victorious grin.

Jake leaned back and sank into the seat, then in frustration nodded forward, then backward, slamming against the headrest. His blue eyes stared straight into the night. The events of the evening swirled through his mind like a movie reel. Finally, he snapped out of the trance-like state.

"OK, girl. Get me home," he spoke softly to his car.

He tried starting it again. Unexpectedly, it turned over on the first try.

"Bam!" he cheered.

Upon arriving home, Jake entered the side door that opened directly into the kitchen. The house was dark except for a small amount of light spilling from the living room. On the breakfast table sat a plate of meatloaf and vegetables Grace had left for him, and as usual, her Bible rested in the center.

Jake wasn't hungry but sat down anyway to the plate his mother had left. Tapping his fork on the table, he glanced at the nearby wall where the family's keys hung. Lamplight from the den fell on the red "J" of his keychain dangling among the other keys, taunting him. So many thoughts raced through his mind. *This is my senior year and I'm sitting at home eating cold meatloaf…in the dark. I should be at that party. I should be there with Morgan.* Jake's mind could not grasp how Eric Williams had gotten the upper hand in both major areas of his life right now – the race and the girl. *This is not the way it's supposed to be.* Voices from an unknown source began to confirm these thoughts. *You're right, Jake. This isn't the way things are supposed to be. Just take the car. It's your car. You deserve it, Jake.*

The voices ceased with the opening, then closing, of the front door. Mitch had come home.

"Hey," Jake heard Grace gently speak to Mitch, realizing she must have been in the living room the entire time.

"Hey," Mitch quietly responded.

Grace remained silent for a few moments.

"Forget your cell?" she asked. "I tried calling you a few times but didn't get an answer."

"No. I've been talking to that not-so-bright coach of ours," Mitch said.

Grace sat up. "Coach Scott?"

Jake raised his head and listened.

Embarrassed, Grace responded, "He's a friend from church, Mitch. I can't believe you did that."

Mitch stood over Grace with his hands on his hips. "Jake needs to be playing for somebody who understands what he's capable of."

Grace lowered her head and spoke softly. "JC Scott is a good man."

"Well, he's a lousy coach. If he weren't, he wouldn't still be coaching high school," Mitch ranted.

Grace raised her head and looked Mitch in the eyes. "He would've finished that game two touchdowns ahead had Jake obeyed him," she pointed out.

Surprised by her bold response, Mitch was speechless. With his head bowed, he turned and walked toward the bedroom. The sound of the door closing came soon after Grace sat in silence, turning her thoughts toward God's word that was hidden in her heart.

Jake rose from his seat, leaving his plate untouched. Heavy-hearted, he walked across the living room floor toward his room.

Realizing Jake had overheard the conversation between her and Mitch, she called to him. "Jake…"

Jake stopped but did not speak.

"You did good, baby," she encouraged him.

Feeling beaten, he commented, "You don't sound like you really think that."

"You did what you thought you had to do."

Grasping what she meant, he turned to her. "Thanks, Mom."

"I love you," she reassured him.

Jake nodded and walked to his room. Except for a hint of moonlight making its way through his window blinds, darkness pervaded Jake's room. Unnatural shadows crept downward from the ceiling. Jake sat on the end of his bed and stared straight ahead. The clock on his dresser read 11:11 p.m. His mind replayed the night's conversation with Morgan.

I know a party happening later Friday night. Wanna go? He recalled the voice of that beautiful brunette who had caught his attention. On his wall the darkened forms of professional athletes looked down on him from their posters. *You had her,* the voice in his head painfully reminded him. Jake's eyes dropped. He stood, determined to go to the party…in the Trans-Am. It was fixed now, after all. New thermostat, belts, hoses – the works. He wasn't going to be made a fool of any longer by anyone – especially Eric.

Jake quietly made his way to the kitchen, careful not to alert his parents. Just as before, the "J" keychain hung in the small beam of light from the next room. As Jake reached toward the key, he hesitated, standing in the dark, struggling against the temptation and weighing the consequences.

He carefully deactivated the security alarm, gently opened the door and closed it slowly behind him. He sprinted toward the barn. As he opened the massive door, moonlight filled the dark space. Jake's figure, a lone silhouette, stood before the covered form of the Trans-Am. Slowly, he approached the car. His fingers grasped the tarp that covered it. After a moment of hesitation, Jake pulled it away. The shiny, red-and-white Trans-Am rested in front of him. His hands traced the contours of the hood as Jake walked around the front of the car, just as he had done when he was a boy. To ensure that he entered the party with the total look, he removed the T-tops. Finally, he opened the door and slid inside.

The leather seat creaked. With one hand around the steering wheel, Jake inserted the key into the ignition. He paused, thinking. The voice encouraged him. *You deserve this.* It continued to urge him. *He owes you.* Jake's hand moved to the gear shifter. He looked toward the darkened house. Morgan's words rang out. *Don't let me down, Jake.* His hand moved quickly to the key and turned the ignition. The Trans-Am roared to life. A plume of white smoke rolled from the exhaust pipes, illuminated by the red glow of brake lights. Jake checked his rearview mirror and watched the smoke dissipate. Shifting the car into drive, he slowly rolled down the dark driveway, waiting to turn on the headlights until the tires hit the pavement. Once he was far enough away from the house, Jake stomped the accelerator, smiling. The Trans-Am screamed forward into the night. With the wind in his hair and music blaring on the radio, Jake felt himself slipping back into his reigning position of big man on campus and star football player. Life was waiting to be *lived* and enjoyed – not cautiously treaded through while bowing to overbearing people and ridiculous rules. It was time to take charge...

Chapter 8

Entitlement...A mental state that is so prevalent today. I was the poster child for this syndrome. "I deserve it. He owes me." This is what I believed. The voices I heard fueled that belief, fully convincing me of it. The party being held in another county seemed harmless. I could just lay low and go undetected. The only thing I had on my mind was taking first place back in Morgan's mind and heart. I couldn't understand at all her attraction to Eric, especially compared to what she had in me. There's that ego puffing up again. Once I got out of my driveway, all fear was left behind. After all, what could possibly happen? And if something did happen, who's gonna tell, right? Two little words...social media. Were it not for my dad, it could have been the death of me.

As he approached the party, Jake could see that although it was well after midnight, the end of this social event was nowhere in sight. Hundreds of teenagers were scattered over the field near the blacktop road. Vehicles streamed in and out of the makeshift parking area. A group of sports cars was parked in a circle. Jake drove slowly behind a cluster of girls walking toward the party; they were clueless that Jake drove behind them. One of the girls broke away from the group. "That's Morgan!" he said out loud. "What are the chances?" Jake pulled alongside her.

He was sure the low rumble of the engine would draw her attention. Either she did not hear him, or she had chosen to ignore him. Seeing that she wasn't going to acknowledge him, he spoke up.

"Need a lift?" he asked with a grin. Morgan looked at him and stopped. Jake's grin turned into an uncontainable smile. He motioned for her to get in. Apparently playing hard-to-get, she hesitated, but after a moment climbed into the passenger's seat. Morgan gave the car a quick once-over before even opening her mouth. She first looked through the open T-top. The moon's white glow escaped the dark clouds that had covered it. She rubbed her fingers along the red leather seat.

"Whose car?" Morgan inquired.

Jake shrugged. "Mine."

Morgan smirked. "I thought you were grounded. Did you sneak out?" she asked.

"Uh, I guess you could say I stole it," Jake confessed.

They both giggled. Morgan nodded with approval as she sat with Jake, now saying nothing, the car still idling in the field. Jake glanced in the side-view mirror and noticed they were being watched by Morgan's ride to the party, Eric.

Elated, he looked at Morgan. "Where to?"

"Anywhere," she replied.

Excited by her free-spirit response, he again looked in his side-view mirror and winked at Eric. Jake could tell by the look on Eric's face he was not happy. Leaving the premises, they passed a blue SS Impala with its hood raised. The driver was Robbie James, a junior at Morgan's former school. He had a terrible attitude and was always looking for a fight. Giving Jake a hard, cold look, Robbie nudged his sidekick, motioning him to look at the Trans-Am as it passed by.

Very soon, the field party was miles behind them, and the Trans-Am rolled through the mostly deserted downtown. A shopping strip comprised primarily of mom-and-pop businesses – a dry cleaner, a bank and the town's city hall – each displayed homemade, paw-shaped wooden signs that read "Tiger Country." The streets were completely dark and quiet. Morgan ran a hand through her hair as a gentle wind blew into the car.

"So…you in the habit of stealing cars?" Morgan asked.

"That depends."

Morgan raised her eyebrows.

"Right now it's working out pretty good," he kidded.

Amused by his answer, she turned away and allowed the wind to continue blowing through her hair.

"Your dad's pretty intense," she said bluntly.

"You noticed," Jake replied.

"He's loud, too," she added.

Jake conceded with a chuckle. "He's a good guy, just passionate about football, I guess," he said, looking at Morgan for affirmation. "He could have gone pro, but he married my mom in college. Soon after she got pregnant with me, and he had to give it up. So…"

"So, you're his second chance."

"I guess," Jake agreed loosely.

Jake shifted the focus onto Morgan. "What about your parents?" he asked, stopping at a red light.

"What about them?"

Their conversation was drowned out by the sudden humming of a car next to them. Jake looked past Morgan to find Robbie James behind the wheel. The sleek car that Jake had passed when leaving the party pulled to a stop on Morgan's side. Disgusted, Morgan turned away from him.

"Dude...that's a sweet classic!" Robbie yelled. "Where do you keep the crank handle?"

"Same place you keep your remote control!" Jake retorted.

Morgan suppressed a laugh.

"You're funny, bro! Let's see what's under the hood," Robbie challenged, revving his car into a high-pitched squeal.

Jake shook his head. "I'll pass," he conceded. "Besides, the lady doesn't want to go to jail tonight."

"Go back to the party," Robbie suggested. "No cops out there."

Jake glanced at Morgan, secretly hoping for a way out. A naughty smile crossed her face.

"Sounds like fun," she said, approving Robbie's challenge.

The light changed to green. Jake reluctantly turned his car around and headed back to the party. He remained silent, but there was plenty going on in his mind. The battle raged. He knew he had taken a huge risk by sneaking out in the car while grounded from it. If anything happened, or if he were to get caught, the privilege to drive *any* car could be revoked. He looked at Morgan and saw nothing but excitement on her face. She seemed to have no fear whatsoever about his racing. She was not going to be a way out for him. In fact, her desire to see this happen added pressure to accept the challenge. For Jake, pride overshadowed good judgment.

They returned to the party site. Word of the impending race began to spread. The drivers had decided on Ridge Road, another area known for drag racing. Cars immediately left the field and proceeded one by one onto the county road and toward the race site.

Now at the racing location, Jake and Robbie lined up their cars side-by-side.

Jake looked at Morgan. "This is where I have to ask you to get out of the car."

Morgan poked out her lips in disappointment. "Awww...OK," she replied.

The two engines idled. A large crowd of teenagers had gathered. Eric Williams designated himself to start the race, hoping to see Jake fall victim again – this time to an unknown predator. If it were to happen, he wanted to make sure he had a great view.

"Drive down Ridge Road until you reach the caution sign, then turn around and come back," Eric instructed Jake and Robbie. Pointing toward his feet, he said, "The race ends here!"

Both boys revved their engines. Jake tapped his index finger on the steering wheel and inhaled shallow breaths. Eric bent down toward Jake's window. "Don't let it get overheated," he said with pouted lips.

"Thanks for the tip," Jake replied.

Jake looked at his competitor. Robbie sarcastically blew him a kiss. Leaning in through the open T-top, Morgan looked at Jake with her big hazel eyes and said, "Burn him."

She quickly backed away as Eric moved to the front of the cars. He held up his hands in the air. Robbie raced his engine. Jake joined him. They stared at each other for a moment.

"Ready?" Eric alerted them.

Both drivers peered down the dark road. Jake blinked. His face was stone.

Your time, Jake, a voice reassured him.

Eric's hands dropped. Jake slammed the accelerator. The Trans-Am engine roared into the darkness. A swath of smoke and dust trailed from the rear tires as the vehicles lurched forward. Onlookers screamed with delight. As the cars sped into the night, the drivers glanced at each other to check positions, one car in the lead for a moment, then the other overtaking him. The back-and-forth continued for a few seconds.

Robbie was now in the lead. Jake grinned facetiously at his opponent, pressing the accelerator to the floor. The Trans-Am tires burned again as Jake pulled forward, leaving Robbie and his Impala behind.

As Jake pulled away in the lead, the turn spot grew closer. A yellow caution sign appeared as Jake approached the curve. He applied the brakes, pulled to the right slightly onto the road's shoulder, and then made a wide U-turn back toward the starting line. Once on the straight-away, Jake pressed the accelerator and met the Impala, just now starting its turn. The Trans-Am screamed toward the starting point. Robbie followed suit. Jake watched the Impala in his rearview mirror.

"See ya!" Jake heckled and waved goodbye.

Jake had gained so much momentum that Robbie would never catch up. Jake crossed the finish line a quarter of a mile ahead of him.

Robbie's engine had red-lined.

"Dude, we're going to get laughed out of school!" his sidekick whined.

"Man, forget that!" Robbie cried, looking for a place to exit off the main road.

He slammed on the brakes and turned onto an adjoining county road to escape the shame he was sure to face had he stopped.

"Hey, where's he going?" someone asked from the large group of spectators.

"Probably home to Momma!" another onlooker heckled.

The crowd rushed to the Trans-Am. Eric's friend Aaron was the first at Jake's window.

"Whoa! Pop the hood, bro!" Aaron yelled in excitement.

Jake pulled the hood latch. Aaron raised it as everyone gathered around the front. A beautiful, chrome-filled engine vibrated as it idled. The teenagers gawked. Jake joined them around front. With pats on the back, accolades from the crowd and Morgan on his arm, Jake was on top of the world. He caught Eric out of the corner of his eye. Judging by the look on Eric's face, this was all too much for him to handle. The redhead made his way back to the Challenger and sat inside to watch from a distance. The events of the evening had only fueled his rage.

The party continued into the early morning hours, and then eventually died down. After dropping Morgan off at her house, Jake drove home. He pulled up the driveway, barely taking the car above an idle. The headlights turned off, Jake stealthily backed into the barn and killed the engine. He sat in the dark for a few moments, exhaling a sigh of relief. He didn't tarry, though, knowing there was some cleaning up to do. Jake then wiped down the car, sponged the tires with conditioner and replaced the T-tops.

He took one last look to make sure the car was in mint condition before covering it with the tarp. Jake swept the floor of dusty tire prints, attempting to remove any evidence of the car leaving its spot, then he quietly closed the barn doors. He was exhausted. It had been a long night, and he was ready to get some sleep. The sky was already lit with the first hint of morning. Jake entered the dark house and gently hung the keys in their place. On the way to his room, Jake stopped when Mitch's voice spoke from the darkness in the living room.

"Long night?" Mitch asked.

Jake was startled, causing him to drop his cell phone, shattering the screen and rendering it useless.

"Great. Just great," Jake mumbled, quickly but carefully picking up the tiny glass shards. "I'm so busted."

"You got a second?" Mitch asked.

"Yeah, sure, Dad," Jake replied.

Mitch looked at the broken phone on the floor.

"Hey, don't worry," he said. "I'll get it replaced Monday. You think you can live without it for a couple of days? I mean, I know it's like another appendage to your body, right?"

Relieved his phone wasn't being taken away, Jake said, "Sure. I'll survive."

He motioned for Jake to join him on the sofa. Both remained silent for a moment. Mitch gathered his thoughts. Every muscle in Jake's body tensed.

"Dad, I'm sorry," he apologized.

"For what? You did your best," Mitch affirmed.

Jake was confused.

"The rookies botched the play."

Realizing they were talking about two different things, Jake began to relax.

"The scouts will be back," Mitch assured him.

"Right," Jake agreed.

"Look...Coach Scott...we don't necessarily see things eye-to-eye. But sometimes that's just the way life is, ya know?" Mitch explained.

Jake nodded. "Yes, sir."

"OK, so just do the best you can."

Jake nodded his head in agreement, then rose from his seat.

"It's hard being better than the rest," Mitch said arrogantly. "You have to wait on everybody. It seems like they're all trying to hold you back. Sometimes, we just have to leave the weaker ones behind."

"Yeah."

"Don't lose any more sleep over this...and hey...don't let your mom know," Mitch suggested as he nodded his head toward the shiny red "J" keychain. "She's worried enough."

Jake understood what his dad meant. He walked to his room, threw the decorator pillows off the bed and climbed between the sheets. He released a long-held breath and suppressed a smile as the light of early morning broke across the ceiling. The voice returned. *You're back on top, Jake. Don't worry about things. Your dad's got your back. Rest easy, Jake.*

Chapter 9

Things seemed to have turned the corner. What had started out as a crummy school year was taking a turn for the better. Senior year was looking a lot more like what I had envisioned it would be. Tonight had been awesome. I would spend the weekend recovering from it, but I thought it was so worth it. Monday, and school, would come quickly, and I didn't have a clue as to what I would experience when I got there. The events that would continue to unfold would only fuel the egotistical monster inside me.

The hallways of the high school were crowded with students rushing in, getting situated for the first class of the day. Oversleeping all weekend had left Jake feeling sluggish instead of well-rested. All morning he operated on autopilot. As he walked to his creative writing class, students stopped to compliment him on the victory Friday night. He assumed they were referring to the football game. He offered nods and smiles as gratitude for their encouraging words. Jake snapped out of his zombie state, though, when a teammate yelled his name and ran down the hall toward him.

"Jake, wait up! You gotta see this!" his teammate, Drew, proclaimed.

Curious, Jake waited for him to catch up.

"Dude, I heard you smoked the pants off that guy!" Drew said.

"What guy?" Jake asked.

Suddenly, the faint sound of a roaring engine caught Jake's attention. Following the sound with his ear, he stepped inside a classroom, with Drew following, where several students were gathered around a boy holding an iPhone.

"What's everyone watching?" Jake asked.

"Man, it's all over YouTube!" Drew exclaimed.

"What is?" a clueless Jake asked.

"You don't know?" Drew asked.

"My phone's broken," Jake explained. "And I've sort of been out of it all weekend."

His teammate Marcus chimed in. "The race! You were awesome!"

Jake was stunned. He watched as Friday night's race unfolded before him. *That is surreal. Thank goodness my mom isn't on social media*, he thought.

In the midst of the crowd, Morgan materialized.

"What's going on here?"

"Jake's all over the Internet!" Marcus informed her. "That's what's going on."

Morgan became excited. "Am I on there?" she asked, positioning herself for a better view. Jake couldn't believe she hadn't seen it, either.

"Sorry, just the cars," Marcus said patronizingly. "Maybe next time."

Jake suddenly felt energized. He wasn't expecting to come to school a hero today.

"Can you believe it, Jake?" Marcus asked excitedly.

Not wanting to appear desperate for attention, he casually responded, "I guess. Come on, we gotta get to class."

As Jake and Drew made their way to their lockers, some friends tagged behind, continuing to comment on the race.

"Man, I'd give my left leg to be you for just a few hours," Drew said, biting his lower lip.

"Seriously?" Jake asked.

"Drew's never serious," a voice spoke from behind. Eric, along with his friend Aaron, approached the lockers beside Jake. Jake smirked and shook his head.

"You love playing the devil's advocate, don't you, Eric?" Jake said.

Morgan stood silently, watching the tense situation between the rivals.

"Oh, naw, bro!" Eric said confidently. "I admit, you had a good run the other night."

Jake chuckled. "You noticed," he said, smiling at Drew and Marcus.

"Yeah, you dusted that guy," Eric said.

Trying to play things down, Jake said, "Well, racing was that guy's idea, not mine."

"Wait...Eric, how do you know?" Marcus asked.

"Oh, I was there," Eric said. "I actually participated."

Confused, Marcus asked, "But why were *you* there?" It was odd to him that Eric and Jake were at the same event in another county.

Morgan became uncomfortable. Jake noticed it.

"It's a long story. Besides, it's irrelevant," Jake said, covering for Morgan.

Eric caught on. Although he was upset that Morgan used him for a ride to the party, then left with Jake, he dared not mention it to avoid his own humiliation. He changed the subject.

"Now, I'm asking you to race me…again," Eric challenged. "If you've got the guts to take me on again, that is."

Jake slammed his locker door. "What's up with you, man?"

"I'll tell you what's up! I'm sick of jerks like you who come along just to play ball for a year or two!"

Eric cut his eyes to Morgan, then back to Jake. "You think you can take whatever you want and act like you're better than every-body else!" he vented.

Jake leaned in close to Eric and met him eye-to-eye. "Better than everybody…or just better than you?" Jake said.

Eric tensed. "Saturday night. Hell's Bend."

The crowd grew silent. His suggestion of location spoke death.

Jake stood silent, his eyes fiercely fixed on Eric. "Hell's Bend it is," he confirmed. "Ten o'clock. Don't make me wait."

Eric gave Jake a two-finger salute as he and Aaron backed away. Drew leaned over to Jake. "I've changed my mind about wanting to be you."

Jake looked at Morgan for her reaction to the altercation. Her smile exuded satisfaction with the suitor rivalry.

Drew watched the body language between the two. Just like every other guy in high school, Drew was enamored by Morgan's beauty and intrigued by her mystique. Drew changed his mind. "Then again…who needs two legs?"

He held up a hand to Jake, offering a fist bump. "Later, bro. See you in English." He turned to leave, then hesitated. Looking back to Jake, he posed the question, "By the way, you wouldn't happen to have done your homework, would ya?"

"What do you think?" Jake asked, presuming Drew already knew the answer.

"I think I need some new friends...the kind that do their home-work," Drew jested.

"Get out of here, you parasite," Jake joked.

Jake had been so distracted by the drama surrounding the race, he wasn't prepared for class. He rustled through his extremely unor-ganized locker, trying to find what he needed.

"Are you kidding me!" a voice called out behind him.

Suddenly a smartphone appeared in front of his face with a familiar hand attached to it. Jake grabbed it as his eyes tried to focus on the screen. It was the same video from earlier, except this time, it was on Facebook. He turned around to verify the culprit.

"I knew I knew that hand," Jake said to Ross.

"You snuck out in the Trans-Am?" Ross asked in disbelief.

Jake shrugged.

Ross looked around to make sure no one was looking. "And raced it? And you didn't call me?" he continued in a whisper.

Jake nodded, proudly grinning from ear to ear.

"And you're gonna do it again?" Ross asked.

"Yeah."

"Are you crazy?"

"Wanna come?"

"Absolutely!"

Lauren made her way down the hall toward the two boys. The talk about the race between Jake and Eric had already spread.

"Ross!" she called.

The boys continued their conversation.

"When?" Ross asked.

"Saturday night."

"Time?"

"Ten o'clock."

"I'm in," Ross said.

"The Youth Explosion is Saturday night!" Lauren reminded them passionately.

Ross looked at Lauren. "At seven, right?" implying there was time to do both.

Lauren shook her head in disbelief. "You guys are crazy. You're going to get busted," she warned.

"Thank you, conscience," Jake remarked.

"I can't believe what I'm hearing!" she cried. "I'll see you later, Ross," she said, dismissing them with a wave of her hand. She then abruptly walked away.

"Bye, Lauren," Jake said obnoxiously.

Lauren kept walking, ignoring his facetious farewell. The boys resumed their conversation.

"So, how'd she run this time?" Ross asked enthusiastically.

Jake shook his head, paused for a moment. "Like we always dreamed."

Ross nodded longingly.

Realizing how time had quickly slipped by, they scurried to class, hoping to sneak in unnoticed. As they entered Mr. Anders's class, the voice of Dr. Sharp was ringing over the intercom with morning announcements. Relieved, they tried to situate their things before he finished.

"I realize this will be a very difficult week to focus on your studies, considering it's homecoming week, along with our annual Youth Explosion," the voice continued.

Ross leaned back toward Jake, who sat behind him. "Not to mention the race at Hell's Bend," he interjected.

"Shhh…" Mr. Anders scolded.

Dr. Sharp continued. "I want to encourage you to press on and do what is required of you by your teachers. I'm sure they're making some concessions due to the events we have going on this week. Don't take advantage. I also want to encourage you to be responsible while you're in attendance at this weekend's festivities. Remember, it's a privilege to do these things. Privilege means it's optional. So, with that being said, I expect that no activity will be taking place such as the one this past Friday night in a neighboring county that was brought to my attention by a colleague of mine."

All eyes in the classroom suddenly fell on Jake. He sank in his seat and placed a book in front of his face. He felt his temperature rising rapidly. For once, Jake was relieved to hear Mr. Anders begin his lecture, as it took the attention away from him. This was a rare occurrence, as usually Jake's goal was having all eyes on him.

The school-day ritual continued as usual, followed by after-school activities in preparation for the big weekend ahead.

Across town, as supper time drew near, Sergeant Mayhew and his deputies began funneling into the sheriff's department for their evening shift. Sheriff Howell was still working in his office as the shift change began. There was a knock on his door.

"Come in," he said.

The door opened. Sergeant Mayhew stood in the entryway with cell phone in hand and concern on his face.

"You got a minute?" Mayhew asked.

Sheriff Howell pushed away from his desk and turned to face him. He could see something was bothering Mayhew.

"Sure. Whatcha got?" he asked.

"Something you need to take a look at," Mayhew said, walking toward the sheriff's desk. Handing Sheriff Howell his cell phone, he said, "It came across my newsfeed on Facebook earlier today."

On the phone's small screen was the video of Jake racing the Friday night before. Howell recognized the car immediately. "Oh my word," he said. "Where was this?"

"On Ridge Road in Prentiss County," Mayhew said. "Some kid videoed it and posted it on social media. It's gone viral."

"No doubt," Howell replied.

Mayhew leaned against the desk and watched his boss's face. "What do you think?"

Howell continued watching the video for a few more seconds and then handed the phone back to Mayhew. "I think it's time to pay Mitch a visit," he said.

"Do you think it'll do any good?" Mayhew asked.

"Probably not, but I still gotta try," Howell said. "Tag me on that video so I'll have it on my Facebook page, would you?"

"Sure thing," Mayhew said.

Sheriff Howell stood up. "I'm headed out anyway. I'll go ahead and deal with it on my way home," he said.

"Let me know how it goes, if you would," Mayhew asked.

Sergeant Mayhew left the sheriff's office to meet with the other deputies in the briefing room. On his way, a loud banging resounded throughout the cinderblock hallway. He rolled his eyes. *Wonder who got brought in?* he thought. Entering the briefing room, he saw Galen Daniels and motioned for him.

"What's up?" Daniels asked.

Mayhew handed him his cell phone. "Have you seen this?" he asked.

Daniels watched it for a moment. "That's Jake," he said. "Where is this?" Daniels asked.

"Ridge Road...Prentiss County," Mayhew said. "I just showed it to the sheriff."

"Yeah? What'd he say?" Daniels asked.

"He's actually headed to the Adamses' house right now to talk to Mitch about it," Mayhew said.

"That'll go real well," Daniels said sarcastically. "Was Ross with him?"

"No. I know for a fact he wasn't. I saw him Friday night while I was out patrolling. I go by the McKays' house from time to time to check on them at night. You know, with Margaret being a single mom. Ross was there hanging out with Lauren."

"That's good," Daniels said.

The banging noise from the jail area grew louder and more frequent.

"Who got brought in?" Mayhew asked.

"No one. It's Jed Boozer," Daniels replied.

"He's still here?" Mayhew asked.

"Yep. He hasn't bonded out yet," Daniels said.

The other deputies snickered.

"What's so funny?" Mayhew asked.

Deputy Hollis walked over to them. "You shoulda seen him last night, Sergeant," Hollis said. "4.2."

"Seen what? I was on another call. What'd I miss?" Mayhew asked.

"Nothin'. You didn't miss nothin'," Daniels said.

Deputy Ramon continued laughing in the background. "Go on, Juicy. Tell him."

Hollis looked back at Ramon and said, "Oh, don't worry. I am."

Daniels looked down and shook his head.

Hollis looked back at Mayhew. "Well, you know we got that call from a passerby saying there was a woman with clothes torn, blood all over her, beaten to a pulp and layin' in a ditch."

"Right," Mayhew said.

"Come to find out, it was Boozer's latest girlfriend," Hollis said.

"Oh, my word," Mayhew said.

"Anyway...we picked her up, got her help and took her statement. We headed over to Jed's house to bring him in," Hollis said. "So, we get to Jed's house and The Golden Child here gets to the door first. He lightly knocks on the door like he's selling Girl Scout cookies. I told him to just step aside and let me do it. I bang on the door until someone finally answers it. We go inside the house and start trying to locate Jed. Golden Child starts calling out, *Oh, Mr. Boozer,* ever so gently."

Deputy Ramon sat in the background and held his side, laughing uncontrollably. Daniels continued shaking his head, knowing Hollis was exaggerating.

Ramon decided to get in on the storytelling, jumping up and grabbing Hollis by the shoulder. "Hey, let me take it from here."

"Be my guest," Hollis said.

Mayhew shifted his attention to Ramon.

"So, we find the guy and start cuffing him to take him into custody. We were gonna just take him in wearing boxers and a tee shirt. After what he did to that woman, you know, we thought we'd give him a taste of his own medicine. Daniels starts putting a shirt on him and buttoning it. He finds a scarf…"

Daniels interjected. "Naw, man! Now you know that ain't right, not even close!"

Mayhew laughed so hard, tears streamed down his face.

"Oh, it's real close," Hollis said. "I couldn't tell if you were trying to arrest him or date him!"

The men erupted into even louder laughter.

"Y'all ain't right," Daniels said.

"All right, guys," Mayhew said. "That's enough. Where we going to eat?"

Before the deputies could answer him, Mayhew said, "The Driskills' it is."

"Aw, man, go on!" Ramon said.

Grace served Mitch's favorite supper tonight: spaghetti. Jake ate quickly. Knowing the race video had gone viral, he was afraid word may have spread to his parents. He didn't want to give them time to bring it up if they had caught wind of it.

The doorbell rang. Not expecting any guests, they stopped for a moment and looked at each other, waiting for someone to take ownership of the visitor. No one knew.

"I'll get it," Mitch said. As he walked toward the back door, he tried peering through the window pane to see who it was. The face was familiar – Sheriff Howell. Surprised, Mitch opened the door and quickly stepped outside, closing the door behind him. Sheriff Howell's usually pleasant expression was serious tonight.

"Evening, Sheriff."

"Hey, Mitch. I've got something here I think you need to take a look at."

"Sure," Mitch replied reluctantly. "Something wrong?"

"Well, watch this, then you tell me," Sheriff Howell said as he handed him the phone.

Mitch held the phone and watched the video. Quickly realizing it was Jake racing the Trans-Am, he handed the phone back to the sheriff. "Yeah, that's Jake," Mitch said with a frown. "Where'd you get that?"

"Mayhew showed it to me. It was on Facebook," Howell said.

"I see. Let me see that again."

Hopeful that Mitch was taking it seriously, the sheriff returned the phone.

Mitch watched it in its entirety, then handed it back.

"I don't recognize where that race took place," Mitch said. "Do you know where that is?"

"Mayhew said it was over on Ridge Road in Prentiss County," Sheriff Howell said.

"Oh, OK. So, the race happened outside your jurisdiction?" Mitch asked.

The sheriff realized immediately where Mitch was going with the question. "Yes, it did."

"Well, if it wasn't in your jurisdiction, I don't understand why you're here," Mitch said.

"Mitch, it's not about it being in our jurisdiction. It's about us caring about your family," the sheriff explained. "This is the second time Jake has raced that car in a very short period of time."

"You know what I think? I think you guys have it in for my son."

"No, Mitch. It's not like that at all," Howell said.

"I'll tell you what," Mitch said. "When it's your jurisdiction, then you come to me. Until then, you don't need to worry about it."

"I just thought you'd like to know, Mitch. That's all," Howell said.

"Well, now I know," Mitch said. "Have a good night."

Sheriff Howell stood for a moment, staring at Mitch in disbelief.

"Good night, Mitch," he said.

As Howell walked away, Mitch returned to the dining room.

"Who was that?" Grace asked.

"It was just Sheriff Howell. He was in the neighborhood. He just stopped by to say hello," Mitch said. He cut his eyes toward Jake. Jake sank in his seat a little. He knew what had taken place. Mitch winked at him, letting him know he "took care of it."

"Why didn't you invite him in?" Grace asked.

"He didn't have but a minute," Mitch said.

"Oh," Grace said.

The night remained peaceful. As Jake lay in bed that night, the voice returned. *You got out of another one, Jake. Nothing to worry about. Sweet dreams, Jake.*

Chapter 10

Isn't it amazing how someone can just absolutely rub you the wrong way? Constantly? You can feel animosity toward this person yet not be able to explain why. That's how it was with Eric Williams and me. I couldn't explain it if I tried. I can't even tell you how or why it began. That's the thing about pride. It feeds on jealousy and negative competition. The more we fed that monster, the more it grew. Soon, we would be gobbled up by it.

Spirit week continued with a different theme each day and was filled with rituals and traditions that had spanned decades. The two favorite events were the Thursday night bonfire and Friday night's Homecoming, which included a pep rally, presentation of homecoming court, presentation of football and band seniors, and of course, the football game.

On Thursday night, students, faculty and alumni arrived at the bonfire amid smoke-filled air and the pleasant autumn scent of burning wood. Students hung out while faculty visited with each other, enjoying roasting hot dogs and marshmallows over the fifteen-foot fire. Tonight, the low-lying area where the festivities were held was a sea of blue jerseys and pom-poms, with cars parked in row after row. The jubilant blare of brass band instruments and lively percussion rang out above the laughter and fellowship of those in attendance.

Ross and Lauren sat on a crosstie and shared hot dogs and s'mores. Despite the homecoming activities prevailing that week and the impending game to follow, Lauren's thoughts were fixed on Youth Explosion. Her topic of conversation with Ross was not on the present.

"I cannot wait for you to hear the band we have coming Saturday night!" she said. "I bought one of their CDs last week and I almost have the whole thing memorized! I hate going to a concert not knowing the lyrics to the songs. Oh, and did I tell you? George Preston is going to be the speaker! He's awesome! Such a great communicator."

Lauren's enthusiastic rundown of the guests attending the event seemed to fall on deaf ears.

"Are you listening to me? Ross?"

"Huh? Oh, yeah," Ross responded, his mind far from their conversation.

"Have you heard a word I've said?" Lauren asked, disappointed. "Aren't you excited?"

Ross spoke honestly. "I just don't get into all that like you do."

"That bothers me, too," Lauren replied. "I worry about your salvation, Ross."

"There's no need to worry about me. I'm a good person. I go to church. I do nice things for people. I'm a good student and I don't give my parents a hard time. As a matter of fact, I act better than some of your so-called 'Christian' friends. For instance, Jade Everett is in your Christian club, right?"

"Right."

"Well, I heard last weekend she was arrested for shoplifting at the mall. Her parents had to bail her out."

"I didn't know that," Lauren replied with sincere shock.

"I know you didn't," Ross said. "Not many people do because her parents paid 'hush' money to keep it quiet. And I know for a fact that Jesse Mitchell was pulled over for drunk driving the week before school started back."

"Jesse?" Lauren questioned in disbelief.

"Yes. I don't steal or drink. So, why do I have to wear the 'Christian' label? I'm good by my own right."

Lauren fought through her emotions to respond to his statement. "Ross, none of us are good in our own right. That's why Jesus had to die on the cross in our place. He was the only one good enough. You can't look at the bad choices of others and allow that to determine who Christ is and your need for Him."

"Look, I didn't come here with you tonight to be preached to, OK?" Ross said. "Let's just have fun. If there's something else I need to do, I don't see it. I'm good. You don't have to worry about me," Ross reassured her.

"But I'm worried about..."

"'Sup, Bama Bro?" Jake yelled, interrupting Lauren as he approached them, Morgan at his side. Regardless of his careless disruption, Lauren looked at him with total offense.

Realizing he had walked up on an intense conversation, Jake decided to feed off it.

"Lauren? You look mad," he said in a patronizing tone. "Are you mad?"

"Oh no, Jake," she answered harshly. "Not at all. I just don't care for rude people."

"Rude? I'm not rude," Jake retorted, pointing to himself. "It's just that what I have to say is more important."

"Jake, stop!" Ross ordered. "Hey, Morgan, sorry you didn't make the cut on YouTube in the racing video. I guess you'll have to get your big break another way, huh?" he said, giving Jake a dose of his own medicine.

"What's that supposed to mean?" Morgan asked.

Jake stared at Ross.

"We need to get lined up for the pep rally, Ross," Jake directed, diverting attention from the awkward moment.

Ross stood up, patted Jake on the shoulder and said, "You're probably right," giving him a wink. Jake turned red, his blood boiling over Ross's cheap shot. Jake knew Ross was making fun of him. They only used the phrase "You're probably right" to patronize each other.

As the boys walked away, Lauren sat in awkward silence. She and Morgan had nothing in common yet were practically forced together because of the close friendship between Jake and Ross. Lauren decided to make the best of it.

"So, you want to swap cell phone numbers?" Lauren offered.

"I guess," Morgan said. "So, why do you and Jake not get along?"

Unprepared for her question, Lauren quickly became defensive.

"Because he represents everything bad in Ross's life, and I represent everything good in it," Lauren replied brashly.

Shocked by Lauren's outburst, Morgan became quiet. Realizing her tone was rude, Lauren apologized. "I'm sorry, Morgan. It's just a very touchy subject with me."

Lauren stood up and dusted off her pants. "We'd better get going or we'll miss the presentations."

"Sure," Morgan said. Their walk to the makeshift stage was quiet.

Jake and Ross walked ahead of the girls. Attempting to change the mood, Ross pretended to be Morgan, hanging on Jake's arm.

"Oh, am I in the video, Jakey-poo?" Ross asked. "Let me see! Let me see!"

Jake grew agitated. "Just keep it up, Ross. I dare you."

"Oh, Jakey, you sure can pick 'em. When are you going to learn? Beauty is only skin deep. Vanity is to the bone, bro."

"Oh, yeah? Well, let's see if your pretty-boy face goes all the way to the bone," Jake said as he started rough-housing. They continued their horseplay as they headed toward the stage area to join their teammates in line.

"Wow! Look who's comin'!" said a voice from the sideline. "It's our mighty Eagles' co-captains!" Jake and Ross stopped clowning and quickly turned in the direction of the voice.

"Eric," Jake said under his breath. "Why am I not surprised?" Irritated, he stomped toward Eric and his friends. Ross followed hard after him, hoping to prevent a scene. Judging from past experience, he knew it to be a lost cause. Nonetheless, he continued.

Eric's friends seemed faced with the same dilemma. Jake and Eric were as lethal a combination as gasoline and a match. They came face-to-face as their buddies tried to keep them calm, hoping others wouldn't hear the commotion.

Eric looked around and asked, "So, where's your 'classic car'? Did you drive it here or are you still grounded?"

Jake stood silent, but the flexing of his fists and the clenching of his jaws were clear indicators that he was a time bomb. Ross leaned into Jake and whispered calmly, as if Jake were walking on a land mine.

"Don't let Eric get you all worked up, Jake," Ross advised. "Just save it for the race. Now, come on. We need to get in line," he continued, trying to divert Jake's attention from a potentially embarrassing situation. Jake continued to stare at Eric, although the flexing and clenching ceased.

Ross breathed a little easier. Feeling relieved his intervention had worked, he pulled Jake by the forearm toward the setup. Determined to get in the last word, Jake warned Eric, "You just added fuel to the fire for our race at *Hell's Bend*."

By this time, Lauren and Morgan had caught up with Jake and Ross, hearing only the tail end of the race conversation.

"You guys are crazy to even consider doing this!" Lauren ranted. "Do you realize how many people have died trying to take Hell's Bend? Besides, that's the night of the Youth Explosion! Y'all are being completely irrational. How could you plan something so deadly, not to mention so ill-timed?"

"Well, that's too bad!" Jake retorted.

"Ross promised to go with me!" Lauren informed Jake, pointing to herself.

"Sorry, he'll just have to break that promise. He has something more important to do...with his best friend!" Jake stated firmly, declaring his position in Ross's life above hers.

"What do you mean, more important?" Lauren challenged.

"Would you two stop it?" Ross exploded. "I'm sick of listening to y'all go at it all the time!" His outburst took everyone by surprise. This was certainly out of character for such a passive Ross Kelly. "Here's the deal. The Youth Explosion starts at seven, right?" he asked Lauren.

"Right," Lauren confirmed.

Turning to Jake, Ross asked, "And the race doesn't start until ten, right?" Jake stood silent with his arms folded. "Right?" Ross repeated in a louder voice, demanding a response.

Puffed with pride, Jake reluctantly answered, "Yeah."

"So what's the problem here? There's time to do both," Ross explained. "We can go to the youth thing at seven, then have time to get to the race. Problem solved, right?" Still stunned, everyone stood silent. "Right?" Ross repeated.

"Right," Morgan said, perturbed. "Now can we please move on?"

"Thank you!" Ross replied.

Although the night's events were steeped in school history and were supposed to be fun, Jake's unexpected confrontations with Eric and Lauren had distracted him. He half-heartedly walked through the mid-field presentation of players, resentful that Ross didn't side with him against Lauren, and ever mindful of a well-devised plan of revenge on Eric.

"And finally, your co-captains leading your mighty Eagles this season, Jake Adams and Ross Kelly!" the announcer shouted enthusiastically. The crowd erupted in applause for the team's dynamic duo. Ironically, the best friends stood side by side with inter-locked hands raised, representing a spirit of unity. Cameras flashed throughout the crowd. Most of the audience had either watched them grow up or had grown up with them. This moment in time had a very special place in the school's history. It was bittersweet for the boys. They had looked forward to their senior year for a long time, yet now that it had come, the reality of it being the *last one* was a bit emotional for them, mellowing the boys after the argument only minutes earlier.

Jake fought to block thoughts of the confrontation with Eric. This moment was his; Eric Williams was not going to ruin it. The boys made eye contact with their parents and others who meant so much to them, pointing their fingers at them with their free hand, acknowledging them in the stands. After a few glorious moments basking in the limelight, Jake and Ross turned to each other, performed their handshake they had invented many years earlier, then yelled, "Bama Bros!" The crowd loved it.

The night finally came to a close. Football players and students had made some fun memories. But with the traditions and friendships and cheering also came an increase in the intensity between Eric and Jake and between Jake and Lauren – an animosity that was allowed to grow deeper and wilder. These fierce feelings boiled underneath the surface, needing an escape, needing to warn anyone who would pay attention that danger lay ahead.

Friday morning came early. The hallways at school were quiet, but as the day continued, talk about the big game, along with the crowning of the homecoming queen just hours away, re-energized the students. By lunchtime, minds were alert and mouths were jabbering.

In the cafeteria, a group of football players stood in line with their trays. One of the cafeteria workers, wearing a less-than-fashionable hairnet and clear plastic gloves, methodically spooned out a substance that mimicked red beans and rice. Feeling squeamish, Marcus turned his head.

"I don't even want to know," he said, pulling his tray close, ensuring he didn't receive the food, deeming it inedible. After the guys made their way through the line, they collected at their usual table.

"So, where's Ross?" Drew asked.

"He's helping move some stuff they need for homecoming tonight to the football field," Jake said.

"And you didn't offer to help?" Drew asked.

"What...and miss this fine cuisine?" Jake asked sarcastically.

Drew laughed. Suddenly, his expression changed. Jake noticed. Gauging by the direction of Drew's stare, he realized the reason lurked behind him.

"Drew, what is it? What are you looking at?"

Before Drew had time to respond, Jake felt someone bend down to his ear and whisper, "Hey, could we talk for a minute?" Expecting that it was Morgan, Jake turned around with a large smile, intending a sweet response. He was stunned to find Lauren instead. Confused and deflated, he still managed to reply positively.

"Sure," Jake said.

Lauren hesitated for a moment, looking at the many friends around the cafeteria table.

"Alone...please?" Lauren asked quietly.

"Oh, um...OK, sure," Jake said. They walked to a table in an empty area of the cafeteria soon to be filled with students after the second bell.

"So, what's up?" Jake inquired calmly but anxiously.

Lauren had never approached Jake this way, so her sudden cordial manner made him uncomfortable.

"I want you to tell Ross not to race with you tomorrow night," she requested in a very straightforward manner.

Jake was stunned. "Seriously?" he asked, appalled.

"It's stupid and you know it," Lauren commented. "Just because you want to do something crazy doesn't mean Ross has to join you."

Jake shook his head in disbelief. "Wait...did you two get married and forget to tell me? I mean...you're not even officially dating!" Jake scoffed and pushed himself away from the table, ending the conversation. Pausing a moment, he pulled back. Anger and resentment had built up over the past few months from Lauren's many negative comments and snide remarks. Jake was ready to let it go.

"What...how...how long have you guys really been friends?" Jake asked. "What – two, three years? And you think you know him? You think you care about him more than I do? I know what he is to you. I know what we all are to you," Jake said, pointing around the room. Lauren noticed that people were watching.

Trying to remain brave and composed, she very boldly asked, "What's that?"

As that look of stone seeped into Jake's face and his voice grew louder, he stood abruptly, shoved his chair back and yelled, "Come on, Lauren! What do you think is going to happen here? You can't fix Ross because there's nothing to fix!"

Lauren began to cower.

"That's the difference between you and me," Jake continued. "When you look at Ross, you see someone less than you. When I look at him, I see the best person I know. To you, he's just a potential convert. You have to make him think and feel the way you do, and when he won't, you try to manipulate him through his *real* friends!"

Lauren stood up. As she looked around the room, she realized all eyes were on her. Her face became flushed, revealing the wave of embarrassment that had washed over her.

"You're a class 'A' jerk, Jake Adams!" she yelled defensively. As she walked away, Jake noticed faces around him; he was being judged as guilty.

"Well, looks like somebody forgot to take her medication this morning," Jake said, trying to recover. The reaction of the students was split. While his teammates approved his mockery, the girls recoiled from Jake in disgust.

Lauren was overwhelmed with humiliation and darted out of the cafeteria in tears. Judging by the smirk on Jake's face, he enjoyed watching her suffer. Her request had fueled his ill will toward her. As he made his way back to his table of supporters, he began imitating Lauren's behavior during their confrontation. As the guys joined in the juvenile behavior, Jake focused on the exit through which Lauren had left. *That'll teach you to mess with me, Miss Holier-than-Thou,* he thought. Jake was elated he had the opportunity to put Lauren in her place. The encouragement Jake received from his teammates heightened his obnoxious behavior.

As the reactions subsided, Jake noticed Hamm walking across the cafeteria, his tray overloaded with food and a milk carton clenched between his teeth. Still feeling a rush of adrenaline from his run-in with Lauren, Jake decided to continue his performance. As Hamm walked past the lunch table filled with his teammates, Jake stuck out his left foot. Hamm tripped, his lunch tray sailing through the air, slinging food three feet away. His oversized body plunged to the floor, sliding into the mess that preceded him. His natural instinct was to break his fall with his right knee – the knee that had already sustained serious injury and required surgery a year earlier.

Hamm grabbed his knee and let out a terrible cry. Teachers rushed to his aid. Jake stood in shock. His antics had gone further than he intended. He made a quiet exit from the cafeteria, hoping to leave unnoticed. His little prank had gone undetected by most. Unfortunately for Jake, though, there was one who witnessed the mean-spirited trick. Still fuming from the humiliation Jake had caused her friend Lauren, Lizzy Cambridge immediately reported Jake's cruelty to Dr. Sharp, who in turn alerted the head football coach. Coach Scott was already upset with Jake because of his cruel behavior, particularly toward Hamm. Now he was infuriated.

The school day couldn't end soon enough for the overly-excited student body. For the female students, there was a lot of primping to be done. Unhappy with her wardrobe and needing a good diversion from the emotional trauma inflicted by Jake, Lauren texted Lizzy and told her to meet her at *The Snooty Owl* after school to help pick out something to wear to homecoming.

Jake arrived home from school expecting to grab a quick shower and get a pep talk from his dad before leaving for the pre-game warm-up. As he entered the back door with his backpack slung over his shoulder, he found Mitch and Grace sitting at the kitchen table. The expressions on their faces were grave.

"Someone die?" Jake asked, completely oblivious to what was going on. He had ditched his last couple of classes after lunch to avoid any fallout from his escapades in the cafeteria.

"Coach Scott called," Grace said quietly.

"And?" Jake questioned.

"You've been suspended from tonight's game," Mitch said.

Jake shook his head in disbelief. "What?" he asked, dropping his backpack to the floor.

"You tripped a boy in the lunch room on purpose. He was injured," Grace said, over-emphasizing her words.

"How bad?" Jake asked.

"Bad enough to have to be taken to the ER!" Grace exclaimed.

Shocked, Jake searched for a retort. "It was just a stupid prank!"

"Well, that stupid prank has him at the hospital as we speak!" Grace said firmly.

"But it's homecoming! I can't miss homecoming! It's my last one!" Jake cried.

Seeking a rational resolution, Grace said, "Then let's go to Coach Scott and apologize and see if we can't come up with another option of punishment." Jake raised his eyes toward Mitch, looking for help. Mitch shook his head.

"No," Mitch answered. "No, we won't." He stared at Jake intently. "Let them lose," he said, savoring the words as they left his tongue. Both Grace and Jake looked at Mitch, confused. "Make that coach understand what he has without Jake. Let them lose tonight."

Incensed, Grace stood. "This doesn't have anything to do with winning or losing, Mitch. You are completely missing the point here!" Grace yelled. "Your son intentionally tripped that boy and caused him harm, not to mention the embarrassment he must have felt!"

Mitch stood up to be eye-level with his wife, who clearly didn't understand. "It was a prank, Grace," Mitch continued. "It just got out of hand, that's all. I'm sure Jake didn't mean for the boy to get hurt, right, Jake?"

"It was humiliating!" Grace hammered.

"That coach already has it in for *your* son!" Mitch yelled defensively.

Fed up with his defending Jake's negative behavior, Grace said sarcastically, "Well, it was a joint decision between him and the principal, so I guess Dr. Sharp has it in for him, too!"

Trying to defuse the situation, Jake said, "Guys, it's no big deal. I'll go and talk to him."

Mitch quickly turned to Jake. "No!" Then, addressing Grace, he said, "No, he won't." He turned his attention back to Jake. "This moment could determine the rest of your life. You have to stand your ground."

Grace was in absolute shock. "Sometimes, I really don't understand you."

Grace walked to the back door and grabbed her keys from the hook on the wall. She paused, then turned to the still-shocked Mitch and Jake. "I need to get some air. Supper is in the oven and the timer is set. I'm sure you can take it from there." Trying to recompose herself, she calmly and quietly made her exit.

The awkward silence in the kitchen was deafening. Father and son said nothing. After a few moments, Mitch retired to his shop, while Jake made his way to the front porch. He sat in deep thought. Except for once during his sophomore year, Jake hadn't missed a game during his high school career. To still be at home at five o'clock on a Friday night this time of year felt strange to him. He snapped out of his reverie when the text tone on his phone sounded. It was Ross.

What's going on, Bama Bro? Marcus texted me and said Ethan's starting as QB tonight. What's up with that? Let me hear from you.

Jake stared at the text. He had no idea how to respond. His mind raced back to the incident in the cafeteria with Hamm, then to the confrontation between his parents. He chose to cling to the words of his dad that rationalized his behavior. Finally, he texted back.

Coach Scott just overreacted. That's all. It'll all blow over. He needs to learn a lesson tonight.

Lauren and Lizzy met at The Snooty Owl. The popular clothing and home décor boutique was owned by two local sisters and had been an overnight success when it opened two years earlier. The shop's trendy clothes were displayed on antiques throughout the store.

While Lauren was trying on a dress that Dawn, a co-owner, chose for her, Lizzy started a conversation about the events from earlier that day.

"So, are you feeling better?" Lizzy asked.

"I guess," Lauren said. "I was a fool for even thinking he would be reasonable."

"Well, he was wrong for humiliating you like that," Lizzy said sympathetically.

"I really tried to talk with him today and give him the opportunity to do the right thing," Lauren said. "He didn't. So, I decided to take things into my own hands."

Lizzy sat up straight. "How?"

"Oh, I just may have made a phone call to a certain Sergeant Mayhew, and I just may have shared some information about a possible race planned for tomorrow night…at Hell's Bend…at 10 p.m.," Lauren said dramatically.

"Now that took guts, girl," Lizzy said. "What if Ross finds out you did that? He will be *so* mad."

"He won't. Sergeant Mayhew promised he'd never tell. Anyway…if it saves Ross's life, it's worth it, right?"

"Yep, you're right," Lizzy said. "Not to mention, that was a great way for you to get back at Jake for what he did to you."

"His day is coming," Lauren said.

"Yeah, maybe even sooner than we think," Lizzy said.

Puzzled, Lauren asked, "What do you mean?"

Smiling, Lizzy said, "Let's just say, I've got your back."

Lauren turned her attention away from the full-length mirror and looked at her impish best friend.

"Erin Elizabeth Cambridge, what did you do?" Lauren asked.

Lizzy winked. Lauren's text message tone sounded. As she read the words on her phone screen, her eyes grew large.

"Are you kidding me?" Lauren exclaimed.

"What?" Lizzy asked.

Stunned, Lauren said, "Jake has been suspended from tonight's game!"

"No way!" Lizzy said. "From homecoming?"

"I gotta call Ross," Lauren said. "He'll know if it's true or not."

After a couple of rings, Lauren remembered, "Oh, he's in warm-up practice. I'll just text him later."

"So whatcha thinkin'?" Lizzy asked Lauren, concerned.

"I think he deserves it," Lauren said judgmentally. "But now I'm worried about us winning our homecoming game."

Lizzy began to question her decision to snitch.

Seeing that she was second-guessing herself, Lauren said, "You did the right thing, Lizzy. Jake deserves it."

Lizzy looked at Lauren, eyes wide.

Lauren smiled. "I figured it was you who told. You despise his actions as much as I do."

The news put a little more energy into Lauren's swirl and twirl as she admired the outfit she was modeling. Nicole, Dawn's older sister, entered the store, returning from afternoon carpool at Lee County Academy.

"Oh, girl! That's adorable on you!" Nicole raved. "Homecoming?"

"Yep!" Lauren replied. "Thanks. I love it!"

"Dawn pick that out for ya?" Nicole asked.

"She did," Lauren said.

"Perfect!" Nicole said. "My sissy does good, doesn't she?" she said, bragging on her younger sister.

Lizzy grew impatient. "Lauren, I don't mean to rush you, but we've got to hurry up."

"I know, but I love playing dress-up," Lauren said. "Are you not gonna try on anything?"

"We got her fixed up last week," Dawn said.

Surprised, Lauren asked, "And why did I not know about this?"

"Cause you were all up in Ross's Kool-Aid. Duh!" Lizzy replied.

Lauren grinned.

Text messages continued to light up Lauren's phone.

"I've gotten three more texts about Jake being suspended," Lauren said, looking at her phone.

"I'm getting them, too," Lizzy said. "Word travels fast."

Taking one last twirl in the colorful print dress, Lauren said, "I'll take this one."

"Yay!" Lizzy cheered, standing. "Cause we gotta go!"

"Here, let me help you with that zipper," Dawn offered.

"Thank you," Lauren said. "I need to hurry up and get to the bottom of the news about Jake."

After quickly making her purchase, Lauren and Lizzy exited the store. "Thanks, y'all, for all your help!" Lauren said.

"You're so welcome, sweetie!" Dawn replied as she and Nicole waved good-bye.

"Have fun!" Nicole said.

Once Lauren and Lizzy made their exit from The Snooty Owl, Dawn and Nicole wondered about the news of their alma mater's quarterback.

"So what could he have done to get suspended?" Dawn asked.

"With Jake Adams, there is no telling," Nicole said.

Jake sat in shock over the conversation that had taken place minutes earlier. Suddenly, the oven timer sounded in the kitchen, breaking him from his trance.

"Dinner," he whispered. Jake walked inside to the wonderful aroma of baked chicken. "My favorite." As he removed the glass dish from the oven, Mitch walked in the back door with greasy hands and sweat rolling down his face.

"Hey, turn on the water for me, would you?" Mitch requested.

"Sure," Jake responded as he quickly set the hot dish on the countertop. He turned on the water and grabbed the dishwashing liquid from under the sink. Seeing that his dad's hands were too grimy to hold the bottle, Jake squirted some in his hands for him.

"Thanks, son."

"You're welcome."

The awkwardness from earlier had returned. Grace had never left them to themselves like that. Not on a bad note anyway. Dinner was quiet. Neither knew what to say following the showdown that had taken place.

After piling their dishes in the sink, Jake looked at the time. "Oh, man. The game's already started," he said under his breath.

Jake sat in his favorite spot on the back porch with earbuds hung around his neck while he searched for the game on the local station's Internet stream. He faced the sun and watched it set into the late summer sky, anxious for the announcers to bring the game to life.

Chaotic cries erupted from the crowd. The crackled voice of one of the announcers responded in disgust.

"That's the third offensive turnover for the Eagles in the first quarter."

"Yes, it is, John," the second announcer commented. "They better tighten up out there." Jake sat quietly with no emotion, staring out across the expansive yard.

"Unfortunately, we're seeing some bad judgment calls by a very inexperienced QB. Senior quarterback Jake Adams was suspended for this game due to an uncited team violation," the announcer informed the audience. Jake inhaled a long breath while he contemplated the situation. As the game continued, Jake's mind wandered. Before him, the sun touched the horizon.

"So the Bulldogs take the ball again as the clock ticks down. Bulldogs fourteen. Eagles zero. This is not what the Eagle fans were expecting here tonight, John."

"No, it wasn't. It's never easy accepting a loss, especially homecoming night."

Still in a state of shock, Jake arose and went inside the house. He searched the kitchen cabinets for a snack to follow his supper. The closing of a car door caught his attention. Grace had returned home. As she entered the kitchen, she dropped her purse on the counter.

"Hey," Jake said.

"Hey," Grace replied, trying to force a smile. She knew Jake's plundering habits for sweets after a meal. "There's some chocolate pie in the fridge," she informed him.

"Oh, thanks," Jake responded. "So, where you been?"

"The game," she answered. Jake stopped. His lips pursed.

"Coach got what he asked for," Jake said arrogantly.

Grace hesitated. "We all get what we ask for."

Jake chuckled. He had no response for that. "I'm not really hungry. I'm going to bed." As he walked toward his room, Grace unloaded the dishwasher. Jake hesitated for a moment, expecting to hear Grace utter a verse of scripture to back up her point...but nothing. He walked on. Plopping down on his bed, he placed his hands behind his head. Moonlight streamed through the windows, revealing the collage of athletic posters on the walls. Quarterback Jay Barker, who led the Alabama Crimson Tide to the 1992 national title, stared down at him. Jake stared back. "What are you looking at?" he asked rhetorically.

It had been a strange evening. "So glad this night is over," Jake mumbled.

A chore list awaited Jake the next morning, beginning with yard work. Jake mounted the family's riding lawn mower. To drown out the noise of the mower, he placed his earbuds in his ears and rocked out to songs that helped block out all of the negativity from the day before. As he made the third loop around the yard, a 2010 Nissan pickup sped up the driveway and came to a screeching halt. Ross forcefully put the gear shift into park and slammed the door, revealing an unusual anger. He stormed toward Jake, pointing his finger at him and yelling. Jake stopped the mower and put it in neutral as Ross continued his rant. Jake pointed to his earbuds, indicating he couldn't hear what was he was saying.

Ross reached out and snatched one of the earbuds out of Jake's ear. "Can you hear me now?" he yelled.

Jake grimaced but gave him a thumbs-up. Ross reached past Jake and turned the ignition key to "off." The lawn mower died. Jake removed the other earbud.

"I said don't ever do that again!" Ross ordered.

"It was bad, huh? But hey, that was Coach Scott's call, not mine."

"I'm not talking about the game! I'm talking about Lauren!" Ross shouted. "What were you thinking, you self-absorbed jerk?"

Realizing Lauren must have told Ross about his confrontation with her in the cafeteria, Jake sighed and shook his head.

"You and Lauren...it'll never work," Jake said.

"That's not up to you! I like her. Get it? I enjoy spending time with her. So, get used to it!"

Ross walked away. He was very serious, Jake suddenly realized.

"OK. I'll make it up to her!" Jake said desperately.

Ross stopped and turned around. "Some things, you just can't take back." Once again, he moved toward his truck. As he opened the door, he hesitated, then slammed the door shut. His anger escalated. "You really want to make it up to her? Come to the Youth Explosion tonight."

Jake was taken aback, feeling as if the breath had been knocked out of him.

"We got..." Jake stopped and looked around, making sure his parents were not within hearing distance. "You know...Eric," he whispered.

"We'll leave early if we have to," Ross assured him, leaving Jake no way out. Jake shook his head again in disbelief. Ross approached him again.

"You know, she really does care about you. She wants you to go."

Jake replaced his earbuds and smirked. Ross was livid. He grabbed Jake's earbuds, yanked them out and hurled them across the yard. Jake stared, wide-eyed. Ross stepped in close to Jake, his nostrils flaring. "You owe me...and her." He returned to his truck. Jake sat in shock.

"I'll pick you up at six-thirty. No excuses," Ross remarked.

Stunned, Jake leaned forward on the steering wheel and watched Ross drive away.

Chapter 11

It's amazing how pride and arrogance can cause you to make such an erroneous decision. One bad choice. Not just one bad choice, but one bad choice made after several people had warned you not to make it...on several occasions. That one bad choice would reap such damage and destruction that could never be undone, nor could the consequences ever be reversed. That horrible choice I made after multiple opportunities to choose differently... Mine would be a choice that would forever change many lives, and I imagined that I would never be able to live with what I had done.

Lauren stood outside the gymnasium in the late summer air, waiting for Jake and Ross. She gazed at the stars between glances at her phone to check the time. *Where are they?* she thought. *I knew Jake would do this. He's such a terrible influence on Ross.*

"Aren't you coming inside?" a voice spoke behind her. "The band has already started."

Lauren turned around to find her friend Lizzy.

"I know. I can hear them," Lauren said. "I'm waiting on Ross. Just save three seats, OK?"

"OK," Lizzy responded. "But you're missing out on some great music."

"I'll be inside as soon as Ross gets here," Lauren assured her.

Lizzy walked back inside. Lauren paced back and forth in front of the gym entrance. Frustrated, she chided herself. *I knew I should have brought Ross with me.* She looked at the stars again and closed her eyes. *Please God,* Lauren prayed. *Don't allow Jake to keep Ross from coming tonight. He needs to hear the gospel. Please get him here, Lord.*

The sound of squealing tires startled her. Lauren opened her eyes and saw Ross's truck nearly fly into the school parking lot. He pulled up beside her and rolled down the window. Before Ross could say a word, Lauren began to question him.

"Where have you been? I was getting worried about you."

"I know," Ross explained. "I'm sorry. We lost track of time."

"Yeah, Lauren," Jake added, filled with sarcasm. "Sorry about that."

Lauren looked at Jake in disgust, a look she found herself using only toward Jake.

"Let's just get this over with, OK?" Jake continued.

Frustrated, Lauren urged, "We need to get inside. It's already started."

"OK. Let me find a parking space," Ross said.

The lot was packed. Ross had to park quite a distance away and walked quickly to get to Lauren. Jake intentionally walked slowly, obviously trying to further frustrate Lauren.

Ross stopped and turned to Jake. "Come on, Jake. Hurry up. We're already late."

Jake continued moving slowly. Lauren looked at Ross with discontent.

"Seriously?" she asked, aggravated by Jake's juvenile behavior.

Feeling helpless, Ross threw his hands up in frustration.

Finally, Jake caught up with them. He looked at Lauren and smirked.

"Let's just get inside," Lauren said.

Ross and Lauren entered the gymnasium with Jake lagging behind. Multicolored lights crisscrossed the gym. The air vibrated with amped instruments and microphoned voices as the Christian band led hundreds of students in praise and worship. Throughout the enormous arena, students danced, clapped and raised their hands, enthusiastically singing spiritual lyrics at the top of their lungs. Lauren spotted the ever-vigilant Lizzy wildly waving to get her attention. Lauren acknowledged her as she led Ross and Jake to their saved seats.

Concerned that someone would recognize him at the Christian event, Jake kept his head down as he followed them. Once at their seats, Lauren and Ross remained standing while a very uninterested Jake sat down and propped his feet up on the chair in front of him. Lauren joined with the others in the worship service. Ross stood beside her with his hands in his pockets and observed those around him. Jake scoped out the room. His attention was captured by an attractive teenaged girl staring at him from across the aisle. He offered her a grin. She returned the smile and gave him a short wave. Jake checked the time on his phone. It was 8:30 p.m.

The worship continued. Jake, in his boredom, continued checking out the audience. Mostly high school students. A fairly large amount of adults, too. A group of girls in one section, obviously at their first concert, acting giddy and giggling. A few yards to the left stood a group of older girls, dancing and lip-syncing every lyric perfectly. Behind them Jake noticed his buddies Marcus and Drew waving at him. Jake halfway waved back. As the band wrapped up with their final tune, the school's headmaster, Dr. Sharp, joined them on stage. Taking a mic, he encouraged the audience to show their appreciation for the worship experience.

"Let's give it up for the band!" he exclaimed.

The audience erupted with cheers and applause.

"Well, if that doesn't cause you to get your praise on, I don't know what will!" Dr. Sharp said.

The crowd laughed at the elderly gentleman's attempt to use the latest lingo.

"They'll be back in a little while, but for now, I want you to help me welcome our speaker for the evening, George Preston!"

Cheers erupted again. George Preston was well known for his ability to effectively communicate the gospel to young people. His approach was always relevant and well-received by youth all over the country. Preston paced across the stage as he addressed the crowd.

"Man! What a good-looking group!" he said.

Jake rolled his eyes.

The crowd applauded him again and took their seats. Jake checked the time on his phone – 8:45 p.m. He exhaled. Preston opened his Bible and began to speak.

"Tonight, I want to talk to you about God's guardrails against Hell."

A holy hush fell across the room. No matter its connotation to the listener, that word had a tendency to affect people this way.

"Oooh...did he just say that?" Preston joked.

The audience chuckled.

"I'm going to start by sharing a story with you that Jesus shared in the form of a parable. The passage is taken from Luke 16:19-26. I'll be reading from the New King James version."

The fluttery ruffling of pages echoed through the gym.

"Man, I love that sound," the speaker commented. "Kudos to you for remembering to bring your Bibles."

Embarrassed that he didn't bring his, Ross leaned in close to Lauren to look on with her. Lauren accommodated him and placed half the Bible on his lap. He smiled at her gesture. Preston began reading:

"There was a certain rich man who was clothed in purple and fine linen and fared sumptuously every day. But there was a certain beggar named Lazarus, full of sores, who was laid at his gate, desiring to be fed with the crumbs which fell from the rich man's table. Moreover the dogs licked his sores. So it was that the beggar died, and was carried by the angels to Abraham's bosom. The rich man also died and was buried. And being in torments in Hades, he lifted up his eyes and saw Abraham afar off, and Lazarus in his bosom.

"Then he cried and said, 'Father Abraham, have mercy on me, and send Lazarus that he may dip the tip of his finger in water and cool my tongue; for I am tormented in this flame.' But Abraham said, 'Son, remember that in your lifetime you received your good things, and likewise Lazarus evil things; but now he is comforted and you are tormented. And besides all this, between us and you there is a great gulf fixed, so that those who want to pass from here to you cannot, nor can those from there pass to us.'

"The rich man in this story had it made," Preston said after finishing the Scripture reading. "Life was easy, so he didn't really see his need for salvation. Is that you tonight? Most of you guys have it pretty easy – nice clothes, popularity, a decent ride."

Jake leaned over to Ross and held up his fist. Ross immediately met Jake's with his own.

"I know you have real-life pressures, don't get me wrong," Preston continued, "but for the most part, you really have it made.

ou have a zippity-do-da life. Everything pretty much goes your way. Many times, just like the rich man, a life of luxury can blind us to our need for a Savior. The scripture says, '...every day Lazarus was laid at the gate of the rich man.' Every day the rich man was given an opportunity to respond to him. But his response was always, 'Not today. Maybe I will tomorrow.' What is the Lazarus in your life? What Lazarus is God allowing to be laid in front of you daily as a guardrail to keep you out of the eternal place of fire? I can tell you that there is probably more than one. You see, it is God's desire that none should perish. He has made every effort to give us that opportunity, but God will not dictate our choice to us. He gives us free will. In His great love for us, He has set guardrails in place to steer us toward Himself. What is the Lazarus God has placed at your gate?

"The first guardrail I want to point out to you is the Christian witness. Perhaps you're here tonight because a friend who's concerned for your soul invited you to come. That's a good friend. Are they your Lazarus?" Preston asked.

Ross glanced at Lauren and smiled. Elated that Ross acknowledged her, she smiled back.

"Another guardrail is the preacher. How many of you have grown up in church, attending services Sunday after Sunday, hearing the preacher share truth? Or how many times have you participated in VBS, Bible drills, or attended youth camps? All have been opportunities to hear truth. Has that been your Lazarus?"

Jake yawned and stretched dramatically, desperately wanting those around him to notice his extreme boredom. He glanced at the same girl he had made eye contact with earlier. She caught his gaze and smiled at him. Jake grinned. Lauren noticed the exchange and turned her head in disgust.

"A third guardrail is the word of God itself," the speaker went on. "Hebrews 4:12 says that God's word is alive and powerful and sharper than any two-edged sword. God's word that you have hidden in your heart is a vital, incorruptible seed that helps to guard you if you allow it to do so. Is that your Lazarus?"

Ross listened intently.

"Another guardrail set in place is the Holy Spirit. He is a gentleman, leading us away from destruction and to salvation. Has the Holy Spirit been your Lazarus? When the witness shared, when the preacher preached, when the word of God was spoken, what has been your response?"

The room was silent. Students listened wholeheartedly as truth was shared.

"Our biggest guardrail is the cross of Christ. You see, without Jesus, you cannot have a relationship with God. Scary, huh?"

This thought-provoking question triggered heads to nod in agreement across the large room, including Ross's.

"But God loved us so much that He sent Jesus, His one and only Son, to pay the penalty for our sins. He sent Jesus so that we could have an incredible relationship with Him now and eternal life after this one. Romans 5:8 says, 'But God demonstrates His own love toward us, in that while we were still sinners, Christ died for us.' Get this...the result of sin is death, eternal Hell, but the gift of God is eternal life through Jesus Christ His Son."

Jake nodded condescendingly while noticing Ross hanging on Preston's every word. Jake didn't like Ross being interested in God. He liked Ross just the way he was.

"In our worst state, Christ chose to die for us. Now *we* have a choice. The cross of Christ demands a response. What will you say to this Lazarus that has been laid before you? Will you heed this guard-rail? Will you say yes and choose Him, or will you be like the rich man and say, 'Not today. My life is fine just the way it is right now. Maybe I will tomorrow.' The truth is, we aren't promised tomorrow. God's word says that today is the day of salvation."

Preston laid down his Bible and walked to the edge of the stage.

Bending down, he said, "Listen...God loves you very, very much, but He will let you go if that's what you want."

Ross squirmed. He began to sweat. Lauren recognized the conviction Ross was experiencing. Jake looked down and scoffed at Preston's statement.

"Don't miss the guardrails! Don't plow through them into utter and eternal destruction to a real place called Hell. Make no mistake; eternity is forever."

The band joined Preston on stage.

"In just a moment, we're going to give you an incredible opportunity – an opportunity to change your life forever."

Youth pastors from area churches, as well as school staff members, made their way to the front in anticipation of the privilege of leading others to Christ.

Jake checked his phone once more. It was now 9:15 p.m. As the band continued to play, youth flooded the makeshift altar, seeking counsel from spiritual leaders who awaited them. Ross stood still and stared at the floor. Jake nudged him and showed him the time on his phone. Ross glanced at the phone, then returned his gaze to the floor. Confused, Jake nudged him again, motioning his head toward the exit.

"We've got to go," Jake said.

Ross hesitated.

"What's wrong with you, Ross? Did you not see the time? We've got to go!" Jake repeated.

Ross nodded in concession and turned to Lauren. "We've got to go."

"What? You're still going?" Lauren asked in disbelief.

"I promised him. That's how I got him here."

Jake leaned over and joined the conversation as the altar call continued.

"Hey, it was fun," Jake chimed in sarcastically. "Thanks for letting me come."

Lauren shook her head and inched away from Ross. Ross struggled. He hated having to choose between the two of them.

"Dude, we still have to get the car," Jake reminded him, easing into the aisle to leave.

Ross leaned over to Lauren, took her hand and said, "I'll see you at church in the morning, OK?"

He squeezed her hand, then followed Jake. Lauren stared at her empty hand and refused to watch him leave.

"He was so close," she whispered, tears rolling down her face.

A group of nearby students noticed Jake and Ross leaving and motioned to the students behind them. Word about the race had made its way around school. It was no secret what was taking place at ten o'clock at Hell's Bend. Soon a small mob was following the boys out of the gym.

Jake and Ross climbed into Ross's truck.

"You ready?" Jake asked. Ross stared ahead for a moment.

"Ross, what are you waiting for?" Jake asked again. "We've got a race to get to!"

Ross continued to sit in silence for a moment.

"You buy any of that stuff?" Ross asked.

Jake turned and looked Ross straight in the eyes.

"No. They don't even know what they're selling. One second God loves everybody...the next second He's killing everybody. I mean, which is it?"

"Yeah, you're right," Ross replied.

Ross turned the ignition. As soon as he put the truck in reverse, students began banging on the windows. The boys rolled down the windows to see what the commotion was about.

"You guys still racing tonight, right?" one student asked.

"Yeah," Jake replied, pumped with pride. "We're actually headed to get the Trans-Am now."

"We're right behind ya!" another student said. "We'll be there to cheer you on!"

"Thanks," Jake said. "Appreciate that."

The conversation excited Jake and Ross. It was the shot of adrenaline they needed to put at bay the nervousness that was now overtaking them.

The ride to Jake's house was silent. Each boy contemplated in his own mind how events might unfold that night.

Minutes later Ross pulled into Jake's driveway.

"I'll just be a sec," Jake yelled to Ross as he unlocked the side door into the kitchen. He planned only to step inside and grab the Trans-Am key attached to the red "J" keychain, but he noticed a note on the kitchen counter.

Hey, sweetie, just wanted to remind you that your dad and I are with the Kellys at an anniversary party just outside of town. I'm so glad you and Ross decided to attend the Youth Explosion tonight! I know you'll get a blessing out of it. I'll have my phone with me if you need me. We'll be home late – maybe around midnight? Ross is welcome to spend the night if he wants to. I cleared it with Kate. Love you!

Jake was relieved. He had forgotten about their parents' plans for the evening. This was great! There would be no chance of them finding out about the race. They weren't anywhere close by. He reached for the keys. A twinge of guilt rose inside as he thought of her words…*I'm so glad you and Ross decided to attend the Youth Explosion tonight!* Ignoring the feeling, he grabbed the keys, ran out to the car and jumped inside, where Ross waited for him.

Turning the ignition, he looked at Ross and said, "Let's do this."

Ross turned up the radio as loud as they could tolerate it. Jake sped out of the driveway, tires spinning, burning rubber, headed to the race he hoped would shut Eric Williams down once and for all.

Chapter 12

Have you ever heard of the "ripple effect"? You drop a pebble into a body of water, and it creates multiple ripples that continue on and on. That's the same kind of reaction I would see from this night forward. My terrible, selfish decision would cast pain and heartache into so many far-reaching areas I would never, ever be able to comprehend. It seemed for the rest of my life I would find living unbearable. The most difficult thing for me to process was the numerous opportunities I had been given to choose differently.

Hell's Bend was in a rural, sparsely-populated area of the community. The house closest to the notorious curve was occupied by a humble, God-fearing family, the Morrisons.

It was routine for the wife, Tonya Morrison, to bathe at night, slip into her pajamas and slide under the covers of her bed. On this particular evening, she felt impressed by the Holy Spirit to remain dressed in the clothes she had worn that day and sleep on top of her covers. She recognized the still, small voice that spoke to her, but didn't understand why it had done so. Her husband, Lewis, a 6'5" gentle giant, had tucked their girls into bed.

"I told the girls you would come kiss them goodnight," Lewis said, entering their bedroom. He noticed the difference in his wife's nightly routine. "Are you still not ready for bed?" he asked.

"I'm ready for bed, but I don't know why I'm doing it like this," Tonya said.

Confused, Lewis said, "I'm not following you."

"I just felt strongly the Holy Spirit told me to do it this way. I don't know the 'why,' but I know His voice, so I'm obeying," Tonya said with conviction.

"Well, the Lord has told you to do crazier things than this before," Lewis said, chuckling.

Tonya giggled. She stood up and gave him a kiss on the cheek. "Thanks for understanding. I'm going to kiss the girls goodnight."

"Did I say I understood?" Lewis asked. "I didn't say I understood, 'cause I don't."

Tonya laughed as she walked away.

Lewis looked around the room as if he was expecting to see something. Whenever Tonya heard that "voice," it usually proved to be true.

"Oh, dear Lord," Lewis said. "What are You about to do now?"

The white-and-crimson Trans-Am roared down the road and stopped in front of a waiting crowd of teenagers. Eric's black Challenger was parked in the midst of the excited onlookers. Jake eyed the situation, then turned off his headlights and killed the engine. Ross studied Jake, who had spotted Morgan standing close beside Eric.

"I still don't know where I stand with that girl," Jake said.

"Well...right now she's standing by Eric," Ross said. "Don't waste your time on her. She's poison."

"Yeah, I know. I think that's what makes her so attractive," Jake said.

The boys got out of the car. Eric saw them and walked toward the two. The crowd slowly surrounded Eric and Jake as if they were heavyweight fighters about to spar. Morgan was enthralled with the intensity of the moment.

"Well, if it's not the 'Bama Bros,' " Eric said sarcastically. "Thought you were gonna be a no-show...like last night's game."

"Sorry to disappoint," Jake replied.

Eric's sidekick, Aaron, stepped forward to start the race.

"You guys know the rules," he said.

Morgan edged close to Jake and nodded hello. He grinned at her. Although he didn't like the games she played, he had a hard time resisting her.

Aaron continued his instructions. "Make the curve at Hell's Bend, turn around at Hardin's Grocery and race back. First one to cross this line..." he pointed to the ground, "...wins! Got it?"

"Got it!" Eric said.

"Yup!" Jake replied.

Jake and Ross walked toward the Trans-Am. Eric followed them.

"Hey," Eric called.

Jake and Ross turned to see what he wanted.

"You taste that?" Eric asked.

Jake squinted his eyebrows.

"That's your foot...in your mouth," Eric answered.

Jake stepped closer to Eric. "That's not where I'm gonna put it."

"Nice," Eric responded.

As he walked toward his Challenger, Eric yelled out for all to hear, "Don't scratch Daddy's car!"

Laughs trickled from the crowd.

Jake turned to Morgan. "See you in a minute."

"Don't take too long," she replied seductively.

While Jake climbed into the driver's seat of the Trans-Am, Ross entered on the passenger's side.

"This ain't gonna be like racing that Impala," Ross said.

"You got that right," Jake responded.

From inside the car the boys watched in silence as Eric's Challenger, which faced them, roared to life. Jake looked worried, and Ross could see it in his face. It made Ross uncomfortable, this failure in confidence. Jake was the leader. Ross followed. He didn't know how to handle such an unusual situation. He attempted to lighten the mood.

"Hey, Bama Bro," Ross said.

Jake looked at him. Ross pointed his finger toward the roof of the car. "This thing has windows on the ceiling," he said, flashing his cute boyish grin.

Jake couldn't keep a straight face. He burst into laughter. Relieved that it had the effect he was shooting for, Ross laughed, too.

"I had forgotten about that," Jake said.

The less-than-serious moment helped release the tension that had built. Suddenly a blinding light flooded the car as Eric turned on his headlights. Jake and Ross immediately put their hands in front of their eyes to block the intense glare.

"What's up with that?" Ross asked.

"He's just putting on a show," Jake responded.

Eric's black Challenger backed into a Y-turn, aligning it with the Trans-Am. Reality began to set in. Jake's resolve was wavering. He placed his fingers around the key and allowed the red "J" keychain to rest in his hand. It sparkled in the minimal light that remained.

This moment could determine the rest of your life, he thought to himself.

Jake shook himself free of the trance-like state and looked at Ross.

"Our time," Jake said, turning the ignition.

Ross nodded in agreement.

The Trans-Am now purred, and its headlights shot two bright beams into the dark, desolate road that lay ahead. Jake looked through his window at Eric, who returned his gaze. Jake nodded. Eric revved his engine. Jake smirked, acknowledging Eric's immaturity. Aaron walked between the cars and tapped the hoods for attention.

"All right, dudes," he said.

He looked at Jake, then to Eric, making sure they were both paying attention. He slowly backed away toward the front of the vehicles while the onlookers peeled to either side. Jake focused on the road. Aaron raised his arms above his head, ready in a moment to signal the race's start. Ross nervously fumbled at his seat belt.

"It won't lock," Ross said nervously.

"Try again," Jake said calmly.

Ross tried again to no avail, causing him to become even more anxious.

"You've got to stay calm, Ross, or it won't work," Jake said.

Frantic, Ross looked at Jake helplessly. Jake turned his attention back to the road. Ross struggled to steady his hand. He tried again. Finally, it locked. Ross exhaled a long-held breath and faced forward. Relieved, he sighed and sank into the seat. Jake nervously tapped his thumbs on the steering wheel while gunning the accelerator. At last, Aaron's arms dropped. The cars shot forward and darted down the open stretch of County Road 1498, leaving a crowd of screaming witnesses behind. The sudden burst of speed pinned Ross back in his seat. He looked at Jake, wide-eyed. Jake and Eric quickly checked each other's positions while also eyeing the road. The Challenger pulled away, taking the lead. Jake glanced at the speedometer, which had quickly shot past 65 miles per hour. The tachometer touched the red zone before the automatic transmission shifted into a higher gear. The Trans-Am was catching up with the Challenger. Side by side, the drivers checked each other again. Jake grinned while pushing the accelerator even closer to the floor. The car inched forward as the speedometer needle ascended. Seventy-five miles per hour, 85... The car began to vibrate.

"Whoa," Ross said nervously.

"She'll level out," Jake said.

Sergeant Mike Mayhew sat in a dark patrol car just off County Road 1498, concealed by a large group of pine trees. The volunteer fire station's gravel lot was a perfect spot to monitor the notorious drag-racing strip. On his way to the clandestine area, Mayhew had seen a clump of headlights and the soft, small glows of a hundred cell phones. Suspecting Ross Kelly might be involved in tonight's escapade, the sheriff's deputy wanted to personally follow up on the tip. He felt responsible for the young man he had mentored for five years. Jake Adams's white-and-crimson Trans-Am suddenly flew past, followed by another speeding vehicle. Mike Mayhew already knew the driver of the lead car, and his heart sank; Ross would be in the passenger's seat.

Jake glanced into the rearview mirror, checking Eric's progress. He was regaining momentum. Jake gripped the steering wheel. The Trans-Am leveled out as it passed 100 miles per hour. Jake stomped the accelerator. The needle soared. Neither driver wanted to brake. Suddenly, without warning, blue lights burst from the darkness.

They filled Ross's side-view mirror. "Cops!" he yelled frantically.

Jake craned his head and saw a Lee County Sheriff's Department SUV moving closely behind them.

"No way!" Jake exclaimed in disbelief. "Somebody tipped them off!"

And I bet I know who, he thought, Lauren's prudish, impudent face filling his head.

"911, this is Lee-40. I'm attempting to stop two vehicles at a high rate of speed headed eastbound on 1498," Mayhew reported while peeling out of the lot, tires squealing and gravel dust billowing behind his vehicle.

"Lee-40 eastbound on 1498 at 22:40," the 911 dispatcher confirmed.

Mayhew immediately recognized the dispatcher's voice. It belonged to Nick Michaels. Mayhew was relieved. Michaels was one of the best in the business – calm, experienced. Mayhew felt at ease knowing Michaels was the one on board for this kind of situation. He accelerated quickly to ensure the teens remained in sight. So far, neither driver heeded his blue lights.

"Subjects are not stopping," he continued to the radio. "I'm in pursuit."

"All units, 10-33 traffic on S-O dispatch," Michaels radioed the entire sheriff's office personnel.

With the airwaves now clear, Mayhew could summon help if needed and get the situation under control.

A different voice now crackled from the radio. "Lee-40, this is Lee-42. I'm coming up 1409...headed toward you." Mayhew smiled. Hollis was on the way.

Two miles into the race, Eric Williams conceded and pulled into the parking lot of Crossroads Church. Sergeant Mayhew pulled in behind.

Jake laughed aloud as he watched in the rearview mirror.

"Ha-ha! Eric choked!" he yelled jubilantly. "What a coward!" Without hesitation, Jake continued the dark course. The Trans-Am barreled recklessly down the last few miles that led to Hell's Bend.

"What are you doing?" Ross asked desperately, not believing his eyes. Jake had won; why was he not stopping?

Jake didn't respond. The speedometer continued to rise.

In the church parking lot, Mayhew reported to Nick Michaels the information on Eric's vehicle. "911, I've got the black Challenger, Lincoln George Tom 432, stopped at Crossroads Church, at County Road 1349." Then, addressing his fellow officer, "Lee-42, if you're still at 1409, the Trans-Am is still headed eastbound at a high rate of speed toward you."

The dispatcher repeated the information to confirm it, then asked, "Lee-40, give me another description of the car still going."

Mayhew quickly replied, "It's a Trans-Am, white and other in color."

The sergeant exited his car and approached Eric. Following protocol was hard for Mayhew on this one. He wanted so desperately to continue trailing that Trans-Am and make sure Ross was OK. He struggled to put it out of his mind and focused on the driver who had made the decision to stop.

Soon, Deputy Daniels joined in to help. He, like Mayhew, was certain if there was a race taking place that night, Jake was involved. He had purposefully chosen to patrol the area during the alleged race time. "911, this is Lee-44. I'm coming up on the intersection of County Roads 1349 and 1498."

County Road 1349 was directly across from Crossroads Church, where Mayhew had Eric detained.

"I'll take over the pursuit of the Trans-Am," Daniels said.

Mayhew overheard the dialogue. He looked toward County Road 1349 and saw Daniels's headlights at the stop sign. The officers flickered their lights to acknowledge one another. Mayhew shined his flashlight in the direction Jake was headed. Daniels sped onto the road and soon caught up with the Trans-Am he had helped only a week earlier when it overheated. Daniels felt heartsick knowing the danger that lay ahead. Like Mayhew, he, too, struggled to stay calm and focused.

Daniels keyed his mic. "911, this is Lee-44. I'm behind subject now. Lincoln Frank George 452. Lee-42, we need to get him stopped ASAP. He's headed toward Hell's Bend."

Jake checked his mirror again. A different set of flashing blue lights had appeared. The blaring siren pounded his eardrums.

"Where did *that* guy come from?" Jake asked anxiously.

Ross watched the patrol car in the side mirror as sweat rolled down his face.

"We are so dead!" Ross shouted.

Deputy Hollis decided on a tactic used regularly in this kind of pursuit – stop Jake before he got any closer to the notorious spot where several people had already lost their lives.

"This is Lee-42," Hollis reported. "I'm deploying the spike strip."

"Strip deployed between 1349 and 1409 at 22:46," Michaels confirmed.

Knowing he had little time, Hollis removed the accordion-like device from its vinyl bag. He positioned himself just a few feet from the road and laid it in Jake's path. Only milliseconds later the Trans-Am roared near the mark.

"Look out!" Ross yelled.

Trying to avoid the spike strip, Jake jerked the steering wheel to the left. The tires hit the shoulder of the road, slinging rocks and dust everywhere and into the path where Deputy Hollis stood. The officer jumped out of the way and barely escaped injury.

Jake leaned his head out the window, looked back toward Hollis and yelled, "Loser!" He laughed at the deputy's failed attempt to stop him.

"Man, are you crazy? You almost killed that guy!" Ross yelled.

Galen Daniels witnessed the ordeal. While it unnerved him to see his friend involved in such a close call, his heart was heavy with fear for the young men in front of him. He knew they had done everything within their power to safely stop the teens. Now, the only hope he saw was calling off the pursuit.

"This is Lee-44. Subject has gone around the spike strip. I'm calling a 10-25 due to high rate of speed."

Daniels refused to be responsible for a pursuit that led to tragedy. It wasn't worth the risk. On a personal level, he prayed Jake would slow down quickly and make that curve safely.

"All units, 10-33 traffic is lifted. Pursuit has been called due to high rate of speed encountering Hell's Bend at 22:48."

Deputy Daniels slowed his vehicle.

"Yes!" Jake cheered as he watched the blue lights fade away.

Daniels turned around in a nearby driveway and returned to check on Deputy Hollis. Daniels found Hollis visibly shaken from the encounter with the Trans-Am.

"Juicy, you all right?" he asked.

"Whew! That was a close one," Deputy Hollis said. "I'll be fine."

"Good thing you been going to CrossFit. Otherwise, you might not have been agile enough to dodge that bullet," Daniels joked.

"Real funny...4.2," Hollis said with humorous vengeance.

Deputy Daniels laughed. "I'm glad you're all right, man," he said, patting him on the back.

"Yeah, I just hope those kids will be," Hollis said, concerned.

Daniels radioed Mayhew. "Lee-40, this is Lee-44. We're returning to Crossroads Church to assist. We're headed your way."

"10-4," Mayhew confirmed.

Back on County Road 1498, Jake celebrated his perceived victory.

"What are you doing?" Ross asked in disbelief. "The cops backed off! Slow down!"

Jake didn't respond. The speedometer continued to rise. Jake checked the mirror again to make sure they were in the clear.

Although the deputies were long gone, Jake did not ease up. In fact, outrunning the cops seemed to fuel Jake's adrenaline rush.

Daniels and Hollis drove to the church where Mayhew had detained Eric.

As Mayhew filled out the citation, he glanced at Eric sitting quietly in his car. Given Eric's reputation, Mayhew expected him to be difficult. Instead, he witnessed a very remorseful and humble Eric. *Maybe this "bad boy" wasn't so bad after all.* A bit of compassion stirred in the ol' softie.

Mayhew knew with the power of his position as sergeant, he had the ability to make decisions outside the box. He always took into consideration not only the effects of the subjects' bad choices, but also the effects of his own judgment as well. His decisions could determine the course of others' lives. His goal was always to enrich those lives, not destroy them.

He deliberated for a moment, then decided to show mercy and tore up the citation. Eric stared at him, puzzled.

"Son, I'm going to cut you some slack tonight," Mayhew said. "You made the right decision."

Eric breathed a sigh of relief. He couldn't believe it.

"I'm sure there'll be some consequences to face with your parents," Mayhew continued. "But it could have been a lot worse had you chosen to continue down that road. You know where it leads."

Eric wasn't sure if the sergeant was talking figuratively or literally. Either way, he knew Mayhew was right.

"Yes, sir," Eric replied respectfully, hoping Mayhew wouldn't change his mind about the ticket.

Jake continued speeding down the dangerous route, ignoring the warning signs of the deadly Hell's Bend just ahead. Ross looked at the speedometer. It now read 130 miles per hour. The car began to feel as if it were gravitating away from the road. Fear gripped him.

"Jake, I'm scared," Ross said, his voice trembling.

Jake saw sheer terror in Ross's eyes and fear radiating from his face as his best friend held on tightly to the passenger's-side door handle. Jake was overcome with an enormous sense of responsibility for him. Then Jake turned his eyes back to the road. His feelings of victory changed quickly once he focused on the sight ahead. He had been so distracted by the police pursuit that he missed the bright orange danger signs along the road. Terror overtook them both. Their view now was the guardrail that marked the beginning of the notorious Hell's Bend.

Jake checked the speedometer. There was no hope of taking that curve at the speed he was going. Instinctively he slammed on the brakes. The Trans-Am went into a tailspin and was now out of Jake's control. Still traveling at an outrageously high rate of speed, the car plowed through the galvanized steel. The newly-restored, red-and-white 1979 Trans-Am became airborne. Inside the classic car, the boys' world turned upside down.

"Jake!" Ross cried as he desperately sought to grab anything to stabilize himself. Jake yelled, gripping the steering wheel while his body was fiercely yanked against the seatbelt. His mind filled with a thousand images. Suddenly he was with Ross playing basketball at age twelve, guzzling Gatorades. No, no…he was in church with his mother. Voices echoed in his ears. Was he actually hearing them, or remembering them? *How many sermons have you heard the preacher preach?*

"Ahhh!" Jake screamed violently. The pressure of the seatbelt against his chest was unbearable.

He and Ross were now removing the dusty tarp from the Trans-Am. *Wanna take her for a spin?…She purrs like a kitten… Like a lion!*

Jake tried to brace himself against the door as glass exploded throughout the car.

You in the habit of stealing cars? The red "J"…Coach Scott… *This is more than a game…*

The car rotated in mid-air. Ross looked at Jake, horrified, his mouth moving but his cries inaudible to Jake.

There are bigger things at stake here than you can understand… Dad…Jake threw the football…Eagles quarterback…bursting through cheerleader paper…the cafeteria…Lauren…*I want you to tell Ross not to go with you tomorrow night…*

Shattered glass flew around the boys, impaling everything in its way.

Youth Explosion…George Preston…*God loves you, but He will let you go…*

As the Trans-Am rotated one last time, the catch broke on Ross's seatbelt. The boys looked at each other, terror ripping through their veins.

"Help me!" Ross screamed. Inertia from the tumbling vehicle snatched him through the passenger door window. Jake heard his mother's voice: *We all get what we ask for.*

"Ross!"

Jake frantically grabbed for Ross's arm, but he was no longer inside the car. *Some things…you just can't take back.*

The terrible sounds of metal crushing and glass shattering suddenly ceased. Jake's Trans-Am was no longer tumbling. He closed his eyes and shielded his face with his arms as the car skidded through the open field for what seemed like an eternity before passing between two pecan trees. It came to an abrupt stop when it slammed head-on into another pecan tree to arrive at its final resting place.

Jake's mind no longer raced. He was alone and still. The world was silent. Jake had no idea where Ross was. All he knew was that he was trapped inside a twisted mess of metal.

Back at the church, the deputies had joined Mayhew and Eric.

"Son, what in the world were y'all thinking?" Daniels asked.

Eric sat quietly and said nothing.

"I've tried talking to that boy," Daniels said, shaking his head, wondering what else he could have said to Jake Adams to stop his dangerous behavior.

"We all have," Mayhew replied. "Nothing gets through to him."

Nick Michaels, the dispatcher, was back on the radio.

"Lee S-O Zone Two, Road 1498 at Hell's Bend, 10-50 with injuries, one subject possibly 10-7...the vehicle's possibly on fire."

Despite dealing with this almost daily, the deputies cringed as they heard the 10-codes they hated the most – injury...and death.

"It's them," they said in unison.

"Oh, please, Lord, no," Mayhew whispered.

The officers immediately jumped in their patrol vehicles to head back toward Hell's Bend.

Eric heard it loud and clear. He grabbed the steering wheel with his hands and laid his head against it. He knew it was Jake and Ross. "This can't be happening," he said softly.

Hollis was already on the radio. "Lee-42 responding. En route to the 10-50."

"Lee-42 en route to the 10-50 at 22:57," Nick Michaels confirmed.

Daniels followed suit. "Lee-44 responding. En route to the 10-50."

"Lee-44 en route to the 10-50 at 23:58," Michaels stated.

Deputy Mike Mayhew was still with Eric at his car. "I'm right behind you guys," he replied into his microphone. He looked at Eric. "Son, you need to go home."

Shocked, Eric replied, "Yes, sir."

Mayhew sped off.

Eric started the Challenger and spun out of the parking lot, headed toward the finish line and the kids who were sure to be waiting on the winner.

A minute later, the crowd appeared, standing around in anticipation, placing bets on who would win. Eric fired into their midst,
slammed on his brakes and shoved the gear shift into park. Assuming
Eric's crossing the finish line meant victory, the young people
started cheering.

Eric slowly exited his car. The cheers faded as his friends saw his
white-as-a-ghost face. They quickly quieted down and rushed to him.

"Eric, what's wrong?" Aaron asked.

Eric felt nauseous and crouched down beside his car. "There's
been a wreck."

His voice was so soft that Aaron asked him to repeat himself.

"Jake and Ross…they wrecked…at Hell's Bend," Eric said. "The
cops were waiting for us. Someone must have tipped them off. I
stopped, but Jake kept going. Next thing I know, someone comes
over the radio saying there'd been a wreck at Hell's Bend."

"How do you know it's them?" Aaron asked.

"I just know it is. Jake wouldn't stop. They called off the chase
just minutes before the call came over the radio," Eric explained.
"You should have seen the look on those guys' faces. It was like they
knew something else that they weren't telling me."

"What guys?" Aaron asked, becoming agitated with the news.
"You aren't making sense!"

"Mayhew and a couple of deputies," Eric said, his voice trembling.

"Come on," Aaron said. "Let's get down there!"

The frenzied crowd began loading up in cars and the backs of
trucks and sped off toward Hell's Bend to check on their friends.

Aaron looked at Eric. "You don't need to drive. Give me your
keys and climb in the back," he ordered.

Without argument, Eric crawled into the back seat. Morgan joined Aaron in the front. She recalled having exchanged cell numbers with Lauren a couple of nights earlier. Immediately she texted her.

The night sky was completely clear. Light from a half moon revealed the wreckage. A faint chirping of tree frogs in the distance was the only sound. The ominous odor of gasoline permeated the air. A gray, wispy funnel of smoke rose from what was left of the Trans-Am's crumpled hood. Orange-and-yellow sparks flew from the mangled metal.

In the distance, the sound of one siren quickly multiplied. Help was on the way, but there was a long, difficult night ahead.

Chapter 13

Extreme...over the top...out of control. These are just a few descriptions of me that night. In my self-centered mind, nothing was going to stop me from beating Eric and shutting him down once and for all. I look back and just can't believe to what lengths I was willing to go just to win a race. The guy behind the wheel of the car that night makes me sick. I still can't believe it was me. How did I become so narcissistic? How could I even think that I could act like that and get away with it...with man, or God? I quickly went from thinking I was invincible to wishing I was invisible.

The horrific sound of metal crashing and twisting jolted the Morrison family from their sleep.

"Jesus!" Tonya cried out prayerfully.

"Dear God, help us!" Lewis proclaimed.

The reason for the Holy Spirit's bizarre impression on Tonya earlier that evening was now becoming clear. The pitter-patter of tiny little feet entered the couple's master bedroom.

"What was that noise, Momma?" the elder daughter, Ashley, cried fearfully.

"I'm not sure," Tonya said as she comforted her.

Lewis quickly swooped up their youngest, Emily, in his arms. Her body trembled.

"You stay inside with your sister," Lewis instructed her. "Your momma and I are gonna go see what's going on."

Tears in her eyes, the little girl nodded her head.

Tonya reassured her. "You'll be just fine."

As the Morrison couple ran out the front door, the girls watched out the living room window and embraced each other. The couple ran down the hill toward the aftermath in the field below them.

The view ahead of them was devastating.

"Oh, Lord, help!" Tonya yelled.

First responders made it on the scene within minutes. Mayhew, Daniels and Hollis each alerted dispatcher Nick Michaels of their arrival. The officers exited their vehicles quickly with flashlights in hand. Daniels and Mayhew looked at each other. Without hesitation, both officers sprinted toward the Trans-Am. Instinctively, Mayhew aimed for the passenger side where Ross was expected to be, as did Daniels toward Jake.

Hollis charged toward the car as well but was diverted by the commotion of the Morrison couple running toward him, praying aloud with fervency.

Unsure of their intentions, Hollis ordered them to stop.

"You folks are going to have to stay back!" Deputy Hollis said, waving his flashlight in front of them to get a better look at who they were. "This is a very dangerous situation!"

Laboring to breathe, Lewis said, "Don't worry, sir. We're just here to pray."

While Deputy Hollis was surprised by the unusual response, he respected it.

"Well, OK, but you need to do it from right here," he said, pointing to the spot where they stood. "I can't allow you to get any closer. It's for your own safety."

Mayhew and Daniels carefully approached the car. The smell of gas was overbearing. Mayhew looked in through the glassless window on the passenger's side only to see an empty seat.

"Oh, no," Mayhew said. His face paled. He knew from Eric that Ross had been with Jake. *Ross must have been ejected.* His heart sank. He couldn't recall there ever being a time in all of his years in law enforcement when someone ejected from a vehicle survived. He struggled to not succumb to his emotions but to stay focused on the task at hand.

Daniels leaned in through the window opening of the driver's side and found Jake Adams – still, eyes closed, his head turned away. His chest looked like it was moving, though. Daniels shined his flashlight around the interior. The mangled mess indicated Jake was undoubtedly trapped.

Peering at Daniels through the car, Mayhew asked, "How is he?"

"Unresponsive and pinned in," Daniels said.

Sergeant Mayhew pressed the button on the radio clipped to his shirt. "911, we've got one ejected and one entrapment. The smell of gas is overwhelming. Get me medics and fire department and get them here quick!"

While Mayhew looked for Ross, Daniels labored to get a response from Jake.

"Jake, can you hear me?" he called. No answer. Shaking him, he pleaded, "Jake, please answer me, son!"

Daniels continued to work with Jake while vehicle after vehicle loaded with panicked teens raced down County Road 1498 toward

Hell's Bend, desperate to reach their friends. As they approached the intersection of CR 1409, the sight of swirling blue lights caused them to stop at once. Deputy Ramon had blocked the road, suspending traffic near the wreck site.

Parked on the other side of the dangerous curve, Trent Maze, an off-duty EMT, grabbed his medical bag and ran toward the wreckage.

Recognizing him, Hollis called his name and waved his hand in the air, attempting to get the EMT's attention.

Trent noticed him quickly. "Hey, I heard you guys call over the scanner," Trent said. "I figured I'd be the closest one to you. What can I do to help?"

Pointing toward the car, Hollis said, "Head over there and ask Daniels. I'm not sure what's going on with the subjects inside the car."

"Gotcha!" Trent replied. The EMT ran to Daniels to see how he could assist.

"Please, God, don't take him," Daniels prayed under his breath. His heart was pounding so hard, he could feel his pulse in his throat.

The EMT bent down beside him. "How's he doing?"

"Oh, man, Trent! Glad you're here!" Daniels said with relief. "He's trapped and unresponsive. It doesn't look good to me."

"Let me take a look."

As Trent tended to Jake, more teens concentrated at the roadblock. News of the accident was traveling fast.

About an hour had passed since Youth Explosion had ended. To reward themselves for their hard work and celebrate the successful event, Lauren, Lizzy and some of the other FISH club members stopped at their favorite yogurt spot. After enjoying a snack and sharing testimonies from the night's successful event, Lauren headed home. While driving, she debated driving out to the race site. She checked her phone for the twentieth time, hoping to have a missed call or text message from Ross, but there was nothing. Pride swelled inside. *If he doesn't think enough of me to call and let me know he's OK, then I'm not going to check on him.* Her mind shifted to the conversation with Sergeant Mayhew the day before about the pending race. Feeling jaded, her thoughts turned cold. *I hope they get caught this time. It would serve them right.*

She pulled into the driveway and walked to the back door. As she unlocked the door, her phone's text alert sounded. Lauren's heart leaped, thinking it might be from Ross. She looked at her phone and was surprised to see it was from Morgan. Lauren stared at her phone in disbelief as she read the text.

Jake and Ross have wrecked at Hell's Bend. I knew you would want to know right away.

Hysteria set in. Lauren ran inside screaming for her mom. Margaret sat on the couch reading, waiting for her daughter to get home. Startled, she jumped up and followed Lauren's cries.

"What's wrong?" Margaret asked.

Lauren was so emotional she couldn't speak. She handed Margaret her phone.

"Oh, God, help us!" Margaret said prayerfully. She grabbed Lauren and hugged her tightly.

"Mom, I knew it!" Lauren wailed. "I knew it!"

Margaret mind's raced to figure out what to do next. She pulled Lauren back and looked at her.

"Lauren, sweetie, I know you are terribly upset, but we've got to hold it together."

"I've got to get down there!" Lauren cried.

"No, Lauren! I don't want you going down there!" Margaret ordered.

"Mom, please!" Lauren begged.

"Absolutely not!" Margaret said adamantly. Realizing her voice was raised, she forced herself to regain control of the situation. "Sweetheart, we have got to calm down." Taking Lauren by the hand, she pulled her to the couch. "Here, sit down," Margaret said.

Margaret handed Lauren the box of Kleenex sitting on the end table.

After regaining her composure, Margaret thought aloud, partially to convince herself she was doing the right thing.

"I need to call Grace. They were at an anniversary party with the Kellys tonight, but it was out of town." She began to second-guess her plan of action. "Oh, my, I don't know what to do!" She thought for a moment. "Well, if it were one of my children, I would hope someone would call me right away."

She picked up her cell phone from the coffee table. Unnerved, she searched for Grace's name on her call list. Then, taking a deep breath, she pressed the green button.

Grace's phone rang, but she never knew it. She had placed it on silent mode while attending the twenty-fifth wedding anniversary celebration for some former classmates.

During the drive home from the party, Grace and Kate chatted in the back seat.

"Could you believe the surprised look on Lisa's face?" Grace asked.

"It was priceless," Kate agreed. "I loved the idea of their children surprising them with the reception."

"You started to tell me about this outfit you have on tonight," Grace said. "Love the color. Is that the one you found at *Sparrows on Main*?"

"Yes," Grace said. "My sweet friend, Marie, helped me pick it out."

Kate said. "She is just the cutest thing!"

"They're all adorable. That place is addictive."

"I went in to model for them on my birthday a few months ago," Kate said. "When I walked into the store, they presented me with a crown and little petit fours to celebrate...so sweet. They made it very special."

"You must shop there plenty to get treatment like that," Grace laughed.

"Shhhhhh," Kate said, holding her finger to her mouth and looking toward Lance. They both giggled.

Mitch and Lance looked at each other and rolled their eyes as their wives talked ninety-to-nothing.

"It's so hard to decide what to wear this time of year," Kate said. "It's not autumn yet, but it's the end of summer when you're sick of summer clothes."

"I know," Grace said. "But that outfit is a great in-between."

"Mitch, I just love that tie," Lance said, waving his hand toward his friend. "It really brings out your eyes."

"What? This old thing?" Mitch said, playing along. "Oh, and I really like your sports coat, Lance. It's perfect for this in-between time of year."

"I got it at *Buzzards on Veterans*."

"You two stop it," Grace ordered.

The guys laughed. Mitch placed his hand on Grace's knee and winked.

"You know we're just messing with you," Mitch said.

"That *is* a pretty catchy name for a boutique," Lance said. "I wonder how they came up with it."

"It's a sweet story, actually," Kate said. "One of the store owners, Lynn, lost her husband to cancer a couple of years ago. He told Lynn before his death that he would watch over them like a little bird; hence the name Sparrows."

"Bless her," Lance said sympathetically.

"It reminds me of an old Southern gospel song," Kate said. "*His eye is on the sparrow and I know He watches me.*"

"I remember that old song," Grace said, taking her phone out of her purse. "I'm gonna check in with Jake."

There were several missed calls from Margaret, and she was suddenly concerned. She quickly tapped on Margaret's number to return the call.

As Margaret pondered about what to say once she reached Grace, Lauren replied to Morgan's text: *My mom won't allow me to go. What happened? Is Ross OK? Please let me know what's going on!*

Morgan stood outside, leaning against Eric's car, nervously twirling her hair, while Eric stayed in the back seat, still numb from the nightmare he had helped create. Morgan felt her phone vibrate. She looked at the alert. It was Lauren. After reading Lauren's text, Morgan responded: *They were racing. Cops were ready for them. Eric stopped, but Jake didn't. They went through the guardrail at Hell's Bend. They put up a roadblock so we can't get through to check on them.*

She paused for a moment. The reality of the situation overwhelmed her. She ended her message: *Lauren, I'm really scared.*

Lauren waited impatiently on Morgan's response, chewing her nails down to the quick, while Margaret allowed time to pass before calling Grace again. Finally, Morgan's text lit up the phone screen. Lauren could hear Morgan's emotions coming through her message. Her admission of fear shocked Lauren. Lauren responded: *Me, too.*

Morgan stared at Lauren's text, empathizing with her. The sound of another roaring engine startled her. She looked up and saw Marcus and Drew running toward them. Morgan watched their reaction to the grim situation.

Seeing that his mentor, Deputy Ramon, was overseeing the roadblock, Marcus darted straight to him.

"Ramon, please!" Marcus cried. "Let me get to them!"

Deputy Ramon grabbed him. "I'm sorry, son, but I can't let you do that."

"You don't understand!" Marcus cried. "They's my boys!"

"I know, Marcus, but there's nothing you can do to help the situation," Ramon said sympathetically.

"I got to know they all right," Marcus said through tears.

"Look, you guys just need to go on home, OK?" Ramon said. "I'll keep you posted."

Morgan watched Marcus plead with Deputy Ramon to let him through. Tearing up herself, she updated Lauren: *Marcus is ballistic! It's really hard to watch.*

Margaret looked at Lauren and stroked her hair away from her face. Feeling helpless, Margaret said, "We need to pray."

As Margaret and Lauren prayed for the boys, the Morrisons continued doing the same at the wreck site.

The EMT, Trent, felt hopeless. He looked at Daniels and said, "There's barely a pulse."

Daniels paced in the deep grass and began to pray.

Resolved to continue caring for Jake as much as possible, Trent examined the gash on Jake's head. Blood oozed out of the deep cut approximately three inches long. After treating the injury, Trent wrapped gauze around his head, hoping the pressure would stop the flow of blood.

Mayhew combed the area looking for Ross, calling out for him.

"Ross! Can you hear me?"

The light beaming from his flashlight pierced the darkness just steps ahead of his feet. As he walked through the overgrown grassy area, he prayed for a miracle.

"Ross!" he called.

"M...M...Mayhew..." Ross tried to utter from his parched lips. He felt like he was screaming, but he knew only a whisper actually emerged from his lips. Suddenly he saw the beam of a flashlight. Then a face appeared above him.

"Oh, no," Mayhew said.

Ross raised his head as much as he could. "Mike," he called. "How's Jake?"

Mayhew stared at him. Then, pressing the button on his radio, he said, "911, this is Lee-40. We have a 10-7. Please advise ME-1 and send one of our CID units."

Mayhew had taught Ross all the 10-codes, and a "10-7" meant a death had occurred.

Ross screamed. "Jake! Please, God, no!" He shook his head back and forth in denial. His best friend wasn't dead.

"Oh, Ross," Mayhew whispered.

Several miles away, Lauren, too, whispered Ross's name as she sat beside her mother, dabbing away tears.

Margaret's phone rang. It was Grace returning her call. Startled, her mind searched for what to say. She heard Grace's voice on the other end of the line.

"Hello, friend," Grace said with reservation.

"Grace," Margaret responded anxiously.

Grace could tell by the tone in her voice something was up.

"Margaret, what's wrong?" Grace asked. Mitch and Kate turned toward Grace when they heard her words. Lance peered at her through the rearview mirror.

Margaret chose her words carefully. "Are you guys headed home?" she asked.

"Yes, we are. Why?" Grace asked.

"I don't want to alarm you, Grace, but we've gotten word that Jake and Ross may have been in a wreck," Margaret said.

Grace gasped.

"Honey, what's wrong?" Mitch asked.

Grace held up her finger to him as she listened to Margaret.

"A girl in Lauren's class texted her saying they had wrecked at Hell's Bend. Apparently, they were racing," Margaret said.

Grace's imagination raced. Words were difficult to form. She dropped the phone slowly away from her mouth as she muttered, "Thank you...for letting us know. I'll see what I can find out. If you hear anything else..."

"Absolutely, Grace! I'll be praying, friend," Margaret said. "Lauren and I are worried sick!"

But Grace didn't hear her friend. She looked to the front seat at Mitch, who was still turned toward her.

Tears flowed down her face. She looked at Mitch, then Kate, then Lance. "That was Margaret. She said someone texted Lauren saying our boys have been involved in an accident," Grace said as she struggled to breathe.

"What kind of accident, honey?" Mitch asked.

"A car accident...at Hell's Bend," Grace said. The words "accident at Hell's Bend" equaled "fatality" to them. That statement cut through them like a serrated knife.

Kate immediately took her phone from her purse.

"I'm calling Ross," she said. As she listened to the rings, she pleaded for Ross to answer.

ant wail of sirens grew closer as emergency agencies, more law enforcement officials, arrived on the scene, including Sheriff Howell. Another emergency had detained him from arriving sooner.

Ross watched as a misshapen form of black smoke poured across the road in the direction of the approaching help. The wispy, porous mass was as wide as the county road and now covered it, hovering about twenty feet above it. Ross rubbed his eyes, trying to understand what was looming ahead of him. A large form began to emerge. In a matter of milliseconds the cloud-like smoke morphed into a huge, demonic figure over seven feet tall with glowing red eyes. The smoky figure glided toward Ross with long, powerful strides. Ross panted. His heart raced. His eyes grew wider as the monstrous figure drew nearer.

The gray-black smoke began to dissipate from the demon's body, revealing a dark cloak and dragon-like armor. Ross found the sight grotesque. An unnatural fire took to the air behind it. The world around him began to burn away like paper held to a flame. Left behind was now a black landscape dominated by flames and glowing embers. The hooded demon bent to its knee and looked Ross in the eyes, paralyzing him with fear. It reached for Ross, who screamed in fear with every ounce of his strength. With its oversized hand, the demon lifted him high off the ground. Ross fought against the foul-smelling beast, but his struggle was no match for the powerful being. While dangling in mid-air, he looked down in the field below, trying to find Mayhew, Jake's body, anyone… anyone…please! What was happening? Where did this demon come from? Instead of the wreck site where he had just been snatched, Ross saw below something that he did not comprehend. A body lay amid the tall field grass, mangled and lifeless, brain matter scattered nearby.

Ross tried to understand what he was seeing. He stared at the familiar body. And the familiar clothes. *It's me. I'm the one who's dead, not Jake.* Ross struggled in vain to break free from the supernatural grip of the demon. The ground began to quake. The ground behind them separated. Smoke billowed from the enormous opening. The heavy odor of sulfur was overbearing. Vibrant red-and-orange hues appeared, followed by hot molten lava that oozed from the large crevice. Sounds of faint screams and cries escaped, sending a chill down Ross's spine.

His soul now dangled over the opening in the earth. The heat was such that Ross had never felt before, worse than a thousand Southern summers. He continued to struggle to break free as he begged the demon to let him go. He suddenly realized what was happening. Sermons and scriptures he had learned throughout his life reverberated through his brain. They were no longer just words and sentences he had been encouraged to memorize. Ross knew what his fate was about to be.

Refusing to accept it, he cried aloud to the Almighty.

"Please, God! Please give me one more chance! I'm so sorry I rejected you! Please, save me!" He felt as if the words left his mouth, danced in the air, then quickly dropped into the abyss below.

The demon howled a debilitating, screeching laugh, then released Ross into the opening. As he dropped, he was able to grab the side of the earth. His body burned as it pressed against the lava and embers. He gasped for air. The demon watched him suffer with tremendous delight. Finally, his scaly, filthy foot kicked Ross's hand, causing him to lose his grip. Ross's screams went unheard as he plunged into the eternal lake of fire. The demon continued to laugh as it lowered itself inside the opening behind Ross. Once again, the earth began to quake as the gap closed, leaving things as they were before…as if nothing had ever happened.

After tending to Jake's head wound, Trent had gone over to see if there was anything he could do for Ross. In only a few minutes, he returned to the car with the news that Ross was gone. Daniels's emotions overtook him with the words of the EMT. They were so final – so complete. Ross was dead. There was no possibility of ever again seeing life in that young man. Daniels wiped a tear away. This business never got any easier, especially in a small town where law enforcement knew almost everyone.

Suddenly, he noticed sparks spewing from the hood of the car. Smoke followed.

"Hey! Get a fire extinguisher over here!" he yelled to Hollis.

Hollis ran to his vehicle, grabbed an extinguisher and hurried back to the car.

The sparks and smoke increased.

"Spray down the whole area!" Daniels shouted.

Deputy Hollis tried spraying the extinguisher. "It's jammed!"

Daniels reached for it. "Let me try." After wrestling with the mechanism, Daniels finally was able to release it.

While the deputies doused the hazardous area with the freezing cold substance, Mayhew stared at Ross's lifeless body. Sheriff Howell approached him from behind, observing the disturbing scene. Scattered around were tissue and brain matter. Looking at Ross's wounds and shattered skull, there was no doubt in his mind that Ross was dead.

Recognizing him as the young man Mayhew had mentored, he patted his shoulder and commented sorrowfully, "Mike, I am so sorry."

Mayhew's mind immediately raced with memories of the seven years he had worked with Ross, gotten to know him, helped him. He was overcome with emotion.

"Come on, Mike," the sheriff said. "Hold it together."

"This just can't be," Mayhew whispered.

Suddenly, a light appeared through the dandelion grass of the field. He fished through the weeds for the object. It was Ross's cell phone. Mayhew picked it up and looked at the screen.

"Mom" calling. The words were eerie, and Mayhew froze. *It's Kate,* he thought. Taking a deep breath, he answered the phone.

As Kate prayed for Ross to answer, the ringing stopped. There was silence on the other end of the line.

"Ross, honey, are you OK?"

Mayhew struggled to keep his composure. "Kate, it's Mike."

Stunned that it wasn't Ross, she asked, "Mayhew?"

"Yes," he said.

"Please tell me Ross is OK!" she begged.

Calmly, the distraught sergeant responded. "Kate, I need you to listen to me. Ross has been involved in an accident. I need you to go straight to the hospital right now, OK?"

"Mike, what happened?" Kate asked frantically. Tears began to stream down her face. She pulled the phone down to her chin and looked at Lance.

"It's true. Our boys have been in a wreck!"

Lance pulled to the side of the road as Kate returned to the phone conversation.

"Just listen to me, Kate," Mayhew said. "You need to go to the hospital right now."

"What about Jake?" Mitch asked desperately.

"What about Jake?" Kate asked Mayhew. "We're with the Adamses. Is he OK?"

"Jake was driving," Mayhew said.

Kate looked at Mitch. "Jake was driving," she said.

The simple statement dealt a painful blow to Mitch. Immediately, he was consumed with guilt.

"You all need to go straight to the hospital," Mayhew said firmly.

"OK...we're on our way," Kate said. "Mike, please don't let anything happen to my baby!" she pleaded.

Mike struggled to stay calm. "Just do what I said, all right? They'll tell you more when you get there."

Kate laid the phone down. "Lance, go straight to the hospital."

Lance floored the accelerator, turned on his hazard lights and darted toward the medical center.

Mitch grabbed Grace's hand. Grace wrapped her arm around Kate. "We need to pray."

Kate placed her hand over the front seat to rest on Lance's shoulder. Seeing the awkwardness on Mitch's face, Lance boldly placed his right hand on Mitch's arm and continued steering with his left hand. Desperation brought Mitch to a place of acceptance of the prayer circle.

Mayhew stared at Ross's face. He ended the call with Kate and placed the phone in his pocket to give her later. He thought his face might explode in tears. Sheriff Howell grabbed Mayhew's shoulder. "You did good, Mike. That's the absolute hardest part of our job, right there."

A large burst of colors suddenly erupted into the night air, and the silence of the field was interrupted by a deafening boom. The deputies' attempt to extinguish the sparks from Jake's car had fallen short, and it exploded into flames. The sheriff and sergeant rushed toward the Trans-Am.

The unexpected explosion thundered through the atmosphere, creating an outcry of emotion among the young people waiting just up the road for more news on their friends. Marcus and Drew took advantage of the distraction and sneaked around Deputy Ramon. Seeing the Morrisons praying, Marcus realized he knew them from his church. He and Drew joined them in prayer.

Inside the blazing car, Jake's body lay limp.

The prayers of the couple and young men rang out across the open field. The EMT and law enforcement were forced to back away as the heat intensified. The car's crimson-and-white paint began to bubble and melt. Volunteer firemen arrived and raced to get their equipment in place to put out the blaze.

Jake's body was still, and his eyes remained open. His breathing was almost undetectable. Hovering above him, the smoldering demon appeared, returning for its second victim. Jake was overcome with terror as the ludicrous beast stared, laughing. The malicious emotions that emanated from the demon began to overtake Jake. The onset of despair and death drained what little bit of life remained within him. The demon leaned over Jake's motionless body, sucking the very life breath from him, initiating suffocation.

Deputy Daniels attempted to reach Jake again, but to no avail. He could see, though, that Jake was silent and was not moving at all.

"I think he's dead!" he called out.

Tonya Morrison turned to the deputy and yelled with confidence and boldness, "No!"

All eyes turned to her. Her husband, Lewis, dropped to his knees and raised his hands toward Heaven.

"He is not dead!" he cried. "He shall live and not die and declare the works of the Lord!"

Tonya fell to her knees and clasped her hands together.

"Spare him, Lord!" she pleaded. "Give Your angels charge over him to keep him in all his ways!"

The couple began praying in a language no one around them understood.

"What are they saying?" Drew asked.

"They are praying in the Spirit," Marcus said. "It's very powerful. Don't let it scare you."

Skeptical, Drew asked, "Is that scriptural?"

"Very scriptural," Marcus replied.

"OK," Drew said reluctantly.

Marcus and Drew continued praying aloud with them, pleading desperately for Jake's life to be spared.

The demon leaned closer to Jake and smiled its wicked smile, assuming victory was close at hand. Behind it, the world burned away, revealing the fiery landscape of perdition. Jake's eyes filled with horror. Ross's voice echoed among the other tormented souls. The demon reached into the car for Jake.

Outside, the prayer warriors begged.

"Answer the pleas of Your children, Lord!" Lewis cried.

"Jesus!" Tonya pleaded. "Save him! Commission Your angels to him, Lord!"

Suddenly, a blinding white flash blew by the car window, a warring angel within it, ordered to intervene on Jake's behalf. The angel drew its flaming sword and effortlessly smote the demon, sending it back to Hades.

In the meantime, a fire engine arrived. All eyes were drawn to it as the group of firefighters hurried to assist.

The present world returned. Jake continued to gasp for air. The warring angel grabbed the glassless door, ripped it from the charred vehicle and sent it sailing across the field. The loud crash caught everyone's attention. They stood awestruck as they witnessed the car door skid across the ground at unnatural speed.

"What in the world!" Sheriff Howell yelled.

The angel leaned in to Jake, placing its mouth over his, and breathed life back into his lungs. Jake regained consciousness. The angel's bright light blinded him. The angel then lifted away the dashboard, allowing Jake to pull himself free. Jake propelled himself through the opening the angel had made, his legs still ablaze.

"Help me!" Jake cried.

Galen Daniels ran to the driver's side of the car and grabbed Jake under the arms, struggling to pull him away from the burning vehicle.

Trent, the EMT, grabbed a blanket and followed behind Daniels.

Jake looked intently at Daniels. "Don't let me die, Daniels!"

"Don't worry, Jake," he replied calmly. "I'm not gonna let you die!"

As Daniels's adrenaline fueled his energy, he pulled Jake clear of the burning car. Quickly, the EMT smothered the fire on Jake's legs with a blanket.

Realizing the extent of Jake's injuries, Trent radioed for the hospital helicopter. "EMT One to Care Flight...we have an MVA. Requesting assistance."

"Copy, EMT One. What is your location?" the pilot requested.

"Location is field area below Hell's Bend," the EMT worker responded.

The pilot hesitated for a moment, trying to envision how that could have occurred. Hell's Bend was all too familiar to him, having made many trips to the site, but never to the field area below it.

"We are en route."

Trent began communication with the doctor headed his way.

"Victim is an eighteen-year-old male, Caucasian, with severe burns to the lower extremities. Possible pneumothorax and possible concussion. He is verbally cognitive."

"Is the victim stable?" the doctor asked.

"Yes," the EMT answered. "C-spine precaution has been taken. Give me your ETA."

"Ten minutes," the pilot said.

Lauren and Margaret had prayed every prayer they could think of. Emotionally drained, they sat in silence, cuddled together on the couch, and waited for an update on the tragedy that had them paralyzed mentally and emotionally. Startled by the alert tone on Margaret's phone, she grabbed it, hoping to receive some kind of encouraging news. It was from Grace.

Confirming to you there has been a wreck involving Jake and Ross. We are headed to the hospital now. Please pray! We have no idea what we are about to walk into.

Margaret put her hand over her mouth, a gesture she commonly made when receiving bad news.

"Who was it?" Lauren asked, trembling.

"It was from Grace," Margaret replied somberly. "They're headed to the hospital."

"Please, Mom. Can we go?" Lauren pleaded.

"You bet," Margaret replied. "Go get ready while I get in touch with a neighbor to come stay with your brother."

As Lauren washed her face in the bathroom, she received another text from Morgan. *Car is in flames!*

Once again, Lauren was hysterical. "Mom! The car is on fire!"

Margaret grabbed Lauren and hugged her tightly, trying to comfort her the only way she knew how.

"Let's go now," Margaret said.

The emergency medical team continued to care for Jake as they waited for Care Flight to arrive at the scene. Within minutes, just as the pilot had reported, the chopping sound of the helicopter's rotor blades cut through the air while its searchlights beamed through the darkness. Anxious teens waiting for updates of their friends' conditions watched the sky as the chopper closed in. The emergency workers on the ground stopped and watched it circle around the wreck site, ensuring all was clear. The weather conditions were perfect. Clear skies and low winds made for an easy landing.

The medical team aboard Care Flight, clad in blue jumpsuits resembling pilot uniforms and wearing royal blue helmets with clear shields and headsets, exited the helicopter and hastened to Jake's aid.

Trent finalized his report to the doctor. "No change from the initial assessment."

A very feminine, gentle, strawberry-blonde flight nurse sat at Jake's head and gently positioned it between her knees, keeping Jake's neck and spine aligned.

"Hey, fella. I'm Gabby," she said.

Jake lifted his eyes and saw a young woman leaning over him with a big smile. Gabby's expression and demeanor calmed him. He smiled back at the flight nurse and acknowledged her introduction by nodding his head.

"This is my partner, Heath," Gabby said as she motioned toward him with her head.

Jake raised his head slightly and shifted his eyes, trying to find him. He focused on a man wearing an identical jumpsuit and head-gear. Heath smiled and waved at him. Jake quickly relaxed his head.

"What's your name?" Gabby asked.

"Jake...Jake Adams."

"Very good. Well, don't worry, Jake Adams. We're gonna take very good care of you," she assured him.

"How bad are my legs?" Jake asked as he tried to raise his head again to glance at them.

"Hey, just relax. Everything's gonna be all right. You just need to lie back and let us do our thing, OK?"

"OK," Jake agreed.

"What about Ross?" Jake asked.

"Who's Ross?" Gabby asked.

"My best friend," Jake replied. "He was in the car with me."

Gabby looked at Heath. Heath looked toward the open field at the wreck site. Noticing an area taped off, he quickly looked back at Jake, making sure he wasn't looking in the same direction. Then, making eye contact with Gabby, he slowly shook his head, indicating Ross hadn't survived.

"I'm sure he's in better shape than you are right now," Gabby said, trying to keep up Jake's morale.

As the flight nurses continued to care for Jake, Ann Sullivan, the Lee County medical examiner, and a pair of criminal investigators took samples around the site of Ross's death.

"So, where do you go to school, Jake?" Heath asked as he administered an IV, keeping Jake calm and his mind alert.

"Lee County Academy," Jake answered through shallow breaths.

"Oh! The mighty Eagles, huh? That's my alma mater," Heath said.

"Really?" Jake whispered.

"Yep. Class of '95," Heath said.

"Are you cold, Jake?" Gabby asked.

"A little," Jake replied.

"OK. I'll take care of that," Gabby said.

She took off her jacket, placed it over Jake's upper body and gently tucked it under his arms.

The flight nurses continued to blend casual conversation with their medical assessment.

"Are you hurting anywhere else?" Heath asked.

"Not that I can tell, except that my head hurts," Jake said quietly.

Gabby removed the bandage from Jake's head the EMT had applied earlier. She found a deep gash and checked for excessive bleeding. The wound appeared to be clotting well on its own. Gabby gave it a fresh dressing and covered it with a clean gauze bandage.

The nurses gently but quickly pushed a stretcher underneath Jake and secured his head to protect his neck and spine. As they completed the assessment and prepared to get him to the helicopter, Jake stared at the sky. Somehow, in the midst of the trauma to his body, he was able to comprehend its clarity and how defined the constellations were.

"One...two...three...lift," Trent instructed the group.

They carried Jake to the chopper against the strong wind created by the fierce rotation of the whirling blades. The nurses carefully slid him through the doorway and secured him for the flight. The medical team joined him and prepared to care for him as they journeyed back.

As the royal-blue-and-white helicopter made its ascent, the doctor communicated Jake's condition to the ER. The view of the wreck site below from the helicopter's perspective was terribly grim. Smoke from the fiery crash filled the sky. The '79 Trans-Am that had taken years for Mitch to restore was now a charred monstrosity of twisted metal. The driver's side of the car was a large, gaping hole created by supernatural force. Across the field lay a white sheet covering the earthly shell of Ross Kelly, whose soul had been taken by demonic forces. Tiny circles had formed across the Hell's Bend area as emergency workers, bystanders and classmates interlocked hands in fervent prayer, crying out to God over the tragedy.

Chapter 14

From this night forward, our community would lose all semblance of normal life. My selfish refusal to slow down – and, more importantly, the aftermath – would consume the thoughts and behaviors of so many people in this little town. Routines would be interrupted for an incredible amount of time. We wondered if life would ever feel normal again.

Margaret and Lauren made it to the hospital before anyone else. The emergency room waiting area was nearly empty. The medical staff had experienced a calm night so far, but calm was about to change to chaos. The McKay women were scared for their friends and craved any kind of news on them. In the middle of the waiting room was a large, round counter that almost formed a complete circle except for a small area in the back for staff to enter and exit. Wearing a badge stating her name was "Ruby," a beautiful, middle-aged, African-American woman in maroon scrubs sat behind the desk, entering information into a computer.

"Excuse me," Margaret said before she and Lauren even reached the desk.

Ruby looked up from her work with a pleasant, serene smile. She placed her hand atop Margaret's and asked, "How can I help you, dear?"

Margaret stumbled over her words for a moment, realizing she looked and sounded worried.

"Take your time," Ruby said calmly.

"We have friends on the way here," Margaret said. "We'd gotten word about a wreck involving two of my daughter's classmates."

The three turned to the sudden sound of people behind them rustling to check in through security. The Adamses and Kellys had made it there in record time. Grace ran to Margaret and embraced her. Lauren hugged Kate as she cried uncontrollably. Mitch and Lance quickly made their way to Ruby to find out the condition of their sons. Within minutes, a sea of distraught classmates, school faculty and church family began pouring into the once-empty waiting area. A woman in her mid-fifties with short, red hair and wearing a black pantsuit approached the families. She lowered her pink designer reading glasses and smiled at them. "Who would be the Adamses?" she gently asked.

"We are," Mitch answered quickly, wrapping his arm around Grace. Trying to identify the lady, Mitch focused on the lanyard that hung around her neck. Beside her photo ID was the name Nell. Her title was *Patient Care*.

"OK," Nell answered. "And the Kellys?"

Kate stepped closely to Lance's side. "Right here," Lance replied.

"Very good," Nell said. "If you two couples would follow me, please."

Anxiously, the Adamses and Kellys followed close behind her until they reached a hallway and the family counseling rooms.

"I'll be placing you in separate rooms," Nell explained. "Someone will be by shortly to bring each of you up to speed on your child's condition."

Pastor Glenn corralled the remainder of the group while the parents separated into two rooms.

Nell instructed the Adamses to enter the first room on the right. Grace and Kate looked at each other and began to cry. After a brief embrace the two separated. Nell then led the Kellys to the next room. Grace and Mitch watched as their friends walked away. Kate looked back at Grace and mouthed the words *I love you*. Through tears, Grace did the same. Each couple closed the doors behind them and waited silently for the news.

Officials continued their protocol at the wreck site. A friend to both the Adamses and Kellys, Vic Spears happened to be the next wrecker in rotation call and hurried to the site to transport the Trans-Am. At first, he didn't recognize the car. He stood silently and stared at the opening on the driver's side where the door used to be. Scratching his head, the veteran tow-truck driver tried to wrap his mind around what he was seeing. Sheriff Howell watched him from a few feet away.

"Can't figure that one out, huh, Vic?" Sheriff Howell said.

"How'd that happen?" Vic asked.

"You wouldn't believe me if I told you," Sheriff Howell replied. "Can I give you a hand with it?"

"Nope, I got my system down pat," Vic said. He looked more closely at the charred vehicle. "Oh my goodness. I was afraid something like this was gonna happen. That boy shoulda had a knot jerked in his tail the last time he pulled a stunt. Mitch, too."

"I hear ya," Sheriff Howell agreed. "I tried to talk to Mitch myself."

"How's the boy?" Vic asked.

"Not good, Vic. Bad burns," Sheriff Howell said. "Just so you know...Jake wasn't alone."

Vic froze. "Oh, no. The Kelly boy?" he asked.

"Yeah," the sheriff replied.

"Is he all right?" Vic asked.

Sheriff Howell shook his head.

"Oh, my word." Vic lowered his head.

"If you don't need me," Howell said, "I'm gonna head out. We've wrapped things up here."

"OK, Sheriff. I'll probably see you at the hospital."

The ER had now filled with even more people, most of whom were there on Jake's and Ross's behalf. The Adamses felt as if they were waiting an eternity to get news of Jake's condition. Grace sat quietly, praying under her breath, while Mitch impatiently paced the floor. Finally, a shallow knock on the door startled them.

"Come in," Mitch said.

Grace stood as a man in a white lab coat entered the room. With white hair and blue eyes, the doctor was a small-framed man with a serious and somber demeanor. This made the couple uneasy.

"Please, sit down," the doctor directed them.

Mitch and Grace sat side-by-side on the couch, holding hands for security.

"I'm Dr. Gills," he said. "I'm going to get right to the point of things, because time is critical."

Grace and Mitch each felt the other tense.

"Jake is alert and talking. All of his vitals are good," the doctor informed them.

They breathed a sigh of relief.

"However, he has sustained some very serious injuries," Dr. Gills continued.

"What kind of injuries?" Mitch asked anxiously.

"On the minor side, he had a gash in his head, and he has a punctured lung. Those things are fairly easy to remedy. His head's been stitched...but he has severe burns to his legs."

"Oh, no!" Mitch lowered his head.

"How bad are they, Doctor?" Grace asked nervously.

"Beyond fourth degree, mostly, I'm afraid," the doctor said gently.

"No!" Mitch screamed through clenched teeth.

Grace tried to comfort him, but he pushed her hand away. He stood and walked across the room, his back now facing them.

"So, you're telling me my son is going to lose his legs?" Mitch asked.

"That's not my call," Dr. Gills replied, "but I'm going to be honest with you. It's very possible. The doctors at the Firefighters' Burn Center will determine that."

"Wait...the doctors where?" Mitch asked.

"The Firefighters' Burn Center," the doctor repeated. "It's located at The Med in Memphis. We can't treat his burns here."

Grace looked straight ahead as she suddenly felt a supernatural shield over her head, encasing her. Peace permeated the air around her.

"What's next, Dr. Gills?" she asked.

"Well, we've already done one procedure. It's call a fasciotomy," the doctor said.

"What is that?" Mitch asked.

"It's a procedure where we cut through the fascia of his legs to relieve tension. It prevents loss of circulation to his tissue and muscle," Dr. Gills explained. "You see, burns cause terrible and immediate swelling. It was absolutely necessary."

"Is he in pain?" Grace asked.

"Not at the moment. He's on high doses of morphine, so he's fine," Dr. Gills assured her. "We've already made arrangements to transport him."

"Can we see him?" Grace asked.

"Of course, but just for a few minutes. I'll have Nell give you more instructions."

"Thank you, Doctor," Grace said.

"You're very welcome," he said, nodding, then left the room.

"I want a second opinion," Mitch said firmly the moment the door closed.

"What?" Grace asked.

"Jake can't lose his legs!" Mitch cried. "His legs are his future!"

"Mitch! Be thankful! Jake is alive!"

Grace reached for Mitch. He began to cry and took her in his arms.

"You're right, honey. You're right."

Suddenly, a sickening scream came from the room next to them. Mitch and Grace looked at each other. It was Kate. They could hear Lance's cries underneath Kate's gut-wrenching squall. The Adamses began to weep. Ross...

Kate's screams echoed into the ER waiting area. Margaret recognized the voice.

"Oh, no. It's Ross," Margaret whispered, tears streaming. Lauren curled into a fetal position against her mother. "Ross! Noooooooo!"

230

Jake's and Ross's friends gradually realized, one by one, what was happening in the nearby room. Some wept aloud, and some simply shook their heads and looked toward the floor, the realization too difficult to process at the moment. Pastor Glenn was extremely distraught and struggled to console those around him.

Grace and Mitch rushed out of their room to run to their friends. The Kellys grabbed them and embraced them. Grace stroked Kate's back as she prayed over her friend.

"Pastor Glenn is in the waiting room," she whispered. "You want me to get him?"

"I'll get him," Mitch said. He needed an excuse to step out. He was suffocating from the emotions swirling in his head.

Minutes later Mitch returned with David Glenn and Ann Sullivan, the county coroner. Kate bristled when she saw the word "coroner" embroidered on the woman's jacket. This was not happening. It couldn't be happening. She had just seen her boy hours earlier.

Everyone sat down to listen to "Sully." She looked at each one of them with comforting eyes. Her kind and gentle spirit and compassion for people had been a huge factor in her long tenure of public service.

She introduced herself, then asked, "Who are the parents?"

"I'm Lance, Ross's dad," Lance said, pointing to himself. Then, pointing to Kate, he said, "...and this is my wife, Kate, Ross's mom." His voice broke.

Sully placed her hand on Kate's knee. "I'm so sorry for your loss."

"Thank you," Kate whispered.

Sully smiled gently. "I'm here as I usually am with all accidental deaths. Do you understand what was explained to you about Ross's accident?"

t that Ross was thrown from the car and that he died from an open skull fracture," Lance replied.

"That's correct," Sully confirmed. "I'll work closely with the law enforcement agency that's heading up the investigation. They'll probably do a reconstruction of the accident. That might be helpful in answering any questions you may have about it."

Sully very gently continued explaining the cause of death due to the nature of Ross's injuries.

"Do you know which funeral home you'll be working with?" Sully asked.

"Yes," Lance said.

"As a parent, I would advise you not view the body today," Sully continued.

Kate began weeping. All she could think about were Ross's big brown eyes. *I'll never see them again.* Her mind raced to remember the last time she saw them. She had seen him that morning. And then for a few minutes that afternoon, when he raced in to shower before meeting Lauren at Youth Explosion. Then he shot out of the house, waving at her quickly. Lance tried to comfort her. Looking to Pastor Glenn, Sully asked, "Would you pray for us, please?"

Through tears, the preacher agreed. "Certainly." Placing his hands on the Kellys, he began to pray. "Father, we come to you right now, not asking for comfort, for comfort can't come right now, and not asking for joy, because joy can't come right now. But we ask, Lord, that you send us your peace in the midst of this storm. Your peace that passes all understanding. Be close to us during this time. For we ask it in Jesus' name. Amen."

After the heartfelt prayer, Sully embraced the four parents and told them good-bye. As she walked out of the room, Nell passed her, returning for the Adamses.

"The doctor sent me for you," Nell said. "They're ready for you."

The Adamses were torn emotionally. They wanted to see their son but hated to leave their friends, who had just lost theirs. The pastor picked up on it right away.

"Hey, you guys go. I'll take care of your friends," he said.

"Thank you," Grace said as she embraced Kate once more. Grief-stricken and incapacitated, Kate was slow to respond.

Mitch looked at Lance, completely at a loss for words.

"You get back to that boy," Lance said.

Unsure of how to respond, Mitch reached out his hand to Lance. "I'm sorry, man. I'm so sorry."

"I know," Lance replied.

The Adamses locked hands and followed Nell into the ER waiting area. The couple was bombarded with friends and relatives desperate to hear any news. Coach Scott tried to control the crowd as the Adamses pushed through and fought to keep up with the patient care attendant. They entered through large double doors where numerous observation rooms lined the hallways. The white, blank walls were a maze. Their hearts raced as they followed Nell to the room where Jake was being cared for. They had no idea what to expect. What would they see? What should they say? Grace trembled.

Finally, Nell stopped in front of a large sliding glass door covered by a royal blue curtain.

"Are you ready?" Nell asked.

Mitch and Grace each took a deep breath. "Ready," Grace said, nodding her head.

Nell pulled back the curtain, then slid open the glass door. She stepped just inside the room and motioned for the couple. Immediately, they fixed their eyes on Jake, lying underneath a blanket in the cold room. Relieved to see him awake and alert, Grace rushed to him.

"Jake," Grace cried as she kissed his forehead.

"I'm so sorry, Dad," Jake said. "I totaled the car."

"That's an understatement," Mitch said, trying to make light of the situation.

"It's just a stupid ol' car," Grace said.

"Your mom's right," Mitch said. "That car is the least of our worries. We're just glad you're alive."

"Where's Ross? Is he OK?" Jake asked.

Caught off-guard by his question, Grace and Mitch were in shock. They hadn't prepared themselves for Jake's asking about Ross. The couple looked at each other for a moment. Realizing the dramatic pause was awkward and revealing, Grace spoke up. "Oh, I'm sure Ross is going to be just fine, honey. You just focus on getting better."

"Is he back here?" Jake asked.

"No, son. He's not," Mitch said, not wanting to lie but certainly not ready to tell Jake.

The nurse tending to Jake caught on quickly to the situation and jumped in to help.

"Now, Jake, you just need to rest," she said. "Just relax and let that medicine take full effect."

"OK," Jake said.

"Are you in pain, son?" Grace asked.

"Physically, no," Jake said.

Grace looked over her son's body. His left foot wasn't completely covered by the blanket. She had difficulty understanding what she was looking at. His toes were so badly burned they looked like marsh-mallows that had been held over a campfire too long. But incredibly, she felt no pain seeing her son's badly burned body. She questioned herself, wondering how she was not breaking down at this moment. She could only assume it was God's mercy covering her.

Grace stroked Jake's hair and studied his face as he talked to his father.

Dr. Gills entered the room. "OK, guys, we have everything lined up with the burn center at The Med. The ambulance is outside, ready to transport him. You can have a couple more minutes, but we need to hurry."

"OK, thanks," Mitch said.

"Doctor, may we ride in the ambulance with him?" Grace asked.

"Only one of you can ride," Dr. Gills said.

Mitch looked at Grace. "You ride with Jake. I'll follow in the car."

Grace nodded in agreement. Relieved, she turned to Jake and said, "I'll be with you the whole way."

Mitch and Grace stepped out while the nurses prepared Jake to be moved. She was overcome with emotion. "Everything is moving so fast."

"I know," Mitch said, holding her.

Two minutes later Jake was being rolled into the hallway, sur-rounded by an orderly and a nurse, and Grace and Mitch. They were soon met by a long line of familiar faces waiting to see them off. Friend after friend offered their hands and encouraging words. Jake held out his hand, giving high fives. Suddenly, Morgan appeared beside him.

"Stop, please," Jake said.

The orderly stopped pushing. Jake looked Morgan in the eyes.

"You OK?" Morgan asked.

"I'm OK," Jake replied.

"I'm so sorry about..."

Grace coughed, interrupting her.

"About what?" Jake asked.

Morgan froze. She looked at Grace. Understanding what Grace meant, she struggled to change her story.

"Everything...I'm so sorry about everything."

"We need to move on, Mr. Adams," the nurse advised.

"Bye, Morgan," Jake said.

"Bye, Jake."

As the nurse rolled Jake down the path to the ambulance, people continued to tell Jake good-bye and to wish him well. Just outside the door, mixed in the crowd, were Sheriff Howell and Vic. They had made it in time to see the family before they left. Mitch saw the two men and was immediately taken back to the conversations with them about Jake's racing. The guilt was becoming unbearable. He quickly cut his eyes away and turned to Grace.

"Here, honey, let me help you in," Mitch said.

All of a sudden, she realized, "Oh, Mitch, we don't have any kind of overnight bag."

Pastor Glenn's wife emerged from the crowd. "Don't worry, friend, I'll go to your house and pack you and Mitch some things."

"Thank you, Jeannie," Grace said, relieved.

The ambulance pulled away, and people continued waving good-bye. Grace gave them a thumbs-up though the passenger window. Then she looked straight ahead, taking deep breaths. She looked into the back of the ambulance, hoping to get a glimpse of Jake. His silence made her uneasy.

"Is he OK?" Grace asked.

"He's just fine, Mrs. Adams," the EMT assured her. "I gave him another dose of morphine to keep him comfortable. He's just resting."

She stared out the window as the medical center grew smaller, and eventually the town disappeared into the night. Grace had no idea when she would return, nor what she and her family would be facing when they did. She whispered yet another prayer.

Chapter 15

In a matter of moments, everything changed. The only thing I had going for me at the moment was the fact that I was kept heavily sedated. For now, my mind was in a safe place, but it wouldn't stay there for long. The reality that I was about to face would be incomprehensible and almost unbearable.

The ride to Memphis was an hour and a half long, but to Grace and Jake, and Mitch riding behind, it seemed to take days. School friends and church friends caravanned behind the ambulance to The Med, a tier-one trauma center in the heart of downtown.

Upon arrival at the burn unit section of the immense hospital, Grace found a medical team had already assembled and were ready to take Jake under their wings. The first person to greet the Adamses was charge nurse LaVelle Armstrong. The sassy, Southern, African-American woman welcomed them literally with open arms.

"Hey, sugar," Nurse Velle said, offering Grace a hug. "I'm Nurse Velle, and we are gon' take real good care of yo baby."

Surprised yet receptive of the friendly woman's greeting, Grace returned the hug.

"Now, I just need you to sign something here, then we can move on," Velle said.

As Grace signed the form, orderlies brought in Jake behind her. She turned to watch him being wheeled through stainless steel double doors, keeping her eyes on him until he was out of her view. Tears filled her eyes. Velle watched her with a sincere look of compassion.

"Sugar, it's gon' be all right," she assured her.

"I know," Grace whispered.

Grace handed Velle the form.

"Now, y'all gon' have to make yourself comfortable in the waiting room for now," she explained. "As soon as the doctor's made his initial assessment, he'll come up there and consult with you, OK, sugar?"

"Yes, ma'am," Grace said, wiping away tears.

Mitch walked in after parking the car, then Velle escorted him to the waiting area of the burn center's critical care unit. As soon as they entered, Grace stood in shock at the number of people who had set up camp. She scanned the room. Recliners lined the walls, used by families who had almost taken up residency here. Grace realized most had been there for quite some time. Then reality hit. *We could be here for a while ourselves. Oh, Lord, please. Don't put me on a shelf.* Those words were her way of telling God not to stop using her.

Frantic family members and friends poured into the waiting room to join the Adamses during their wait. After asking Mitch and Grace about Jake's status, all 25 of them formed a prayer circle in the middle of the room. Many took turns praying aloud, through tears, for Jake, his parents and the Kelly family they had left behind in horrific mourning. After a time of prayer and a couple of worship choruses, the circle disbanded.

Finally, a voice over the intercom called for the Adamses. Mitch and Grace hurried to the desk, where they were greeted by a doctor in blue scrubs and a lab coat. The embroidered name read *Dr. Edward King*.

Reaching out his hand to Grace, he said, "Hello, Mrs. Adams. I'm Dr. King."

"It's very nice to meet you," Grace said softly, shaking his hand.

Mitch offered a handshake as well. "How's Jake?"

Dr. King motioned for them to enter a nearby room. Once inside, Mitch and Grace sat down close beside each other. Dr. King sat and began to share with them what they were potentially facing.

Dr. King began to speak sincerely and honestly. "Jake is stable, but his burns are very severe."

"This sounds really bad," Mitch said.

"It is, Mr. Adams. I'm not going to sugar-coat this. The good news is that I fully expect Jake to live. The worst news we have here is that a double amputation is absolutely necessary."

"Oh, please...no," Mitch said, his face in his hands.

Grace placed her arm around Mitch. "Honey, it's going to be all right. Didn't you hear what the doctor said? He fully expects Jake to live!"

Ignoring Grace, Mitch looked at the doctor again. "So, you're not even gonna try to save his legs?"

"Mr. Adams, trust me," Dr. King said. "Amputating is the last thing we want to do, especially on a young man like Jake."

"You don't understand. Football is Jake's future. If he has no legs, he has...nothing."

"Mr. Adams, I know this is difficult, but—"

"No, you don't know," Mitch said firmly. "And difficult doesn't begin to cover it."

"Mitch, please," Grace pleaded, trying to calm him.

"You need to understand," the doctor continued. "Jake's legs were burned through the bone in most places. If we left them intact, they would be brittle and serve him no good purpose. Not to mention the fact that he is at very high risk for infection in this condition."

"So, you're saying there's no hope," Mitch said.

"Oh, there's hope, Mr. Adams. Technology today with prosthetics is amazing."

Not wanting to listen to the doctor's other options, Mitch stood and walked across the room.

"I'm sorry, Doctor," Grace said. "He's just taking this so hard."

"I know," the doctor softly replied. "It's all fresh, and a very hard blow."

"It's not just Jake's legs," Grace said. "It's much worse than that. In the car wreck, Jake's best friend was killed."

"Oh, my…I'm so sorry to hear that," Dr. King said sympathetically.

"Well, it gets worse. Jake was racing. The sheriff's department got involved and, well, Jake decided to try to outrun them. We're just hurting on all levels right now," Grace said.

"I can't begin to imagine," Dr. King said.

Grace leaned in closely to Dr. King. "You do what you believe is best."

"Trust me, Mrs. Adams, to take away a young athlete's legs is the last thing I want to do. It's a terrible burden to bear, but it's my responsibility above all things to save his life."

"I understand," Grace said.

"So, when will you do the surgery?" Mitch asked.

"I'll have to look at my schedule, but probably in just a few days," Dr. King answered.

"Can we see him?" Mitch asked.

"You'll be able to see him at the next visitation time, but that's several hours away," Dr. King said.

Mitch nodded.

"As I told you earlier, because of the burns, he's highly susceptible to infection," Dr. King said. "You will have to wear protective clothing and a face mask while visiting. You'll be instructed on what to do when you get down there."

The doctor rose from the chair. "I'll let you get back to your support system."

"Doctor, just one more thing," Grace asked.

"Certainly," Dr. King said.

"Will we be able to share with Jake about the surgery ahead of time?"

"I'm afraid not, Mrs. Adams. We're keeping him heavily sedated – he's in a tremendous amount of pain. He won't be coherent enough to understand. Besides, it would only upset him and potentially make his pain worse."

Grace nodded slightly. "I understand. Thank you for everything."

"I only wish I could do more," Dr. King said sincerely.

When Mitch and Grace walked back into the main area of the waiting room, friends and family flocked around for an update. As Grace shared the doctor's report with them, the mood immediately turned somber – more devastation to the already tragic situation.

Those who had traveled to The Med with the Adamses for support tearfully said their good-byes.

It was just a few hours before dawn. Mitch and Grace found an empty space as their makeshift sleeping quarters for the next few hours.

Morning soon broke. Grace awoke. A little disoriented, her mind raced as she looked around the room, trying to remember where she was. *It really did happen*, she thought. Tears began to roll down the sides of her face as the events of the night before replayed in her mind...the horrible sight of Jake's burns...Kate's awful screams echoed in her mind. She placed her hand over her mouth to muffle the cries trying to escape. She turned to Mitch, who lay staring at the ceiling.

"Did you get any sleep?" Grace asked.

"Not really," Mitch replied.

The two stood and embraced each other. Exhaustion prevented them from entering any further conversation.

The smell of coffee permeated the room. Coffee was a familiar place to start. They walked together to the small kitchen area and fell in line to get a cup. The room was full of weary and worn people, all there for the same reason. Little conversation took place.

A voice called over the intercom. "Could someone with the Adams family come to the front desk, please?" Mitch and Grace looked at each other, wondering who would be there so early. Puzzled, they chose to go together. As they rounded the corner to the front desk, they broke into smiles.

"Pastor Glenn! Coach Scott!"

Both men stood smiling. Pastor Glenn held out an overnight bag. "Jeannie packed this for you guys."

"Oh, bless her!" Grace said, taking the bag and offering him a hug.

"And just in time," Mitch said. "We literally woke up just minutes before you arrived."

"How are you guys this morning?" the pastor asked.

"I guess numb is the best way to describe it," Grace said. Mitch nodded.

"I'm sure you're both exhausted," Pastor Glenn said sympathetically. "I'm so sorry I didn't make the trip up here from the ER."

"You were right where you needed to be," Grace assured him.

"Thank you for understanding," he said. "It was a tough spot, you know. My heart was torn between two families who mean a lot to me."

"Same here," Coach Scott said.

"Grace is right," Mitch said. "You were needed where you were."

The four returned to the kitchen area for coffee, then found a place to visit.

"How are they, Pastor?" Grace asked.

"In shock," Pastor Glenn said.

"I wish I could be there with Kate right now," Grace said tearfully.

"I know you do."

A voice over the loudspeaker announced the visitation time. Because Jake was allowed to have multiple visitors, Mitch and Grace invited the men to join them. Both were excited to have the opportunity to see him. They made their way to the burn step-down unit and dressed in protective garments.

Soon they were escorted through the stainless steel double doors into the U-shaped unit where patients who required close care were kept.

Grace sat in an aluminum chair in the nurses' station. Knowing the pastor and Coach Scott's time was short, she offered them the opportunity to go in with Mitch first and give the men some time alone with Jake.

"Would you like to sit in my office while you wait?"

Grace quickly looked in the direction of the familiar voice. It was Velle from the night before. "I know you must be exhausted. You'll have more privacy in there. Plus, my couch is a lot more comfy than this ol' hard chair."

"Yes, thank you," Grace said.

They stepped inside the office where Velle made Grace feel at home.

Velle sat beside Grace. "How you doin', sugar?"

Attempting to be optimistic, Grace replied, "I'm OK, I guess, under the circumstances."

"Well, sugar, whatcha doin' under there?" she asked with conviction.

Confused, Grace asked, "Excuse me? Under where?"

"You said under the circumstances."

"Yes," Grace said.

"Sugar, do you know Jesus?" Velle asked very bluntly.

"Oh, yes, ma'am, I do," Grace replied.

"Then you know God is still on His throne, so you don't belong under those circumstances, sugar. They belong under yo feet."

Seeing her point, Grace giggled. "You know, I've never heard it put that way before. And you're absolutely right. God is still on His throne."

"We gon' take real good care of yo baby," Velle said.

"Of course you are," Grace said confidently.

"I'll tell you a little secret," Velle said.

"What's that?" Grace asked.

"Yo baby is gon' have the best nurse we got caring for him."

Grace raised her eyebrows.

"Mm-hum. His name is Joe Bill Anton. He a big ol' muscle-bound thang with bright blue eyes, a baby face and the sweetest smile. He has a heart that is so tender and compassionate. Very humble and soft-spoken. To tell you the truth, I believe he was hand-picked by God Himself for yo baby."

"Why do you say that?" Grace asked.

"He been through a lot," Velle explained. "More than ten men would experience in a lifetime, and came out a mighty warrior for the Lord."

"That's so encouraging," Grace said.

"I be honest with you," Velle said. "I didn't really know what a good nurse Joe Bill was when I hired him, but when I heard his testimony, I knew he was God-appointed for this place."

Grace smiled. "I've been praying for that. Godly people helping Jake. I know it will take that for him."

"The Lord know exactly what that baby need...more than his own momma know."

"I'm sure Nurse Anton is someone very special then," Grace said.

"Oh, he very special," Velle said.

"Well, I can't wait to meet him then," Grace replied. Taking a deep breath, she said despairingly, "I'm afraid it's going to take someone very special to help Jake through this. I feel like my words, no matter how sincere, always come up short."

"The Lord promises to use everything for our good. This situation will be no different. You'll see."

"It's hard to see it right now," Grace commented, "but I do believe it."

"For we walk by faith..." Velle said.

"...and not by sight," Grace said, completing her statement.

The deep sound of male voices echoed in the nurses' station outside Velle's office.

"Sounds like my crew," Grace said. "Come on out here and let me introduce you."

"That'd be nice," the nurse said.

"Mitch, honey, you remember meeting the charge nurse here, Nurse LaVelle Armstrong, right?"

"Certainly," Mitch replied.

"But everybody call me Velle, baby," she said.

She then introduced the others. "Well, I'm anxious to get in to see Jake," Grace said, "so I'll see you all in a few minutes. Was he responsive at all?"

"Not really, honey," Mitch said. "He's on so much pain medication, he's just kinda in and out of it."

Grace felt a little deflated. "Well, at least I'll get to be with him."

She dismissed herself to walk to Jake's room. Unaware that Joe Bill Anton had walked up behind her, Grace bumped into him, causing her to lose her balance. Instinctively, he caught her.

Grace was embarrassed. "I am so sorry."

Looking at the person whose hands had caught her, she immediately recognized him by Velle's description.

"You must be Mr. Anton," she said.

"That would be me. But please...call me Joe Bill," he said.

Velle laughed. "Now that's a fancy way to meet."

Those standing around snickered. Grace was still embarrassed and moved close to Mitch. He patted her on the arm.

"It's nice to meet you," Grace said. "Nurse Velle speaks very highly of you."

"Oh, really now," Joe Bill asked, looking at Velle.

"Now, don't go gettin' the big head," Velle said. "I told her you wuttin' fit for nuttin' and that I just hired you for eye candy around here."

They all giggled.

Conditioned to Velle's humor, Joe Bill commented, "Y'all, it's the truth."

"That's what they said when they hired me to coach football," Coach Scott said, sucking in his gut, imitating Joe Bill's grand stature.

The giggles turned to laughter.

Grace excused herself and gently opened Jake's hospital room door, careful not to disturb him. She sat at Jake's side and watched as he slept. Combing her fingers through his hair, she ached over all that had happened since last night, and for the fate of her son. Everything was happening so quickly. As she continued brushing his hair with her hand, endless questions ran through her mind. *How will he react? How do we help him adjust? Will he be angry with me?*

"Oh, son, I hope you can forgive us."

Chapter 16

Two tragic, life-changing events in one day, happening simultane-
ously...A surgery was about to bury a son's dreams; a funeral would
bury another's son...and my best friend. In an ironic and cruel twist
of fate, the people of our small town would be so closely-tied to both
events that they would be forced to choose between the two. The
answer was obvious, though. Death is so final, and Ross's parents
needed the support. Looking back, I regret their having to choose. I
regret even creating the situation in the first place. Surely this would
be the worst I'd have to endure.

"I just talked to Lance," Grace said, returning to the waiting room.
"How are they?" Mitch asked.

"Kate's not doing very well, I'm afraid," Grace said. "But Lance is doing OK. He's trying to be strong for her." Tears welled in her eyes. "I'm so heartbroken that Kate and I can't be there for each other right now. It just seems so unfair."

"Well, it's probably for the best," Mitch said.

Grace was confused. "Why would you say that? They're our best friends! Mitch, why haven't you called to check on Lance?"

Mitch looked Grace square in the face. "Do you really think he wants to hear from me?"

"Of course he does, honey," Grace said. "He asked about you."

"It's just too painful right now," Mitch said.

"Whose pain? His...or yours?" Grace asked.

"What's that supposed to mean?" Mitch asked defensively.

"I'm just not sure who you are feeling sorry for right now," Grace said.

"Grace, our son is about to lose both legs! His football career is over!" Mitch ranted.

Grace quickly and firmly took both of Mitch's hands. "Mitch, they are burying their only child today! At least we still have Jake!" Grace exclaimed.

"And why are they burying their son today?" Mitch asked. "Because of our son!"

Grace began to understand. "You can't think like that."

"Grace, I can't face Lance. I don't know what to say! How do you offer comfort to a friend who's lost his son when your own son is responsible?"

"Mitch, he is one of your dearest friends!" Grace said. "It's not like we don't know each other."

"I just think that if I were Lance, I would be the last person that I would want to talk to," Mitch said.

"Well, you're not Lance," Grace said.

"Grace, I don't have anything to give right now," Mitch said. "I've got my own grief to deal with."

Grace needed Mitch to look outside himself. "The best way to deal with your own pain is to reach out to someone else whose pain is worse," she said.

Agitated, Mitch said, "OK, Grace. If that works for you, then fine, you do that. But my way of dealing with it is different. Don't judge that. I'd rather not talk to anyone, all right?"

Silence fell between them. Their conversation was going nowhere positive, leaving Grace feeling hopeless. Trying to convince her husband to grieve the way she wanted him to was draining her.

Waiting for Jake's surgery to begin was agonizing – but not as agonizing as the pain the Kellys experienced watching the funeral directors close the coffin lid on their teenage son. Nothing had ever felt so final to them. Kate and Lance looked over the casket, Kate's hands tightly clutched to her chest, grasping in desperation for a last-minute miracle that might bring back her baby. Lance stood beside her, his hand bravely touching the lid as it was slowly lowered. Neither cried at the moment, their bodies still in such shock that no tears would flow.

Grace blew kisses at Jake as his hospital bed disappeared through the double doors leading into surgery. Kate blew kisses to Ross as his coffin disappeared through double doors leading to the funeral home chapel.

Grace and Mitch embraced one another, shedding a few tears and offering comfort to each other, with thoughts of how living with an amputee was about to drastically change their lives. Kate and Lance held each other, now weeping uncontrollably, their minds racing to comprehend life without Ross.

Friends and family at the hospital stood as Grace and Mitch entered the CCU waiting room, walking unsteadily to the recliners to wait during Jake's surgery. Back home, friends and family stood and watched in sorrow while emotionally-drained Kate and Lance Kelly entered the chapel and walked to the section of pews reserved for them.

Grace reclined in the oversized chair and tried to rest for a while. As she lay back and closed her eyes, her mind somersaulted between the two families' situations. She battled negative feelings of worry, heartache and fear. Unable to shut them off, she decided to read. She pulled a book from her brightly-colored tote. The title was colorful and attention-getting...*Praying God's Word*. She whispered the book's prayers softly on behalf of their cherished, heartbroken friends, who were saying sorrowful farewells to their only son.

May Your unfailing love be their comfort, according to Your promise to Your servants. Let Your compassion go to them that they may live, for Your law is their delight. Their souls faint with longing for Your salvation, but their hope is in Your word.

The soft, comforting female voice of the anesthesiologist promised not to leave Jake's side as she administered medication through the IV. Meanwhile, the comforting soprano voice of Ross's classmate Lizzy sang to his parents of God's promise to never leave them nor forsake them. Ross's teammate Drew skillfully accompanied her on the acoustic guitar. Those listening were amazed at the young duo's ability to usher in the presence of God.

The receptionist at the desk called out for Mitch and Grace. Mitch hurried to the desk where he was handed the phone. Grace sat up and straightened her chair. He nodded his head in agreement several times, then finally said, "OK, thank you." Grace and their friends eagerly waited to hear the news.

"He's asleep," Mitch explained. "The surgery's begun."

A fleeting moment of fear iced Grace's veins. She took a deep breath and nodded in acceptance.

A family member of the Kellys, who was also a pastor, walked to the pulpit and set down a piece of paper. On it were the words he had planned to share with the mourners. As he began to read Ross's obituary, his hand shook and his voice quivered. The man followed the reading with two funny stories of Ross that he had always cherished. The audience smiled.

In the waiting room, the hands of the wall clock seemed to be at a standstill. Grace held her Bible in her lap, nervously strumming the corner of the pages with her fingers. Mitch's eyes were on his phone's web browser, searching for articles about the upcoming SEC football Saturday.

Inside the chapel of the funeral home, the voice of Pastor David Glenn echoed as he jubilantly shared stories of Ross. He had been the only pastor Ross had ever known. He had watched Ross grow up in that church and was able to recall legions of stories about the young man. The pastor, with his animated personality and knack for story-telling, brought to life the mischievous but lovable Ross everyone knew. Some laughed at the beginning of a story, knowing what the outcome was going to be. After the first three tales, Pastor Glenn grew serious. Through tears, he shared some hard truths regarding the reality of what today's funeral represented.

―――――――――――

"Scalpel," Dr. King called, beginning the surgery to remove Jake's legs. Covered in blankets, his body lay limp on the cold, steel table. The surgeon made the initial incision.

―――――――――――

Knowing many of those in attendance would be young people, including Ross's teammates, Pastor Glenn felt led to use an analogy that would affect them and make them realize their mortality.

"In any given football game, you are going to have sixty snaps on one side of the ball. In only three to six of those will you have the chance to impact the outcome of the game. The issue is that you never know what three to six plays will come. The same is true in life. Say you live to be the age of normal retirement, which is age sixty-five. If every day is a game and you produce three to six plays each day, in your lifetime, you could potentially have one hundred forty-two thousand, four hundred and forty-six opportunities to impact the outcome of these life-changing events. Some of those events will be incredible...and some – like today – will be horrific. Lance...Kate... the best play you ever made in preparing for this was the day you each chose to accept Jesus as Savior. The second best play you ever made was the day you each chose to make Him Lord of your lives and chose to raise your son in 'the nurture and admonition of the Lord.' Knowing that you gave him that foundation, that you lived it out in front of him, will bring you peace in the days ahead."

"Sponge," the surgeon requested. He carefully dabbed the incision area.

Grace reached inside her bag and pulled out a pair of white earbuds. As she tried to plug them into the phone to listen to her collection of worship music, her hand trembled, making it difficult to insert. Mitch noticed her struggle.

"Here, honey, let me get that for you," he said.

His tenderness provoked compassion in her heart. The hopelessness she was feeling earlier started to diminish. Mitch did have a tender side. She enjoyed it immensely whenever it surfaced, but she was hungry to see that side more often.

The pastor continued. "Those two decisions will determine how you overcome this tragedy. John chapter 14 tells us this...*Let not your heart be troubled; you believe in God, believe also in Me. In My Father's house are many mansions; if it were not so, I would have told you. I go to prepare a place for you. And if I go and prepare a place for you, I will come again and receive you to Myself,*

am, there you may be also. And where I go you know,
you know.

"Here is our hope…Life is a vapor. The unbearable pain of today will last only for a little while. God will heal you day by day as you allow Him, and life will have the potential to bring happiness. Weeping may endure for the night, but joy is surely coming in the morning. Now, our question becomes this…Until that day comes, how do we mourn?"

"Suction," Dr. King said. "How's his breathing?"

The anesthesiologist gave him a thumbs-up.

"Good," he responded, acknowledging the anesthesiologist's positive report.

Mitch looked out the window of the CCU waiting room as he sipped coffee. Grace tried to pass the time by updating the status of Jake's progress on a health-related social media site and responding to encouraging messages they had received. She was overwhelmed by the number of people reaching out to her family…many of whom they didn't know.

Pastor Glenn answered the question he proposed. "In Psalm 30:11, David said, '*You have turned for me my mourning into dancing; You have put off my sackcloth and clothed me with gladness.*' Lance, Kate, family, friends: There is coming a time in which you will dance again. Your gladness will return to you."

"Gigli saw." Dr. King slowly lowered the buzzing instrument until it met Jake's severely burned limb. Upon impact, fragments of bone spewed into the air. Dr. King steadied his right arm with his left hand.

Mitch walked to the restroom to splash cold water on his face. The wait was nerve-racking. He looked at himself in the mirror as he wiped his face with a paper towel. He struggled with the view. Thoughts of missed opportunities to intervene in Jake's irresponsible decisions flooded his mind. *If only I had stopped him. If only I had confronted him. Things could have been so different.* He was about to lose his mind with guilt. *If I had swallowed my pride, we might not be here today. The Kellys wouldn't be having a funeral for their son.* He rubbed his face, trying to change the focus of his thoughts.

Ross's senior teammates, who had played alongside him on the football field, served as pallbearers. They exited the limousine clad in their game-day jerseys and khaki pants. The boys silently formed a line behind the hearse and waited to carry their friend to his final destination. Family and friends gathered close to Kate and Lance under the green funeral home tent as Pastor Glenn shared final words of encouragement.

The buzz of the Gigli saw ceased. Dr. King checked with the anesthesiologist to make sure Jake remained stable. After tying off the veins, he closed off the stumps of Jake's legs.

Grace gazed out the window, her mind and heart still split between two places. Mitch re-entered the waiting area.

"Any word?" he asked.

Disappointment on her face, she shook her head.

Mitch offered her a hug. Grace gladly embraced him.

The minister offered a final prayer. "Lord, teach us to number our days, for we do not know how many we are given or what each of them may hold. "

While the casket began to lower into the ground, Lauren laid her head on her mother's lap and wept. Kate, exhausted from crying, sat still and stared at the casket as it disappeared from view. With his arm around his grieving wife, Lance stared at the casket as well.

Ross's funeral service had ended. So had Jake's surgery.

"OK, we're done here," Dr. King commented. "Good job, everyone."

The casket softly thumped the bottom of the opening in the ground. At the same moment, Jake's severed, charred remains struck the bottom of the pathology receptacle.

The phone rang in the CCU waiting room. Once again, a voice called out for the Adams family. Grace and Mitch looked at each other, anxious and terrified.

"I'll answer it," Grace said. Although Grace trusted the Lord for a good report, she became nervous as she reached for the phone.

"This is Grace Adams."

She listened to the report from the other end of the line. A smile, accompanied by tears, swept her face.

"Wonderful. Thank you very much," she said, then hung up the phone.

Mitch, along with the others who had waited with them, watched Grace as she walked toward them.

"The surgery is over. It was very successful. Jake's being taken to recovery, and Dr. King will be here shortly to tell us more."

Although the news was good, everyone remained silent. It was bittersweet. Jake had made it through the surgery successfully, but now he would be a different young man.

The limousine transporting the Kellys drove away from the grave site. The couple had made it through the service, and it was beautiful, but they had left a huge part of themselves behind.

Jake awoke to find a kindly, older gentleman standing over him. "Morning, buddy," Dr. King said.

Jake looked around the dim room. Mitch and Grace stood at his side, dressed in their protective garments. Jake reached up to touch the strange object in his nose. Confused, he stared at Dr. King. The surgeon produced a pen light and shone it into Jake's eyes.

"What's your name?" Dr. King asked him.

"Jake Adams," he replied. Thinking for a moment, he said, "My feet hurt."

Mitch and Grace looked at each other. Dr. King nodded hesitantly. "They'll do that," he said, looking back at them.

Jake turned to his mother. She smiled through her face mask. "Hey, baby," she said softly.

Her eyes began to tear.

"Jake, do you remember anything?" the doctor asked.

Jake closed his eyes. "Fire."

Mitch leaned toward him and put his hand on his head. Grace began to cry.

Jake's voice quivered. "My feet hurt."

"It'll pass," Dr. King said.

Jake tried to raise his head, but he was too weak.

"You sustained third and fourth degree burns, son," Dr. King said.

Growing panicked, Jake tried to raise his head again. He began to recall more from the wreck.

"Ross...where's Ross? He was with me." Jake was becoming more agitated. "Ross was in the car with me." His mind raced back to the night of the wreck. "The car flipped. Ross was thrown out! Is he OK?"

Mitch dropped his head. Tears streamed down Grace's face.

"Someone answer me!" he demanded.

Gathering all the courage she could, Grace responded, "Jake, honey, I'm sorry. Ross didn't make it."

Jake froze. Her words froze in mid-air. He couldn't comprehend them. "What? Ross is dead?"

"I'm so sorry, son," Grace cried.

"No!" Jake screamed. "He can't be!"

Jake managed to lift his head and looked toward his feet. "Why can't I move my feet?"

Something didn't look right. Jake grabbed the sheet covering his legs and threw it to the side. What was he seeing? "My...my..." With as much strength as he could muster, he flailed his head from side to side. "No, no, no!"

Grace reached for Jake to console him, but he slapped her hand away.

"Please, son," she cried.

Dr. King buzzed the nurses' desk.

"Can I help you?" a voice responded.

"I need some help in here, please," Dr. King replied.

Joe Bill came quickly with a syringe and immediately injected it into Jake's IV. The medication quickly took effect, and Jake soon began to calm down.

Mitch and Grace embraced each other. Their son's reaction was upsetting.

"It's all going to be all right," Dr. King encouraged them. "It's just going to take some time."

Lauren lay in bed hours after her normal wake-up time. Her face hurt. Her sinuses hurt. Her entire body burned with grief and hatred. She heard the bedroom door open slightly and knew her mother must be looking in on her.

"No. She's still sleeping. She's exhausted." Lauren's mother was talking to someone. Lauren realized after a moment that she was on the phone.

"I know! It's wonderful news! And Grace said that there were no complications. I'm so thankful!"

Margaret and Pastor Glenn's wife, Jeannie, rejoiced over the phone as they discussed the outcome of Jake's surgery.

"Have you spoken to Grace this morning?" Lauren heard her mother say. "And how are she and Mitch holding up? I hope they were able to rest...I know. Grace is such a rock." The words grew fainter as her mother walked away.

"I hope to make a trip to The Med later this week to see them. If you would, put me on the supper list for the Kellys for Friday night. I'll be glad to help with anything else that comes up. OK. I'll talk to you later. Bye."

Now Lauren heard a soft tapping on her door. Emotionally, she felt so numb she didn't even bother answering.

"Are you awake?" Margaret asked softly, sitting on the side of Lauren's bed.

Lauren rolled over to face her. "Yes, unfortunately," she said.

"Your eyes are swollen," Margaret said. "Poor baby." She placed Lauren's head in her lap and stroked her hair. "Did you get any sleep at all?"

"No. I had bad dreams all night."

"I know you're hurting, sweetheart," Margaret said sympathetically. "I hate it for you so much."

Lauren began crying again. "I just wish Ross had listened to me. He would be here right now."

Margaret reached for the box of Kleenex on the night table and offered one to Lauren.

"I made you some hot tea," Margaret said as she continued to smooth Lauren's hair. "It might help. You are so stuffed up from crying."

"I don't think I'll ever stop crying," Lauren said.

Margaret set the box of Kleenex on the night table and helped Lauren sit up.

"I was just talking to Mrs. Glenn on the phone. We're taking the Kellys dinner Friday night. You want to go with me?" Margaret asked.

"Yes, I would like that," Lauren said.

Margaret hesitated. "She also told me that Jake's surgery went well, but Jake isn't taking it well at all."

"Good," Lauren said hatefully.

"Good?" Margaret questioned.

"Yes. Good," Lauren said firmly. She suddenly became bitter. "I hope he feels bad for the rest of his life for what he did."

Margaret was stunned at the anger in her child's voice.

"Lauren, you don't mean that."

Lauren sat up. "Yes, I do. It's Jake's fault that Ross is dead. I wish he had died instead."

"Lauren, that's enough," Margaret said. "I wanted to encourage you to go visit Jake with me, but I can see that you are quite resentful toward him."

"You would be too if you were me." Lauren looked Margaret in the eye. "I hope that every time he looks at his legs, or whatever is left of them, he'll have to remember what he did to Ross!" Her voice grew louder with each word. Then, becoming stone-faced, she said, "I hope Jake doesn't make it to Heaven, either."

"Lauren, that's enough!" Margaret rebuked. "You have no idea the implications of what you just said! That's not right and you know it."

"It may not be right, but it's how I feel," Lauren said. She turned and faced the wall. "Please leave me alone. I just want to be alone."

Margaret was concerned about Lauren's attitude toward Jake. She felt helpless and stood to leave. "I pray God will change your heart...I'll bring you that tea now."

Grace and Mitch remained in CCU, waiting. It would be another day or two before they could return to Jake's room due to the high risk of infection. Though hard to accept, Grace made the best of it by looking for productive things to do.

She immersed herself in Bible study. The area around her seat was cluttered with multiple bags and baskets of food and spiritual resources. Grace had felt so privileged with her opportunities to share her abundance with others in need. So many who waited in the room with Mitch and her were from other states and had come in such a rush to get to their loved ones, uncertain of their condition, that they had only the shirts on their backs and what money was in their wallets.

A voice interrupted Grace's studying.

"Excuse me," spoke a soft, feminine voice. "Would you mind if I borrowed one of your books to read?"

Grace lifted her eyes and saw a refined, well-dressed, blonde-haired woman. "No, not at all. Help yourself."

"Thank you," the lady said. "I need something to keep my mind occupied. I'm afraid I didn't come very well prepared."

Grace grinned. "I'd venture to guess most of us didn't."

The lady smiled.

"I've been here a few days, so I've accumulated quite a bit," Grace said with a wink.

Her demeanor quickly set the lady at ease.

"I'm Mary," she said.

"It's very nice to meet you. I'm Grace."

"So, why are you here?" Mary asked, thumbing through the books in Grace's bag.

"My son was in a car accident," Grace replied. "He sustained severe burns on his legs – so severe, they had to amputate both of them."

Mary stopped searching. She was shocked. "That is horrible," she said barely above a whisper, holding her hand to her chest. "You must have been devastated."

"Certainly, and I still am," Grace said.

"But...you're so...so...calm," Mary said.

"I've had a little time to process things; I still don't have my mind wrapped around it, but the Lord has sustained me," Grace said.

"Apparently so," Mary said. "And I thought *my* situation was bad."

"Your situation *is* bad or you wouldn't be here. The levels of injuries and longevity of recovery don't lessen the pain and fear we face," Grace said empathetically.

"Well, God was merciful to us. My daughter was in a car wreck as well, but the doctors seem to think her injury is primarily a broken bone requiring surgery. It's still very nerve-racking, though."

"Yes, I'm sure it is," Grace said. "Any time our children must undergo anesthesia, it can be scary."

Both ladies turned to their reading and became absorbed. Grace was interrupted every few minutes by people asking for a snack from her basket, which she kept available for everyone.

Grace struggled to stay focused on her reading. She hadn't spoken to her dear friend, Kate, in quite some time. Grace couldn't begin to understand what Kate was going through. Not hearing her voice left her feeling empty. Knowing she wouldn't hear Ross's voice again was gut-wrenching. While her own circumstances kept her thoughts occupied, the Kellys were still present in her mind. Grace picked up her phone and typed out a text to Kate. *Praying for you, sweet friend. I hurt for you and miss you terribly! Love, Grace.* Pressing "Send," Grace whispered under her breath, *Please God, let her see this.*

Grace's message remained unread in a sea of text messages. The outpouring of love and care for the Kellys was incredible. Lance and Kate were exhausted and filled with a grief they had not imagined was possible. As people continued to provide for them – not just meals, but other needs as well – the Kellys functioned in a robotic state as they forced smiles and repeated the same brief dialogue.

Friday came. It was the McKays' turn to furnish the evening meal for Lance and Kate. Although they longed to see the Kellys, Margaret and Lauren felt a deep sense of dread on the way to the home. Knowing Ross wasn't going to be there sickened Lauren. She never went there without expecting to see Ross. The harsh reality enflamed her emotions.

"I don't think I can do this, Mom," Lauren cried.

"I know, dear, but it's for them, not us," Margaret reminded her.

"Yes, but it's so hard."

"I think seeing Kate will be good for you, Lauren."

"I can't bear to see her like she was at the funeral home," Lauren said. "It was horrible."

"I understand, but we all have to face these difficult days," her mother said calmly.

They pulled into the driveway. "OK," Margaret said, "take a deep breath."

Lauren closed her eyes and followed her mom's instruction.

"Now, let's go love on the Kellys," Margaret said.

Lauren wiped tears from her face and exited the car. They removed several platters from the back seat of the car and walked toward the house.

Lance met them at the back door. Seeing the McKay women, he smiled.

"I didn't know you guys were coming tonight," Lance said. "Here, let me help."

"You're good, Lance," Margaret said, shaking her head. "Lauren and I can manage just fine."

Lauren worked quickly to get inside and set down the food items on the kitchen counter. Quickly offering Lance a hug, she asked, "Where's Mrs. Kate?"

"She's sitting on the couch in the living room, sweet girl," Lance replied.

Without a word, Lauren walked to the living room. As soon she saw Kate, Lauren began to weep. Kate quickly turned to her and pulled her into her lap. Lauren had become like a daughter to the Kellys. As they cried together, Lance and Margaret stood silently in the kitchen, listening. Not sure of what to say, Margaret offered a hug to Lance and said, "I'm praying for you continually."

"I know," Lance said. "And thank you. Come on – I know Kate would love to see you."

Margaret nodded in agreement as they walked to the living room, where Kate and Lauren comforted each other. Margaret and Lance quietly sat in the chairs adjacent to them and indulged them as they grieved together.

Chapter 17

*Up to this point, it seemed that time was in fast-forward motion –
our families had little time to process what had happened. But now,
time had begun to slow a bit. Acceptance was a difficult thing. During
this period, being kept heavily sedated was a gift for me. I was kept
from having to deal with what I had done, but the day was coming
soon when I would be forced to deal with every single consequence
of that night.*

Some time had passed since the surgery. With the threat of infection now minimal, the Adamses were allowed to return to stay
with Jake in the hospital room. Jake had finally come out of the heavy
sedation and reality was setting in. Physically, Jake was recovering
well, yet he was plagued with feelings of guilt, anger and fear. He
continued playing the blame game and feeling sorry for himself.
Some of the more easily-intimidated members of the nursing staff
walked on eggshells around him. The wretched daily routine wore
on Grace and Jake. It was a vicious cycle. And he was in agony. Jake
was on the highest dose of morphine allowed, but it only briefly controlled the horrendous pain. Jake writhed in misery between doses,
calling out to Grace for comfort.

This morning the nurse injected another dose into his IV. It moved
quickly through Jake's system, relaxing him and placing him in a

deep sleep. Grace sat quietly by his bed with her eyes closed. She was exhausted from trying to comfort him. Her mind was plagued with so many things: medical bills, keeping the floral shop in business during her absence, getting their home equipped for a wheelchair. But the main thing wearing on her was her precious friends, Lance and Kate. Negative thoughts invaded her mind...Why had they not responded to her texts? Grace's immediate response was to run to God's word for refuge and assurance. She pulled her bag of spiritual resources from underneath the chair. As she thumbed through them, the face gracing the cover of a DVD box caught her eye. She recognized renowned Bible teacher Beth Moore, and Grace's mind raced back to the Sunday morning she had given the set to Kate. Although thinking of her friend caused Grace's heart to ache, seeing Beth's smile brought her a sense of peace. Over the years, Grace had gained much insight into God's word through Beth's teachings, and she suspected these DVDs would have the same effect. Grace opened the DVD case. On the very top of the five discs was Session One, titled *God's Purpose for You*. Grace felt joy trickle inside her. While she firmly believed circumstances in life had purpose, she needed to hear it. She moved to the little oasis she had created for herself in Jake's room. Loading the DVD into her laptop, Grace was ready for the Lord to speak to her.

As Beth spoke, Grace became entranced in her words. After listening for at least half an hour, Beth's words grabbed Grace:

I hope to prove to you in the next few minutes that absolutely nothing is allowed to come to you and into your life through the permissive will of God that does not have some bearing on God's purpose for you in your own generation. I want to prove that to you biblically...that not one single thing...any hardship that you go through...any temptation that should come your way...anything you've experienced...as a child of God, who was so loved in His mother's womb...before you even knew He existed, He said over you, "Child, do you have any idea how loved you are?" before you served Him for one second. Before you had your first unselfish thought, God completely, lavishly and fully and unchangingly loved you. And absolutely nothing gets to touch your life, nothing, that is not in keeping with God's purpose in your own generation, nothing. Nothing.

Grace sat in awe. It was exactly what she needed to hear. She needed to be reminded that everything they were going through had purpose and was a part of God's plan. She recalled Romans 8:28 – *"Now we know that everything works together for good for those who love God and are called according to His purpose."*

Beth's words spoke hope into the circumstances the Kellys were experiencing. *Kate needs to hear this,* Grace thought.

Kate had turned off her phone. After Ross's death, the texts and phone calls had overwhelmed her and Lance. Although she knew people meant well, she had chosen not to respond to them...at least not now. Kate lacked the strength and focus to even try. For days now she had stayed in bed. Numb from endless tears and sleepless nights, she stared out her bedroom window. She had lost her ability to function and her will to live.

Lance knocked softly on the door. He second-guessed himself in doing so, but was concerned about Kate. The silence scared him. Once Ross's service was over and the meals stopped and visitors became sparse, Kate had become a recluse. Her vivaciousness had disappeared, causing Lance even more heartache. He feared the Kate he'd loved for over twenty years would never return. He had already lost his son. He didn't want to lose her as well.

"Honey, can I come in?" Lance asked.

Kate said nothing. Emotionally drained, she lacked the strength to respond. Lance walked in and sat on the bed beside her. He watched her with difficulty as she stared out the window, hardly blinking.

"Can I get you anything?" he asked softly.

Kate slowly moved her head left to right. Lance caressed her hair.

"I hope you don't mind, but I invited Pastor Glenn to come over."

"Why?" Kate asked, barely above a whisper.

"Because I'm worried about you. A lot of people are. I thought it would do you good to talk to him."

"I don't want to talk to anybody," Kate replied.

"You need to talk to someone," Lance said. "It's so hard to watch you like this."

"Well, I guess you're gonna have to get used to it," Kate said. "There's nothing anyone can say to make the pain go away."

Lance felt hopeless. Not wanting to push too hard, he said, "I'll call Pastor Glenn back and tell him it's not a good time." He walked toward the door to leave. He paused. His eyes filled with tears. "I'm hurting too, you know."

The morning routine began at 7 a.m. Joe Bill made his rounds to check on his patients. Now it was Jake's turn. The weighted door into Jake's hospital room whistled as it opened.

"Good morning, Mr. Adams," a deep-toned voice called out softly but cheerfully. The muscle-bound man pulled back the curtains and let the sunlight brighten the dim hospital room.

Jake was less than enthused. "Who are you...and pull that curtain back!" he ordered with his hands over his face, attempting to block the sun from his eyes.

"Aw, c'mon," the nurse said. "It's a beautiful day! You'll feel better, trust me."

Annoyed, Jake asked again, "Who *are* you?"

"My name's Joe Bill, and I'm gonna be your nurse and your new best friend," he said sarcastically.

"You're a nurse?" Jake asked.

"Yup. Why? Does that surprise you?"

"Well, yeah," Jake said. "You don't look like any nurse I've ever seen."

Joe Bill laughed. "I'll take that as a compliment."

"Seriously, you look like the Incredible Hulk without the green skin," Jake said with a half-smile. "I don't remember seeing you."

"I've been in here several times," Joe Bill said. "You're just usually too drugged to remember." He stood beside Jake. "Well, I have a series of questions I'm supposed to ask you to make sure you're cognitive, but I can tell by the way you're running your mouth you ain't got no problem."

"You're quite a comedian, aren't you?" Jake said facetiously.

Joe Bill placed the blood pressure cuff around Jake's arm, pumped the bulb and listened through his stethoscope.

"What day is it?" Jake asked.

"Shhh..." Joe Bill said.

"Excuse *me*," Jake murmured.

After taking Jake's vitals, Joe Bill answered, "Sunday."

"Wow, that's weird," Jake said.

"What is?" Joe Bill asked.

"I've been here a week and can't remember it," Jake said.

"It's weird for sure, not being able to remember days at a time, but it won't be long until that won't bother you anymore."

"Oh, yeah?" Jake asked. "And how do you know?"

"Just trust me – I know," Joe Bill assured him. "Can I get you anything before I go?"

"You can get me the channel and time Alabama plays Saturday," Jake replied.

Joe Bill looked at Jake. "Wait...you're an Alabama fan?" he asked.

"You're not?" Jake replied arrogantly.

"Not hardly," Joe Bill replied. "Ole Miss. Bama's off this week."

"Are you serious?" Jake was disappointed.

"As a heart attack," Joe Bill answered. He turned to leave but stopped.

"Oh, and by the way...we play Bama the next Saturday...at *our* house," he said, smiling.

"You say that like I should be worried," Jake said.

Joe Bill shook his head and laughed.

"What's so funny?"

"Nothin'," Joe Bill said. "I just think it's going to be an interesting football season."

"Yeah, well, you Rebel fans don't need to get your hopes up," Jake said condescendingly.

"Aw, now...you gotta have hope," Joe Bill said.

"Whatever," Jake said. "How long you gonna be in here?"

"Leaving now," Joe Bill said. Untouched by Jake's rude behavior, he added, "Buzz me if you need anything."

Joe Bill walked out of Jake's room and into the nurses' station. Nurse Velle was leaning over the counter discussing a patient's chart with another nurse. Joe Bill stood next to Velle.

"He's something else."

Velle didn't have to ask who Joe Bill meant. "You got that right," she said. "He gon' be a tough nut to crack."

"Naw...he just needs someone that understands him," Joe Bill said compassionately.

"Well, if anybody understand, baby, it's you," Nurse Velle said, patting him on the back. "You should talk to him."

"All in God's time," Joe Bill said. "He's not ready."

"I don't know how to get to that boy," Nurse Velle said. "He won't let me in."

"Well, I just found you a way in," Joe Bill said. "He's an Alabama fan."

Velle gasped. "Fah real?"

"For real," Joe Bill said.

"Well, hallelujah!" Velle said, her hand up in the air. "There is hope for that baby after all! With that hard-nose kid cheering with me for my Tide, football season will be a little more exciting!"

The Lee County Academy Eagle football team struggled in practice. The talent in their second-string players behind Jake and Ross worked hard to fill their roles, but the team's ability to focus and remember plays suffered terribly. On this particular day, Coach Scott noticed it more than usual. It was time to boost his weary team's morale.

Coach Scott blew his whistle. "OK, guys, we're gonna call it a day."

The players and assistant coaches looked at him, shocked. Coach was a drill sergeant. He had allowed a mercy period the week of Ross's funeral and Jake's surgery, but had pushed the guys hard ever since to make up for the time they lost.

As the team walked off the practice field with helmets in hand, Coach Scott called out to a few of his players. "Riley, Collins and Hamm, I need to see you in my office ASAP."

Puzzled, the guys looked at each other, wondering what they had done wrong. On the way to the field house Marcus, Drew and Hamm discussed what he could possibly want, then sat down in Coach Scott's office and waited. Finally, Coach Scott entered the room and closed the door. He sat in his swivel chair and looked at each one of them. The silence was uncomfortable for all of them.

"I know you guys are having a tough time. I am, too. But I really need you to step up."

Marcus spoke up. "Coach, we doing all we can do."

"Don't misunderstand me," Coach said. "I know you're working as hard as you can. I'm talking about leadership."

He walked around to the front of his desk and leaned on it. "I need another team captain."

Knowing that Marcus and Drew had already been made team captains following the accident, Hamm looked at his teammates, then his coach, pointed to himself and mouthed the word *Me?*

"Yes, you," Coach Scott said. "A captain must be a good leader. You meet that qualification."

"Coach, I never thought..." Hamm scrambled for words.

"That's awesome, Hamm!" Marcus said.

"Good choice, Coach," Drew said.

Coach Scott nodded. "You guys will lead us not only on that field, but through this storm."

Looking at Marcus, Coach Scott said, "You're our lead man, Marcus."

"I don't know, Coach," Hamm said, his voice quivering. "Those are some tough shoes to fill."

Coach Scott said, "You fill your shoes...no one else's."

Marcus nodded in agreement. "I get the picture."

Kate looked through pictures of Ross in the scrapbooks she had put together over the years. She had worked diligently to complete them as a part of Ross's graduation present. She had caught up over the summer and only lacked pictures from events that were yet to take place. Instead of adding pictures during this senior year, she was returning snapshots used for the slide show at his funeral.

There was a knock at the bedroom door.

"It's open," Kate said solemnly.

Lance walked in and found her looking at the colored pages filled with pictures, stickers and journaling. His heart sank. Quietly, he joined her on the bed and looked with her, commenting on the event taking place in each one.

"It will never be complete." Kate spoke barely above a whisper.

"What, honey?" Lance asked.

"Ross's scrapbook. It will never be complete," Kate explained. "No senior basketball season. No senior baseball season. No senior prom.

No athletic banquet. No graduation. Lance, we will never have a picture of us with our son in his cap and gown. It's so unfair."

"Kate, please, don't torture yourself like this," Lance said, hugging her closely.

"I *am* tortured, Lance. This is the only way I have left to see those brown eyes and sweet smile again. I can't hug him. I can't hear his voice."

She began to cry. "Oh, my baby. I miss my baby, Lance."

She became limp. Lance scooted off the bed onto the floor to hold her. They both were crying now.

"We can only live through this one day at a time, Kate. One event at a time, trusting the Lord to give us the grace and the strength to get through each one."

"I don't even want to think about it," Kate said. "It hurts too much."

"Then don't think about it," Lance said. "Just grieve. That's all you need to do right now is grieve." Lance pulled her face toward him. "Grieving is a gift. It helps us heal. It's good to grieve, but you can't allow it to control you."

"I don't think I'll ever be able to laugh again. Or sing...or even smile," Kate said in despair.

"I can't believe that," Lance said through tears. "If I never hear you laugh, or sing...If I never get to see you smile, Kate, then I'm a dead man."

Kate continued to sob uncontrollably. "Lance, I wish I could die."

Lance felt helpless. He was without words. Finally, he said, "Kate, that's God's call...not ours."

Kate's statement scared Lance. He knew this was more than he could handle.

Chapter 18

Weeks passed. The new normal for everyone in our community was best described as unwanted, invasive, shoving itself down our throats. The students and faculty at Lee County Academy walked the hallways dazed for the most part. The laughter and horseplay that usually took place on the school grounds had ceased. The campus was a mortuary with walking corpses.

Mr. Kelly forced himself to work while Mrs. Kelly grew more hopeless each day. Pastor Glenn spent many extra hours seeking the Lord's wisdom for how to meet the needs of not only his own flock, but others outside the walls of his church as well. He felt the burden of the community hurting around him. My family was with me at the hospital, day after day. So monotonous. Our stay felt like it would be infinite. But God was working on behalf of all of us. Needs were going to be met. Hope was going to reappear. Healing was going to come.

L ance sat on the enclosed patio, a dead stare in his eyes. Once again, his efforts to lift Kate's spirits and encourage her to seek counsel had failed. Needing to be encouraged himself, he dialed Pastor Glenn. The preacher answered immediately.

"Hey, Lance," Pastor Glenn said, hopeful his call would bring good news.

"Hi, Pastor," Lance said.

The pastor could hear the discouragement in Lance's voice. "Kate still hasn't changed her mind?"

"She's just not ready," Lance said.

"Well, just give her some time. It's only been a few weeks," Glenn encouraged. "We'll keep praying."

"OK," Lance said. "It's just so difficult watching her like this. I know we need to grieve, but I can't grieve over losing Ross because I'm battling fear that I'm going to lose Kate, too." His voice began to break. "I'm afraid she's never going to be the same. It's wearing me out, Pastor!"

"That's just it, Lance. She *won't* ever be the same. Neither of you will," Pastor Glenn said. "But it's up to both of you to let God heal you and somehow use it for good."

"I hope to do that," Lance said. "I can't let Ross's death have been in vain." After a moment of silence he said, "I just always thought if we suffered something tragic, we would mourn together…not apart."

"People grieve differently, Lance," Pastor Glenn said. "Don't lose heart. God sees your pain. Remember His word…*He is near to the broken-hearted.*"

"Thank you, Pastor," Lance said.

"Stay in touch with me, OK?"

"You know I will," Lance said.

After ending the call, Pastor Glenn sat silently, aching for his friends. Feeling helpless, he began to pray.

Father, this is a God-sized job. I am guiding them as best as I know how, but I feel like, except for Your truth that I share, my words are empty. Lord, I cannot identify with their pain. I'm thankful for that, yet at a disadvantage. Show me, Lord. Lead me. Help me help them.

Glenn returned to his studies in preparation for Sunday's sermon. His phone's text alert sounded. It was JJ Jasper, his friend and national Christian radio host.

Hey, Pastor Glenn. Someone shared with me today about the tragedy you and your congregation have suffered recently. Wanted to let you know that Melanie, our girls, and I are praying for you and your church. If there is anything we can do to help, please let us know.

"Would you look at that..." David said. "God, You are incredible. Thank you for answering so quickly."

God's answer was crystal clear...and perfectly timed. Pastor Glenn called JJ right away.

The phone rang only a couple of times before being answered.

"JJ, man, thank you for answering so quickly," David said, laughing.

"Well, I knew when I saw your name, it must be important," JJ said. "What can I do to help?"

"I need you, brother," Pastor Glenn confessed. "The parents of the young boy we lost are really struggling. I'm going to be honest with you – so am I."

"You just tell me what I can do, David, and I'll do it."

"That would be awesome. I know you have so much on your plate and your own family who needs you. What a blessing to have you reach out like this."

Their conversation was productive and encouraging. As they ended the call, David knew the Lord was working on their behalf and that He would work out all the details.

Then, feeling like air had been breathed back into his lungs, Pastor Glenn sat back in his desk chair, closed his eyes and lifted his hands up to Heaven, saying, "You **are** the God who truly sees."

Jake's high risk of infection after another skin graft surgery sent Grace back to camping out in the CCU waiting room. Her spirit was somewhat uneasy, a feeling not uncommon when she had to return to this area. Although CCU had become her mission field, Grace certainly preferred to be with Jake, ministering to him.

Once again, Grace set up camp. This time, she had to relocate. Bodies constantly shifted and changed with the flow of new patients brought to the trauma center.

Grace noticed an older gentleman watching her as she fell into her normal routine. She caught a glimpse of him and realized he was a newcomer. Once again, she played the role of the hospitality committee chairman for the waiting room.

"Hi. I'm Grace," she said.

"Hello. I'm Robert."

"Nice to meet you, Robert," Grace said.

"Same here," he said.

"You haven't been here long, have you?" Grace inquired.

"Not long at all. Just a couple of days."

Robert read the title of her book, *Praying Through the Tough Times*.

"Are you a Christian?" Robert asked.

"Absolutely," Grace responded. "Are you a believer?"

"Yes, I am," Robert said confidently.

Grace saw deep concern on his face. He moved closer to her. Grace put her book away. She could tell Robert wanted to talk and welcomed the opportunity to encourage him, but this was very different.

"Who do you have here?" Grace asked.

"It's my brother, Keith," Robert said.

"What happened to him?" she asked.

"Keith was mauled by his pit bull," Robert said.

Grace gasped. "Oh, my! That's terrible!"

Robert shared the details of Keith's tragedy. "Sadly, my brother has an addiction to cocaine. He snorted a line of it, then walked out on his front porch. From what we can tell, he accidentally fell off the side of the porch and burst his head open. His pit bull ran to him and began to lick the wound. It was bleeding badly. After the dog got the taste of blood in its mouth, it went crazy and literally ripped Keith's face off. It's a miracle he made it here alive."

"Absolutely it is!" Grace affirmed.

"Oh, it's bad. He's in awful shape," Robert said sadly. "I think they've given him about a forty percent chance of survival."

"We will just pray, believing in faith that Keith will beat those odds," Grace said.

Robert sat silently for a few seconds as he leaned forward with his elbows on his thighs and rubbed his hands together. "Mrs. Grace, I'm worried. I don't think my brother is saved. Right now, I'm so scared he's going to die. If he does, well, I'm pretty sure I won't see him in Heaven." Robert began to weep. "I'm so afraid it's too late for him."

Grace leaned up and put her hand on his back. "We will just have to pray extra hard for God's mercy," she said.

"Could I ask you to do something?" Robert asked.

"Sure," Grace said.

"I know this is a lot coming from someone you don't even know, but I feel like you may be the only one who could intervene," Robert said.

"Ask me," Grace said, not sure what to expect.

l you mind going with me to the next visitation time and sus with my brother?" Robert asked.

Grace was stunned. She didn't want to refuse but couldn't imagine how that would unfold. Nonetheless, she was more than willing. "Yes, I certainly will."

Robert was elated. "We get to see him in about an hour."

Grace was a little nervous and anxious, but the drastic change in Robert's demeanor encouraged her to press on and do it. She knew the Lord would guide her through it.

"I'm going to get some coffee," Robert said. "Can I bring you some?" he offered.

"No, thank you. I'm just fine," she said.

Robert excused himself. Grace began to pray about the witnessing opportunity she would soon have with Robert's brother.

"Oh, Father, I have no idea what I'm going to face inside that room. Lord, please go before me now. Prepare the way. I feel this is a divine appointment orchestrated by You. Fill me with Your Holy Spirit and empower me to do this...in Jesus' name."

Grace took out her Bible and reviewed verses appropriate for the God-given assignment. Robert returned to his seat but remained silent, praying under his breath.

Soon, the visitation was announced. Robert rose to his feet quickly, anxious to get to Keith.

"You ready?" Robert asked.

"Yes, sir," Grace replied.

The two took the elevator to the Critical Care Unit where Keith was being cared for. They followed the signs down the maze of hallways that seemed endless. Finally, they entered a heavily-monitored area. Keith's room was tiny and filled to capacity with equipment used to sustain his life.

Grace stood at Keith's left side. Robert stood on his right. She was shocked at Keith's appearance. He looked like a mummy. Bandages wrapped around his face and head literally held it together. The only visible parts of Keith's face were his tear ducts, which were filled with tinges of blood, and his nostrils and lips. His hands were bandaged as well. The man moved very little. He had just returned from surgery, and Grace knew he must be quite sedated from medications. She was concerned how well Keith would comprehend what she was saying. She pushed those thoughts aside and entrusted the meeting to God. Although Grace was alarmed by his condition, she acted as if it were completely normal. Because time was very limited, Grace started a conversation right away. Her mind raced as she tried to find a way to begin. This was tough. They had never met and communication was difficult. At once, the words began to flow.

"Hi, Keith," Grace said softly. "My name is Grace Adams and I've gotten to be friends with your brother."

Keith remained still.

Grace continued. "I'm here because my son was in a terrible accident. I met your brother in the waiting room. He shared your story with me."

Still no movement. The awkwardness grew. Grace pushed through it and began to share the gospel.

"As your brother and I talked, I could tell right away that he loves you very much. We talked about our salvation. Keith, Robert is very concerned that you don't know the Lord and that if you die, you will not go to Heaven. He asked me to come and share the gospel with you, so I'd like to do that."

Keith showed no signs of coherency.

"Keith, I'm going to share truth with you. I know you can't speak to me, but if you agree with what I'm saying to you, would you please squeeze your brother's hand?"

Robert looked at Grace in shock. "He squeezed my hand." Grace became excited, which fueled her energy to continue.

"The Bible says in John 3:16, 'God so loved the world that He gave His only Son, that whosoever believes in Him will not perish, but will have eternal life.' So Christ was born of a virgin and lived a sinless life. If you believe that, Keith, would you please squeeze Robert's hand?"

"He's squeezing my hand!" Robert whispered.

"Jesus was beaten beyond recognition and suffered a cruel death on the cross, where He took on all the sins of the world, once and for all. If you believe that, Robert, would you please squeeze your brother's hand?"

Grace saw tears form in the small bandage openings.

"He's squeezing it," Robert said.

"But Keith, He didn't stay dead. On the third day, He rose again, conquering death, Hell and the grave. He now sits at the right side of God, waiting to be told when it's time for Him to return for His children. If you believe that is truth, Keith, please squeeze Robert's hand."

Through tears and broken speech, Robert said, "He's squeezing my hand like crazy."

Grace looked down at Keith. The tear ducts tinged with blood were filled with tears. Mucus drained from his nostrils. Saliva formed on his lips. She caught movement out of the peripheral vision of her left eye. She looked to see what the movement was. Keith's right foot moved side-to-side in a fast motion. Robert continued to weep, and

Grace knew that Keith's response to God's gift of salvation had been, "Yes, Lord." She looked at Keith and smiled as her eyes filled with tears. "Welcome to the family of God, my new brother."

Grace and Robert stood by Keith rejoicing until the visitation ended. They said their good-byes and made their way to the waiting room. They felt like they were walking on air, and they couldn't stop laughing. Surely, the presence of the Lord was with them.

Mitch munched on goodies from a gift basket, assuming Grace was somewhere nearby. He soon spotted her with a man he didn't know, walking toward him with the big, sweet smile he loved. This was completely heartwarming to Mitch. He stood and hugged his wife. It had been difficult being away from each other, working extra hours at the flower shop so Grace could stay with Jake.

After a lengthy embrace and a couple of pecks on the lips, Grace introduced Mitch to Robert.

Robert turned to her. "Mrs. Grace, you were my angel today. I want you to know that."

"You're sweet, Robert, but it was all God in that room," Grace said.

"I understand that, but He sent you to do it," Robert said.

"I was honored to serve Him," she said.

"I think I'm gonna head down to the cafeteria and find me something to eat," Robert said as he rubbed his stomach. "Y'all care to join me?"

"No, thank you," Grace said, looking to Mitch for confirmation.

"Yeah, but we appreciate your offer," Mitch said.

"All right. Well, I'll be back shortly," Robert said.

Mitch and Grace sat down beside each other. At that moment, a fleeting thought crossed Grace's mind. *Lord, please don't put me on a shelf.* She could hear herself saying that to God when she walked through those CCU waiting room doors for the first time. *Now, that was the craziest thing I have ever said to God,* she thought. Grace laughed out loud.

Mitch was puzzled. "What's so funny?" he asked.

"Oh, nothing," Grace said.

Curious, Mitch asked, "What was your new friend talking about? And where were you earlier?"

Grace hesitated. The encounter she had just experienced left her searching for words to explain. "I just had one of the most incredible experiences of my life. I sit here in total awe, first, because of what just took place, but even more mind-boggling is that God allowed me to be a part of it."

Grace shared with Mitch the miraculous event she had witnessed. She concluded by asking him, "Is that not absolutely incredible?"

Although Mitch saw it was very special to her, it made him very uncomfortable. He didn't know how to respond and certainly couldn't elaborate.

"Yeah, Grace, that's…that's…sweet," Mitch said.

Disappointed, Grace asked, "Sweet? I just had the privilege of leading a man to Christ – a man with his face ripped off – and the only word you can come up with is 'sweet'?"

"I'm sorry, Grace. You're right. It was a wonderful thing for you," Mitch said as he struggled to be more impressed.

"Not for me, Mitch. For Keith! For Robert! That wasn't about me!" Grace began to cry. It was so hard not being able to share experiences like these with Mitch and have him rejoice in it. It burdened her terribly. She knew her response had probably made Mitch feel bad.

"I'm sorry, honey," Grace said. "I'm just tired and emotional. I shouldn't expect you to feel the same way about it as I do. I mean, you weren't even in the room."

"No...I'm sorry I'm not as excited about it as you wish I were," Mitch said.

Their conversation ceased. Silence fell between them. The reality of the difference in their spiritual maturity surfaced in times like these. In normal, day-to-day life, they avoided it for the most part, but sadly, in this very difficult time when Grace really needed Mitch to be there for her, he couldn't. Mitch felt frustrated and agitated. Grace felt frustrated and alone.

Next day, the Adamses were allowed back in Jake's room. Grace always felt relieved when she could return to her son. Although she knew he was in good care, she still wanted to be at his side.

Lauren was ready to try school again. Until this week, she could focus on nothing. Everything in her room reminded her of Ross – movie tickets on her bulletin board, pictures of him on her dresser mirror... Last week she removed all of these mementos, but her brain still felt dangerously scattered. Just as she was able to concentrate on something other than Ross or the race, she'd hear a song that reminded her of Youth Explosion, and that would make her think of Ross. Thinking of Ross sometimes actually brought a smile to her on the inside, then Jake Adams suddenly swept it aside, filling her brain, forcing out her sweet, gentle boyfriend and filling in every crevice with hatred and revenge and... gratitude. Lauren had no problem admitting to herself that she was glad Jake was hurt and in the hospital for such a long time – glad that he was no longer whole. Lauren didn't know, nor did she care, if she would ever have to see him again, but one thing was for sure – Jake Adams would no longer be the arrogant, obnoxious, friend-stealing thief who for some reason drew so many to him.

Still dazed and drained, she pressed on to catch up on her schoolwork. During her high school years, she had worked incredibly hard to maintain a 4.0 GPA. Her ultimate high school goal was to be valedictorian of her graduating class. Now...she found herself struggling to even care about her long-time dream of leading her class academically.

While Lauren gathered books from her locker, she felt movement beside her. Glancing to her right, she saw a very harried Eric Williams. Eric had struggled terribly since the wreck. His school attendance had been sparse. He had no one he felt he could talk to. Searching for answers to ease the pain he was battling, he went to Lauren.

"You look awful," Lauren said.

"Nice to see you, too," he said.

Lauren noticed a horrendous odor from Eric's mouth.

"Have you been drinking?" she asked.

"Shhh..." he said, quieting her, forcing even more alcohol fumes toward her.

Lauren waved her hand back and forth in front of her face. "Please!"

"Look, I really need to talk to you."

"What for?" she asked, still waving away the repugnant smell.

Eric looked around, then stopped at an empty classroom across the hall. "Come in here with me?"

"I guess," Lauren said reluctantly.

"What?" she asked shortly, wanting to get to her next class.

"I don't know. I've just felt horrible ever since the wreck, you know?"

"We all have, Eric," Lauren said unsympathetically.

"I know," he replied, "but, I mean, I feel really bad. Like the whole thing was my fault."

"How was it your fault?" Lauren asked. "You're the one who pulled over. Jake's the one who kept going and wrecked, killing Ross."

"I just feel like I instigated it," Eric said.

"So, you're on a guilt trip," Lauren explained. "What do you want me to do about it, huh?"

"Nothing...I just thought you could help me, you know? Like tell me what I need to do."

"Well, I'll tell you what *I* would do. I wouldn't worry about it. Jake Adams is the murderer here, not you."

"Yeah, but I feel like I need to do something," he said. "I just thought you being over the Bible club, you might could help me. Just forget it. Forget I said anything." He ran out of the room.

Lauren stopped in her tracks...*I just thought you being over the Bible club, you might could help me.* Conviction seeped in. She'd had the opportunity to speak truth to Eric, who was known for being "the lost boy," and she'd blown it. Not knowing how to rectify what she had done, she directed her mind back to Jake. Anger and hatred won out over conviction. *Eric doesn't have anything to feel bad about. It was all Jake's fault.* Lauren walked to her next class.

The afternoon's football practice was slow and unproductive. Coach Scott saw the efforts on the field were in vain. Blowing his whistle, he yelled, "Hit the showers!"

Marcus knew it was too early to end practice. Something must be up, but his concern ended there. Then he and the other team captains were ordered to Coach Scott's office.

"What now," Drew said to Marcus.

Marcus merely shook his head in reply.

They walked into Coach Scott's office and took a seat. Coach Scott sat on the end of his desk – his normal spot when he was prepared to chew a player out. Oddly, his demeanor was calm.

"Boys, I know you're struggling. I know it's hard, but you've gotta get tough. We are so close to the play-offs. It's a miracle we're in it after that loss early in the season to Prentiss County."

"Coach, we don't know what else to do," Marcus said.

"I know, Marcus." Coach Scott stood up and placed his hands on his hips. "I been thinkin'," he said. "What you guys need is some inspiration."

"Some what?" Hamm asked.

"Inspiration," Coach Scott repeated. "Look, our game this week is at home. That means an early night. So...get a good night's sleep after the game, 'cause come Saturday morning, the four of us are taking a road trip."

Curious, Drew asked, "Where to?"

Coach Scott grinned. "The Med."

"Yes!" Marcus yelled as the young men stood and gave each other high fives.

Lance sat in his oversized brown leather recliner and stared at the ceiling. He was emotionally drained and at a loss as to how to deal with the pain and how to help Kate. He recalled the words of JJ Jasper at a church breakfast only a month earlier:

How you deal with the worst day of your life, which for me was losing our son, is determined by the best day of your life, which is the day I received Christ as my Savior.

Lance began to weep as he remembered the day he accepted Jesus into his heart as a young boy. He knelt on the floor beside the coffee table and began to pray.

"Thank you, Jesus, for dying for me at Calvary so that I can experience Your healing power during this terribly painful time in my life. And I thank You for the eighteen years You gave me with my son. Thank you for the memories and pictures. Thank you for Little League and kindergarten. Thank you that Ross was an affectionate child who gave lots of hugs and kisses, and for his adorable giggles. Thank you for his big, brown puppy-dog eyes that would melt my heart. Thank you for trips to the beach where he and I built sand castles during the day and went crab digging at night, and his love for trying out different kinds of shrimp gumbo when we would go out to eat. Thank you for our trips to the mountains where we canoed and fished. Thank you for all the boo-boos I got to kiss and broken bones I got to pray over. Thank you for high school football, where I got to watch him play the sport he loved so much, and watching SEC football, cheering on our Crimson Tide together. Now, Lord, I ask that You help Kate and me embrace the healing power of Your precious blood and show us how to grieve the right way so that we are pulled closer together, not farther apart. In Jesus' name."

Lance lingered in his prayer posture until his tears dried. He raised his head and opened his eyes. Straight ahead were bookshelves that lined the wall. They were full of spiritual resources they had accumulated over the years, along with several series of chapter books that Ross loved to read over and over again. Mingled in between these were framed family photos and collectible pottery pieces. One book stood out to him, almost appearing to have a glow surrounding it. The book was *Losing Cooper.*

Kate must have placed it there, he thought. Lance stood and walked to it, never taking his eyes off the book. Pulling it from the shelf, he focused on the sweet, blonde-headed little boy he'd never met, but who felt so familiar. He sat back down and began reading.

After reading only a couple of chapters, the doorbell rang. Once he opened the door, Lance couldn't believe his eyes. On the porch was a small-framed man, standing less than six feet tall, with blondish hair and rimless glasses. Dumbfounded, Lance said nothing. He immediately recognized him as JJ Jasper.

"You look like you've seen a ghost," the man said, almost laughing.

"Oh, I'm so sorry," Lance said. "I'm just surprised, I guess. Please...come in."

As JJ stepped inside, he pointed to the book in Lance's hand. "I hear that's really good," JJ jested.

Lance chuckled. "Yeah, so I've heard. Please, have a seat."

"I tell you what...it's a beautiful autumn day. How 'bout we take a walk?"

"Even better," Lance said. He placed the book face down on the coffee table and walked outside with JJ.

They began to stroll down the leaf-covered driveway. "I hope it's OK for me to drop by unannounced like this," JJ said.

"Actually, your timing was perfect," Lance said.

"Apparently," JJ said, alluding to Lance meeting him at the door with his book in hand. "I'm headed out of town but just felt very impressed to come by and see you before I left. I spoke to your pastor the other day and told him someone had shared with me about your tragedy. I want you to know that my family and I are praying for you guys."

"You don't know how much I appreciate that," Lance said. "Thank you."

"Well, our hearts break for you," JJ said.

"Ours do for you as well," Lance said. "I was at the Brotherhood Breakfast the morning you spoke about Cooper. I met you briefly, but I know you meet a lot of people."

"Lance, I actually remember meeting you. When I shook your hand, I felt a connection, but I didn't have any idea why," JJ said. "Now, I do."

"That's amazing," Lance said.

"I know you're hurting, Lance. It's unnatural for a child to die before the parent. It's like a searing hot poker to your soul," JJ shared.

"That's a very accurate way to describe it," Lance said.

"But, Lance, you know, the character of God's nature doesn't change. He's still a good God. Mel and I know what's at the bottom, and we know Who's there waiting for you, to catch you with open arms."

JJ's words were like a warm blanket wrapping itself around Lance's heart. They brought comfort and hope. To hear JJ openly discussing his own pain showed Lance he had already experienced so much healing.

They came to the end of their walk and the sharing of their hearts. JJ placed his hand on Lance's shoulder and said, "There is hope to grieve well, Lance. When I talked to Pastor Glenn, he shared with me how your precious wife is struggling."

Lance teared up. "Yes, terribly. I don't know how to help her."

"Well, he and I discussed the possibility of Melanie and I meeting with you and Kate...when she's ready. I would love for Mel to have the chance to talk to her."

Lance smiled. "That would be incredible! Thank you."

"You bet," JJ said. He looked at his watch. "I need to get on the road, but we'll keep in touch." Handing Lance a card, JJ said, "Here's my number. Call me anytime if you need me."

"I appreciate it, JJ. Be safe traveling," Lance said.

Lance waved good-bye as JJ disappeared down the street. Then, looking to the sky, he said, "God...all I can say right now is... You rock!"

Chapter 19

The human brain is amazing. Even after suffering physical and emotional trauma and experiencing absolute upheaval in the world as we know it, still we can rearrange and adapt. Things were feeling a little more natural. This was due greatly in part to the incredible medical staff the Lord had surrounded my family and me with – especially Joe Bill and Nurse Velle. I mean, what are the chances that my charge nurse would be a die-hard Alabama fan? I was seeing the blessing in them, but I still had no clue just what a blessing they truly were.

It was 7 a.m., and Joe Bill had started making his rounds. Jake was still sleeping. Softly knocking on the door, Joe Bill entered with a humble smile on his exterior, but wearing a suit of armor underneath, ready to deflect Jake's cutting remarks he shot like fiery darts. Joe Bill drew open the curtain covering the large double window, allowing the morning sunshine to pierce the darkness in the room. Jake flinched. As usual, he threw up his arms, attempting to block the light.

"C'mon, Joe!" Jake said.

"Aw, now, Jake, you know the routine," Joe Bill said.

"Doesn't mean I like it." Jake was agitated.

Grace walked in not far behind Joe Bill, a wrapped sausage biscuit in her hand.

"Jake, son, I could hear you at the nurses' station. Would you please keep your voice down?" She turned to Joe Bill. "Good morning!"

Shifting his attention back to Jake, he continued.

"OK, rundown of questions, then I'll leave you alone. What's your name?"

"Jake Adams."

"Where are you?"

"Joe Bill's Torture Chamber," Jake said sarcastically.

"OK, comedian. And why are you here?"

"Because I'm an idiot."

Joe Bill laughed. "I ain't touchin' that one." He made a couple of notes, then asked, "Can I get you anything?"

"Sure...an order of buffalo wings, cheese fries with ranch dressing, a large sweet tea – and the channel to watch my Tide take down your Rebels, forward slash, Black Bears, forward slash, Land Sharks."

"I'll get your order in down at the cafeteria," Joe Bill chuckled.

It was good to see Jake smiling and joking, even if he was a smart-aleck. The staff that worked with him so closely every hour, every day obviously had a lot to do with his upturn.

Grace was perhaps the most enthused about the turnaround in Jake's demeanor.

Her phone rang, and she answered it more chipper than usual.

"Do I have the right number?" Pastor Glenn laughed on the other end. "Because the last person I talked to on this phone sounded gloomy."

Grace smiled. "Funny, Pastor. Actually, we're having a good morning around here."

"Now, that's what I've been waiting to hear," the pastor said enthusiastically. "Hey, want to hear some more good news?"

"Of course!" she answered.

"Kate is coming with Lance for counseling tomorrow."

"Oh, that *is* awesome news!" Grace said excitedly.

"I was able to get JJ and Melanie Jasper to meet with them. I'm sure you're familiar with their testimony."

"Yes! That will be so good for both Lance and Kate," Grace said, feeling encouraged.

"Well, the whole thing has God's fingerprints all over it, that's for sure," he said.

"He's working all around," Grace said.

"Absolutely," Pastor Glenn agreed. "Well, I just wanted to check in with you and see how things are going. I'm glad y'all are having a good day."

"We are. Thank you for calling…and for letting me know about Kate," Grace said. "I'll be praying."

Coach Scott and team captains Marcus, Drew and Hamm walked into the nurses' station in the burn step-down unit. They quickly noticed the staff wore scrubs decorated with various collegiate teams' logos.

"Wow!" Marcus said. "They take their college football serious around here."

"Some of these fans are gonna be pretty disappointed this year... like them Dawgs," Drew said condescendingly.

"You know that's right," Marcus said, giving Drew a high five. Aggravated by his remark, one of the nurses who pulled for Mississippi State quietly stepped behind them and shook her cowbell loudly, causing the boys to jump sky high. She then threw in a big, "Go Dawgs!"

The others started laughing at the boys' reaction.

"You asked for it," Coach Scott said.

They entered Jake's room and found him completely absorbed in the *College GameDay* pre-game show on ESPN. Jake was so focused on the statistics the commentators were talking about, he didn't notice his visitors right away.

Marcus cleared his throat, then said, "Excuse me, but is that any way to treat your guests?"

Jake turned his eyes toward the familiar voice.

"No way!" Jake said, surprised.

"In the flesh," Drew replied.

Jake's teammates and coach walked to his bedside, exchanging high fives.

"So, what's up with the whole nursing staff in college football getup?" Marcus asked.

"Dude, they take college football very seriously around here," Jake replied.

"Looks like it," Coach Scott said.

Jake noticed Hamm. He recoiled, remembering that the last time he had seen Hamm was when he was rolling on the floor of the cafeteria – after Jake had tripped him.

"One of them was wearing an Oregon Ducks cap," Drew said. "Somebody needs to talk to 'em."

"To each their own, I guess," Grace said, walking in behind them.

"Mrs. A!" the boys shouted simultaneously, gently hugging her.

"How are you boys?" she asked, smiling.

"Awesome," Marcus said. "Just glad to see this guy."

Grace looked at Coach Scott. "It was so good of you to come and bring them."

"Glad to do it," Coach Scott said.

"Oh, Hamm, it's so good to see you walking around!" Grace said gratefully as she gave him a hug.

"Yes, ma'am. I'm doin' real good," Hamm said, smiling. Looking at Jake, he said, "Can't keep a good man down, right, Jake?"

Jake's face became flushed with embarrassment. Trying to pass it off, he quickly responded, "Yep."

The door opened again. This time it was Joe Bill and Nurse Velle.

"How y'all doin'?" Velle asked, greeting Jake's visitors. She walked toward Jake with her hands behind her back. "I got something for you, baby," she said with a grin.

"What's that?" Jake asked.

She brought her hands around to the front of her body and held up a crimson-red Alabama football jersey with the number fifteen on it, representing each national title Alabama had won.

"Oh, wow!" Jake yelled. "That's so awesome!"

"Hey...me and the coach...we tight," Nurse Velle said with a wink.

"Let me help you get it on," Grace offered.

They worked to get it over his head atop the Alabama t-shirt he was already wearing to cheer on his Tide today on TV.

"How's that?" Jake asked, looking at the others.

"I guess I can stomach it for a day," Joe Bill said, stepping toward Jake with a white Styrofoam "to go" box and a white Styrofoam cup. Handing them to Jake, he said, "There ya go."

Curious, Jake asked, "What's this?"

"It's the order you placed a little while ago. Remember?"

"I was actually kidding, but I'll take it!" Jake said.

Jake set the cup on the table by his bed, then lifted the lid on the box. Steam rose into the air, along with the delicious aroma of buffalo wings and cheese fries.

"Are you kidding me?" Jake asked, surprised.

"Dude! That's a dream meal!" Hamm exclaimed.

Leaning forward with a small container in his hand, Joe Bill said, "And here's your ranch dressing for the fries."

"Oh, Joe Bill, you thought of everything!" Grace said sweetly.

"Just looking out for my boy," Joe Bill said. "Besides, I thought a good meal would help soften the blow of his Tide losing to my Rebels today," Joe Bill said, his thumb on his forehead and four fingers waving in the air. "Fins up!"

Agitated at Joe Bill's behavior, Nurse Velle interrupted. "Oh, look at yo fins up and yo Rebels. Y'all so messed up. You don't know what you are. First you Rebels, then Black Bears and now Fins Up!" she mocked as she held her hand in the same gesture.

The friends in the room laughed at their horseplay.

Grace noticed Jake joining in the laughter. She was glad to see him having such a good day.

A minute later, Mitch joined the crowded hospital room.

"What's going...my goodness!" he said, surprised by the unexpected visitors. "Hey, guys! So good to see you!" Mitch shook the coach's hand.

The crimson-red jersey caught Mitch's attention. "Wow! Look at you, man. You been shopping while I was gone, huh?"

"Actually, Nurse Velle brought it to me," Jake said.

"No way," Mitch said in disbelief.

He noticed the writing across the jersey. "Nick Saban? How?"

Jake shrugged. "She said she knows some people."

"Looks like it."

"I'm an Alabama gal, you know," Nurse Velle reminded them. "Well, I gotta go get some work done so I can rejoin this party in a bit and watch the Tide wipe out them Rebel land, black shark, bear fins or whatever you call 'em!"

"I'm gonna do the same," Joe Bill said. "Jake, you need anything else?"

Jake stopped chewing for a moment. He placed the chicken wing in the box and held up his hands. "Moist towelettes."

Marcus snickered with his hand over his mouth. "Man, you rotten," he said.

"So, Jake," Drew said. "How far up are your legs missing?" He pulled the blanket away from his friend's legs, catching everyone off guard.

"Drew!" Coach Scott called out.

Marcus glanced at the amputated legs...one above the knee, one below, both wrapped in white gauze fabric. Immediately, he passed out.

"Catch him!" Grace yelled.

Jake laughed.

"Son, that's not funny!" Mitch rebuked, trying to curb his own laughter.

"Yeah, it is. Hang on. I'll get a nurse," Jake said, pressing the button that alerted the nurses' desk.

Grace hurried around the bed to tend to Marcus. She sat in the floor and placed his head in her lap.

"You rang?" Joe Bill asked over the speaker built into the hospital bed.

"Yep – we got a man down in here," Jake said sarcastically.

Hesitant, Joe Bill replied, "Ooo-kay...I'll be right there."

"And bring your smelling salts with ya," Jake added.

Drew stood back and watched. "I'm such an idiot," he whispered.

Coach Scott patted him on the back. "You just weren't thinking... again," he joked.

Drew placed his face in his hands.

"Ah...he'll be all right," Coach said.

Joe Bill entered the room and moved quickly to Marcus. A few seconds after waving the smelling salts under his nose, Marcus began to cough.

"Oh, thank goodness," Grace said with relief.

"Just lie still for a minute," Joe Bill instructed him.

"Don't worry," Marcus said lightly.

"Marcus, you OK?" Mitch asked.

"I guess," Marcus replied.

"How many fingers am I holding up?" Mitch asked playfully.

"Dude, I don't even know where you are," Marcus said.

"That's better," Mitch said. "How 'bout I order us some pizza while Marcus recovers? It should be here by game time."

"Sounds good to me," Coach Scott said.

Marcus recovered, and thirty minutes later the pizza arrived. The Adamses and their guests each took a seat with their food and turned up the TV's volume, waiting for the football game.

"Game on," Jake said. Grace and Mitch looked at each other, and Mitch winked, their hearts full that Jake's attitude was better, and that he was now surrounded by his friends.

The commentators sat behind the well-known *College GameDay* desk, giving fans background information leading up to game time, while college football fans stood behind them with shakers and hand-made signs, waving and cheering.

"And today, the Alabama Crimson Tide plays against the Ole Miss Rebels in Oxford, Mississippi. It's a beautiful day here at The Grove," one announcer said.

"Yes, it is," another added. "It has been eleven years since Ole Miss has enjoyed a victory over the Tide. Each year, Rebel fans are hopeful, but by game's end, they are usually left with their hopes dashed. Their 'hope tank' is full as they are coming into this game a three-point favorite against the Crimson Tide," the first announcer said.

The game started, and Jake and his friends enjoyed watching, talking in short bursts during commercials, but not missing any plays. Shortly into the game, things were unfolding in the Rebels' favor. Although Joe Bill was outnumbered as an Ole Miss fan, he wasn't alone. Coach Scott joined ranks with him in cheering them on. Alabama couldn't seem to get their momentum going. Everything was lining up in Ole Miss's direction, but the Tide fans in the room doubted it would last.

The game was intense. Nurse Velle came in to catch some of it.

"How we doin', baby?" she asked Jake.

"Not good," Jake replied.

Nurse Velle looked at the score. "Are you kiddin' me?" she said loudly.

"Shhh…" Joe Bill said.

"Don't you shush me!" Nurse Velle said, her hands on her hips.

"Can't hear," Joe Bill explained.

The game was nerve-racking, for the Tide fans in particular.

"Come on, Bama!" Jake yelled in frustration. "What's your problem?"

"Jake, son, calm down," Grace said.

The Alabama quarterback threw an interception, putting the ball into the hands of the team that already had the lead.

Drew lashed out. "Are you for real? Bench him!" he yelled. "He's horrible! Oh, y'all just wait! Just wait!"

Coach Scott placed his hand on Drew's shoulder to calm him. "You're a little overboard, Drew."

Pointing at the television screen, Drew continued his rant. "Y'all just wait 'til next year when my boy Jake gets there!"

Everyone looked at Drew in shock.

Drew continued, totally unaware of the repercussions of his comment. "That quarterback is going down!"

"Oh, my gosh, Drew," Marcus whispered as he shook his head.

Joe Bill lowered his head and prayed for wisdom in how to respond.

Mitch stepped in. "Drew, that's enough."

"Next year they won't know what hit 'em when Jake gets out there, huh, Mr. A?"

Jake sat still, red-faced, looking at Drew. Tears began to fill Jake's eyes.

"Shut it down, Drew," Jake said.

Everyone grew silent. Drew looked at their faces, then to Jake's. He thought about his comments. Again, he looked at Jake. Feeling the heat of embarrassment and shame, he quickly looked at Coach Scott, who only shook his head. There was no recovering from this.

"Oh, Jake, I'm so sorry," Drew said.

Jake stared at his legs. "Just get out," he said through clenched teeth.

"Please, Jake. I'm so sorry. I don't know…"

"Just get out, now!" Jake cried.

Drew looked around the room again. Then, grabbing his hair in his hands, he said, "Please, Jake. I'm so…"

"Leave now!" Jake yelled.

Coach Scott quickly grabbed Drew and said, "Come on, son. We need to go."

Grace stood and looked at Coach Scott, mouthing the words *I'm sorry.*

Coach Scott shook his head and motioned with his hand, letting her know it was OK.

Marcus followed them out the door, his head down.

Grace sat on the edge of Jake's bed as he sobbed pitifully.

"What was that boy thinking?" Mitch said, facing the window. Tears rolled down his face. It was a horrible blow to him as well.

"I'll get him something to calm him down and help him rest," Joe Bill said.

The room quickly emptied except for the Adams family.

"How could such a great day turn so bad, so quickly?" Mitch asked. He slammed a fist against the wall. "Why? Why any of this?"

"Mitch, please," Grace begged.

Joe Bill returned with medication to help Jake rest. As he poured pills from a little white paper cup into Jake's hand, he glanced at the television screen. The game had ended and the score read Ole Miss 28… Alabama 14. Joe Bill's team had won for the first time in over a decade, but it meant nothing to him in light of the pain his patient was enduring.

Jake awoke ahead of the 7 a.m. routine. Joe Bill entered the room and found him in his bed with the back raised, staring straight ahead.

Not moving his gaze, he said to Joe Bill, "Well, you not gonna gloat?"

Joe Bill silently began his normal protocol by pulling back the curtains. "No, Jake. I don't gloat. I just choose to let the score brag for me."

Stunned at the nurse's direct response, he refrained from continuing the conversation.

Grace returned to Jake's room after getting breakfast. She sat quietly in the chair beside Jake's bed as Joe Bill finished his rounds with Jake.

"Call me if you need me," Joe Bill said ritualistically, yet sincerely.

"Thanks, Joe Bill," Grace said.

"You're welcome," he said smiling.

Grace turned her attention to Jake. "Son, I got a call this morning from Drew's mom. She was crying. She and Drew have been up all night aching over what happened."

As soon as Joe Bill reached the nurses' station, he realized he had left Jake's chart in his room. He retraced his steps, and as he started through Jake's door, he heard Jake's voice break.

"He ought to be! That was just cruel!"

Joe Bill's heart sank. He stood by the door and listened.

"Son, I'm not going to downplay how painful that was for you... for all of us. But you know Drew. You know how he is, and you know he loves you."

Jake gave no response.

"I've thought through the words in his rant, and you know what? I hear him bragging on his friend, Jake Adams," Grace said. "Did you notice that?"

"I guess, but you don't understand! It was so in my face!"

Jake began to cry. Joe Bill continued to listen. The sound in Jake's voice was different. This time, it wasn't a tantrum.

"I feel like I've lost everything, Mom! I mean...why did that one choice have to cost me everything? I lost my best friend. I lost my legs. And by the way...has Morgan ever called me since I've been here or visited?"

Grace hesitated. "Not that I know of, son."

"See? But do you blame her? I mean...what girl would ever want this?" He threw back the blanket, revealing his partial legs.

They both began to cry. "Jake, baby, you don't know how sorry your father and I are for what you're having to go through. It does seem like a lot to lose, son, but regardless, I know God has a plan in all of this. We just can't see it right now."

"I'll never see it," Jake said hopelessly.

Joe Bill could hear the pain in Jake's voice. He knew...Jake was ready.

"It's time," Joe Bill whispered under his breath.

Chapter 20

I had returned to the muck and mire of hopelessness. I hated feeling this way, but impossibility filled my entire body. For a day I was on top of the whole world; my friends had come to visit, and there seemed to be a light at the end of this twisted, ugly tunnel in which I traveled. With one well-meaning but unthinking remark, I again had a partial body, which naturally meant a partial future. I could think of nothing that could boost myself back to that wonderful high I felt the day before.

Later that morning, Dr. King dropped by to check on Jake. He was a work in progress, like all his patients, but Jake was going to take a little longer than he had suspected. And upon entering the young patient's hospital room, the doctor knew there would be the daily sarcastic rant.

But there wasn't.

"What?" Dr. King asked. "No Dr. Scissorhands remark?"

Jake said nothing.

Dr. King began his assessment. "You know, Jake, you're going to experience a lot of different emotions during the next few weeks. Let them run their course. It's a healthy process."

"So you're a psychiatrist, too?" Jake asked, frowning.

"Jake!" Grace admonished.

Dr. King chuckled and waved to Grace not to worry. "Oh, no. Not at all. I've just seen enough to know."

"Well, you don't know everything," Jake said.

"That's for sure," Dr. King replied. "But Jake, my goal for you is not just for you to do well physically. I want you to be whole... mind, body and spirit. I know you've been through a lot and are still going through a lot."

"Don't even try to act like you know what I'm going through, Doc, because you don't," Jake said.

Dr. King pulled the blanket back over Jake's legs. He sat down on the edge of the bed.

"Well, I do have a *bit* of an idea, son," Dr. King said. "You see, a few years ago, I lost my wife of thirty-five years in a car accident."

Jake turned to him in shock. Grace glanced at Dr. King's left hand. His ring finger was bare.

"Doctor, I'm so sorry," Grace said.

"Thank you," he said. "I really struggled. You see, I was driving the car," Dr. King said.

"I had no idea," Jake said, feeling ashamed for his attitude.

"What happened, Dr. King?" Grace asked.

"We were driving home late from out of town. I had been at a meeting, and Sarah, my wife, had gone with me to do a little shopping. We should have stayed overnight, but I insisted on driving back home. I fell asleep at the wheel. We went off the side of the road and the car slammed into a tree on Sarah's side."

"That's terrible," Grace said.

"It was devastating," Dr. King said. "I thought I'd never get over what I had done. If only I had chosen to stay overnight, things would have been a lot different, I thought. But then I realized – God is sovereign…in all things. Jake, it's no different with you. Yours was a bad choice. You know that. But God was still in control."

Grace was inspired. Having spent very little time around Dr. King, she hadn't been sure if he was a believer or not. His nature led her to believe he was, but now, his testimony left no doubt.

"So much truth in that, son," Grace said.

Jake nodded.

Dr. King finished examining Jake. "Everything looks good. You're healing well, Jake."

"Good," Jake replied.

"I'll check in with you a little later, OK?" Dr. King said.

"K," Jake said.

For the first time, Dr. King left and Jake was smiling. The progress felt good.

"I'll walk you out, Doctor," Grace said.

"Sure," Dr. King replied.

Stepping out to the nurses' station area, Grace touched his arm. "Dr. King, thank you for your transparency today. I can tell it made a difference."

"Empathy is a gift," Dr. King said. "It just comes with a price."

"So true," Grace said. Then, with a sudden boldness, she asked, "Dr. King, are you a believer?"

Dr. King smiled. "For about forty years now," he said.

"I thought so," Grace said.

"If you ever need me – for anything – don't hesitate to call," Dr. King said.

"Thank you."

Another day began to wind down. Grace left Jake for a few minutes to get dinner in the cafeteria and to catch a breath of fresh air.

It was also time for Joe Bill's supper break. He had prayed for some time about how to reach out to Jake when the time was right. He had a plan and was ready to put it into action. He entered Jake's hospital room with a wheelchair and accidentally pushed it against a wall, startling Jake.

"Man, what are you doing?" Jake asked.

"Get up," Joe Bill said. "I'm getting you out of here for a while."

"Why?" Jake asked.

"I think you could use a change of scenery."

Joe Bill looked in Jake's small closet and grabbed a shirt. "Here, throw this on."

"Why?" Jake asked.

"Because that gown you're wearing is a little drafty," Joe Bill said.

"Where we going?" Jake asked.

"I'll tell you when we get there," Joe Bill said. "Now move it. My supper break will be over before we get out of here."

Jake gave up. "Just use a blanket," Joe Bill said. "The weather has cooled down since you've been out last."

As Jake situated himself in the wheelchair, curiosity got the best of him. "Where we going, Joe?"

"I said I'll tell you when we get there," Joe Bill said firmly. "It's a surprise."

He wheeled Jake into the nurses' station area, looking around to see if the coast was clear.

Detected by Nurse Velle, she yelled, "Where you think you—"

Joe Bill held a hand in the air, motioning for her to hush.

"Excuse me?" Velle exclaimed.

Placing his finger over his lips, Joe Bill continued to silence her.

Appalled by his gesture, Velle placed her hands on her hips.

Joe Bill looked at her and softly said, "It's time, Velle. It's time."

"It's time? Time for what?"

Suddenly, it dawned on her. "Oh! It's time!" she declared. "OK, baby. You go ahead on, then!"

Joe Bill gave her a "thumbs up" and wheeled Jake through the hallway's steel double doors.

A very confused LPN looked at Velle, her eyebrows raised.

"It be OK," Velle said. "'Cause it time."

"Nurse Velle ain't happy about this at all," Jake said as he and Joe Bill continued down the next hall.

Joe Bill wasn't worried in the least. "Aw...she be ah-ight."

As they continued down the hallway, two young student nurses walked toward them.

One made eye contact with Joe Bill, looked down at Jake, then whispered something to the other.

Joe Bill bent down to Jake's ear and said, "Hey...you see that nurse looking at you?"

"What nurse?" Jake asked, straightening up in his chair.

"Right there. The blonde on the right." Joe Bill pointed.

"No, she wasn't," Jake said.

"I'm telling you...she had her eye on you," Joe Bill commented.

"No way," Jake said.

"Uh...way," Joe Bill said.

"No, she wasn't!" Jake exclaimed.

"Yes, she...wait...Jake, she's looking at you." Overly animated, Joe Bill pretended to talk to the nurse in question. "Oh, wait, what?

Tell him to call you?" he said, holding a pretend phone to his ear. "See, Jake? I told you."

The student nurse became embarrassed and looked the other way as she walked speedily past them.

"You're playing me," Jake said.

"No...*she* might be playing you, but I'm telling you...she wants your phone number."

"So, where we going?" Jake asked, brushing off Joe Bill's silliness.

"You ask me again and I'm gonna punch you in yo throat."

Joe Bill strolled Jake out into the courtyard area of the hospital. Jake looked around, shocked at how different the outdoors looked since his accident. The colors had gone from a vibrant green with colorful flowers in bloom, to earth-tone shades of brown, green and red. Leaves were falling all around him as they made their way to the place Joe Bill had scouted out for them. On a nearby picnic table sat a small duffle bag.

"What's in the bag?" Jake asked.

"You a nosey somethin', aren't ya?" Joe Bill asked.

He parked Jake's wheelchair and locked the brakes, then unzipped the bag and pulled out an official, collegiate-size, Nike football and handed it to Jake.

"Sweet!" Jake said. "What am I supposed to do with this?"

"Well, what do you normally do with it?" Joe Bill asked.

"Pass it," Jake responded.

"Well, OK then. Pass it," Joe Bill said, running backward to get in catching position.

Jake attempted to throw the ball, but it fell an embarrassingly short distance away.

"Oh, that was awful!" Jake yelled.

"You're OK. You've lost strength being laid up for so long. You'll work your way back up to it. It's just gonna take some time." Jake had never known such an encouraging man.

"I haven't thrown like that since flag football," Jake said, making fun of himself. "So, did *you* play?"

"Yup – five years," Joe Bill said, passing the ball back to Jake.

Jake passed it again, this time a little further and straighter.

"There ya go!" Joe Bill said, passing it back.

Jake positioned his hand tightly, trying to get a better grip. Then he passed it back. "What positions did you play?"

"Linebacker on defense and running back on offense."

"Cool!" Jake replied.

Jake and Joe Bill continued passing back and forth, and Jake gained distance with each pass.

"See, you're gettin' your game back!" Joe Bill shouted, encouraging him. "You'll be back to full strength in no time."

After only a few more passes, Jake grew tired.

"That's it for me, man – I'm out," Jake said, breathing heavily.

"You sure?" Joe Bill asked.

"Positive," Jake replied.

Joe Bill sat at the picnic table beside Jake's wheelchair. He pulled a towel from his duffle bag and wiped the sweat off his face. Then, offering it to Jake, he asked, "You wanna use it?"

"No, thanks," Jake said.

Joe Bill laughed as he reached inside his duffle bag and pulled out another towel and handed it to Jake.

"Here, this one's for you," Joe Bill said.

As Jake reached for it, he noticed the words *Ole Miss* embroidered on it.

"Uh...again....no, thanks," Jake said.

"What?" Joe Bill asked.

"I'd rather be sweaty," Jake said.

"Are you kidding me?" Joe Bill asked in disbelief. "Are you that eat up?"

"Yes, I am," Jake replied.

"Boy, you somethin' else," Joe Bill said, placing the towel back inside his duffle bag.

The two sat quietly for a few minutes, taking in the early autumn view. Joe Bill knew the moment was right, so he began to speak.

"Jake, I want you to know that I do have an understanding of what you're going through."

"Yeah? How's that?" Jake asked.

"Well, I was in an accident, too. I want to share my testimony with you, if that's OK," Joe Bill said.

Jake looked at Joe Bill. Curious, he said, "OK...shoot."

"OK. So here it goes," Joe Bill began. "Me and my brother were cutting limbs out of a tree for a good friend of ours. We were just kinda doing it as a favor.

"I had climbed up the tree about ninety feet and rappelled down to the limbs we had to cut out. I was cutting the limbs and throwing them down, going back and forth through the tree. My chainsaw was on a lanyard rope hooked to my climbing belt. Once I finished cutting away the bad limbs where I was, I turned off the chainsaw and let it dangle by my side. I didn't realize it, but the chain of the saw nicked my climbing rope. You see, the chain is sharp enough to cut, even when it's not running. As I rappelled down to the next set of limbs to be cut, the rope broke. I fell about fifty feet.

"I thought I just got the breath knocked out of me. My brother ran over to me yelling to stay down. I didn't realize it, but I had broken both my legs and my back. I hit my head up against the tree when I fell, so I had a pretty good head injury. I remember telling my brother to help me up, so he helped me up. Then I said, 'Put me back down!'"

Jake laughed.

"And man, it hurt!" Joe Bill continued. "My legs were like spaghetti. I could see 'em twisted. I started going into shock. It seemed like it wasn't any time 'til the ambulance got there. Right away they cut off my clothes. I was lying there completely naked. It was a really quiet neighborhood, but it seemed like everybody came out of the woodwork. And here I am...I'm worried about being naked in front of everybody. I had that on my mind. I kept telling the EMT to please cover me up. They were checking my vitals and couldn't believe that I was still conscious and talking. But when they put the air casts on me, they had to move my legs and get them centered, and they had to put me onto the spinal board. *That's* when I started hurting the worst. That lady EMT told me it was going to really hurt and to take a deep breath and let it out while she pulled my legs around. I could hear my bones crunching. When she did it, I just grabbed her and chunked her."

"Oh, snap!" Jake exclaimed.

"Well, when somebody hurts you, your instinct is to get them off of you, ya know? So anyway, my brother ran over to help, and they held me down. They got me back on the board and into the ambulance. I told them, 'You gotta give me something!' I was fading in and out. I was in shock. I was arguing with them. 'You need to give me something! You're not supposed to let me hurt!' I remember I could feel every bump during the ride, and I was making fun of the driver, saying he couldn't drive. Finally, the paramedic said to give me something. I think it was probably morphine."

"That's some good stuff," Jake said.

"I was completely fine after that. When I got to the hospital, I thought I was gonna be there in the ER for a couple of hours and get a cast and go back to finish the job with my brother. Dr. Gills was my surgeon."

"Mine, too!" Jake said.

"Wow! Well, he said, 'Joe Bill, you've messed yourself up pretty good. We're gonna do emergency surgery on you.' I didn't know it then, but in the beginning, they had called me Humpty Dumpty. All the king's horses and all the king's men couldn't put me back together again. After a while, at some point, I was in a coma. Part of it was induced so my body could rest, and part of it was from trauma.

"Then I got a blood clot – it traveled to my heart and lungs. Basically, it gets in your bone marrow and in your bloodstream and you drown in your own blood. The strain on my lungs from trying to breathe on my own caused me to go into cardiac arrest. I actually coded a couple of times. That's when they put me on life support and a ventilator.

"From what my family said, I was hooked up to a bunch of machines. My head was swollen like a basketball." Joe Bill held his hands out around his head. "When that accident happened, I was in the best shape of my life. I was running six-and-a-half miles a day, lifting weights. I didn't smoke or drink. I had thought about trying out for our local semi-pro football team."

n," Jake said empathetically. "So...you had a football dream, too."

"Yup," Joe Bill said. "After a few weeks, the doctor called in my family and told them that because I had a living will, they were going to take me off life support. He told them to call our extended family and to make arrangements for my funeral. My family asked for a little more time so they could call in some people to pray. They weren't giving up. Looking back, it's so funny because of all the people from different faiths, different denominations who came in to pray over me. About thirty minutes to an hour later, they started taking me off the machines. All of a sudden, I was in a white room. I was very comforted; it felt like a mother comforting me. It may have been my angel."

"Seriously, you think so?" Jake asked.

"Yeah, I do," Joe Bill said. "I just felt deep comfort. I didn't see anything or anybody – I just knew I was in a good place. I have no idea if it was while they were praying or not, because I had no idea of time while I was in the coma. I thought it had only been minutes or hours, but it was months."

"Whoa!" Jake interjected.

"I know, right?" Joe Bill said. "A voice told me, 'Joe Bill, you gotta go back.' Real soft. I knew it meant to go back to my body, and I said I didn't want to go back. 'I don't want that. It hurts.' I was in dire pain. A second time, a real soft-spoken voice, it said, 'Joe Bill, you gotta go back.' I was in an argument, almost a debate, with the voice. I was trying to make my point. 'I don't want to go back. It's agony. I'm good where I'm at. I like it here. I want to be here.'

"Third time, 'Joe Bill, go back.' It was like taking a deep breath into some cold water. That's exactly how I felt. It's the only way I know how to explain it. I woke up from the coma. I had a ventilator tube in me. I didn't know what was going on. I felt pain right away. I was hurting all over. I was hurting in my chest. I couldn't breathe cause they had taken me off the ventilator. I looked around. I had wires all over me. I had a chest tube, a catheter, I had drain tubes on my legs, casts on my legs, my back was in traction – everything you could think of.

"Finally, the nurse went and got the doctor. My sister said they were running around and didn't say nothing to nobody. All of a sudden, the doctor said to hook me back up to help my breathing. They started giving me oxygen and put me back on the ventilator. I was coherent. I remember him asking me, 'Who are you? How old are you? Do you know what happened to you?' I knew everything. I told him, 'You don't know where I've just been.'

" 'Yeah, you were in a tree accident,' he said. I said, 'No...I was in a place that...you know...I mean, it was real.' I wanted to tell him that I didn't care about the accident. I wanted to tell him where I was at. And I know I was in a good place. The nurse taking care of me went out to my family, excited, and said, 'I don't know what y'all did, but get back in there. He's awake on his own. He's breathing on his own. But we're hooking him up to assist him in his breathing so his lungs can heal, and we've got him on oxygen.' They were ecstatic! My whole family was walking in...crying. Some of the people I didn't even know.

"I wanted to know what was going on, but I couldn't speak because of the tubes down my throat. I wanted to write but I couldn't. They prayed over me again. I was thinking it was just a bunch of crazy people. That's what I thought at the time. I got to where I could breathe on my own. They were going to amputate my left leg.

Everyone that came by to see me, when they would ask me, 'Is there anything I can do for you?' I told them I wanted them to pray for me that I won't lose my left leg. They would say, 'OK, we will.' I'd say, 'No...I want you to pray right now!' "

Jake laughed; he could picture Joe Bill saying just that.

"If they asked me, that's what I wanted. My leg had turned a bluish-black color because it had gotten infected. People laid hands on me and prayed for me and had the faith to believe it, and I was saved. So I believed it for my leg. And, as you see, I've still got my leg. I went through a strenuous time in physical therapy. I wanted out of the hospital. I couldn't rest."

"I understand that," Jake said. "For example...having this annoying nurse come in every morning at 7 a.m. and—"

"You better watch it," Joe Bill said. "Eventually, I got to go home. I had a hospital bed. I couldn't walk for eighteen months. I had a home health nurse. Prayer saved me, no doubt. It works. Even in the little things. In scripture, Jesus said, *You have not, because you ask not.* And you don't have to pray big elaborate prayers. You just talk to Him like you would your best friend. I guess I had to go through some things in my life, that's why God allowed it to happen.

"Dr. Gills said, 'We called you Humpty Dumpty because we didn't know how we were going to put you back together again. We had to call in specialists because there were some things we couldn't do. You were a puzzle.' He said, 'All the king's horses and all the king's men couldn't put Humpty Dumpty back together again.' "

Then, pointing up to Heaven, Joe Bill said, "I said, 'Yeah, but I had a *king* that could and He's the King of kings.' The King of kings put me back together again. I gained a lot of strength and was humbled by it. You know, we're not promised a fairytale life, but we are promised that He won't forsake us."

Jake and Joe Bill sat quietly for a few moments.

"So, you really believe in all that 'God' stuff?" Jake asked.

"You bet I do!" Joe Bill said. "I'm living proof...He's real. No doubt in my mind."

Jake nodded. "Did you ever get angry at God?"

"For what?" Joe Bill asked.

"For your accident," Jake said.

"Nope. Never did," Joe Bill said.

Feeling that he had shared all he was led to share, Joe Bill stood up. "Come on...let's get you back. Nurse Velle has probably already put out an APB for us."

Jake chuckled. "You're probably right."

As they wheeled back inside the hospital, the same nurses passed them again.

"See," Joe Bill said. "There she is again."

"Shut up, Joe!" Jake said.

"I think she's stalking you, man," Joe Bill said.

"C'mon, man!" Jake said, agitated.

"I'm just saying..." Joe Bill said.

As they pushed through the steel double doors, re-entering the burn step-down unit, they were met by an unexpected visitor.

"Eric?" Jake said, surprised.

"Hey, Jake," Eric said.

The moment was awkward. Even Joe Bill could sense the situation was strange.

"How 'bout I roll you into your room so you guys can catch up," he suggested, trying to break the ice.

"That'll be good," Jake said.

Joe Bill got Jake back to his room and then he left. So now only Jake and Eric were in the room. Eric shuffled his feet for a few moments, and Jake looked at his lap, avoiding eye contact.

"Jake, I just want to say that I'm so sorry for what happened. I'm sorry for the way I acted leading up to the wreck."

"It's not your fault, Eric," Jake said. "I was the one driving the car."

"Yeah, but if I hadn't kept taunting you about racing me, it might never have happened. You know, it seemed like such a big deal at the time, but once the wreck happened, I didn't even like my car anymore. As a matter of fact, I traded it in for an older model."

Jake was dumbfounded. "Oh, yeah? What'd you get?"

"A '68 Camaro."

They laughed at the irony.

"So...we straight?" Eric asked.

"Very straight," Jake assured him.

Chapter 21

Cool things were happening. I was feeling stronger in every way. God was putting encouragers in my path almost daily. He created a friendship with Eric that I never would have expected. And those were just the things that I could see. God was working all the way around. He's the ultimate multi-tasker.

Lance and Kate Kelly pulled into the parking lot of their home church. Although Kate was ready to receive help, Lance could see she was anxious. He took her hand. "Honey, you're doing the right thing."

Attempting to smile, Kate said, "I know."

Lance got out of the car, and as he had done for over twenty years, he opened Kate's car door. As they began to walk toward the side entrance to the church offices, Lance noticed a gold Yukon sitting in a parking space. The back windshield was decorated with a row of decals representing each family member. Second from the right was a figure representing a boy with a halo. *That's Cooper*, he thought.

"The Jaspers are already here," Lance said.

"Let's hurry in," Kate said. "I hate to keep people waiting."

The Kellys entered the study where Pastor Glenn and the Jaspers were seated, chatting. Kate first noticed Melanie Jasper. She was a petite woman with auburn hair and blue eyes. She greeted Kate with a sympathetic hug.

Pastor Glenn began their meeting with prayer.

"Father, we praise You today for this meeting ordained by Your sovereign hand. Thank You for going before us. We know You love Lance and Kate more than we ever could. We praise You for what You have done in the Jaspers' lives and for the good You have done through their pain. Now, Father, we give this time to You and we ask that You direct this meeting. We know You have healing on Your mind, and we receive it in Jesus' name...Amen."

"Amen," JJ reiterated.

Pastor Glenn quickly turned the conversation over to the Jaspers.

"Kate," JJ said, "it's nice to meet you, and I'm sure you are aware that Lance and I had the privilege of talking a little while back. We want you to know that we have been praying for you continually."

"Thank you," Kate softly replied.

"My heart breaks for you, Kate," Melanie said compassionately. "I don't know exactly what you're going through because every situation is so different, but I do know loss; and I know how to pray. As I've shared before, even if someone else's five-year-old, blonde-haired, blue-eyed little boy was killed in a dune buggy accident, I still wouldn't know exactly what they were going through because family dynamics and lifestyles make things so different."

"That's very true, Melanie," Pastor Glenn said.

As the Jaspers shared what they felt would minister to the Kellys' needs the most, the room filled with an incredible peace. To Lance, it was almost tangible. The story of the Jaspers' heartache and pain bore witness with him and Kate. The way the Lord had shown JJ and Melanie how to grieve opened the Kellys' hearts to receive it.

"Statistics show that eighty-nine percent of marriages fail after the death of a child," JJ said. "We didn't want to be part of that statistic, and we don't want you to be, either."

Lance took Kate's hand and gently kissed it.

"You get up and you pray when you don't feel like it," JJ said. "You read your Bible when you don't want to. Those were lifelines for us."

Melanie nodded her head in agreement.

Suddenly, without warning, Kate erupted in tears.

"I can't stop asking God why. Why? Why? Why?" Kate cried. Then, looking at Lance, she asked, "Do you remember what I endured to get pregnant? Then the issues I had during pregnancy? We were so happy, Lance! Thankful! We thanked God every day for our Ross! And then… with each pregnancy that followed, miscarriage after miscarriage, diminishing our hope for more children of our own. Then, the final blow of my doctor recommending we not try anymore. I accepted that! I praised God for the one we were blessed with and accepted it. No anger…no bitterness. Then…He takes away our son? Our only child?"

Pastor Glenn quietly placed a box of tissues on the table in the middle of the group. Each person took two or three as they sobbed with her.

Kate confessed, "I don't understand. I'm really struggling here. I don't know how to get past it. I am so afraid my friendship with Grace is never going to be the same. I'm scared I am going to resent Jake so much that I can't love him anymore. I'm worried that I will never be able to face Mitch and genuinely smile. I know that's so wrong. I'm ashamed to even admit it, but it's the reality of where I am right now."

While difficult to hear, the group was glad to hear her release the thoughts.

Pastor Glenn spoke in response. "Kate, you have nothing to be ashamed of in what you are feeling."

"That's right, honey," Lance affirmed, pulling her close.

"Fortunately, you don't have to have all the answers to your concerns right now," the pastor said. "All you need to do right now is grieve so you can heal."

"Very well said, Pastor," JJ said.

"It feels like the pain will never go away," Kate said. "When will my grieving end?"

"Sweetie, it will take time," Melanie said. "There were times that I would think I was doing good, then I'd be ambushed again by grief. It would come in waves. Smells, accidentally setting six plates instead of five. My bones were in agony. For some time, I seemed to have only a few good minutes or hours. Calling out Cooper's name, forgetting he wasn't there."

"I find myself doing the same things," Kate said.

"Melanie, what are some things you can suggest that can give Kate some realistic expectations?" Pastor Glenn asked.

Melanie focused her attention on Kate. "Don't expect too much out of yourself the first few days and weeks. Let others come beside you and help. Dig deep in the word. Draw close to God. His word says that *In this world you will have trouble*, but then it goes on to say, *take heart, for I have overcome the world*. That's how we get to know Him. There is a purpose in every circumstance. Sometimes you may see it quickly. Other times you may not see it this side of Heaven. It's not always painless, but His plan is perfect, and you just have to hold on tight to Him and trust Him and let those around you come beside you. I'm a personal griever. I don't grieve well in public. That was so difficult for me, but I'm so thankful that I allowed friends to come alongside me."

"I just can't envision ever seeing in this lifetime a purpose in this or good coming from it," Kate said.

"Let me encourage you," Pastor Glenn said. "Are you aware that at least one of Ross's classmates has accepted Christ due to this devastation?"

"Really?" Kate asked, surprised. "Who?"

"Eric Williams," he replied.

Kate and Lance looked at each other.

"That's incredible!" Lance said.

Looking to the Jaspers, the pastor explained. "Eric Williams was the young man who was racing against Ross and Jake when the accident occurred."

Understanding the magnitude, JJ and Melanie were awestruck.

"Eric was smart enough to pull over when the police arrived," Pastor Glenn continued. "Oddly, he pulled over in the parking lot of a church called *Crossroads*."

"Isn't that something," JJ commented.

"There was another life changed because of this, too," Pastor Glenn said.

"Ross's teammate and co-captain, Marcus Riley, surrendered to preach because of the way he's been affected by it," Pastor Glenn said.

"I had no idea," Lance said.

"And those are just the ones that you know of," JJ pointed out.

"And I know there will be many more to follow," Pastor Glenn said.

"I've encouraged Kate, when she's ready, to read your book," Lance said to JJ. "It has helped me beyond belief. I'm so thankful for the Lord's sovereignty in this situation. He knew the pain that was headed our way, and He placed you in our path just ahead of it. I'm so thankful that you two had the courage to write *Losing Cooper*."

"Thank you, Lance," JJ said. "We feel like our book is God's way of allowing us to give the devil a black eye."

The others chuckled.

"I know that what the Lord has done for us, He will also do for you," JJ concluded.

After a closing prayer, hugs and final words of encouragement, the families departed.

As the Kellys drove home, Kate turned to Lance and touched his arm. "Today has been a good day."

Overjoyed by his wife's statement, he smiled. "It has, hasn't it?"

Another surgery. Another trip to the Critical Care Unit. Grace hoped this would be the last one – not only for Jake, but for herself. Waiting between visitation times had become excruciatingly tiresome. She searched the waiting room for a place to rest. An elderly lady sat in a corner alone. Grace had noticed her earlier this week but hadn't had the opportunity to introduce herself. The woman appeared weary. Compassion for her swept over Grace, and she stepped close to introduce herself.

"Hello, I'm Grace Adams."

"I know who you are," she replied bluntly and with an unusual accent.

Surprised by her statement and dialect, Grace sat in the recliner beside her. She wasn't sure how to respond.

The lady smiled at Grace. "I'm Eloise," she said.

Grace relaxed. "So, Eloise, what brings you here to this less-than-desirable vacation spot?" Grace asked, also smiling.

"Well, I didn't book it by choice. My son, Rick, is here. He was in a really bad motorcycle accident two months ago. Severe head trauma. The doctors gave me little hope, but somehow, by the grace of God, he's held on."

Grace placed her hand on Eloise's arm. "Oh, my! I'm so sorry you're having to go through this," Grace sympathized. "But it seems there may be a miracle in the works," she tried to encourage her.

"Perhaps," Eloise replied with little emotion. "He's still in a coma. It's so hard not being able to communicate with him."

"I can't imagine," Grace commented. "My son's accident was tragic beyond belief. Severe burns in a car accident led to surgery to amputate both legs; but we are extremely blessed that we have always been able to talk to each other. Where do you live?" Grace asked.

"Louisiana," Eloise said. "Baton Rouge, actually."

"That explains the accent, then," Grace said, chuckling. Cajuns had a dialect all their own.

"What accent?" Eloise asked seriously.

Grace blushed. She placed her hand over her mouth. "I didn't mean to offend..."

Eloise laughed. "I'm teasing. It's just funny to me when someone from the South tells someone else they have an accent."

Grace thought for a second, then laughed aloud. "You're right!" She thought about how far away Baton Rouge was. "So you're hours away from home," Grace said. "I feel even more blessed because our home is only about an hour and a half away."

Eloise nodded in agreement. They sat quietly for a while. Eloise lay back in her recliner with a thin hospital blanket over her lap. Grace sat and breathed prayers of thankfulness for the blessings that were revealed to her in the last few moments.

"I've been watching you," Eloise said, staring at the ceiling.

Another awkward statement to which Grace was unsure how to respond. "What do you mean?" she asked reluctantly.

"I've just been watching you," Eloise repeated. "I remember the day your family got here. All those people followed you up here… praying, singing…then they loved on others, too. Me included."

She looked at Grace with a look of complete sincerity. "Mrs. Adams, it's been a blessing watching you minister to others who are hurting. I mean, we have people from area churches and minis-ters come by and say kind words, or bring a nice supper, but you are reaching out to others in the midst of your own pain. That's really something."

Grace was speechless. She wasn't sure how to respond to such sweet words about herself. "I appreciate that. We are very blessed with a church family who truly practices being the hands and feet of Jesus. And let me just tell you, friend, if you see anything good in me at all, it is surely the Lord working through me. I am nothing without Him."

Eloise smiled. "Your humility is quite refreshing. I understand what you are saying, but it still takes a willing vessel."

"You are very kind, Eloise," Grace said. "Could I get you any-thing? You live so far away. You must have needs. That's not a quick road trip."

"I thank you, but I have everything I need," Eloise assured her.

Grace took Eloise's hand, smiled at her and said, "Well, if you think of anything, please, don't hesitate to ask."

"If I do, you will be the first to know," Eloise replied.

Eloise returned her gaze to the ceiling, but Grace still watched her. She saw exhaustion in Eloise's face. The rigor of managing life from a recliner, a small suitcase and a public restroom for that extended period of time, combined with her age, had obviously taken a toll on Eloise's body. Grace arranged the woman's pillow and covers to save Eloise the effort. Eloise patted Grace's hand.

"Thank you, dear," Eloise said. "You really are an angel here."

Days passed. Grace and Mitch were once again allowed to stay in Jake's room with him. Autumn continued pushing summer aside, and the temperatures dropped. Rain made the days gloomy. Late after-noon appeared to be night as the storm clouds cast darkness throughout the sky. Opening the curtains did little to help. The weather made Jake's pain worse.

This particular rainy day was special: it was Jake's nineteenth birthday. Grace, Nurse Velle and Joe Bill had planned a surprise celebration.

Filled with boredom, Jake continually flipped channels with the television remote.

"Nothing to watch. Nothing to do," Jake mumbled.

In an effort to keep Jake from suspecting anything, Grace patronized his self-pity. "Son, I'm sorry your birthday is such a bummer this year."

There was a light rap on the door.

"Come in," Jake said unenthusiastically.

"It's just me," Mitch said. He had taken off work early to spend some time with Jake on his birthday. In one hand he carried a gift bag, and in the other, Jake's favorite frozen drink from a local coffee shop.

"Yeah, baby," Jake said, eyeing the cup's logo.

"He needed something to perk him up," Grace said. Although she tried to talk normally, Grace was a bundle of nerves, excited for the upcoming surprise.

Mitch handed Jake the gift bag.

"What's this?" Jake asked.

"Why don't you look and see?" his father said.

Jake haphazardly pulled multiple layers of tissue paper out of the bag and threw them on the floor, digging to get to what was inside. Grace picked up the paper from the floor, shaking her head, wondering how much longer she would have to pick up after her son.

Jake pulled from the bag a crimson-red Alabama hoodie. "Sweet!" he exclaimed.

"I figured you could use a new one for football season," Mitch said.

"Can't have too many of those," Jake said.

"I bet you can," Grace joked. "That's sweet, honey. You did good." She kissed Mitch on the forehead.

"Get a room," Jake said, pulling the hoodie on over his gown. "Well? How do I look?"

"Like a hospital patient in an Alabama hoodie," Mitch said.

"Good. That's the look I was going for," Jake replied.

Another knock at the door...Grace knew this had to be the knock she was waiting for.

The door opened. It was Nurse Velle and Joe Bill, carrying a cake and a brightly wrapped gift.

"Happy birthday, baby," Velle said, setting the cake on Jake's lap.

"Thank you, sugar," Jake replied, winking at Joe Bill.

"Look at you in yo Alabama hoodie!" Nurse Velle said.

"You like that, huh?" Jake said.

"Sho do!" Nurse Velle replied.

"Happy birthday, Jake," Joe Bill said, handing him his gift.

"Thanks, Joe," Jake said. "Y'all didn't have to do this."

"You're right – we didn't," Joe Bill said. "So that should tell you how special you are to us."

"Oh, Joe Bill, y'all are special to us, too," Grace said.

Nurse Velle clapped her hands together and said, "Now, fah my gift..."

The door opened. In walked a man completely hidden by a huge bouquet of crimson-red, gray, black and white latex balloons, along with three football-shaped foil ones. Nurse Velle took the balloons from the man to reveal his identity.

Jake's eyes grew wide as saucers. Mitch and Grace couldn't believe who was standing in their room.

"What?" Jake cried. "The head football coach of my Alabama Crimson Tide?"

"In the flesh," Nick Saban replied.

"No way!" Mitch shouted as he walked over to shake the coach's hand.

"It's very nice to meet you," Mitch said.

"Nice to meet you, too," Coach Saban replied.

Walking toward Jake, he held out a large bag. Jake reached inside and pulled out a shadowboxed University of Alabama football helmet with a red number 15 on the side.

"Oh, snap!" Jake said loudly. "Look at all the names!"

"It's signed by every player of this year's team and each member of the coaching staff," Coach said.

"Awesome!" Jake exclaimed.

"So, how you like my gift, baby?" Nurse Velle asked.

"What do you think?" Jake asked.

"Nurse Velle, how in the world did you pull this off?" Mitch asked.

"Hey, I tol' you this Bama gal knows some peoples," Nurse Velle said. "I gots me some connections."

"Nurse Velle and I go way back," Coach said.

"Yep. Waaaaay back," she added. "I tol' you we's tight."

"How is that?" Mitch asked.

"I was at the hospital in Tuscaloosa before coming here," Nurse Velle said. "I took care of some of those babies that played for the Tide."

Joe Bill couldn't pass that up. "Babies...you said it. I didn't."

"Watch it, you ole Land Bear. Don't you even get me started."

"It's not Land Bear, Velle – it's Black Sharks," Joe Bill said.

Nick Saban looked at the two of them, confused.

Velle cupped her hands around her mouth and whispered, "He pull fah Ole Miss."

"Oh, gotcha," Coach Saban said, winking.

"We prayin' fah him," Velle said.

While the football coach visited with the Adamses, someone else knocked at the door.

336

"Can't wait to see who this is and what they're bringing me," Jake said jokingly.

"Well, whoever it is, it can't top this guy," Mitch said, opening the door.

Suddenly, Mitch's smile fell.

"Hey, uh...come in," Mitch said awkwardly.

Lance Kelly entered the room. Jake and Grace were stunned. Mitch slowly returned to Grace. Grace placed her hands over her mouth in quiet disbelief and shock, then on her chest.

"Oh, my goodness, Lance," Grace said, walking to him and giving him a hug.

"Mr. Kelly," Jake called out with shallow breaths.

Nurse Velle, Joe Bill and the birthday guest could tell the moment was awkward but didn't understand why. Joe Bill looked at Jake. Jake looked at him and mouthed the words *Ross's dad*.

Grace pulled Lance closer to Jake and introduced him to Velle and Joe Bill.

"And finally, this is—"

"Heavens!" Lance said. "Roll Tide!"

"Roll Tide," Coach Saban said, shaking Lance's hand.

"I guess I should have known you would recognize him," Grace said.

"Yeah," Lance said. "I sort of see him every Saturday."

Everyone laughed.

Lance stepped close to Jake's bed. "Hey, son. How you doing?"

"OK, I guess," Jake replied.

"This is such a wonderful surprise, Lance," Grace said. "I just can't believe you're here."

"Well, I haven't missed a birthday party for Jake in twelve years. I guess I didn't want to break tradition, right, Mitch?" Lance said.

"Right," Mitch half-heartedly replied.

"I got you a gift, but I'm just gonna go ahead and tell ya…whoever got you that hoodie has great taste, cause that's the same thing in this gift bag."

Everyone laughed again. Mitch continued to sit quietly and remained evasive. Not fully understanding the situation, Coach Saban said, "You guys must share a brain."

Trying to save face, Mitch replied, "Yeah, looks like it."

Feeling the tension, Joe Bill decided to add some comic relief. "So, Coach, what happened to your team last Saturday?" he said, winking and inconspicuously pointing to Nurse Velle.

The keen coach picked up on Joe Bill's intentions right away. He decided to join in the fun. "Joe Bill, I don't know. Those Rebels really got the best of us."

Appalled, Nurse Velle placed her hands on her hips and yelled out, "What! Coach, are you kiddin' me? You gon' dis my Tide with a statement like that?"

Unfamiliar with Nurse Velle's personality, Lance looked at Grace and Jake for explanation, but the looks on their faces told it all. Joe Bill's stunt worked well. The conversation quickly turned to last Saturday's game, getting Mitch and Lance engaged in a conversation that was normal and comfortable for them.

"Settle down, Velle, before your dreadlocks uncurl," Joe Bill kidded.

Finally, Nurse Velle had had all she could take.

"That is it! Oh, you done did it now, Joe Bill Anton!" Pointing toward the nurses' station, Nurse Velle ordered, "You get yo Rebel self back out there and get to work! The party is over fah you!"

"Yes'm," Joe Bill said. "But it was worth it."

As Joe Bill turned to leave, he looked at Jake and winked. Seeing through Joe Bill's little stunt made Jake smile. He winked back.

"Well, folks, I gotta head out," Coach Saban said. "But listen, it's so good to meet all of you, and Jake, son, I wish you all the best," he said as he shook his hand farewell. "I'll be keeping up with you through Velle, OK?"

"Thank you so much for coming, Coach," Jake said. "This was really cool."

"Hey, it was my privilege. By the way – I do expect to see you on our campus in the near future."

"Plan on it," Jake replied.

"Mr. Saban, this was really special," Grace said. "You were so kind to drive all this way."

"It really was," Mitch agreed.

"I was glad to do it," Coach Saban said. "And please – call me Nick."

"Coach, it was an honor," Lance said.

"I'll show you out, baby," Nurse Velle said.

Once Nurse Velle and Coach left the room, the tension returned. Lance and the Adamses remained silent. No one knew exactly what to say.

"Well, I guess I'll be going, too," Lance said. "Jake, happy birthday, son."

"Thank you, Mr. Kelly," Jake said. "I really appreciate you coming."

"Mitch, it's good to see you," Lance said, offering him a handshake.

Slowly, Mitch returned the shake. "You, too, man. Thanks for stopping by."

Grace's heart broke watching the two old friends struggle to have a conversation. "I'll walk you out," Grace said.

"Grace, you don't have to do that," Lance assured her.

"I know, but I want to."

Once they were in the main area of the hospital, Grace stopped.

"Lance, I'm sorry. I don't know what to say."

"No, it was probably a bad idea for me to come unannounced."

"No, Lance. We have to start somewhere. This was a good place," Grace said. "How's Kate?"

"She's actually doing a little better," Lance said.

"I'm so glad," Grace said. "Pastor Glenn had shared with me about your meeting with the Jaspers. I've been praying for you both."

"I know," Lance said. "We met with them last week, actually, and I believe that is totally the reason for the change I'm seeing in her."

"I really miss her, Lance," Grace said. "I've texted her several times, just to let her know I love her and that I'm praying for her."

"She loves you, too, Grace. Just give her some time. She's coming around."

"I'm trusting the Lord that she will," Grace said. "Please give her a hug for me."

"I sure will," Lance said.

As Lance walked away, Grace took a deep breath. As difficult as it was seeing him for the first time, and as awkward as it was trying to have a conversation, she felt in her heart that tonight was a huge step in the right direction...and she thanked God for it.

Lance returned home to find Kate curled up on the couch with a book in front of her face. He was elated when he saw the book was *Losing Cooper*. Leaning over the back of the couch to give her a kiss, he looked at the page she was reading. "How far have you gotten?"

"I just finished Melanie's chapter," she said. She bookmarked her stopping point and set the book on the table. "So, how did it go?"

Lance joined her on the couch. "It was OK. Very awkward at first, but I think it will prove productive. Hey, I got to meet the Alabama football coach while I was there."

"Alabama? As in Crimson Tide?" Kate asked in disbelief.

"Yep!" Lance replied. "Nick Saban himself."

"Where?" Kate asked.

"Jake's hospital room. Apparently, the charge nurse – who is quite a character, by the way – is a buddy of Nick Saban's."

"What are the chances?" Kate said.

"Kate...Grace really misses you."

Kate began to tear up. "I miss her, too, Lance. Terribly."

She laid her head on Lance's shoulder and began to weep. "I feel so bad that I didn't go with you. I haven't missed a birthday with that boy since he was five years old."

"Shhh..." Lance whispered, calming her. "You know, it's not too late. You could call."

Kate thought for a moment. "You're right. It's not."

Lance pulled his phone from his pants pocket. "Go for it."

Kate sat up and wiped the tears from her face. She took the phone and tapped on Grace's number. Her hands shook.

Grace's phone came to life, lighting up the dim hospital room. Who in the world would be calling her this late? Her phone indicated it was Lance.

Expecting to hear his voice, Grace answered, "Hey, brother, did you forget something?"

It had been weeks since Kate had heard her friend's voice. Hearing it now brought her to tears.

Grace recognized her best friend's cries. "Kate? Is that you?"

"Yes, Grace. It's me."

Grace couldn't believe her ears. "Kate! It's so good to hear your voice!"

Jake and Mitch sat up quickly and listened.

For several minutes there was no talking, only sobs between best friends.

Finally, Kate said, "I wanted to wish Jake a happy birthday."

"Of course!" Grace said. "Hang on." She handed the phone to Jake, who was unsure of what was happening.

"Kate wants to talk to you, son."

Slowly, Jake put the phone to his ear. "Hello?"

"Happy birthday, sweet boy," Kate said, using the same phrase she used every year on his birthday.

Jake began to cry. "Thank you, Mrs. Kate."

"Jake, I'm so sorry I didn't come to see you today. Will you please forgive me?"

Jake thought that was a crazy question.

"I understand. There's no need to apologize."

"I won't miss next year, I promise," Kate said.

"OK," he said.

"I love you, Jake," Kate said sincerely.

"I love you, too, Mrs. Kate," Jake said. "You want to talk to my mom again?"

"Yes, absolutely," Kate replied.

Jake handed the phone back to Grace. She took it and stepped outside the room to talk. "I miss you so much, Kate."

"I know. Me, too," Kate said.

"I've texted you so many times," Grace said, wanting to make sure she knew.

"I know," Kate cried. "I'm sorry I never responded. I've just been struggling so badly."

"I know," Grace sympathized. "I pray for you every day."

"Thank you," Kate said. "I feel it."

The conversation quieted, except for the sound of gentle sobs.

Finally, Kate said, "Well, I guess I'll let you go. I just wanted to tell Jake happy birthday and say hello."

"OK. I love you, my sweet friend," Grace cried.

"I love you, too, Gracie. Good night," Kate said.

As the days passed, they seemed to grow longer. The sorrowful reality of everything that had taken place settled deep into Jake's mind; so did depression. Seeing Mr. Kelly had been very painful for Jake. Guilt ate at him like a monster every other minute. He grew quiet, withdrawn, and his sense of humor disappeared.

Joe Bill prayed, asking how he could help give his buddy a spiritual lift. He sought the Lord for guidance in helping this young man, who he believed was appointed to him by God. As Joe Bill prayed, the Lord brought to his remembrance his own deep depression while still in the hospital. Suddenly, a name came to mind. There had been a nurse who had cared for him and was the inspiration for his desire to become a nurse. She had shown him a YouTube video of a man born into adversity but who had overcome incredible obstacles to live an almost completely normal life. *That's it!* Joe Bill thought. He walked to Nurse Velle's office and knocked on her door.

"What you want now?" Nurse Velle asked with irritation in her voice.

Catching her short tone, Joe Bill cracked open the door and peeked in, flashing his white teeth with his bright baby blues. Nurse Velle looked up to see her favorite employee.

"Hey, baby. What you need?"

"I was making sure I wasn't going to get something thrown at me before I came in," Joe Bill said.

"Oh, never mind me. I thought you was gon' be somebody else that's been gettin' under my skin all day," Nurse Velle explained. "You safe, baby."

"OK, cool," Joe Bill said as he walked into the tiny office. "You got your laptop here by chance?" he asked.

"Yeah, right here," Nurse Velle said, reaching behind her.

"Awesome," Joe Bill said.

"So, what you gon' do with it?" Nurse Velle asked as she handed it to him.

"Well, I've been worried about Jake," Joe Bill said.

"I noticed he different lately," Nurse Velle said.

"It's got depression written all over it," Joe Bill said. "I've been praying about what to do to help him."

"And you got an answer?" Nurse Velle asked.

"Yeah. That's why I need your laptop. I want to show him a video that my nurse showed me," Joe Bill said. "It helped me so much. I think it'll help Jake, too. I just hope I can find it."

"You just the sweetest thing on planet earth, Joe Bill."

Joe Bill grinned. "Spread that around," he said.

She laughed. "Oh, no I ain't," she said. "You my best kept secret."

Joe Bill started typing. Curious, Nurse Velle looked over his shoulder to see what had inspired him so much. Several videos appeared.

"Oh, wow," Joe Bill said. "I didn't expect there to be so many to choose from."

"He must be pretty popular," Velle said.

"It's been quite a while since I've looked at it, but I think I'll recognize it when I see it," Joe Bill said.

He scrolled down several search results.

"And there it is," Joe Bill said excitedly.

"Well, that didn't take long, did it?" Nurse Velle said.

"I didn't expect it to," Joe Bill said confidently. "I knew the Lord had reminded me of it."

Joe Bill hit play to watch a couple of minutes of it to confirm it was the right one. While doing so, he explained to Velle what the video was about. She was dumbfounded.

Joe Bill stopped the video and closed the laptop.

"OK, I'm going in now while it's slow and there aren't any visitors," Joe Bill said.

As Joe Bill stood to leave, Nurse Velle stopped him.

"Hey, you let me know how it goes, OK? An' I be prayin'."

Joe Bill tapped lightly on Jake's door and listened for a response.

"Come in," Jake said.

Joe Bill entered Jake's room. It was dark except for light from the muted television. Jake stared at the TV screen.

"You trying to read their lips?" he asked Jake.

"No, just not interested, I guess," Jake said.

Noticing the laptop, he asked, "What's up with that?"

"I want to show you something." He sat on the bed beside Jake and placed the laptop in front of him.

"I want you to listen to me, all right?"

"K," Jake replied.

Joe Bill continued. "Jake, you know my story. You know I empathize with you in what you're going through."

"Right," Jake said.

"I know you're struggling. I know what depression looks like... and feels like."

Jake looked down, ashamed that Joe Bill had recognized it.

"Don't be embarrassed," Joe Bill said. "It's not unusual at all for depression to set in after a traumatic accident like you've experienced. I went through the same thing while I was in the hospital."

"Really?" Jake asked.

"Yup. One day my nurse noticed, just like I've noticed with you. She showed me a video of someone, and it helped me begin to pull out of it. I want you to see it. Will you watch it?"

"I guess," Jake said. "It's not like I have anything else to do."

Joe Bill started playing the video. Jake watched in amazement at the man's unique story. Born with no legs and only part of an arm,

Clay Dyer became a professional fisherman and an assistant football coach at a high school in Arkansas. Jake sat mesmerized at his ability to text on his phone by using his mouth and to cast a fishing rod with his partial arm and chin. Jake didn't move a muscle while the man shared how he questioned God once around age five. He asked his dad, "Why would God make me this way?" His dad responded by saying, "I don't know, son, but what I do know is that God doesn't make mistakes." He realized that God created him that way *on* purpose, with *great* purpose.

Clay explained about his salvation experience, acknowledging it was his best decision in life.

Jake couldn't believe his accomplishments. "He has fewer body parts than I do," Jake said.

"Yup," Joe Bill replied. "Makes you count your blessings, huh?"

"Yeah, it does," Jake said.

After the video ended, Jake thanked his friend. "That was really inspirational."

"I thought so, too, when my nurse showed it to me," Joe Bill said.

"Copycat," Jake kidded.

"No need to reinvent the wheel, right?" Joe Bill said.

"Nope, not when it works," Jake said.

There was a knock on the door.

"You expecting someone?" Joe Bill asked.

"No. You?"

"Wise guy," Joe Bill said as he opened the door. "Come on in, sir," Joe Bill said.

Jake wasn't sure if he was seeing correctly.

"Daniels?" Jake asked. Other than Lance, Galen Daniels was probably the last person Jake expected to come visit him.

"Hello, Jake," the sheriff's deputy said timidly. "I hope it's OK... me just dropping in like this."

"Yeah, of course," Jake said.

"How you feelin'?" he asked, walking over to Jake's bedside.

Joe Bill quietly left the two to visit.

"I didn't expect to see you here," Jake said, fighting the feeling of awkwardness. "So, how are all the guys down at the department?"

"They're good. Same ol' guys," Daniels said. "We've all been praying for you."

"Thank you," Jake replied. "I can feel 'em."

Daniels' brows furrowed. Jake's demeanor was different... pleasantly different. While Daniels was enjoying it, it was a little uncomfortable.

The two struggled to make small talk.

"I'm sorry you haven't seen me before now, Jake," Daniels apologized.

"Trust me, your timing in coming is perfect," Jake said.

"Why's that?" Daniels asked.

"Because, Daniels, I owe you a huge thank-you and a huge apology, but had you come sooner, you probably wouldn't have gotten them."

Daniels was shocked.

Jake's voice quivered. "Daniels, I can't thank you enough for saving my life, especially after I treated you so terribly all these years."

"It's OK, Jake," Daniels said.

"No, it's not OK," Jake replied. "For years, you tried to speak good things into my life, but I only responded by mocking you and making fun of you. I was so disrespectful. Can you ever forgive me?"

Jake's admission of guilt and unsolicited apology caught Daniels off guard. Regardless, Daniels's forgiveness flowed freely.

"You bet," Daniels replied, offering a fist bump.

Jake smiled inside. Another relationship had been redeemed.

Chapter 22

The day had finally arrived. It was a shocker. Dr. King, in his dry humor, works like that. Regardless, I was ecstatic! So many mixed emotions. I had no idea what to expect. I was just glad to be moving on to the next phase. I follow that by saying my hospital stay couldn't have been better. I was leaving behind family. And I knew beyond the shadow of a doubt…it wouldn't be the last time I would see them. You don't walk away from relationships like the ones formed here. Anxiety would creep in, as would fear, but I knew I had to face them all.

"One…two…three…" Jake counted through grunts and heavy breathing as he worked out, using a rubber band system to do bicep curls. Dr. King's entrance didn't hinder him whatsoever.

"I'm about sick of all this exercise!" Dr. King exclaimed. "You're making me feel guilty!"

Jake chuckled at his doctor's comment, making him lose count.

"I have a ten-pound band with your name on it," Jake informed him.

"You're a real joker," Dr. King said, grinning ear to ear.

Jake took notice. "What?" he asked. "Why are you smiling?"

Dr. King sat on the end of Jake's bed. Jake's workout slowed as he watched the doctor's demeanor change.

"I have good news and I have bad news," Dr. King said.

"I'm used to it," Jake said.

Dr. King nodded. "I guess you are. Good news...your dad is on his way to pick you up."

Jake leaned forward in his chair. "Don't mess with me," Jake warned.

"You're going home," Dr. King said with a big smile.

Jake looked to the ceiling and raised his fists into the air. "Thank you!"

"Bad news," Dr. King continued. "You can't have my wheelchair." He grinned. "BUT we got you something a little sleeker."

The door to Jake's room swung open. Through the doorway, Joe Bill rolled in a new athletic wheelchair.

Elated, Jake commented, "Not bad! Not bad at all!" He was amazed, looking the wheelchair over top to bottom.

"Jake," Dr. King said.

"Sir?"

"Get out of my chair."

"Gladly!"

Joe Bill helped the frail young man into his new ride. He wiggled around, adjusting himself in the seat. Looking up at Dr. King, Jake smiled. "Thanks, Doc."

"You're very welcome, son," Dr. King said.

Jake immediately began locating all the settings on the wheelchair and made adjustments to suit him.

"It's fast," Dr. King warned. "Don't flip it." Jake stopped and looked at his doctor, who had become a friend, and extended his hand. Dr. King smiled as he shook it. He turned to exit the room, but stopped. After a brief pause, he looked at Jake seriously.

"You were given a second chance, son. Make the most of it." He exited the room.

Jake sat quietly as the strong words echoed in his mind. He looked around his gift-littered room – cards, many of which were hand-made by elementary students from his school and church, flowers with wilting blooms, balloons mostly deflated, half-empty gift baskets once filled with snacks and crossword puzzles. Finally, he eyed the huge banner above the big double window where Joe Bill drew the curtain every morning. The vibrant letters spelled out the message *Get Well Soon*, surrounded by signatures of his fellow students from Lee County Academy. All of these gifts reminded him he was about to return to his hometown, where he was loved and missed. The thought comforted him.

He wheeled himself out to the nurses' station to tell the staff good-bye. Each one had taken such good care of him during the long stay. The hugs and well wishes were interrupted by a familiar voice.

"Well, I haven't seen Jake show this much affection since he was about five years old!"

Jake turned around to find his dad.

"I haven't seen *that* in a while either!" Jake commented.

"What's that, son?" Mitch asked.

"A smile," Jake replied.

"It's hard not to smile on a day like today. I get to take my boy home!"

"Well, get him outta here quick!" Nurse Velle shouted. "He ain't been nothin' but trouble since he got here!"

"Agreed!" Joe Bill said, smiling.

"Seriously?" Jake retorted. "Now, Nurse Velle, I thought we were tight! Every Saturday we watched our Tide play together," Jake said.

"I know dis," Nurse Velle said. "I jus' messin' with you," she said, hugging him. "Roll Tide, baby."

"Roll Tide, sugar," Jake replied with a wink.

Jake turned to Joe Bill. "And you, you redneck Rebel lover. Who was it that slipped in my room after his shift late at night and brought me milkshakes, huh?" Jake asked.

"Guilty as charged," Joe Bill said. "But hey, at least it was my treat."

"Yeah, I believe they call that a bribe?" Jake asked. "After all our talks, I could really do your manly reputation some damage, Mr. Nice Guy. You were just trying to keep me quiet."

"You're right," Joe Bill said, giving Jake a fist bump. "I've got an image to protect."

As the chuckles died down, Jake grew serious.

"You two have been the highlight of my stay here," Jake said. "Thank y'all. I don't know how I would have gotten through this without you both." Tears welled in his eyes. "You've been good friends."

Nurse Velle was caught off guard by Jake's emotion. Although she didn't fit the normal description of a charge nurse, this sassy Alabama woman was a very tender-hearted gal. Over the years, Velle had said good-bye to many patients who had become special to her, but this one was extremely difficult. Bending down to Jake's level, she offered a hug. "You gon' be OK, baby."

Joe Bill stepped up from behind her.

Locking hands, Jake said, "I appreciate you, man."

Joe Bill looked at him with his pure blue eyes and said, "It's been my privilege. In spite of everything that has happened, Jake, you still have a very bright future ahead of you. All that you have experienced these past few weeks doesn't change God's plan for you a bit. In fact, it will only funnel into those plans. You understand what I'm saying to you, boy?"

The tears in Jake's eyes began to roll down his face as he nodded in agreement. Everyone watching was moved and stood speechless.

"Now…get outta here, ya pest!" Joe Bill ordered, quickly shifting the mood. Everyone's tears and sniffles turned into laughter.

For the first time in a long time, the staff saw joy in the Adamses' faces. A milestone had been reached.

A band of staff members from the burn step-down unit followed Jake and Mitch to their truck. Joe Bill helped Mitch load Jake's luggage and belongings while Jake gave final hugs and snapped selfies with his cell phone.

The ride home was peaceful, the excitement almost tangible. Going home seemed surreal.

"So, why didn't Mom come with you?" Jake asked.

"She wanted to make sure everything at home was perfect for you," Mitch said. He played it down, not wanting to give away the surprise homecoming celebration that awaited Jake. While Jake and Mitch drove home, Grace and several friends worked diligently to get everything in place for Jake's party. Although she had paid close attention to every detail, her anxiety kept breaking her concentration. She had delegated responsibilities to several ladies who had come early to help. Stopping for a moment to think through everything left to do, she looked around the kitchen and observed her faithful friends working together with joy and enthusiasm. It overwhelmed her. She called for their attention and gathered them together.

"I can't thank you ladies enough for being here to help. I'm so excited, I can hardly stand it!"

"Well, Lauren and I are glad to be here to help...and celebrate. Aren't we, Lauren?" Margaret said, placing an arm around her less-than-excited daughter, giving her the opportunity to say the right thing.

Forcing a positive response, Lauren said, "Yeah, sure."

Her response wasn't very believable. Fortunately, no one caught on to the sarcasm in her voice, except for Margaret.

An odd knock at the kitchen door got Grace's attention. She opened it to find Kate with her hands full of paper goods for the party.

"You made it!" Grace cheered.

"Of course I did," Kate said, searching for a spot to set down the bags. "I wouldn't miss this for the world. When Margaret called and asked me to help, you know I immediately offered to bring paper goods. I'm a terrible cook!"

"No, you are not," Grace said.

Kate continued to ramble, nervously explaining why she was late and something about not being able to find plastic spoons anywhere in town. She suddenly noticed Grace laughing.

"What's so funny?" she asked.

"You are!" Grace answered as she continued to laugh. "Oh, I've missed you!" she exclaimed.

Kate's personality had returned. Grace feared her friend's wit was lost and their friendship strained forever because of the tragedy.

"Oh, I see. You aren't laughing *at* me, you are laughing *with* me, right?"

"Ri-i-ight!" Grace sarcastically agreed. "Just set the bags on the counter and we'll figure it out."

Things had come together very nicely in a short amount of time. Friends and family members arrived in masses, it seemed, with food and decorations ready to quickly set up. The excitement increased when they hung a "Welcome Home" banner on the front lawn. People from school, church and their neighborhood began to line both sides of the street leading to the Adamses' driveway, holding homemade signs of support.

Everything was falling into place, and Grace felt relief. What seemed to be a daunting task earlier had not been too difficult after all. She took one more look around the kitchen, double-checking everything, and breathed a sigh of relief.

"We pulled it off," said a voice from behind her. Grace turned around to see Kate, along with the other ladies who had been instrumental in setting up for the big celebration.

"Yes, we did," Grace confirmed. "I'm so blessed to have such sweet friends." She was overcome with emotion.

"We are blessed to have you, Grace," Margaret said, returning the compliment.

Grace's phone alerted her to a text message. It was the text from Mitch she had been waiting for. *We are 10 minutes from home!*

"Everyone, take your places!" Grace said excitedly. "They're only ten minutes away!" Her nervousness returned. *Just breathe,* she reminded herself.

"You're a wreck!" Kate said, taking Grace's hands, trying to calm her. "Everything is turning out fine. We'll make sure everyone is in place."

The sea of people lining the street extended almost the entire block. A minute later, the Adams men in their black Ford F-250 turned onto Orchid Circle.

Mitch and Jake had been talking about college football's SEC West standings. They were suddenly silenced by the muffled sound of cheers. People were everywhere.

"What is going *on*?" Jake asked. His eyes were wide with excitement.

"They're all here to welcome you home, son."

"Oh my gosh! Do I know this many people?"

Mitch was shocked by the number of supporters. "This *is* amazing!" he said under his breath, scanning the faces just inches away from his window.

"This is insane!" Jake added.

"Wow, I can't believe how many people showed up for this!" Mitch admitted.

"Hey...I'm a popular guy," Jake joked.

"Infamous is more like it," Mitch said.

Jake continued to look around in amazement. "Unbelievable. Just unbelievable. Hey, there's my boys!" he shouted, seeing his teammates in the crowd. As Mitch drove past the players dressed in their blue game-day jerseys, they rushed toward Jake's side of the truck and climbed on the sides and hood, escorting it down the street through the crowd of people who waved their signs, cheering and whistling.

"Welcome home, bro!" Marcus said with excitement. Jake rolled down his window.

"Hey, man! What are y'all doing?" Jake asked in disbelief.

"What does it look like we're doing? We havin' a par-tay, bro!" The football team began to chant, "Jake, Jake, Jake," motioning for the rest of the crowd to join them. Mitch drove into the driveway, and the crowd tightened. He exited the truck with difficulty, pushing his way through the mass of people to the back of the truck.

"Hey, Mitch," Lance said, waiting for him by the tailgate. "If it's OK with you, I'd be honored to unload Jake for you. Please?"

"That would be fantastic." Mitch was filled with emotion and lowered the gate. Lance pulled the wheelchair out of the truck and forced a path through the crowd. He opened the passenger side door and stood face-to-face with Jake.

"Mr. Kelly!" Jake said, surprised.

"Welcome home, Jake," Lance replied warmly.

"Thank you, sir," Jake said.

Lance helped Jake settle into his wheelchair, then motioned for the crowd to make a path to the front door. As soon as Jake became visible, they erupted again in cheers. Mitch and Grace walked on either side of their son. Well-wishers reached in to give Jake high fives and called out words of encouragement. When they reached the front door, Mitch motioned for them to quiet down.

"On behalf of Grace, Jake and myself," Mitch began, "we want to thank you for everything you have done for us. There are no words to adequately express our gratitude. We are blown away. I hope if the time ever arises, we will be the kind of friends to all of you that you have been to us. Thank you."

Although Mitch's speech sounded somewhat rehearsed to her, Grace was thrilled he was willing to get out of his comfort zone and say a few words.

It was her time to speak to the crowd. "Now, there's a lot of food inside, and I know Jake wants to visit with all of you, so let's go celebrate!"

The crowd cheered and slowly made their way into the house. While Jake wheeled himself inside, he panned the room and sighed deeply. Grace noticed.

"Are you OK?" she asked.

"I'm fine, Mom. Just taking it all in." Jake hesitated. "Morgan wouldn't happen to be here, would she?"

"No, son," Grace said sympathetically. "Not that I've seen. I'm sorry."

"It's no biggie."

Grace hugged him from behind and kissed him on the head. Then, pointing to her left, she said, "There's your receiving line."

A big smile spread across his face. He scanned their faces. Toward the end of the line, his eyes fixed on one in particular. It was Kate Kelly. For all these years, Kate had not only been Jake's best friend's mom – she was Jake's second mother. His heart pounded. Although he had talked to her on the phone, he hadn't seen her since before the accident, and Jake was worried about how she might feel toward him. With his eyes fixed on Kate, Jake wheeled past the others in the receiving line.

He stopped and faced her. Kate stooped to his eye level. Tears streamed down Jake's face. The houseful of people quieted.

"Mrs. Kelly, I don't know what to say. I'm so sorry for..."

Kate placed a finger over Jake's lips. Tears began to stream down her face as well.

"Shhh..." she gently quieted him. "We love you very much. Nothing will ever change that."

"I love you, too," Jake said.

"Welcome home, Jake."

As they embraced, Jake finally let go and released all the emotions he had been holding inside. Everyone remained quiet, captivated by the tender moment. Grace wasn't sure how to respond and stood back. Others in the room gathered around them, extended their hands to one another and formed a circle. Mitch stood in the background and observed the amazing occasion. It was too much for him to take. He quietly slipped out the front door to be alone.

Standing on the now-quiet porch, he turned toward a noise in the driveway to see Lance pulling the garbage canister to the street. Mitch was perplexed. He couldn't comprehend the Kellys taking such vital roles in the celebration. Lance wanted to be the first to welcome Jake home. Kate offered Jake sweet words of kindness and love. And now, Lance served him by taking out the trash. Mitch walked to the curb where Lance was stuffing bags of garbage into the waste container for pickup.

"Hey, man," Mitch said.

"Oh, hey, Mitch. What's up?" Lance replied.

"You tell me."

Confused, Lance asked, "What are you talking about?"

"I mean, how do you do it?" Mitch asked.

"Do what?" Lance asked, still puzzled.

"After what my son did to your son, you and Kate are still here. Helping, supporting and caring for us. I don't get it."

Lance stood silent for a moment, then turned to Mitch. "I'm going to be honest with you. It's been very, very hard losing Ross. I can't even begin to put it into words. It's cruel and unusual punishment for us. And I'd be lying if I told you I haven't been tempted to play the 'blame game.' But Mitch, we don't blame Jake for Ross's death. Ross made the choice to get in the car that night. I've asked myself, if Ross had been driving and Jake had died, how would I want you to feel toward me? God says if I show mercy, I'll be shown mercy. Even bigger than that, if I want God's forgiveness, I must forgive others."

"That's admirable, Lance, but it still seems impossible," Mitch said.

"God's word says that with Him, all things are possible," Lance said. "Mitch, God – in His great sovereignty – went before me and began to prepare me for what I was about to face, as a Father."

"What do you mean?" Mitch asked.

"Do you remember that Brotherhood Breakfast I invited you to a few months back?" Lance asked.

"Yeah, vaguely," Mitch replied.

"Well, that morning was a divine appointment for me," Lance said.

"Wait. Divine appointment? What's that?" Mitch asked.

"It's a God moment, Mitch," Lance explained. "A time that God Himself sets up for one of His children."

Mitch still didn't grasp what his friend was saying.

"JJ Jasper was our speaker that morning," Lance continued. "Guess what he spoke about."

"Oh, I couldn't," Mitch said.

"He shared his testimony about losing his only son, Cooper, and how God moved in their grieving process," Lance said.

"Wow," Mitch said.

"I bought his book that day. I had planned on reading it but never could seem to get to it. One day, after Ross died, I was really struggling. Out of desperation, I cried out to God. I yelled at Him, actually. I felt so helpless and alone. Kate was a mess. I felt like I was failing as a husband because I couldn't help her. I couldn't even help myself. The Lord reminded me of the Jaspers' book, *Losing Cooper*. I also remembered something JJ had said at Brotherhood that morning."

Entrenched in Lance's story, Mitch asked, "What was that?"

"JJ said, '*How you deal with the worst day of your life, which for me was losing our son, is determined by the best day of your life, which is the day I received Christ as my Savior.*'" Lance paused for a moment. "Mitch, that is absolutely true," Lance said as he began to cry. "So, I went back to the cross and I thanked Jesus for dying for me there and I thanked Him for the eighteen years He gave me with my son."

Mitch's heart was so full that he began to cry.

"Then I prayed that He would help Kate and me embrace the healing power of His precious blood," Lance continued. "I looked up and saw *Losing Cooper* on the bookshelf. I know it sounds crazy, but it was almost as if it were glowing, sitting there. I took it from the shelf, sat down and started reading it. I had read only a couple of chapters when my doorbell rang. Guess who it was?"

Mitch shrugged.

"JJ Jasper," Lance said, grinning.

Mitch was stunned. "No way."

"Yep," Lance said. "I couldn't believe it. We went for a walk and talked for a while," Lance continued. "He's so full of compassion. Very personable. Just having someone listen who you know understands made so much difference for me. I went home and finished reading the book in one sitting."

"And?" Mitch asked.

"Life-changing," Lance replied. "You know, when people try to say things to comfort you, you appreciate it, yet you resent it. But when someone who has been where you've been says it, it's profound and fills your heart with hope. That day, I started to heal."

"I'm really glad," Mitch said sincerely. "You know, I accepted Jesus into my heart as a ten-year-old boy."

Lance was surprised. "You've never shared that with me."

"I know," Mitch said, ashamed. "You see, I was raised in the belief that you got saved, went to church and tried to do good. That was it. When I got to be a young adult, the church thing bored me, but my job didn't. So I began spending more time with work. Soon, not going to church felt normal. I know it broke Grace's heart. I know she kept praying for me. It's just that I always thought that was all there was to it."

"But Mitch, that's not all there is," Lance said.

"I'm realizing that now," Mitch confessed.

"It's not about a religion, Mitch. It's about a relationship."

Mitch nodded. "I've watched Grace grow in her relationship all these years, and I've felt almost jealous. But Lance, that pride...it kept me from trying because I was so embarrassed."

"Don't walk in that any longer, friend," Lance said. "Let me walk alongside you and hold you accountable. And you can start by helping me cook Brotherhood Breakfast next month."

Mitch laughed. "You got it."

He looked down and became quiet. "I'm sorry I haven't been there for you, friend. Not calling you before the funeral, not checking on you in the days that followed. I just couldn't believe that after what happened, you would even want to talk to me. I was afraid you would think, *The nerve of that guy*, you know? And the day you came by to visit us at the hospital, I was rude. It wasn't on purpose, but I was ashamed and didn't know what to say. The guilt was unbearable."

"You wanna talk about guilt?" Lance asked. "I've had unbearable guilt."

Mitch looked confused. "Why would you feel guilty?"

Lance hesitated. As he responded, his voice began to break. "Because I don't have assurance that Ross is in Heaven."

Mitch was speechless.

"Kate and I always had Ross in church. Church camp, revivals, Bible drills, you name it. But I don't recall a time that he ever asked us about being saved. To my knowledge, Ross never made a profession of faith."

"Oh, but Lance, how could you think that?" Mitch asked.

"Easy," Lance said. "There was never a time that we had a conversation with him. There was never a time that he walked the aisle to receive Christ. There was never a time that he was baptized." Lance paused. "How did I miss that? I really struggled with that out of the gate as I traveled back in time in my mind, thinking of all the memories we had with Ross. That major event that all believing parents should expect to experience and celebrate – it never happened."

"What did Kate say about it?" Mitch asked.

"I've never brought it up," Lance replied. "She's struggled so terribly through this, the last thing I wanted to do was put that on her. I just dealt with it on my own."

"Lance, I'm so sorry," Mitch said.

"Finally, I talked to Pastor Glenn about it."

"And what did he say?"

"He said that we were faithful to train him up, that it was a decision he had to come to on his own at some point, and that I can't dwell on that."

"He's right," Mitch said.

Lance looked at him. "Practice what you preach."

Mitch looked up at Lance after his reprimand. Lance grinned. Immediately getting his point, Mitch smiled. "You're right."

"Mitch, we've been friends for almost twenty years. We raised our boys together and made a lot of wonderful memories. We love your family. I refuse to allow the enemy to take any more from us than he has already taken in this situation. The pain of losing our son would only be compounded if we lost your family, too."

Mitch began to cry again. "Lance, we've agonized over losing Ross. He was like a second son to us. I guess I just don't understand... well, I've never seen this kind of love put into action before. And now, what I'm realizing is that the reason I'm surprised by it is because it's the opposite of what I would probably do. I was projecting onto you how I would have felt. You're a much better man than me, Lance."

"Oh, don't give me too much credit. All I know to tell you, brother, is that it's not me, but the love of Christ in me."

"I just don't know what to say," Mitch said.

Lance placed his hand on Mitch's shoulder. "Don't say anything. Just let us continue to love your family."

"Under one condition," Mitch cited.

"What's that?" Lance asked.

"You allow us to love yours."

"Deal," Lance said. After a manly hug with strong pats on the back, they joined the others inside and continued celebrating Jake's homecoming.

As the evening came to a close and guests began to leave, Jake took the opportunity to tell everyone thanks for their love and support. Soon he asked his parents if he could be excused for bed. The day had been long and tiresome, draining him physically, mentally and emotionally. He longed to snuggle under the covers in his own bed again. His excessive exhaustion made it more enticing.

The Kellys, along with a few other friends, stayed afterward to help clean up after the celebration had ended, then said their good-byes. Mitch closed the door behind them and turned to Grace. He embraced her like he hadn't in a very long time.

"There've been a lot of hugs today," Grace said.

"Yes, there have, and I've been involved in several of them, too," Mitch replied.

"I noticed that," Grace said with a grin.

"I'm going to turn in for the night," Mitch said. "Are you coming?"

"Not right now," Grace replied. "I think I'm going to sit up for a little while and let my mind settle down."

"OK. It has been quite a day, hasn't it?"

"It's been a spectacular day! Our son is home! And I want to write it all down in my journal before I forget every incredible detail."

"I'll see you in the morning," Mitch said.

After Mitch retired to their room for the night, Grace walked to the kitchen table, picked up her Bible and prayer journal, and took them to her chair. Thoughts of the wonderful day continued to run through her mind as she situated herself in her favorite spot and spread her chenille throw over her lap. She closed her eyes, took in a deep breath and let it out slowly.

Oh, Lord. What an incredible day You gave us today. Thank You for the many blessings of it: faithful friends, Jake coming home and especially for the continued healing I saw today. I know You will be faithful to complete what you've started.

Grace opened her eyes and looked straight ahead. Her eyes caught sight of her brightly-colored bag on the floor by the bookshelf. *Someone must have set it there while we were organizing for the homecoming.* A warm feeling spread over her as she gazed at it. She had lugged that tote on her arm from hospital room to CCU so many times she had lost count. It sat still stuffed with the spiritual resources she and many others had used to draw strength from during very dark and questionable days. Still wound up from the excitement of the day, Grace walked across the room and unpacked it.

One by one, she pulled each book from the bag, reading each title and author. Each one brought to mind a specific memory, face and need as she stowed it away on the shelf. As she put away the book *Praying God's Word* by Beth Moore, a small white piece of paper slipped out and floated to the floor like a feather. Curious, Grace picked it up and noticed a note written in very neat penmanship.

Thank you very much for your generosity in sharing your resources with me in the CCU waiting room. This book, along with your unwavering faith displayed through our conversation, brought me great comfort and peace during my unsettled moments as I waited to receive word of my daughter's condition. I pray that as your son and your family heal, God would continue to pour out His mercy on you. I know He has a huge plan for all that you have endured. Thank you again for being such a blessing to me in the midst of your own sufferings.

Love, Mary

Quickly Grace's mind raced back to the time that she and Mary sat together and talked. She did not realize the impact she was having on that very refined lady. Joy leaped inside her at the memory as she placed the thoughtful note back inside the book.

Once again, Grace thanked the Lord for His goodness. There still was a long road to recovery ahead of them, but she wanted only to focus on being thankful for the blessings of the day and enjoy it.

Chapter 23

After a restful weekend, I headed back to school. Mixed emotions plagued me. My best friend wasn't going to be there to greet me. The football team was leaving for the play-offs without me. Morgan hadn't talked to me since the wreck. Lauren despised me. On top of all that, I felt incredibly awkward being in a wheelchair – and having no legs. Regardless, I was ready to get back to as normal a life as possible. I had no idea how difficult it was going to be.

Jake opened the passenger-side door of his mother's minivan and shifted himself into the wheelchair. Grace struggled to help him, but it was still a very awkward situation. She took comfort in knowing that making the transfer would eventually become second nature. Once Jake was situated in his chair, Grace breathed a sigh of relief.

"We'll check into a lift," she suggested. "How's that sound?"

"That would be awesome," Jake said.

He wheeled his way around the minivan and watched as a few students rushed into the school.

"You ready?" Grace asked.

"I guess so," Jake said.

Grace was concerned but tried not to show it. Today, even the next few weeks, weren't going to be easy.

"You mind if I do this one on my own?" Jake asked.

"Oh, OK. Well, I'll see you in a bit. Your dad and I will be here for the pep rally."

Jake smiled and pointed to his cheek. A huge grin spread across Grace's face as she bent down to kiss him.

"See you in a bit," Jake said and turned toward the school entrance.

Eric Williams stood outside the front entry, watching.

"Hey, man, let me get the door."

"Thanks. I appreciate it," Jake said.

Grace watched as Jake disappeared inside the school.

"Please be with him, Lord," she prayed. "Help him adjust."

The moment Jake's wheelchair entered the main hallway, a mass of excited students surrounded him. Football players standing nearby started the team chant.

"Good to have you back," Dr. Sharp welcomed him, offering his hand. Jake shook it and smiled. Coach Scott emerged from among the crowd, holding a folded team jersey in his hands.

"Lead us in the pep rally today?" he asked, handing the shirt to Jake.

Jake smiled, his eyes beaming, and accepted the jersey. Students applauded and rushed to pat Jake on the back and shake his hand.

"All right, all right," Dr. Sharp said. "I hate to break up the party, but everyone needs to get to their first period class."

The students groaned and slowly made their way to class.

"I know," he sympathized. "I'm with ya. But hey, we've got to do some work while we're here. Jake isn't going anywhere. Now, let's move!" As he clapped his hands. the students dispersed, quickening their steps.

"You ready to scoot to first period?" Eric asked.

"Sure, but I'm going to make a pit stop first...if you know what I mean," Jake said.

Eric laughed. "All right. You want me to wait on you?"

"You go ahead," Jake said. "I remember how to get there."

———

Eric entered class and saw Lauren at her desk, studying.

"Have you been in here the whole time?" he asked.

"Yep," she answered shortly.

"Why?" he asked.

"Because I have a quiz next period and I needed to study for it," she said. "Besides. there wasn't enough room for me on Jake's welcome wagon."

"That's kinda rude, don't you think?" Eric asked.

"I hardly think so. Rude is humiliating someone in the cafeteria by tripping them, or intentionally interrupting other people's conversations. In fact, if you look up the word 'rude' in the dictionary, you'll probably see Jake Adams's face beside it. He is the epitome of rude!"

"You're wrong, Lauren," Eric said. Lauren remained expressionless while staring at her book.

———

Jake wheeled toward class with his friend Drew Collins. Hurrying to his own class, an underclassman bumped into Jake's wheelchair.

"Watch it, dude!" Drew ordered.

The young boy froze.

"It's OK," Jake assured him. "Don't worry about it."

The student eyed Drew for his approval. "Sorry," the boy said and took off.

They made it to Mr. Anders's creative writing class just in time; the teacher was waiting for them at the door.

"Hey, Mr. Anders," Jake said.

"Good morning, Mr. Adams," he said. "It's good to see you here."

"I bet you never thought you'd say that about me, huh?" Jake asked, smiling.

"I'm sure crazier things have happened," Mr. Anders said, trying to suppress a smile but failing.

Jake scanned the classroom, looking for a place to park his chair. He spotted Lauren and wheeled himself to her.

"Hey, Lauren," Jake said.

"Jake," Lauren replied sarcastically, making a strong 'k' sound at the end of his name, her eyes still on her book. He sensed her hostility and said nothing further.

Mr. Anders began his lecture. Jake was lost. Although Grace had collected his classwork on a regular basis, Jake hadn't kept up with his lessons. The continual, intense pain he struggled with required a regimen of pain pills every four to six hours, and as a result, he was groggy much of the time. Jake tried to take notes while Mr. Anders lectured. The information made no sense. He looked around the room for someone he felt comfortable enough to ask for help.

Although she was guaranteed to give him a hard time, Lauren was normally Jake's go-to person. This morning proved that privilege was no longer his. His frustration soon turned into despair. Jake gave up.

His quickly-written notes were now doodles. Spiritually dark images covered his paper – not images he created in his mind, but images of what he saw that tragic night. Jake fell into deep thought. Before he realized it, class ended.

The bell rang for break. Jake watched Lauren gather her books to leave. He wanted to talk to her but wasn't sure what to say. Any words at all seemed so inadequate.

"Hey, man. Wanna walk to break?" Eric asked.

"Yeah, that'd be great," Jake mumbled. At least Eric was being supportive. Jake watched Lauren once more for any sign that she'd be open to conversation. She glanced at him, then quickly walked out the door.

Once outside, Jake noticed the football team practicing.

"You go ahead," Jake motioned to Eric. "I'll catch up. I want to see how the team's looking."

Jake wheeled himself over to the football field. Coach Scott was leaning on the fence, a whistle in his right hand.

"Practicing early?" Jake asked.

Coach turned to Jake and smiled. "Yeah. Just having a walk-through before we head out. Checking out play formations to make sure they have the basics down."

"That's good," Jake answered.

"So, are you getting along OK?" Coach Scott asked.

"Yes, sir. I'm learning a few tricks in my chair, so it's not so boring." Jake spun around quickly in the wheelchair.

Coach Scott laughed. "Not bad. You should enter the talent show next spring."

Jake smiled. They watched the team walk through two defensive plays.

"So," Jake asked, "do you feel good about how they look?"

"Yeah, I do," Coach answered. "I hear the team we're playing has some key players out with injuries. I'm hoping we can capitalize on that."

Jake watched the team as they walked through a play. Noticing Hamm on the field, he said, "Hamm's looking good. How's his knee been?"

"Good," Coach replied. "We were a little nervous at first, but he's good."

"I'm glad to hear that," Jake said.

"Hamm's really stepped up. He's really proven himself these past weeks...both athletically and leadership-wise," Coach said. Then he turned to Jake and asked, "So...how are you, really? I don't mean physically. I mean how are you emotionally? Mentally?" Jake had never heard Coach Scott speak so sincerely.

"I don't know, really," Jake admitted. "It's been so good being back at school today. I think the newness of that helps to cover up some of the pain that I normally feel. When the newness wears off, I'll let you know," Jake said.

"OK. You know I'm always here for you."

"I know, Coach. I appreciate that."

"When do you start rehab?"

"Next week. I started a little bit of therapy before I left the hospital."

"Oh yeah?"

"Yep. It's painful and frustrating. My therapist's name is Sandy. She is five feet of sheer evil."

Coach Scott laughed. "Well...good! You need someone tough on you. Is she as tough on you as I've been?"

"She makes you look like a teddy bear," Jake laughed. "Seriously... Sandy's awesome."

Coach Scott smiled, then turned serious. "So, are you going to have a prosthesis? They've come a long way with those."

"Yes, sir. It's just going to take some time. I can't be fitted yet because of my burns. Grafted skin takes a long time to heal – it tears easily. It's a long, tedious process."

"I see," Coach Scott said. "Well, don't give up. You'll get there before you know it."

Coach Scott quieted for a moment. Looking down at Jake, he said somberly, "I'm so glad you're here today and are willing to be a part of the pep rally."

Tears began to fill Jake's eyes. "It's just hard being here without Ross, and knowing it's my fault that he's not here."

"Jake, son, you can't think like that. It was just one of those things. You didn't force Ross to ride with you. He made a choice, too."

"People keep saying that, but I can't help but feel responsible," Jake said. "Coach, thanks for asking me to be a part of the pep rally. It means a lot."

"It would be wrong for you not to be a part of it," Coach replied. "You are one of us."

"Hey, Coach! We need you over here!" a voice called out from the field.

"Let me see what's going on over there. I'll see you in the gym."

"You bet," Jake said.

Jake continued watching his Eagles practice, yelling out words of encouragement as they completed plays successfully. The bell rang, signaling the end of break. Jake felt his stomach knot up as he wheeled toward the gymnasium. He was in turmoil. Although he had been made to feel wanted, he wasn't confident about his participation.

Jake wheeled into the boys' locker room and waited for the team to come in from practice. He looked around the room. It had been a while since his last time in there. He breathed in the air. The smell of sweaty boys and dirty basketball shoes brought back memories. He had missed it. The silence was broken when the players entered, yelling and talking trash. Seeing Jake excited them. Each one took a turn "high fiving" with Jake. Finally, it was Hamm's turn. Seeing Hamm in a knee brace caused Jake to sink inside. *Another stupid choice I made that caused someone pain.* He was at a loss for words.

"Good to see you, man," Hamm said sincerely, hugging Jake.

Stunned, Jake grabbed him roughly and hugged him back.

"Good to see you, too, Hamm," Jake said. "How's the knee?"

"It's OK. The doc cleared me to play," Hamm said.

"Yeah, I heard. By the skin of your teeth, right?" Jake answered. He hesitated for a moment. Looking at the smile on Hamm's face, Jake shook his head in disbelief. While the other teammates got changed for the pep rally, Jake and Hamm continued to make small talk. As Hamm spoke, Jake thought of the pranks he had pulled on him and how good-natured Hamm had always been. *How could he be so nice to me after what I did to him?*

Jake looked at Hamm. "I don't get it."

"Get what?" Hamm asked.

"After what I did to you...you still choose to be my friend," Jake said.

"Aw, Jake. You didn't mean it. You were just messing around. You didn't intend for me to get hurt. It's all good," Hamm said. He leaned in to Jake and added, "Besides...it's probably one of the best things that's ever happened to my social life."

"How's that?" Jake asked curiously.

"Let's just say sympathy can be an awesome tool. I got lots of phone numbers and friend requests on Facebook from chicks, and my number of followers on Instagram and Twitter went through the roof! I'm famous! Your little prank changed my love life forever, bro!" Hamm grinned and winked.

Jake laughed and gave him a fist bump.

"Well, I'm glad you see it that way," Jake said. "So...are we good?"

"You know it!" Hamm said.

"I appreciate that, Hamm. I really do," Jake said.

Coach Scott entered the locker room. "All right, let's get this party started!"

The guys came to attention.

"Listen up," he said. He thought a minute as the boys gathered around. "This team has endured a lot these past months, yet you've been victorious," Coach Scott said. "Your consistency has been awesome, and you've pressed on during difficult times. You have made adjustments both physically and mentally. Now...it's time to enjoy the fruits of your labor. This isn't a time to get complacent. Stay the course, finish strong, and bring that state trophy back with you! Now...all in," he said, directing the team to stack their hands for the team chant.

"Jake," Coach Scott said.

"Yes, sir?" Jake responded.

"Lead us out," Coach Scott said.

"You got it!" Jake replied. He directed his attention toward the team. "Let's do this!" he cried.

"Eagles, Eagles, let's go!" they yelled, lifting their hands in the air.

"OK, let's move!" Coach Scott yelled.

The team ran out of the locker room and onto the gym floor, positioning themselves for their introduction during the pep rally. The student body erupted, waving red-and-blue nylon shakers. Excitement filled the air as the band played the school fight song. The cheerleaders' choreography and pom-poms were perfectly in sync with the beat of the percussion section.

As the team lined up, outfitted in their athletic travel gear, Jake's eye caught Lauren in the stands clapping along. Her clapping slowed, and her expression changed to indignation. Jake knew she had just spotted him. He quickly cut his eyes away. The judgment in her face cut him to the quick.

Jake moved with the team to center court. Jake sat amid the huddle of players as they enthusiastically performed their team chant. The student body followed along, keeping the beat by stomping their feet in the stands. When the chant ended, the team dispersed to their positions for the presentation. Coach Scott approached the mic and asked the rowdy fans to quiet down. After about a minute, they finally did.

"Wow! What a crowd!" Coach Scott commented. "The team, our coaching staff and I really appreciate your attendance today. Your support has been incredible during this season. This is a big day for our guys and our school."

Next he presented each player to the fans. As Jake wheeled to center stage, the crowd rose to its feet with applause.

"Jake!" a student yelled.

That began the chant, "Jake, Jake, Jake!"

Disgusted, Lauren snapped her head toward the young man who initiated it.

"Give the mic to Jake!" another student ordered.

Looking down at Jake, Coach Scott offered the mic to him and motioned his hand forward, giving him the floor to speak. Jake hesitated. He panned the audience, then took the mic from the coach's hand.

"Well…" Jake started. The sound of his own voice startled him. The students laughed. He tapped the mic and held it farther away for his second attempt.

"I'm not much of a speaker, but it's good to be back…most of me, anyway." Awkward chuckles could be heard from the crowd. Coach Scott nodded.

"I wasn't sure how I was going to handle coming back here. Sports have always been my life. I thought maybe I could try theater, but I don't have a leg to break." The students laughed.

"I thought about dancing, but I have no left feet," he said comically.

"Yeah, Jake!" a student yelled. Jake pointed to the guy who had made the exclamation.

"He's seen me dance." The fans' laughter fueled his confidence. Returning to school was going to be much more awesome than he thought.

Coach Scott moved toward Jake to retrieve the mic. Jake looked at him and said, "Come on, Coach. You're stepping on my toes here."

He handed the mic back to Coach and waved at the crowd. A giant grin covered his face. Then he spotted Lauren again. Her face, on the other hand, exuded anger at the support the students were pouring on Jake. She sat in protest with arms crossed and a fixed stare of hatred directed toward him.

Enraged by their show of love and support toward Jake, Lauren forced her way through the crowded stands and stomped out of the gymnasium to the classroom where the Fellowship of Christian Athletes meeting would be held after the pep rally. She paced the floor madly. Her breathing was deep and hard. She collapsed into the teacher's chair and laid back her head. The sound of cheering voices rang out just outside the classroom window. She raised her head to see what was happening. The pep rally had ended and excited Eagles fans followed the team out to load the buses for the big send-off. Jake wheeled toward the two buses, positioning his wheelchair between them and leading the student body and the team in a chant.

"Eagles, Eagles, Eagles!" he called as he punched his fist in the air in rhythm. The fans joined in. His teammates leaned out the bus windows and chanted along with them. The buses began to drive away as the players took their seats. The other students made their way to class, but Jake remained there in the parking lot. At the last second, a head appeared out of one of the bus windows. It was Hamm. He waved bye to Jake.

Then, in an emotional outburst, Hamm yelled, "Stay strong, Jake!"

Jake was taken aback. His chin began to quiver, and a sharp pain pierced his stomach.

He opposes the proud, but gives grace to the humble, his mind recalled. It was a Bible verse he had heard his mother say many times, but he had never really understood it. Now, in this instant, he finally graspedits meaning. The reality was harsh but deserved. Jake waved at Hamm as the buses disappeared out of view; then he sat still and quiet. Although he wanted very much to support his team, it was still very painful.

Chapter 24

*I had been proud and arrogant. I had treated Hamm as less than
human. I bullied, intimidated, humiliated and even caused him injury
that could have potentially put him on the bench for the rest of the
season...all to prove I was a big shot. Hamm was an easy target. He
never retaliated and remained humble. Today, Hamm was the one
riding away on that bus to the play-off game. The injury that I had
caused him could have kept him on the sideline. But somehow, he was
well enough to play, while I – Jake Adams, the big man on campus
– was the one left behind. As painful as that was, things were about
to get worse.*

Some of the students had joined Lauren for the FCA meeting and
were puzzled to find her seated in class alone.

"Why didn't you stay for the rest of the pep rally?" her friend
Hannah asked. "Or tell the team good-bye?"

"There were plenty of people to wish them bon voyage without
me," Lauren scoffed. Uncomfortable with Lauren's attitude, Hannah
changed the subject by directing Lauren's attention outside.

"Look what we're making for Jake," she said.

Disgusted, Lauren asked, "What is it?"

"It's a '79 Trans-Am model car. We painted it to match Jake's," Hannah said. "I worked on it all night trying to have it finished for Jake by today."

Lauren shook her head in disbelief and stormed out of the room. Shocked at Lauren's response, Hannah followed her into the hallway.

"What's wrong?" Hannah asked.

"Seriously?" Lauren asked in an exaggerated tone. Hannah was shocked. "Why would you people waste your time making a gift for Jake?"

Feeling insulted, Hannah didn't respond.

"Wow! Thank heavens! Everything's back to normal! The hero has returned!" Lauren exclaimed dramatically, throwing her hands up in the air.

As Lauren ranted, students at their lockers stopped and watched the scene she was creating. She realized she was making a spectacle of herself but didn't seem to care.

Lauren quieted and stared at the floor. Without raising her head, she said, "You know what...I'm just going to cancel our meeting today. The last thing I want to do right now is hold a 'Jesus' meeting."

The bell rang for the next class to begin.

"What do you want me to tell everyone, Lauren?" Hannah asked. "That you're feeling too much like a hypocrite right now?"

"Don't even get me started on that subject," Lauren retorted. She realized her outburst was making people stare. Embarrassed, she tempered her emotions. "Just tell everyone that the meeting is canceled and to go on to their next class as usual."

She walked away, leaving Hannah to deal with the awkward situation.

Soon, the tardy bell rang. It had been difficult for Jake to watch his team leave without him. He wheeled inside, apathetic that he was late for class. While he searched his locker for his science lab text-book, he saw a figure from the corner of his eye. Instinctively, he glanced to see who it was. It was Morgan. Seeing Jake in his wheel-chair, Morgan slowed her pace. This was the first time they had seen each other since the few moments at the ER. He sat still and watched her as she nervously made her book exchange.

"Hey," Jake said.

"Hey," Morgan said nervously.

"So, how have you been?" Jake asked.

"Good. You?"

"Well, OK, I guess. You know…considering."

At a loss for words, Morgan replied, "Yeah, I guess." A deafening silence settled between them.

"What's wrong, Morgan? Why have you been avoiding me? Why have you been so distant?"

Thrown off by his bluntness, her mind raced for answers. "Oh, you know. I've just been so busy with ballet and school work."

"No. You were doing all of that when we were going out. Just spell it out, Morgan. Shoot straight with me."

She sighed. "OK, I just can't handle this."

"Handle what? The way I look now?" Jake asked.

"Just…you know…this," she muttered, motioning to his wheel-chair. "It's just uncomfortable for me, all right? I don't know how to handle this. I just think we are better off being friends. That's all."

"So, that's it then?" Jake asked.

"Yes, it is. I'm sorry, Jake. I gotta go." She quickly walked away.

Jake sat dazed. Although her answer was what he had anticipated, it was still very difficult to hear. He leaned his head back on the locker door and stared at the ceiling as his mind processed Morgan's words. Her rejection was painful.

A young man running late for class rounded the corner. His momentum caused him to accidentally bump into Jake's chair. Jake's face grew red, and he grabbed the boy's hand and squeezed it. The student stood in shock.

"Watch where you're going," Jake said through clenched teeth.

He thrust the boy's hand away and continued to stare at him. The student was shocked by Jake's reaction and stumbled through an apology as he hurried away.

Jake tried to calm down and gather his thoughts, then wheeled himself to class. He entered the room hesitantly. The science teacher, Mrs. Michael, pointed Jake to an open area away from the occupied desks.

"Science projects are due next week, so get with your partners for the next few minutes and make sure you have everything covered," Mrs. Michael said. Oblivious to her instructions, Jake sat sketching images on a piece of paper as he recounted his conversation with Morgan.

"Jake," Mrs. Michael called. Jake snapped out of his trance-like state and looked at her.

"Why don't you work with Miss Richards's team?" Jake unlocked the wheelchair brakes and spun around to face Natalie Richards. He acknowledged the other classmates in the group, then was stunned to find himself face-to-face with Lauren. He had never seen such hatred in her eyes and quickly lowered his gaze. Immediately, Lauren raised her hand. Mrs. Michael approached their group.

"Yes, Ms. McKay?" she asked.

"I feel ill," Lauren said. "May I go to the nurse's office, please?"

With permission granted, Lauren left class, but she checked out of school instead. Through the classroom window, Jake watched her walk to her car.

"May I be excused?" Jake asked.

"Are you sick, too?" Mrs. Michael asked.

"Not exactly, but it's important," he said.

"Go ahead, then," Mrs. Michael said, looking over her reading glasses.

Jake rushed out the door and into the parking lot.

"Lauren, wait!"

Lauren ignored him. Jake wheeled toward her as fast as he could and caught up to her just as she was opening the door.

"Look, I know you hate me – I get it," Jake said, out of breath. Lauren quickly tossed her backpack into the back seat of the car.

"Do you think I wanted this?" he asked.

Lauren stared at him. "Are you talking about Ross...or your legs?" she harshly suggested.

"He was my best friend!" Jake yelled.

"Mine, too!" Lauren snapped, tears in her eyes.

"I'd do anything to take it back!" Jake cried. "All of it! But it's done!"

"I told you not to take him, didn't I? But you wouldn't listen! You didn't care that you were putting his life in danger! You don't care about anyone except Jake!"

She paused for a moment to catch her breath, then she stepped closer. "Have you ever been to Ross's grave?"

"What?" Jake asked.

"Ross's grave. You've never been, have you?"

"No, but—"

"I knew it," Lauren said. "You don't even think enough about Ross to go pay your respects!"

Jake sat silent with his head bowed. "I'm just trying to figure out how to get going again."

"Looks like you're doing a pretty good job," Lauren scoffed. She reached into the back of her car and produced a worn basketball.

"Here," Lauren said, forcefully tossing it to Jake. He raised his head just in time to catch it. The "Super Ross" emblem on it stared him boldly in the face.

"He left it in my car. You should have it. You should look at it every day so you have to remember!" A stone-like expression enveloped her face as she got in the car. "It should have been you."

Lauren slammed the car door and sped away. Jake stared at Ross's basketball. Lauren's choice of words couldn't have been more cutting.

Jake wheeled back inside the school. Because he sat so low in the wheelchair, he re-entered undetected by the receptionist at the office window. He was now over the edge after the confrontation with Lauren. What a change that was. In the past, their arguments had left Lauren hurting and Jake emotionless. Now, the roles were reversed. There was no way he could go back to class. He wheeled down the hallway and sought refuge in an empty classroom where he sat quietly before a row of plate-glass windows, spinning Ross's basketball in his hands. Each time it stopped, the "Super Ross" emblem faced him, taunting him almost. Voices filled his mind, the same ones he heard during the wreck.

There are some things that you just can't take back. Jake continued spinning the ball in his hands in a dead stare. *She's right, Jake. It should have been you.* Jake recognized it. It was the same voice that had told him to *rest easy.* Jake gripped the ball with both hands and banged his head against it repeatedly. The guilt was overbearing.

"Ahhh!" Jake screamed, hurling the ball through the air. The basketball crashed through the window. Glass shards exploded across the floor and flew onto the ground outside. Jake's cries resounded in the hallway as he continued to yell. Students and faculty ran cautiously toward the sounds of shattered glass and screams. When they reached the room where Jake was, they were in shock. Dr. Sharp and a security guard also ran toward the racket. When Dr. Sharp saw it was Jake, he directed one of the female students to get the guidance counselor. Jake looked at the small crowd that had gathered.

"What's everyone staring at, huh?" Jake questioned them. "Have you never seen broken glass before?"

The students and teachers stood stunned at Jake's outburst.

"Just leave, all right?" Jake yelled.

Dr. Sharp tried to defuse Jake's rage as the security guard cleared out the area.

"He's right – there's nothing to see here," the security guard instructed. "Go back to your classes." The onlookers disbanded quickly. Several students were visibly shaken by what had taken place.

The guidance counselor waded through the dispersing crowd and soon saw Jake in the center of the classroom. René Ogburn had served as guidance counselor at Lee County Academy for seven years. Jake was no stranger to her. The 5'4" brown-eyed blonde, well known for her sternness and lack of tolerance for disrespectful behavior, found herself perplexed with Jake's demeanor. Because she had dealt with Jake's ridiculous antics numerous times in the past, she quickly discerned this to be an unusual situation. Compassion definitely had its place here.

"I'm going to call his parents," Dr. Sharp said.

"Good idea," Dr. Ogburn said. She bent down in front of Jake and spoke very softly.

"Jake, are you hurt?"

Jake just sat there…unspeaking and emotionless.

"Jake, I need you to talk to me," she said gently.

He remained silent.

Dr. Sharp promptly returned to Dr. Ogburn and Jake. "I was able to get in touch with Grace. She said she'd be here shortly."

"Good." Dr. Ogburn examined Jake to ensure he wasn't bleeding. "Let's get him to my office," she said.

Dr. Sharp motioned to the security guard. "It would probably be a good idea for you to join us."

Students in the hallway stopped and stared at the small parade of administrators and Jake. He looked straight ahead, not moving a muscle, as the principal maneuvered his wheelchair down the hall. Dr. Ogburn placed a finger over her mouth, instructing the passing students to say nothing to him.

Dr. Sharp wheeled Jake into Dr. Ogburn's office, where they waited for Grace to arrive.

"Is there anything I can get for you, son?" Dr. Sharp offered.

Jake barely moved his head, signaling to him, "No."

"I'm going to step out and wait for Grace," Dr. Sharp said. "I'll be right outside if you need me."

Dr. Ogburn closed the office door. "Jake, what happened?"

He remained expressionless.

"Come on, Jake. You were having a great day earlier. What happened? Why did you break the window?"

Jake still chose not to respond. There was a knock at her office door.

"Come in," Dr. Ogburn said, standing to greet her visitor.

A very concerned Grace Adams entered.

"What happened?" she asked.

"Grace, we really aren't sure," Dr. Ogburn said. "Let me get Dr. Sharp in on our meeting."

As she left to retrieve the headmaster, Grace sat down beside Jake and watched him for a moment. He didn't acknowledge her entrance into the room.

"What's wrong, son?" Grace asked. "You need to tell us what's going on."

Dr. Sharp joined them in Dr. Ogburn's office.

"I didn't see what happened initially, Grace," Dr. Ogburn said. "A student came and got me out of my office after the fact. However, Dr. Sharp and our school security guard got to the scene pretty quickly."

Dr. Sharp began to speak. "Grace, apparently Jake threw a basketball through a classroom window. Accident or not, we don't know. One of our coaches retrieved it from the school parking lot and brought it to me. Several of us heard the glass shatter and Jake's yell. When I got there and realized it was him, I sent for Dr. Ogburn.

"Jake had been having a good day up until this point. I don't know what happened to cause this, but we want to do everything we can to help. We can't imagine what he's going through right now."

The security guard presented the basketball to Grace. The "Super Ross" emblem faced her. She gasped.

Alarmed, Grace shouted, "Oh my! That's Ross's ball!"

Tears rolled down her face as she grabbed her mouth. She looked at Jake.

"Jake, son, where did you get this?" she asked desperately.

"Lauren gave it to me," Jake whispered as tears filled his eyes.

Grace composed herself. "I'm terribly sorry about this, Dr. Sharp. We will do our best to rectify the situation."

"There's no need for you to apologize, Grace," Dr. Sharp assured her. "Look, we'll have to file a report for insurance purposes, but it will be ruled an accident. There will be no charges against Jake."

"Thank you for that, but if we need to pay for the window just send us the bill," Grace said.

"No, ma'am," Dr. Sharp replied.

"We're just concerned about your family," Dr. Ogburn said. "We want you to know we are here for you, Grace."

"I don't know what to say. I can't imagine how seeing this ball made him feel," Grace said sympathetically.

"Just get him home and let him rest," Dr. Ogburn said. "That's probably the best thing for him right now."

"Absolutely," Grace said.

"I'll help you get him into your car, Mrs. Adams," the security guard said.

As they loaded Jake into the van, the security guard looked around for a place to set Ross's basketball.

"Would you like for me to put the ball in the back, Mrs. Adams?" he asked. Before Grace could respond, Jake grabbed the ball out of his hands. Grace was stunned. She looked at the security guard and mouthed the words *I'm so sorry*. He looked at her with compassion and nodded his head.

The ride home was awkward and silent. Grace tried to get Jake to open up about smashing the window but was unsuccessful.

Finally, Jake broke his silence. "I'm not going back to school, Mom."

"You don't have to go back for a couple of days." Grace said. "I'll get your work from—"

"No, Mom. You're not understanding," Jake interrupted. "I'm not going back ever."

Grace wasn't sure how to respond. "Surely you don't mean that."

"Yes, I do," Jake said firmly.

"But, why?" Grace asked.

"It's just too hard! I'm so far behind in my classes, I'll never catch up."

"We can get you a tutor," Grace said. "I'll help you, son."

"I don't want any help. It's just too hard."

"Is that the only reason?" Grace asked.

"No, but the reasons don't matter. I'm dropping out. I can get my GED. There's nothing for me there now."

Grace was at a loss for words. She felt helpless. The silence returned until they arrived home.

"I'll get the door for you," Grace said.

"No, thanks," Jake replied.

Grace didn't know what else to say or do. She chose to let it go.

She watched Jake get out of the van and wheel himself to the basketball goal, his back to his mother, continuing the silent treatment.

"I'll be in the kitchen if you need me," Grace said.

Heavy-hearted, she entered the house and shut the door. Distraught over the events of the afternoon, Grace called Margaret for encouragement and to request prayer.

Margaret saw Grace's name appear on the phone as it rang. Excited to hear from her, she smiled as she answered her phone.

"Hey, sweet friend," Margaret said.

"Hey, Meg," Grace replied.

Margaret could tell by Grace's voice that something was up. "Are you OK?" Margaret asked.

"Not at the moment," Grace said.

"What's wrong?" Margaret asked.

Grace related the discouraging details of the afternoon.

"You need a break," Margaret said. "Let me take you to lunch tomor-row so we can talk in person and pray together. Will that work for you?"

"That would be wonderful!" Grace said.

"Newk's at noon, then?" Margaret asked.

"Sounds good."

"I'll be praying for you, sister," Margaret said.

They hung up. Margaret's heart grew heavy for Grace once more. It seemed with every step of victory for the Adams family, a negative situation knocked them back. Margaret walked to Lauren's room to share Grace's struggle. She hoped it would soften Lauren's heart toward Jake. Approaching Lauren's closed bedroom door, she heard a low mumbling. Margaret realized Lauren was on the phone. The tone in her daughter's voice was sharp, as if she were upset. Concerned, Margaret leaned in and listened.

"I know, right? Well, I don't understand why everyone is always showing him pity and is so excited he's back. It turns my stomach," Lauren ranted. "And then Coach Scott lets him participate in the pep rally? Seriously?"

Lauren paused to listen to the conversation on the other end of the line.

"What? Morgan dumped him? Shut up!" Lauren said, surprised. "I'd love to have seen the look on his face when that happened!" she said spitefully. "I noticed she wasn't at Jake's homecoming. You know, I thought Morgan was shallow, but after what happened the night of the wreck, I began to see her differently. I'm just glad to see *him* get hurt for a change."

Margaret was disappointed and hurt. Immediately she knocked on Lauren's door, purposefully interrupting the gossip.

"May I come in?" Margaret asked.

"Ummm…Sure, Mom." She turned back to the phone. "I gotta go. Talk to you tomorrow. Oh, and thanks for filling me in. You just made my day." Lauren turned her attention to her mom. "What's up?" Lauren asked.

"Well, I was coming to share with you a prayer need for Grace," Margaret answered, "but after hearing some of your conversation just now, accidentally, of course, I think I'd be wasting my breath."

"Oh, that was Lizzy. We were just messing around."

"I know that's not true," her mother said. "I've been watching you since Ross died. Your words…your body language and attitude toward Jake… They all are filled with bitterness, resentment and such anger."

Lauren became defensive. "And rightfully so, Mom! Jake killed Ross! I told him racing was a stupid idea, but he didn't care. Jake caused all of this! Ross is gone, and now everyone is falling all over Jake like he's some kind of hero, when in reality, he's a murderer!"

Margaret was blown away by Lauren's rage. "You can blame Jake all day long, Lauren, but the truth is…Ross got in that car on his own. No one held a gun to his head."

"Maybe not, but Jake always made Ross feel bad if he didn't do what he wanted him to do. I know! I watched him manipulate Ross all the time!" Lauren's voice grew louder with each word.

"I know you are hurting over losing Ross," Margaret said, more sympathetic now. "I realize he meant a lot to you. But you're allowing that hurt to keep you from seeing the big picture."

"What do you mean?" Lauren asked.

"I'm just concerned about what your real motives were behind wanting Ross to be saved."

Lauren was taken aback.

Margaret explained. "You were always making sure he was at church and inviting him to church events, but why did you really want him there? Was it a genuine concern for his soul, or was it because you had feelings for him beyond friendship?"

Lauren said nothing.

"Pretend Jake had died and Ross had lived. Would you feel as bad about Jake dying as you do Ross dying?"

Lauren dropped her head. "No, I wouldn't. I know that sounds horrible, but I wouldn't have," Lauren admitted. Feeling convicted, she asked, "Does that make me a terrible person?"

"No, sweetie," Margaret said, cupping Lauren's face in her hands. "You're just being honest. The reality of this is that Jake needs Jesus just as much as Ross did. If your motives for wanting Ross to accept Jesus into his heart were pure, then you would be as compassionate about Jake's salvation. But you're not."

"That makes me a hypocrite, huh," Lauren said.

"Yes, sweetie, it does," Margaret said.

Lauren began to cry. Margaret lifted Lauren's chin with her finger.

"You can't do anything to change Ross's fate, but now you have the opportunity to make a difference in Jake's life. Instead, though, you're choosing to be hateful, rude and bitter. You need to look at your behavior and attitude toward Jake and see how it lines up with the word of God, or in this case, how it doesn't."

Lauren continued to defend herself. "You don't understand. He was always making fun of me because of my faith. He belittled my opinion and constantly humiliated me. It's like he got such a kick out of hurting my feelings. Why would I care about someone who treats me like that?"

"Why did Jesus care?" Margaret asked. "He was mocked, humiliated, spat upon, found guilty when He was completely innocent. But He showed mercy. He showed compassion. Lauren, God's word tells you to bless those who curse you. The key here is to choose not to be offended. If Christ had chosen to be offended, He would have never gone to the cross. And we would have no hope." Margaret looked Lauren in the eyes. "When we become offended, we become unproductive for God's kingdom. In essence, you are saying to Jake that your hurt feelings, which are temporary, are more important than his soul, which is eternal."

That revelation was hard for Lauren to realize and accept. "I don't mean to be a hypocrite. I just hurt so bad."

Margaret's heart broke for her child. "I know, sweetie. I wish I could make it go away. One thing I do know is that if you choose to not be offended and turn things around with Jake, you can make something good come from this tragedy. Don't give any more ground to the enemy than he has already taken."

"I don't want to do that, but it's so hard to even look at Jake, much less reach out to him." Lauren paused for a moment, thinking through her mother's words. "I don't want the enemy to win in this, but I can't make any promises. It's going to take some time."

"Well, I have all confidence that you can overcome this, by the power at work inside you," Margaret said. "Now, I'm going to go finish supper."

"I'll be down in a minute to help," Lauren said. Then, hugging her, she said, "Thanks, Mom. I love you."

"I love you, too. Your heart is turned toward the Lord. He'll get this turned around. Trust me – when you step forward in faith and obedience, God will give you the strength and grace you need to turn it around, and He will use it in a mighty way."

Lauren nodded in agreement. "So, what's for supper?"

"Oh, just all your favorites," Margaret said, smiling.

"Spaghetti and meatballs?" Lauren asked.

"Yep," Margaret said.

"Spinach salad?" Lauren asked.

"Uh-huh," Margaret answered.

"Dessert?" Lauren asked.

"Guess," Margaret challenged.

"Chocolate peanut butter pie?" Lauren asked.

"With chocolate graham cracker crust," Margaret added.

"Awesome! I'll fix the salad."

"And I'll let you," Margaret said.

Jake sat silently with Ross's basketball in his lap, staring at the basketball goal. Mitch drove in from work and noticed his son's trance-like state. Their conversation had been difficult in recent days and their relationship strained. Mitch struggled to deal with Jake's condition, what to say, what not to say.

"You want to shoot?" Mitch asked.

"No," Jake said, rolling away.

"You know...the YMCA has a wheelchair league," Mitch said. "Tom Rogers plays on it Thursday nights. I thought maybe we could check it out."

Jake turned around, looked at Mitch and shook his head in awe.

"Well, you're welcome to borrow my chair anytime," Jake replied.

Mitch turned to leave. "Jake, I'm trying."

Jake stopped and rolled back toward him. "Trying to do what?" he asked harshly. "Trying to get to the point that you can look at me? Trying to get to the point of accepting the fact your son will never be an athlete again?"

Mitch was stunned. "I'm trying my best to get over this situation!" he cried.

Jake cringed at Mitch's narcissism. "It's just all about you, isn't it, Dad?" he asked. "Here, catch!" Jake yelled out as he tossed Ross's basketball to him.

Mitch caught the ball. The "Super Ross" emblem caught his eye.

"Try getting over this!" Jake exclaimed.

Mitch felt weak in his knees. He was speechless. Jake wheeled up the ramp that church members had built.

Grace stood by the sink, making a salad. "Supper will be ready at six."

"I'm not hungry. I'm taking my meds and going to bed." He continued past her without slowing.

"OK," she replied gently.

Jake rolled through the bedroom door. He positioned his wheelchair against the side of his bed and pulled himself on top. He winced at the pain in his legs. He reached for the bottle of pills that sat on his nightstand, popped a pill in his mouth and washed it down with a nearby water bottle. He sat for a moment and looked at the bottle of pills. The label read *Take two pills every four to six hours for pain as needed.* He took two more pills. *I just want to go to sleep*, he thought. He replaced the pill bottle and water on the nightstand. Groaning, he situated himself under the covers. He now lay on his back, staring at the poster of University of Alabama quarterback Jay Barker, just as he had done so many times before. *That will never be you, Jake*, a voice said. Tears ran down his temples. He closed his eyes as his body gave way to the medication.

The late afternoon turned into evening. Mitch stepped inside while Grace set the table to eat.

"I was afraid I was going to be eating alone," Grace said.

Mitch offered no response.

"I heard yelling earlier," she asked. "What's wrong?"

"I don't know. Just having a hard time communicating with him right now, I guess."

"So where have you been all this time?" Grace asked.

"The barn. Just thinking."

They sat down to dinner, but neither felt like eating. They picked at their food as they sat silently, each in deep thought. After attempting to eat a few bites, Mitch dropped his fork on his plate.

"I'm sorry, Grace. I'm just not very hungry."

"Me, either," she admitted.

Mitch leaned back in his chair and returned to deep thought. Grace picked up a magazine from a stack of mail on the end of the table. She thumbed through pages filled with pictures showing the latest in prosthetic and orthotic technology. The images of young people sporting high-tech titanium legs were very impressive. For a moment, her heart filled with hope, then she quickly thought of this afternoon's haunting conversation with Jake on the ride home from school.

"I got called to the school today," she said.

Mitch looked at her puzzled. "For what?"

"Jake threw Ross's basketball through a classroom window."

"Are you kidding me?"

"I spoke to Dr. Sharp and Dr. Ogburn about it. They were very kind and sympathetic," Grace said.

Mitch carried his plate to the sink. "Why would Jake do that?"

"He said he's through with school," Grace said.

Mitch stared out the kitchen window.

"He said there's no use. He's missed too much and it's just too painful being back there," she said.

"Lots of people get GEDs," Mitch replied.

Frustrated, Grace closed the magazine. "Talk to him," she said.

"He doesn't even like me," Mitch said.

"He's crazy about you!" Grace cried. "Don't you know that?"

Mitch sat at the table and picked up the magazine. "I just want the best for him. That's all I've ever wanted. What's he going to do now?"

Grace placed her hand on his to stop the page-turning. "Whatever he wants to do. Whatever his father tells him he can do."

Mitch grew solemn. Emotional, he began to crumble.

"I felt so bad about ruining the game for him...embarrassing him in front of everyone. I felt like I owed him," Mitch said through broken words.

He looked at Grace. She didn't understand.

Finally, Mitch confessed. "I knew he was taking the car. I knew it and I let him. I let him because I didn't know another way to tell him that I was sorry!"

Grace lovingly cradled Mitch's head.

"This is not your fault," she said. "And then again, maybe it's a little bit of everyone's fault. But in the end, Jake chose to do it."

Mitch nodded. Grace pulled his head to her chest and held him as he cried.

"I don't know where to go from here," Mitch sobbed. "I don't know how to help our son!"

Mitch's breakdown caught Grace completely off guard, yet she was glad to see it happen. She had been waiting for him to let out every feeling of anger, hurt and guilt.

Holding Mitch close, she noticed an address label on the magazine. *Dr. Edward King, M.D.*

Jake tossed and turned restlessly in his bed. Nightmares plagued him. In one disturbing dream after another, he struggled inside the burning car, swatting at the flames as they crawled up his trapped legs. Screams of anguish erupted from his mouth. Above him, a demon approached outside the window. It winked at Jake and turned from the car, dragging a body by a handful of hair. Jake realized it was Ross. He watched in horror as Ross kicked and screamed while the demon effortlessly pulled him into the fiery inferno of Hades. Ross reached out and yelled, "Jake!" Every ounce of strength and life was inside that syllable.

Jake bolted from his sleep. His mother was calling him.

"Jake!" she called again, knocking this time.

Jake panted. His hair was drenched in sweat. He had fallen onto the floor and attempted to sit up as Grace continued to knock at his door. He winced at the pain.

"Jake, please answer me!" Grace implored.

"I'm OK. I just fell out of bed. I'm fine," Jake replied.

"I heard you yelling. Are you sure you're OK?"

"Yes, I'm OK," he responded harshly. "I just yelled out because I fell off my bed."

"OK…just please call me if you need me," she said.

"OK, Mom! My gosh!"

Frustrated, Grace turned and walked away. There was no use offering any more help.

Jake repositioned himself and looked at the clock. It read 12:37 a.m. He turned over and gazed out the window. *Still a long night ahead.* His body was exhausted. He feared the nightmares would return when he fell asleep. He fought to stay awake. Finally, sleep overtook him. God was merciful. Tonight, the nightmares would not return.

Chapter 25

Has someone ever come into your life, and as far as you could tell, it was only for one purpose? They perform their task, and then they're gone, only to step back into your life with an even greater role to play? That's exactly what Dr. King would do for me. The man I blamed for taking my quality of life would return to help lead me into life.

Grace knocked on Jake's door with one hand, her cell phone in the other.

"Jake, wake up, son. There's someone on the phone who wants to speak with you."

She waited outside his door for a response. The door finally cracked open. A haggard-looking Jake peeked out of the dark room. She handed him her cell phone, and he mouthed the words, *Who is it?*

Grace whispered, "Talk to him."

Jake put the phone to his ear. "Hello?"

"Jake!" a deep, rich voice boomed. "How are ya?"

"Dr. King?"

"Listen…I'm headed to the car show. I'd ask if you like classics, but I already know the answer," he said, chuckling. "I'll pick you up in twenty minutes."

"Uh…actually I'm hurting pretty bad today," Jake said.

"OK. Then I'll make it thirty," he replied. "See you then."

Dr. King hung up before Jake could respond. He looked at Grace, his eyebrows raised.

"I'll have your breakfast ready," Grace said, not giving him a chance to back out. "Do something with that hair. And don't try and pass it off as the messy look."

She took the phone from Jake's hand and pulled the door shut.

Jake was perplexed. *What just happened?*

Realizing there was no way to avoid this outing, Jake started getting dressed. As he sat by the bathroom sink brushing his teeth, thoughts of the nightmares ran through his mind. He pushed them back and refused to allow them to consume him. He wheeled to the kitchen, where Grace had his breakfast ready.

"That seemed so random," Jake said.

"What did?" Grace asked as she poured a glass of orange juice.

"Dr. King calling me. Don't you think that was kinda just outta the blue?"

"Oh, I don't know. You and Dr. King got to be pretty close when you were under his care. I guess he just misses you."

"I guess," Jake said.

Moments later, the doorbell rang.

Grace opened the door to see the elderly Dr. King wearing the heartwarming smile for which he was so well known. And it was contagious. Grace already felt hopeful. She welcomed him inside.

"It's so good to see you, Dr. King," Grace said sincerely as she hugged him.

"It's good to see you, too," he said as he returned a gentle hug.

Jake pushed away from the table and met him at the door.

"Jake, you look good, son," Dr. King said, offering him a firm handshake.

"Thanks, Doc. I appreciate that," Jake said.

"You ready to see some good-looking cars?" Dr. King asked.

"You bet," Jake said enthusiastically.

"Better grab your jacket. It's a bit nippy out this morning," Dr. King said.

While Jake left the room, Grace took Dr. King by the hand. "You have no idea how thankful I am that you're willing to do this."

The doctor patted her arm. "I'm so glad you called me. I've been thinking about Jake…about all of you, actually. I knew it was going to be very difficult, and I was worried about him."

"Thank you for that," Grace said.

"I've been praying for Jake," Dr. King said. "I told the Lord if He wanted to use me in his life that I was willing. And, well, here we are."

They both chuckled. Jake wheeled back into the kitchen.

"What's so funny?" he asked.

"You are, that's what," Dr. King said. "Who gets their jacket, then sets it in their lap and doesn't wear it? Let's get going. I want to beat the crowd."

"Crowd?' Jake asked.

"You'd be surprised at how many fans of old cars there are," Dr. King said.

"You boys have a good time," Grace said.

"Boys?" Dr. King questioned. He looked at Jake and said, "I haven't been referred to as a boy in years! That's why your mom is my favorite person," he said with a wink.

"Yeah, she's pretty special," Jake said.

The light conversation was refreshing to Grace. That was the kind of spirit that Dr. King exuded. She knew calling him had been inspired.

Dr. King and Jake arrived at the Automobile Museum, home of the local annual car show. Rows of classic cars lined the interior of the large building. Dr. King walked beside Jake, keeping pace with his wheelchair. They stopped in front of a Corvette.

"That one's my favorite," Dr. King said.

Dr. King watched Jake look over every inch of the car.

"I had a '67 Pontiac GTO," Dr. King said. "Beat the socks off of a few Corvettes back in the day."

Jake grinned, then looked around. A pink-and-white car across the aisle caught his interest. He wheeled over to it.

"1932 Nash," Dr. King said. "Talk about a success story. Charles Nash was abandoned by his parents when he was six. The courts basically forced him into slave labor for a farmer after that. When he was twelve, he ran away and found a job stuffing cushions for a carriage company. He became president of Buick, then GM. Eventually, he created his own company. Not bad for an orphan, huh? Amazing what the human spirit is capable of."

Jake nodded. His stomach growled loudly. Jake was surprised and embarrassed at the same time. He tapped his stomach with his hand.

"Either you're hungry or you're hiding a bulldog in your shirt," Dr. King kidded. "Come on. Let's get some grub."

The two made their way to a concession stand and took their order out to Dr. King's truck. He let down his tailgate to sit on while they ate. Jake situated his wheelchair in front of the doctor and locked the wheels into place. Dr. King took a bite of his sandwich and watched Jake as he stared into the distance.

"How have you been feeling?" Dr. King asked.

Jake munched on a French fry.

"I hurt," he replied.

"Is that why you're quitting school?" Dr. King asked.

Jake dropped his fry onto his plate. He looked up at Dr. King and said, "I can't pass this year. It's either repeat or get a GED. I'm just going through the motions. Besides, going back was harder than I ever thought it would be. It's so bittersweet. Actually, more bitter than sweet," Jake said. "I feel like I'm just there to hang out."

"Well, you gotta hang out somewhere," Dr. King replied.

"That's just it. I don't belong anywhere," Jake said.

Dr. King wiped his mouth.

"I want to show you another car, but it's not here," Dr. King said.

Puzzled, Jake asked, "Where is it?"

"I'll show you," Dr. King said.

They finished their lunch and headed to another location. Dr. King made a right-hand turn into a familiar parking lot.

"Spears Towing?" Jake asked.

"Yep," Dr. King said.

Jake looked through the front windshield of the truck and wondered why Dr. King would have brought him here. His attention was caught by the opening of the office door. A man with thinning hair and a blue mechanic's outfit emerged. Jake grinned. It was Vic... The life-long family friend waved. Dr. King met him halfway between his truck and the office. The two men talked for a moment. Jake rolled down his window and tried to eavesdrop on their conversation but could hear nothing. A moment later, Dr. King returned to the truck.

"Sit tight," he said to Jake. "We're driving around back."

"For what?" Jake asked.

"You'll see," Dr. King said with a grin.

"You're scaring me," Jake said jokingly.

"Well, a doc who goes around sawing off legs tends to have that effect on people," Dr. King replied.

Jake laughed out loud at his morbid sense of humor.

Dr. King started the truck again, put it in drive and followed the trail that led to the junkyard area. Vic met them around back. Dr. King parked the truck in the midst of hundreds of banged-up vehicles. He unloaded Jake's wheelchair and helped him into it.

Turning to Vic, he said, "Lead the way, sir."

"All-righty," Vic said. "Follow me."

Dr. King pushed Jake's wheelchair over an uneven grassy area mixed with gravel. Jake winced and moaned at the pain from the rough ride.

"We're almost there," Vic said. He motioned ahead. "Just over to our right."

Jake's eyes followed Vic's finger as he pointed to the object Dr. King had brought him to see. Jake squinted as he stared at the charred remains of his '79 Trans-Am. A hunk of black and white metal was all that remained. His face grew pale.

"That's my car," he whispered.

"Yes, Jake. That's *your* classic car," Dr. King said.

Vic excused himself so the two could be alone. "I'll be inside my office if you need anything else. Take all the time you need."

"Thank you, sir," Dr. King replied.

Jake tried to roll closer to the car but struggled on the rocky terrain. Dr. King took over and helped.

"Why would you bring me here?" Jake asked.

"For understanding," Dr. King said.

Jake approached the driver's side window of the totaled vehicle.

"To understand what?" Jake asked, gazing at the melted interior.

"Fourth degree burns. Your legs were nearly burned away...up to the knees."

Jake noticed a black object dangling near the steering wheel.

Dr. King continued. "Above that...perfect. Your torso, your face... smooth as the day you were born. You breathed superheated air...eight hundred degrees...for five minutes without lung damage."

Jake reached into the interior and removed the charred Trans-Am key from the ignition.

"How do you explain that?" Dr. King asked.

Jake examined the key in his hand and the charred letter "J." His heart raced.

Jake rubbed at the keychain with his thumb. Some of the char rubbed away, revealing the bright-red paint.

"You should be dead," Dr. King said. "They should've been picking your teeth out of that melted upholstery. Do you understand that, son?"

Jake spun around.

"I want to understand. But right now, I'm trying to figure out how to get off the toilet without busting my head on the tile floor. I'm trying to figure out if I'm ever going to find a girl who doesn't feel sorry for me."

Dr. King took the keychain from Jake's hand.

"God has some kind of plan for you, boy," he said with conviction. "Something I can't even imagine. But I see it as big as day." He spit on the keychain and scrubbed at the char with an old work rag he found on the ground.

Dr. King continued. "And if you'll let Him heal all that anger and hurt you're wallowing in, you'll begin to see it, too." He tossed the keychain back to Jake. In Jake's hand rested an almost-perfectly-restored red "J" keychain. Not a trace of black remained. Jake clutched it in his hand.

"I think we are done here. Let's get you home," Dr. King said.

During the ride, Dr. King managed to lift Jake's spirits with his corny jokes and crazy hospital stories. Ten minutes later, they pulled into the driveway. Jake hesitated getting out. He looked straight ahead and began to speak.

"At the wreck, when I was trapped...I saw something."

"What?" Dr. King asked.

"Something...I don't even know if it was real, but I can't get it out of my head," Jake said.

"For we are not fighting against people made of flesh and blood, but against the evil rulers and authorities of the unseen world..." Dr. King quoted.

Astonished, Jake turned to the older man, who stared out the front window.

"...against those powers of darkness who rule this world, and against wicked spirits in the heavenly realms..." Dr. King continued. He looked at Jake and smiled. "Here on earth you will have many trials and sorrows. But take heart, because I have overcome the world."

Mitch appeared and unloaded Jake's wheelchair.

"I've heard this stuff all my life," Jake said.

"Then you are without excuse," Dr. King replied.

Mitch opened the door.

"How was the show?" he asked while helping Jake into the chair.

"Lots of old cars," Dr. King commented. "Makes an old man feel young again."

"I'll bet!" Mitch chuckled. "You got it, son?"

Jake gave him a thumbs-up.

Mitch leaned inside the truck toward Dr. King. "Thanks so much for spending time with Jake today."

He turned and walked back to the house.

"Night," Jake said.

As he closed the passenger side door, Dr. King stopped him. He opened the glove box and produced a tattered leather Bible. He passed it to Jake. Jake ran his fingers over the ragged edges of the cover, then across the gold-embossed letters that read *Edward King*. Jake looked at him.

"You're giving me your Bible?' Jake asked.

"It's a weapon," Dr. King said. "Revelation 12."

"Thank you," Jake said as he shut the door and waved good-bye.

"How'd it go?" Grace stood in the kitchen, a look of excitement on her face.

"It was good," Jake said, smiling. "I didn't realize how much I missed talking to him. It was a good day."

"I'm so glad," Grace said.

"I'm pretty tired. I think I'm gonna go on to bed."

"OK. Let me know if you need anything," Grace said.

"I will. Thanks," Jake said.

"Rest well, son," Mitch said.

"OK, Dad."

Jake maneuvered the wheelchair to his room. He took the visibly-worn Bible Dr. King had given him and laid it on his nightstand. He reached into his pocket, pulled out his red "J" keychain and held it in his hand. "I thought I'd lost you forever," he whispered. He held it up for a moment and watched it dangle in the light, then placed it on top of the Bible.

He struggled to change his clothes. The day had been filled with much more activity than had been his usual over the last few weeks, and his pain level was elevated. It was time for his nightly pain pills, but he realized his water bottle was empty. Wheeling down the hall toward the kitchen, he stopped. His parents were talking, and the conversation sounded intense. Jake peered around the corner to listen.

"I don't know what the answer is," Mitch said as he looked through a stack of papers. "Major medical is tapped out and Jake has another surgery next month."

"I could take on more orders at the floral shop," Grace offered.

"You're already working extra hours," Mitch said. "You're stretching yourself too thin."

"Mitch, what if you took that outside sales job Bradley Wilson has been trying to get you to take for a year? It would be a steady income instead of commission," Grace suggested.

"It's steady income, Grace, but comes with a high price. I'd have to travel, leaving you here to take care of the floral shop and Jake by yourself most of the time. I'm not going to leave you stranded like that."

"We need to do whatever it takes, Mitch," Grace said.

"We could sell your floral business," Mitch said. "We could use the profit to pay off the medical bills and have some to live on for a while."

"And then what?" Grace asked.

Mitch sat down and ran his hands through his hair in frustration.

"I don't know. I just don't know."

Jake wheeled back to his room without getting the water. He replayed the conversation he had just overheard. Guilt and condemnation plagued him. Although it was difficult to swallow them without a drink, he hurried to get the pain pills in his system – not only to help him escape the physical pain, but the emotional pain as well. He moaned aloud as he situated himself in his bed. The haunting voices began. *You are such a burden. This is all your fault. Worthless.* Jake turned on his side and faced the nightstand. He stared at the old tattered Bible Dr. King had given him. *Bedtime stories, Jake. They're not real.* Jake opened the drawer and set the Bible and keychain inside. He turned on his back and stared at the poster on the ceiling.

A few moments passed. The pain medication moved through Jake's body, and soon he slipped off to sleep. Smoke began to rise from a table a few feet away, then the smoke turned into flames. The nearby curtains quickly caught fire and spread across the room. Jake looked down to find his legs on fire. He swatted them, trying desperately to extinguish the flames. He screamed out.

His screams awakened him in his bed. He tried to sit up but couldn't. A large shadowy figure stood in the doorway. Jake tried to yell, but no sound came out. The demon moved toward him, shedding its shadowy cloak. The black, armored form stepped toward him, and its lifeless face grinned. Jake managed to push himself up. Then...it was no longer there. Vanished.

Jake sat up. His heart raced as he ran his hands through his sweaty hair. *It was just a dream. It was just a dream.* He collapsed back on the bed. His breathing began to slow. His mouth was parched, so he forced himself into his chair to again make the trip down the hall to the kitchen for a drink.

Once there, he struggled to reach a glass. He gained enough leverage with his fingers to tilt it toward him, then quickly filled it and gulped it down. He slammed the glass down on the counter beside a stack of papers. Medical bills, Jake noticed. Astronomical amounts owed for his hospital care and rehabilitation. The voices returned. *You caused this. It should have been you, Jake.*

Jake rolled down the hallway to the bathroom and turned on the faucet. He stared at himself in the mirror. He heard the voice again. *There's nothing for you here, now. Your life is over.* He splashed his face with the cold water and grabbed a towel from the sink, wiping his face. He threw it on the countertop, knocking over an open bottle of pain medication. Pills bounced all over the sink and onto the floor.

He again looked in the mirror. "It should have been me," he said aloud. He reached for the pills. He paused and looked in the mirror again. An evil version of his reflection smiled back at him. *This is what your soul looks like,* said the voice from Jake's demented reflection. It then winked. Jake pushed away from the sink and fell onto the floor. Terrified, he struggled to get back into his wheelchair. Sweat poured from his face. He wheeled to his bedroom quickly, pushed through the bedroom door and stopped. Spooked from his experience in the bathroom, he sat frozen in place as he looked around his room, moving only his eyes. They stopped on the nightstand drawer, which was pulled out slightly. Another voice spoke – only this time, it was a voice of truth. *It's a weapon.*

Jake rolled himself toward the nightstand and pulled the chain on his bedside lamp. A soft glow overtook the dark room. Slowly, Jake slid open the nightstand drawer. There sat the tattered black Bible with the gold embossing, the red "J" keychain sitting atop it. Placing the keychain on top of the nightstand, he then pulled the Bible out of the drawer and laid it on his bed. He locked the brakes on his chair, picked up the Bible and flipped through the pages until he found the heading that read *Revelation 12*. Jake followed the chapter down to verse seven. He read it aloud as he traced the words with his right index finger.

"And war broke out in Heaven: Michael and his angels fought with the dragon; and the dragon and his angels fought..." Jake looked around his dimly-lit bedroom and into the hall. A dark shadow covered the wall. Jake searched with his eyes, looking for a logical reason for it to be there. He saw nothing; there was no object to cast a shadow.

"This is ridiculous," he said.

He looked back at the Bible and continued to read aloud. "...but they did not prevail, nor was a place found for them in Heaven any longer. So the great dragon was cast out, that servant of old, called the Devil and Satan, who deceives the whole world; he was cast to the earth, and his angels were cast out with him. Then I heard a loud voice saying in Heaven, 'Now salvation, and strength, and the kingdom of our God, and the power of His Christ have come, for the accuser of our brethren, who accused them before our God day and night, has been cast down.' " Then, looking at verse 11, which was highlighted in neon green, he read, " 'And they overcame him by the blood of the Lamb and by the word of their testimony.' "

Jake looked outside his room into the hallway again. The shadow fled. Relief fell across his face. Somehow, Jake understood the power of reading the word of God out loud. Feeling empowered, Jake read through the next several chapters. Before he knew it, it was 12:25. The red "J" keychain gleamed in the light of the lamp in an almost unnatural way. He glared at it for a moment. He picked up the Bible and started to return it to the drawer. He hesitated and instead left it atop the nightstand. After slipping under his covers and adjusting his pillows, a peace enveloped him.

"I need to go to church tomorrow," he said aloud. He was astonished upon hearing the words from his very own mouth, but he was resolved. He set the alarm for 8 a.m. Somehow, he knew tomorrow was going to bring hope.

Chapter 26

I didn't know why I felt like I needed to get to church. I'd never felt that way before…ever. I just knew I needed to. And I was excited about it! So weird…I had run from the Lord for so long, and now, I was about to run right into Him. After so many awful, irresponsible choices, I was about to make a great one.

Jake awoke to the sun peering through his window. His thoughts traveled to the night before. Last night's sleep was the best it had been in months. And it had required no medicine. He looked at the time on his clock. It read 7:30 a.m. It was still early.

Jake's nose caught the aromas of applewood-smoked bacon and coffee. It was like old times this morning with one exception… he planned to join his parents for church. He smiled at the thought of his mom's face when she heard the news. He wheeled into the kitchen and smiled at what he saw. Grace raced around the kitchen preparing Sunday morning breakfast while Mitch sat at the kitchen table and read the college sports aloud. Jake snickered at his mother's attempted interaction in a conversation with Mitch about football highlights from the day before.

"Good morning," Jake said, unusually lively.

His cheerful greeting stunned them.

"Wow! You're up early," Grace said.

Surprised, yet delighted, she walked over to Jake and kissed him on the cheek.

"How would you like your eggs?" Grace asked.

"The usual, I guess," Jake replied as he wheeled to the table. "Hey, Dad, are you done with the sports?" he asked.

"Sure," Mitch said. "I think reading it three times is probably plenty."

"How did you sleep last night, son?" Grace asked.

"Very well, actually," Jake said.

"That's unusual," Mitch said.

"Yeah, I know, right?" Jake said.

Jake continued reading the sports section of the *Daily Journal.* Mitch and Grace eyed each other. Jake's behavior excited them but also perplexed them.

"So, what time we leaving for church?" Jake asked as he continued his reading.

Grace walked to the table with platters of food in her hands. She looked at Mitch again, very puzzled, and said, "Nine-thirty."

"Oh, then I've got plenty of time," Jake said.

"Time for what?" Mitch asked.

"To get dressed," Jake said.

"Dressed for what?" Grace asked.

"Church," Jake replied as if it were a dumb question.

"Oh, of course," Grace replied. "OK, everyone dig in," she said. She chose to drop the subject, concerned that if she went on about his decision to go, he might change his mind.

"Looks like we need to grab our umbrella," Mitch said, folding up the main section of the paper with the weather forecast. "It's going to be a wet one."

Breakfast was peaceful. The three enjoyed conversation while eating, and even laughed once in a while. As Grace cleared the table afterward, she couldn't help but smile.

For the first time in years, all three members of the Adams family arrived at the front doors of the church...together. Elated, Grace couldn't recall the last time this had occurred, except on a holiday. They moved quickly to get inside out of the drizzle. Mitch held an umbrella over them while Grace pushed Jake up the wheelchair ramp.

"Grace!" one greeter exclaimed, hugging her neck before extending his hand to Jake. "Jake, man, it's good to see you."

Jake shook the man's hand and smiled.

"We've been praying for you, Jake," another greeter said. Soon they were surrounded by church family.

The attention was awkward for Jake. He noticed the cemetery across the street where Ross was buried. The conversations around him faded for a moment as he thought of his best friend.

Eventually they moved inside the sanctuary. Jake looked around the large room. Praise music played over the church's sound system, and colorful, detailed announcements were displayed on two large media screens, informing the congregation of upcoming events. Friends continued welcoming the Adamses as they searched for seating. Grace stopped midway up the aisle and took a seat Mitch was saving for her. Jake pulled his chair beside her. A little girl in the pew in front of them stared curiously at Jake's legs. Others in the congregation offered hugs and welcoming words to Jake. Although it made him feel uncomfortable, he appreciated their kindness.

The service began. Those around him sang, but Jake only watched. The songs weren't familiar to him. Afraid that others might notice he wasn't singing, Jake focused on the lyrics on the screen.

Lauren dragged into church late. Not wanting to draw attention to herself, she headed for the first empty seat she saw. Her hair and clothes were damp from the rain. She worked quickly to get her purse and Bible situated so she could join in the worship, unaware that Jake sat two rows ahead.

His wheelchair soon caught her attention. She thought for a moment it must be a visitor. Then it dawned on her who it belonged to. Lauren had worked diligently to avoid him at school, but now she was stuck. She chose to suck it up and stay put. Then, her spiritual battle began.

As the worship leader concluded the final chorus, Pastor Glenn walked onto the platform to share the word that the Lord had laid on his heart. He knew the subject was difficult but necessary to tackle. Pastor Glenn felt strongly convicted that he was led by the Holy Spirit to preach on the subject of death and being eternally separated from God. Realizing it wasn't popular and he could certainly face opposition because of the strong content, he prayed for strength and boldness to be obedient to what he believed the Lord had called him to do.

Scanning the congregation, he took a deep breath and started right in.

"This morning, I am compelled to preach on a subject that is very unpopular – the subject of a very real place called Hell."

From that moment, the preacher had a captive audience, including Jake. The things he had seen at the wreck site were haunting, and he wanted answers.

Lauren, too, perked up at the mention of the subject. In her mind, it was for Jake. He needed to hear a strong sermon on Hell that had the potential to drive him to repentance. She never thought that she might need this powerful message as much as he did.

Pastor Glenn continued. "Preaching on Hell has been left out of most churches. Preachers avoid it like the plague. Some pastors and believers even question its existence. Because it isn't an ear-tickling topic, many scorn those who speak of it. Therefore, it is imperative that I preach this message. The truth is, I would be failing to teach the entire counsel of the gospel of Jesus Christ if I failed to preach this message. I cannot do that. So...it is through a broken heart that I share this with you out of obedience to my Father."

Jake squirmed in his wheelchair as the little girl continued to stare at him.

"First, I want to shatter the lie that Hell doesn't exist," Pastor Glenn said. "Think about it. The salvation offered to us has to be salvation from something. You can't have a need for salvation without having a need to be saved from something. So how can we ignore the idea that Hell exists? Well, the reality of it is that Hell *does* exist. I believe that one of the reasons it is so hard for people to receive the truth of Hell's existence is because it is so misunderstood. Some would ask, how could a loving God send anyone there?"

Jake quickly looked up. This is the answer he had been waiting for.

"The answer is easy," Pastor Glenn said. "He doesn't."

Jake was confused. It wasn't at all what he expected Pastor Glenn to say. Lauren shared in Jake's confusion. Her pharisaical and judgmental attitude had always led her to see things much differently.

The pastor continued. "I'm going to start off by sharing the truth with you about the purpose for Hell. God did not create Hell with man in mind. You see, there was a rebellion – the first ever rebellion – by Lucifer and one third of the angels. God, in His infinite wisdom, knew that evil must be judged, and He judged it at that moment. He created Hell for Satan and all the fallen angels. Then God created man in His own image, and the fall of man was when the second rebellion occurred. Because God had already established the judgment for rebellion, man fell under that just judgment for evil." Then, smiling, Pastor Glenn said, "But...God made a way...the perfect Lamb of God. Christ chose to leave paradise – a place created by God where He could fellowship with man for all eternity – and to instead endure the cross – a substitution for the eternal damnation of Hell. So to say God sends people to Hell...that statement couldn't be any more false, because God has done everything necessary so that no one has to go there. Understand this: No one...no one, was ever meant to go to Hell. We choose it. We choose to reject God, and because He is a good judge, we must receive His judgment. That judgment is eternal separation from Him, in Hell."

For Jake and Lauren, this explanation of Hell was clear. For Jake, as a lost person, it made sense. Everything his mother said versus everything the voices in his head said – they stood in total conflict with each other. But that all faded in his mind behind the truth he had just heard.

As for Lauren, truth had pierced her judgmental and legalistic mentality, and for the first time, she felt peace.

"So this morning, I'm just going to spell it out for you. I'm not going to embellish or even try to paint a picture for you. I'm just going to describe for you, in accordance with God's word, what we know about this place called Hell. I want us to look scripture by scripture at the description God gives us in His word."

A very intrigued congregation, eager to follow Pastor Glenn in the scriptures, pulled out Bibles, tablets and smartphones, waiting to search for each scripture he referenced.

Pastor Glenn stepped to the edge of the platform, bent down toward his flock and asked, "Do you know who taught more about Hell than anyone else?"

Believing the question to be rhetorical, the crowd remained silent.

"Jesus," Pastor Glenn said. "As a matter of fact, it's one of the main topics He talked about in scripture. He even dedicated a whole parable depicting it. It's the parable of the rich man and Lazarus. Turn with me if you would to Luke chapter 16, beginning at verse 19."

Pastor Glenn began to read. "There was a certain rich man who was clothed in purple and fine linen and fared sumptuously every day."

Jake looked up. His mind raced back to the night of Youth Explosion. Although he had paid no attention that night, somehow he remembered that passage and the parable shared by evangelist George Preston. *How could I have remembered that?* he wondered. *I wasn't even listening.*

"But there was a certain beggar named Lazarus, full of sores, who was laid at his gate, desiring to be fed with the crumbs which fell from the rich man's table. Moreover the dogs came and licked his sores. So it was that the beggar died, and was carried by the angels to Abraham's bosom. The rich man also died and was buried. And being in torments in Hades, he lifted up his eyes and saw Abraham afar off, and Lazarus in his bosom."

Suddenly, behind Pastor Glenn, the fabric of this world began to burn away, just as Jake had witnessed at the wreck.

Pastor Glenn continued. "Then he cried and said, 'Father Abraham, have mercy on me, and send Lazarus that he may dip the tip of his finger in water and cool my tongue; for I am tormented in this flame.' "

The flames continued to devastate and burn but were no longer confined to the area behind Pastor Glenn. They now spread at a fast clip in a 360-degree motion around the sanctuary. Jake quickly looked at the faces of those in the congregation and watched for reactions. Nothing. *Am I the only one seeing this?*

Pastor Glenn continued. "But Abraham said, 'Son, remember that in your lifetime you received your good things, and likewise Lazarus evil things; but now he is comforted and you are tormented. And besides all this, between us and you there is a great gulf fixed, so that those who want to pass from here to you cannot, nor can those from there pass to us.' "

In an instant, Jake was transported a second time to the black, filthy landscape of demonic underworld. The area was dark as night, interrupted only by wisps of orange, foul-smelling flames. Superheated winds blew glowing embers and ash through the air, melting everything they landed on. A horrible sound like that of a giant blowtorch filled Jake's ears. And the human wails... Tears filled Jake's eyes, imagining the suffering behind those wretched sounds. The cries of desperation and hopelessness and unending torture were unlike anything Jake had ever heard before.

"Then he said, 'I beg you therefore, father, that you would send him to my father's house, for I have five brothers that he may testify to them, lest they also come to this place of torment.'

"Abraham said to him, 'They have Moses and the prophets; let them hear them.' And he said, 'No, father Abraham; but if one goes to them from the dead, they will repent.' But he said to him, 'If they do not hear Moses and the prophets, neither will they be persuaded though one risen from the dead.' "

Jake watched the rich man, clothed in purple linen and gold jewelry, struggle for a breath of air, then slowly collapse into the glowing coals. The flesh of his hands sizzled and smoked. His clothes started to burn away. His jewelry melted, leaving streams of boiling metal cascading down his now-naked torso. Jake watched as flames licked around him, yet he remained unharmed.

Pastor Glenn's voice rang throughout the sanctuary as he continued the sermon.

"One of the first truths we see about Hell is the torment that came instantaneously. You see that?" he questioned his congregation. "Instantaneously."

This truth gripped every member of the congregation.

"It was a flame so great that the rich man was consumed with fire and he just begged for some semblance of relief. Not a drink of water – just 'dip your finger in water and touch the tip of my tongue,' " Pastor Glenn pointed out. "Guys, Hell is a real place. It's not a figment of our imagination. It's not a Spielberg movie, but a real place."

Flipping the pages of his Bible, Pastor Glenn made reference to another passage of scripture. "We find in Matthew 25:30, 'And cast the unprofitable servant into the outer darkness. There will be weeping and gnashing of teeth.' The torment is so great, you will continually cry without ever stopping. In that same verse, along with Matthew 22:13, we see it is a place of outer darkness. It is a place of complete and total darkness. Why? Because it is absent of the presence of God."

Tears began to fall on faces throughout the sanctuary.

"In Luke 16:23, it says Hell is a place of torments. Not torment, but torments. Plural. You will be tormented by many things. It's a place of sorrow, according to 2 Samuel 22:6, which says this... 'The sorrows of Sheol surrounded me; the snares of death confronted me.'

"In 2 Thessalonians 1:9, it's a place of everlasting destruction. 'These shall be punished with everlasting destruction from the presence of the Lord and from the glory of His power.' Revelation 21:8 says it's a place where men are tormented with fire and brimstone."

The passionate preacher held out his open Bible. "If you want to know what kind of pain it will be, it will be continual pain. Your body is melting yet never consumed."

Jake remained in the spirit world as he witnessed the rich man wail in agony, crawling through the red-and-black coal, leaving a trail of melted flesh as he went. He rolled onto his back, causing a burst of steam to erupt around him. Jake watched in disbelief as the man struggled to lift his body but couldn't. The rich man ground his teeth in pain as the skin burned from his torso, revealing his ribs and muscle. He managed to raise his arm toward Jake and cried out, "Help me!"

Jake stood frozen in fear, incredibly uncomfortable and totally helpless. As the rich man screamed, Jake saw that his throat was filled with the glow of fire from deep within his body. The corners of his lips melted and stuck together while his face burned.

Jake was suddenly swept away from the fiery torment, and the sanctuary was once again before him. Sweating profusely and eyes glazed, he rubbed his forehead. Grace noticed that Jake was visibly shaken.

"Are you all right?" Grace whispered.

Jake simply nodded his head.

Pastor Glenn continued. "Not only will your body be burning, it will be rotting as it burns, according to Mark 9:46. 'Their worm does not die, and the fire is not quenched.' That leads me to my next detail. The fire is never quenched. It never goes out. There is never any relief from it.

"It is a bottomless pit. In Revelation 9:2 God's word says, 'And he opened the bottomless pit, and smoke arose out of the pit like the smoke of a great furnace.'

"It's a place of no rest. Revelation 14:11 says, 'And the smoke of their torment ascends forever and ever; and they have no rest day or night, who worship the beast and his image, and whoever receives the mark of his name.' Understand that when the judgment falls, there will not be a moment's peace.

"Hell is ultimately a lake of fire. Revelation 20:14 and 15 say, 'Then Death and Hades were cast into the lake of fire. This is the second death. And anyone not found written in the Book of Life was cast into the lake of fire.' "

Pastor Glenn walked to the other side of the platform. "It is the agony of unsatisfied desires. Do you know that in Hell, you will have a memory? We just read in Luke that the rich man is told by Abraham, 'Son, remember...' Do you see that? He said, '...*remember* that in your lifetime you received your good things, and likewise Lazarus evil things; but now he is comforted and you are tormented.' With that verse in mind, can you imagine with me for a moment what living in Hell might be like? Consider this as a possibility:

"You will remember every satisfaction you ever experienced on earth, but you will never enjoy them again. And what will be eternally rotating through your mind is every time you heard the gospel... every time Jesus walked up to you in the form of another person and spoke the reality of the love and mercy and grace of the heavenly Father. And you will recall every single time you turned and walked away, every time you laughed, every time you scorned, every time your intellect tried to explain away the existence of Hell. The truth of how Christ made a way for you, and your rejection of it…this will be more tormenting to you than your flesh melting off your body but never being consumed."

The pastor paused a moment and wiped the sweat from his forehead. The intensity of his sermon had his congregation on the edge of their seats.

"Finally, Hell is a place where there is no hope. That moment you realize there will never be an end to it will be the moment you experience complete hopelessness. Do you understand that we could never fathom how horrific Hell is? It defies our imagination and is absolutely indefinite. Yet, in our anger or selfishness we wish for people to go there."

Immediately, Lauren fell under heavy conviction as she remembered the hateful statement she had made to her mother. *I hope Jake doesn't make it to Heaven, either.*

Suddenly, she felt sick in the pit of her stomach.

"You may say, 'Preacher, I don't say that.' What about the times you've said absolutely nothing? Or maybe the words you did say led someone *away* from the cross, instead of *to* it. What about your actions? Do they point people in the direction of the cross that leads to salvation?"

Lauren remembered the confrontation with her mother just days before. She began to recall all the times she had said, thought or wished harm to Jake. Realizing her failures in this, she began to weep.

"Now, let's change perspectives," Pastor Glenn continued. "Let's get personal for a minute. Because every one of us here knows someone who is there at this very moment."

Jake popped the brakes on his wheelchair, turned around and rolled toward the back of the church to the men's room. Lauren watched him. She knew by his expression that he was in turmoil.

Jake burst through the men's room door toward the sink. Pastor Glenn's voice continued to blare from the speakers inside the men's room.

"Chances are that this person is someone you loved and would have even given your life for."

Jake turned on the faucet. As he splashed water on his face, his memory drew up the conversation he had had with Ross when leaving Youth Explosion.

Ross, what are you waiting for? We've got a race to get to!

You buy any of that stuff? Ross had asked.

No, Jake had answered. *They don't even know what they're selling. One second God loves everybody...the next second He's killing everybody. I mean, which is it?*

Yeah, you're right.

Jake had turned Ross away from the cross. He knew that now. Breathing heavily, he looked at his reflection in the mirror. Behind him, the cauterized landscape returned.

"No! Not again!" Jake said loudly.

Again he splashed water on his face.

"Go away. Just go away," Jake said, his face in his hands. "It's not real. It's not real."

A voice whispered his name from behind. Not his given name, but a nickname reserved only by his very best friend.

"Bama Bro."

The hairs stood up on the back of Jake's neck. Reluctantly, he looked in the mirror. Behind him stood a horribly grotesque Ross Kelly. Most of the skin was burned from his face. His half-burned body was riddled with flesh-eating worms. He raised his hand to Jake.

"Help me!" he cried hoarsely, as worms crawled from his nostrils.

Jake was horrified as he watched burning embers sweep across Ross's skin. Heat waves distorted the air. A look of hopelessness overcame Jake's face, and he began to weep uncontrollably.

"I'm so sorry, Ross!" Jake cried out.

Suddenly, Jake awoke from his vision. He peered into the mirror and noticed how haggard he looked. The speakers continued to broadcast Pastor Glenn's sermon.

Fearful the visions would return, Jake quickly wheeled out of the men's room and back into the sanctuary. His hair was wringing wet from the combination of water and sweat.

As Jake fixed his chair back in its position beside Grace, Pastor Glenn took notice of him. Although he continued to preach without hesitation, in his spirit he knew Jake was under conviction. Pastor Glenn's heart was broken for him.

Pastor Glenn spoke honestly with his flock. "I have wept the whole time I've studied this. There is not a passage in scripture that speaks of Hell, Hades or Sheol or any term of Hell that I have not read in preparation for this. The one thing I've come away with is this: Anyone who truly believes this…their life will be eternally changed. So we are not doing a good job of describing it and reflecting Christ, and it falls upon us. But now, both have clearly been revealed today. I knew that there was no way I could stand here and preach this message with any other emotions than horror and sorrow, because in my lifetime, I have come into contact with a lot of people whom I failed to move toward accepting Christ as their personal Savior. As a matter of fact, in my lifetime, I have grabbed people and pulled them away from Christ by my actions."

Seeing herself in that position, Lauren looked at Jake. Tears streamed down her face.

Pastor Glenn continued. "I think about the years I spent in rebellion against God. The dating relationships…the partners and friends I ran with…the things I encouraged them to indulge in with me. Then I think about their eternity that one day will be decided when they take their last breath."

Pastor Glenn sat down on the steps of the altar area just below the platform and shared transparently. "I'll be honest with you. After this study, I'll never be the same, and after hearing this message, I hope you'll never be the same either. Believers, listen to me. Everyone you come in contact with has an eternity in their destiny. What you say makes a difference. How you behave makes a difference. This is saying to the believer, 'You need to do whatever is asked of you to make sure that everyone around you sees the picture of Jesus Christ burning in your life so others will be drawn to Him.' For sure, you shouldn't party with them and tell them it's OK. For sure, you shouldn't lead them into sin and bondage that would lead them away from Christ and tell them it's OK. Your role here on earth is not to merely exist with your fire insurance, but to lead as many as you can to Christ so that one day, they will live in Heaven with their Creator.

"To those of you who are lost today, you have heard truth. Hell is real, but God didn't intend for you to go there. He made a way for you through His precious Son, Jesus. Please understand, it is imperative that you grasp this and look headlong at the finished work of the cross. For you to choose to refuse Christ is to refuse the wonderful destiny God designed for you. When you choose to turn your back on Him, you are choosing an eternity apart from Him. The best part is...you get to choose."

At that moment, Pastor Glenn's and Jake's eyes locked onto one another. Pastor Glenn called for the worship leader to come and start the time of invitation.

Only moments into the music, Jake released the locks on the wheels of his chair. Grace looked at him. He looked toward the altar. Grace's heart raced. Jake began to cry and rolled forward. Pastor Glenn caught sight of him. Jake hesitated, then quickly turned around and rolled out the front doors of the church and down the handicap ramp. The rain began to drizzle again. Jake sat at the edge of the parking lot where it met the street. Making sure he had clearance, he wheeled himself across the street to the cemetery. As Jake struggled through the mud to Ross's grave, church members gathered around Grace to pray. Lauren rose from her seat to join them. She stopped. Pastor Glenn's sermon had brought on conviction that pierced her, forcing her to deal with situations in her life that were far from who Christ was. The hatred and anger she had allowed to control her in this tragic situation was being pushed away by the power of the Holy Spirit at work in her. Compelled to make things right with Jake, she dashed out the double doors of the church and rushed after him.

"Jake!" Lauren yelled.

She knew it was useless. *There's no way he can hear me from here,* she thought. She ran toward the cemetery, not sure what to say. Her overwhelming conviction pressed on her to make things right.

As Lauren ran toward Jake, the congregation continued to pray.

"I'm really sensing the Holy Spirit's movement right now," Pastor Glenn said. "Keep praying!"

As the prayers grew stronger, Jake struggled to push his way to Ross's grave. The drizzling rain turned into a heavy sprinkle. The wheels on the right side of Jake's chair dug deep into the mud. Jake couldn't balance it, and the chair flipped over, spilling Jake into the mud. He was determined to keep moving. Pulling his elbows up under him, Jake crawled toward the tombstone. Suddenly he heard the voices that had spoken lies to rationalize his behavior.

You can't believe this junk!

Jake ignored them as he clawed his way through the sludge toward Ross's fresh grave.

Bedtime stories! Look at yourself! You're a victim of lies!

Jake stopped to rest for a moment. The voices continued their intimidation.

They don't know God. God is love.

Jake looked in the direction from where he heard the voice. Fear ripped through his veins as he saw a cloaked demon on all fours. Its pale face was contorted. It spoke again, but this time, with Jake's voice. *God doesn't send people to Hell. God is within you. He is what you make him. You are God!*

Jake pressed forward. Continuing to use his elbows, he propelled his body toward Ross's grave. He screamed in frustration as he labored to tow his body through the mire. The voices multiplied.

You're a worthless murderer!

You deserve to die!

It should have been you!

Jake climbed onto the mound of Ross's grave, clenching handfuls of mud, crying out, "I'm sorry! It was my fault!"

Lauren ran, almost reaching Jake, calling his name. Her cries were unheard beneath the taunting demonic voices haunting Jake.

God hates you!

Killer!

Invalid!

The pastor continued to lead his congregation in the spiritual battle. Falling to his knees, he raised his hands and cried out, "Please, Lord, answer the prayers of Your children!"

Demons continued to bombard Jake with untruths. Legions of the monster-like beings now surrounded him. Jake threw his body over Ross's grave.

"God, help me!" he begged.

God can't help you! a voice exclaimed.

"Why, God, why?" Jake cried. "Ross, I'm so sorry! This was all my fault! I did this to you! I miss you so bad! Oh, God, how I wish I could go back and change what happened!"

Finally, Lauren's voice pierced through the voices of wickedness. "Jake!"

In a flash of white light, a warrior angel fell onto the back of the cloaked demon that tried to prevent Jake from surrendering his soul to Christ.

In the sanctuary, Grace cried out, "Father, surround them with Your protection!"

More angels joined in the war over Jake's soul. Tall celestial beings clothed in white linen and shining armor...long, white hair flowing from a simple crown of silver...With swords of flame, these creatures of God's goodness battled the demons surrounding Jake. Lauren rushed forward and grabbed Jake. Thunder boomed throughout the sky as a strong storm moved in.

"Jake, I'm sorry!" Lauren cried with humility above the cracks of thunder. "I'm so sorry!"

As Lauren wept, a mighty angel landed a deadly blow, causing a demon to fade away. A second angel grabbed a demon around the neck and pulled it into another dimension, and with a flaming sword, smote a third demon.

Lauren grabbed Jake's face and turned it toward her. "Please forgive me!" she pleaded.

Confused, Jake stared at her. "Forgive you? Are you kidding me? I'm the one who should be apologizing to you! I'm the one who made fun of your faith!" Jake wiped away sweat and mud from his face. "I'm the one who was mean to you. I'm the one who made the stupid decision to race that night. I should have never let Ross get in the car with me. I took Ross away from you. I don't deserve your forgiveness!"

"No, Jake," Lauren said, holding him. "I was selfish. You needed Christ just as badly as Ross did, but I didn't care! I was jealous. My motives were selfish! I'm just as guilty – worse, in fact, because I knew better!" Lauren paused, her heart racing. "Then, after Ross died, I treated you even worse. I wanted you to hurt! I wanted you to feel guilty! I even said I hoped you wouldn't make it to Heaven. What was I thinking? How could I ever say that about someone?" Lauren held Jake's face so he couldn't look away. "I turned my back on you when you needed me most! When you needed Jesus!"

Jake pulled her hands down and held them between his own, turning his face to the sky. In that moment, he was stunned to see a demon and an angel locking arms in a fierce battle. He gasped in shock, causing Lauren to also look toward Heaven. Just then, a second angel tackled the demon from behind, driving it away from the teens.

"Oh...wow...It's like having a ringside seat, isn't it?" Lauren said with wonder in her voice.

"You...you see it, too?" Jake replied in astonishment. "I thought I was going crazy. First it was at the wreck, and then in my dreams, and now visions and voices..."

"No, Jake, you aren't crazy. God allows some of us to catch a glimpse of the unseen world. Apparently He has chosen to allow both of us this view into the heavenly realm."

Looking back down, Jake shook his head and said, "OK, but there's something I still don't understand...What are they fighting over, Lauren?"

"Oh, Jake," she replied, "they are fighting over *you*! Satan wants your soul, but Jesus has sent His angels to fight for you because He wants you for Himself."

Muddy water streamed down Jake's face. "Jesus can't want me!"

"Yes, Jake, He does!" Lauren exclaimed. "For God so loved the world that He gave His only begotten Son, that whoever believes in Him should not perish but have everlasting life! God didn't send Jesus into the world to condemn it...but to save it." Lauren paused. "Jake, I have been a stumbling block to you. I have been a pathetic example of Christ to you. I've been hypocritical, legalistic and even pharisaical at times. Don't look at me, Jake. Look at Christ – the perfect example. He's the one who died on the cross for your sins. There is nothing you have done that Christ's blood cannot cover."

"Lauren, he didn't save Ross!" Jake yelled.

"Ross made that choice," Lauren said. "This is yours."

Frustrated, Jake shook his head. "God doesn't make sense!"

"He doesn't have to…He's God!"

Jake grew calm. His breathing slowed. "I want to know Him," he said.

Lauren looked him in the eyes. "Then, tell Him."

"I don't know how!" Jake said desperately.

"God has made it so easy, Jake!" Lauren began to quote scripture to guide him. "If we confess our sins, He is faithful and just to forgive us our sins and to cleanse us from all unrighteousness."

Jake tucked his head into Lauren's shoulder and called out. "Jesus…I've messed up. I've hurt people. I've hurt You. Please forgive me. Please save me!"

Jake looked into the sky. The heavy sprinkle had turned into a downpour, washing away every trace of mud from his face. Beside him, atop Ross's grave, lay his keychain with the red "J." It had slipped out of Jake's pocket. The rain also cleansed it of mud, revealing the glossy red initial.

Jake began to laugh. "For the first time, I feel clean! I feel free!" he shouted.

Lauren giggled. She remembered. She remembered that feeling of pure joy – the joy that comes with salvation. She began to laugh aloud with him.

They continued to sit on the ground by Ross's grave, their faces toward Heaven and the rain covering them, laughing uncontrollably and celebrating Jake's new salvation and Lauren's renewed faith.

The rain moved out quickly. Soon, rays of sunlight began to stream on them. As the warm sunlight fell upon their faces, they took a deep breath. Lauren cradled Jake's head. Taking a handful of his hair, she said softly, "Welcome to the family of God, my brother." She rested her forehead on Jake's wet hair. He breathed deep sighs of relief. Above them, seven warrior angels stood guard around them. Their flaming swords were drawn and flickered in the sunlight. Glowing white garments flowed about them. Soon, the teens found themselves surrounded by their church family. Victory was theirs.

Chapter 27

For the first time, I celebrated Christmas the right way and for the right reasons and with true understanding. It was like a new holiday had been added to our calendar. Not having my best friend to celebrate it with was sickening, though. Our traditions were forever gone, but I praise God for the new traditions, and that now, they truly have meaning. The start of a new year felt fresh. Although I would spend my lifetime missing Ross, God would give us new opportunities, and knowing Him personally and intimately gave me grand hope that life could be good; I would at some point be able to experience days without guilt. The pain would never die, but the good we would see from our incredible loss would make it much more bearable.

Mitch sat in his home office on Orchid Circle, his back to his desk, staring out the large picture window. A knock at the door failed to break his deep train of thought. The door opened slowly.

"Mitch," Grace's soft voice called as she peeked in to see if he was inside.

Mitch continued to stare out the window. Grace had noticed his mind seemed preoccupied the past few days. She didn't know what to make of it. He had begun to grow spiritually and was becoming more involved with Men's Ministry, but his continual state of contemplation was concerning to her.

"Honey, is everything OK?" Grace asked.

No response. She stepped close and touched him on the shoulder. Her light touch broke the spell.

"I'm sorry. Did you say something?"

"You've just been in deep thought a lot lately. Is everything OK?"

"Yes, sweetie," he said, patting her hand. "I've just been thinking about something that the Lord has laid on my heart."

She was thrilled to hear this. "Do tell," Grace replied excitedly.

He turned to face her. "Sit down," he said.

"OK..." Grace said, not sure what to expect.

"I want to do something, Grace," Mitch said passionately. "Something of substance and with purpose."

Grace was floored; this was very much out of character for Mitch. "Well, that's great, honey, but in what way?"

"I want to make good out of what I did wrong. I'm not going to sit here and rehash everything, but I want to do something to honor Ross. To keep his memory alive for years to come."

"What do you have in mind?" she asked.

"A foundation...a scholarship fund. Something like that," Mitch brainstormed. "I'm just not sure exactly what."

"He was very active with the D.A.R.E. program," Grace re-minded him.

"You know...that may be it," Mitch said. "Of course, I don't want to do anything without talking to Lance and Kate first. I certainly want their blessing on it."

"I'm sure they would be ecstatic about it," Grace said. "Maybe they could give you some ideas."

"I tell you what...Let's get them over here tonight," Mitch suggested.

"I haven't talked to Kate today, but I know she wasn't feeling good yesterday," Grace said.

"Let me text Lance and see," Mitch said as he pulled out his phone. Speaking into it, he said, "Hey Lance...wanted to see if you guys are busy tonight. We'd like to have you over for supper and talk to you about something. Will that work?"

Mitch hit "send," then said to Grace, "You are good with that, right?"

Grace giggled at his backward way of doing things. "It's fine."

Soon, Lance's response came to Mitch's phone. Mitch read Lance's response aloud to Grace. *Hey, brother...I'm sorry, but Kate isn't feeling good. Think she may have a stomach bug. Let's try again soon.* "You were right," he said.

"Oh, I hate she's sick. I'll check on her tomorrow," Grace replied. "Hey, in the meantime, I've got an idea."

"What's that?" Mitch asked.

"How about you talk to Sergeant Mike Mayhew about your idea. He was Ross's D.A.R.E. buddy, remember?"

"You're just full of great ideas, huh?"

"It was your idea, honey," Grace reminded him. "A wonderful one. I know the Kellys will think so, too."

"Let's go down to the sheriff's department and pay the guys a visit," Mitch suggested. "We can talk to Mike then."

Mitch placed a call to the sheriff's office, hoping to catch Mayhew there.

"This is Mike," Mayhew said, taking the call.

"Mike, this is Mitch Adams."

Surprised to hear his voice, Mike replied, "Mitch! Wow! How in the world are ya?"

"Super, actually," Mitch said.

"That's great! How's Jake?" Mike asked.

"Very well," Mitch said. "Better than we ever could have hoped."

"I'm so glad to hear that," Mike said. "So, what's up?"

Mitch told him his thoughts, and they set a meeting for later in the afternoon with the D.A.R.E. coordinator.

Mike Mayhew replaced the phone in the cradle. He sat in amazement at the change in Mitch's attitude and heart. "Wow...I didn't see that coming," he said under his breath.

"Didn't see what coming?" Sheriff Howell asked as he passed by Mike's office.

"You're not going to believe this," Mike said. "Mitch and Grace Adams are coming here at five to discuss ideas about starting a memorial scholarship in honor of Ross."

"*Our* Mitch Adams?" the sheriff asked.

"Yep. Can you believe it?"

"Grace – I can see that happening easily, but not Mitch," Sheriff Howell said.

"Stranger things have happened, I guess," Mike said.

"Not many," Sheriff Howell said.

Mitch and Grace decided to share their idea with Jake. Grace lightly tapped on his door, not wanting to disturb him.

"It's open," Jake called.

She opened the door, pleasantly surprised to see Jake sitting at his desk, studying God's word. "I didn't mean to bother you."

"You didn't," Jake kindly replied, wheeling around to face her. "What's up?"

"Well, your dad and I have an idea we'd like to share with you," she said. "Could you come in here for a minute?"

"Sure," Jake said.

The two of them joined Mitch in his study. Mitch and Grace filled Jake in on their idea to honor Ross and what they had come up with so far. Jake was excited about the idea. The three tossed around several ideas. Jake's input as Ross's best friend enriched the plan greatly.

Mike Mayhew's team of deputies gathered at the sheriff's department and prepared for the evening shift.

Daniels sat at the conference table in the briefing room, reading a text he had received from his wife.

"There you are," Juicy said, joining him at the table. "What you looking at?" peeping at Daniels's phone. Seeing it was from his wife, he asked, "Is that your honey-do list?"

Perturbed at his nosiness, Daniels replied, "Not exactly. Not that it's any of your business."

"So," Juicy said, "I was wondering if you have any jobs you could use some extra help with."

Daniels saw right through him. "You ran out of money building the house, didn't ya."

"Well, sort of...yeah," Juicy confessed.

"I knew it," Daniels said. "How much?"

"How much what?" Juicy asked.

"How much have you spent?" Daniels asked.

Juicy hesitated for a moment, his faced flushed with embarrassment. "About forty thousand," Juicy mumbled.

"How much?" Daniels asked in disbelief.

"Forty thousand...*over* what you quoted," Juicy repeated with more volume. "Don't gloat."

Daniels laughed. "I'm not gloating."

"Daniels, I should have taken you up on your offer," Juicy said humbly. "I'm sorry I didn't listen to you."

"Wow! That sounds like an apology."

"Yeah, I guess it is," Juicy said.

Daniels smiled. "I guess I could use some help."

Relieved, Juicy said, "Thanks, man. I appreciate it." Looking around to make sure no one was standing close by, he said, "Can we just keep this between the two of us?"

"Are you kidding me? Ain't no way!"

Agitated, Juicy hit his fist on the table and said, "Aw, come on, Daniels!"

Daniels laughed out loud. "I'm just messin' with you, partner. It'll stay right here."

Juicy backed off. "You got me," he said, offering him a fist bump.

They were interrupted by a loud-mouthed Jake Adams. "Whassup!"

Daniels and Juicy looked toward the doorway and saw the Adams family standing there, all smiles.

"Jake!" Daniels shouted. "How are you, man?" He leaped toward Jake.

"Not bad," Jake said, giving Daniels a high five.

"Mrs. Grace, how are you?' Daniels asked, offering her a hug.

"I'm doing very well, Daniels. How are you boys doing?"

"We're good," Daniels replied, offering Mitch a handshake.

"So, what brings you guys by here?" Daniels asked.

Mayhew entered the room with Sheriff Howell and another officer.

Mitch turned around. "Mike!" he called out, shaking his hand. "Thanks for meeting with us on such short notice. We really appreciate it."

"I'm glad to do it! I'm pumped about your idea." Mike motioned to the sheriff and the other officer. "So much so that I brought these two up to speed on our conversation."

"Jake, how are you, bud," Sheriff Howell asked.

"Doing great, sir," Jake said. "I'm just glad to be here for a good reason for a change."

Everyone laughed.

"Me, too, son," Sheriff Howell replied.

"I don't know if you guys have ever met Paige. She's the state D.A.R.E. program coordinator," Mike said.

Jake spoke up. "Mrs. Hall," he said.

Lt. Paige Hall, blue-eyed with blondish-brown, naturally curly hair, had been with the sheriff's department for 23 years. She started out as a deputy, but two years later, Paige's heart fell into the D.A.R.E. program.

"Hey, Jake. How are you?" Paige said. "It's been a while."

"Yes, ma'am, it has," Jake replied.

"You look good!" Paige said enthusiastically.

"Thanks, and I hope you've been able to forgive me for that terrible trick I pulled on you at camp several years ago," Jake said.

Surprised, Grace asked, "What trick?"

"Oh, it was nothing. It didn't take long for my hair to grow back out," she said, winking at Jake.

"What?" Grace asked.

"I believe the statute of limitations is up on punishment for that one," Jake said.

"Ha-ha...but seriously, folks," Mike said. "I thought it would be great if we could all discuss your idea and pull this thing together," Mike suggested. They gathered in the conference room.

Paige began the meeting. "I must tell you, when Mike came to me with this, it brought me to tears. I remember Ross very well. Such a sweet young man. Very polite. I was devastated when I heard the news. You know, you get to know these kids who come through here over the years. When we lose one, it's always tragic, but when Ross's death occurred, it seemed more sad than usual. It hit our department really hard." She turned to Jake. "We've been praying for you. We are so thankful the Lord spared your life. When you're ready, I'd love for you to come speak at some of our D.A.R.E. events. Although your accident wasn't drug-related, I know it would make a huge impact on a lot of young kids' lives."

Taken aback, Jake said, "I'd love to do that!"

"Great," Paige replied with a smile. "Now, back to our discussion," Paige said. "First of all, just a little info for you: D.A.R.E. stands for Drug Abuse Resistance Education. It's not just a 'Say no' program. It focuses on good decision-making in all areas of life. D.A.R.E. has a national scholarship, but unfortunately, only one senior student is awarded nationwide."

"I see," Mitch said, disappointed.

Paige sensed his discouragement. "After talking with Mike about your idea, I became inspired. I know your vision is focused on your own school, but I'd love to see this happen locally, somehow."

Mike interjected. "Ross embraced everything about the D.A.R.E. program. Not only did he attend camps and graduate from the course at school, he was a Peer Helper. And he implemented those values in his daily life."

"Ross was a star student," Paige said. "This is a golden opportunity, not just to expand our program, but to honor Ross."

The Adamses exchanged glances, overjoyed. "That would be incredible," Mitch said.

"That confirms what you had on your heart, doesn't it, honey," Grace said.

"Yes, it absolutely does," Mitch said.

"Well, let's get started," Paige said.

The team of people sat together, pooling their ideas until they had a format in place.

"Lance and Kate are going to be so excited," Grace said.

Sheriff Howell turned to Mitch. "This was an awesome idea, friend."

Appreciating his approval, Mitch nodded. "Thanks, Jimmy. That means a lot."

The next day, Grace called Kate to check on her, expecting her sickness to have subsided by now.

"How are you today?" Grace asked.

"Hey, Grace. Still nauseated, but the doctor said I should live," Kate laughed.

"Bless your heart," Grace said sympathetically.

"This, too, shall pass," Kate replied, downplaying her illness.

"Do you think you'll feel like coming over tonight? Mitch and I have something important we'd like to share with you and Lance," Grace said.

"That would be great," Kate said. "We've got something we'd like to share with you, too."

"Great! We'll see you then," Grace said joyfully.

Grace stepped into the doorway of Mitch's home office. "Hey, I just got off the phone with Kate."

"And?" Mitch asked.

"Everything's set," Grace said.

"Fantastic!" Mitch said. "Did you tell her Mayhew was coming as well?"

"Oh, no. I was afraid that might make her suspicious," Grace said.

A few blocks away, Kate struggled to get dressed, fighting the nausea. Lance noticed the squeamish look on her face. "You think this is a good idea?"

"We've got to go, Lance," Kate said. "It's too important."

"Well, if you change your mind, honey, they'll understand," Lance said.

"I know, but it's not going away any time soon,"

———————————————

Grace worked frantically in the kitchen, trying to get everything together. The doorbell rang. Grace peeked out the window. "It's Mike!" she called.

"OK, be right there," Mitch said. He quickly moved to the back door and let their first arriving guest in.

"Hey, man, come on in," Mitch said. "Let's run over this once more before the Kellys get here. Do you mind?"

"No, not at all," Mike replied.

The men sat down at the kitchen table to go over the details.

The doorbell rang again, catching Grace with her hands in dishwater.

"Mitch, honey, will you get that, please?"

After Grace's phone conversation with Kate, she expected to see a very pale and sickly Kate. Mitch opened the door.

"Back door guests are best!" a bubbly Kate said with a large grin. Mitch and Grace were somewhat perplexed, knowing she was battling sickness.

"So, did the doctor give you a diagnosis?" Grace asked.

"Yes, he did," Kate said.

"Did he give you any medicine?" Grace asked.

"Yep," Lance said.

"So, how long did he say you would need to take it?" Grace asked.

"Oh, about nine months," Kate said, grinning ear to ear.

The hosts and sergeant stood in shock. Grace walked toward Kate as tears welled in her eyes.

Taking Kate's hands, Grace whispered, "You're pregnant?"

Kate joined her in her tears, nodding. They embraced as they all burst out laughing. Mitch grabbed Lance and hugged him. New life was breathed into all of them. Out of the corner of her eye, Kate caught Mayhew dabbing tears as they ran down his face.

"Oh, you big baby!" Kate exclaimed through her laughter.

"This woman who was told she could probably have no more children!" Grace said boldly. "Praise the Lord!"

"I told Lance on the way over here…For months I've been dreading facing the upcoming senior events. The spring athletic banquet…prom… graduation. I so desperately want to be a part somehow because we love all of Ross's classmates and want to enjoy it with them, but…such a sting, you know? But today, our news about this baby…I know it is God's gift that will help to take some of that sting out of it because of what He has given us to look forward to."

"That's wonderful that you see God's mercy!" Grace said as she continued to sob. "Do you have a due date?"

"October," Lance said.

"Harvest time," Grace said.

"I already thought of that," Lance commented.

"Well," Grace said, "speaking of the harvest reminds me of food, which is going to get cold if we don't start eating it! So would everyone please get comfortable around the dinner table and I'll serve supper."

Lance looked around the room. "Where's Jake?" he asked.

"He's at Lauren's. A group of them are planning the athletic banquet," Mitch said, feeling awkward after Kate's comment earlier.

"I'm so glad they have each other," Lance said. "They were the two who were the closest to Ross."

"I know," Mitch said. "They have had such a turnaround. It's been incredible to watch."

As they gathered around to eat, Grace looked at Mitch in hopes he would lead in a prayer of blessing. Mitch saw her and gave her a smile and a wink, letting her know he was on top of it.

"Let's pray," Mitch said. "Father in Heaven, we thank You for these precious friends who have gathered with us tonight. We thank You for the wonderful news You have given our dear friends to share, and we rejoice with them. We pray for divine protection over this child and that You would enable them to enjoy every moment to come. Bless this food and the sweet hands that prepared it, and bless our time together. Amen."

The group enjoyed their time together, sharing in the joy of friendship. As they were finishing with dessert, Mitch stood and motioned for Grace to join him.

He began, "First of all, I want to thank my beautiful wife for that amazing dinner. Thank you, Grace," he said with a smile as she walked over to stand by his side. A chorus of hearty "Amens" rang out from around the table. Putting his arm around her, he said, "We are so grateful to all of you for coming to spend your evening with us, but I'm sure a few of you are wondering why you are here.

"Well, what Grace and I wanted to talk to you about tonight is something that has really been on my heart," Mitch continued. "I shared it with Grace the other day. I want to do something to commemorate Ross's memory...something that will go on for years to come. Over the past couple of days, Grace and I have brainstormed about it and prayed about it."

Kate was stunned. "Mitch...How wonderful!"

"That's why Mike is here, too," Grace said.

"My vision was for a foundation or scholarship fund," Mitch said.

"I like it," Lance said.

"I thought of Mike, because for years, Ross was so involved with D.A.R.E.," Grace said.

"You're right," Kate said. "He loved it…and Mike."

"And I loved him," Mike said.

"So we called Mike and put our heads together, and this is what we came up with," Mitch said. "Tell 'em, honey."

Stunned, Grace asked, "Me?"

"Sure. You are much more articulate than me," Mitch said.

"Uh…that would be more articulate than I, dear," Grace kindly corrected him.

"My point exactly," Mitch said.

Everyone snickered.

Grace explained. "OK…so the plan is this: The D.A.R.E. program will set up a foundation in Ross's name—"

"The Ross Kelly Foundation," Mitch interjected.

Grace continued. "People can make charitable contributions that will go toward a scholarship given annually to a senior male student who graduated from the D.A.R.E. program and is characteristic of the things taught through the program."

"That's terrific, but how in the world will that decision be made?" Lance asked.

"This is how it will work. Senior male students will fill out a questionnaire and write an essay on a subject of your choosing. Now, there will be some qualifying factors. For instance, each of the candidates must be a graduate of the D.A.R.E. program and must have been involved as a camper and as a Peer Helper at camps. Ross's former teachers will also make recommendations regarding those students applying for the scholarship. You will read over each questionnaire and essay and take teachers' recommendations. After narrowing it down to three students, you'll personally interview them. From those interviews, the two of you will choose the scholarship winner."

"What do you think?" Mitch asked.

"Wow," Lance said. "That's quite a process."

"It will start at the beginning of second semester. That will give you plenty of time to be done by spring," Mike said.

"And get this," Mitch said. "The scholarship amount will be ten thousand dollars."

Kate began to cry. "I'm so overwhelmed."

Lance put his arm around her. "We are truly blown away."

Kate looked at Lance and said, "Giving the devil another black eye, huh?"

Lance laughed. "Yes, it is!" He noticed confused looks on their faces. "It's an inside joke."

Chapter 28

We hit the time of senior year where things really started rockin'. Along with the passage of some time and the Kellys' wonderful news of a baby on the way, the springtime weather lifted our spirits and helped propel us on to new lives and renewed hope. Our senior prom was now behind us. And, to answer the question you female readers are asking me out loud right now – yes, Lauren and I went to prom together. Now we were looking ahead to the Spring Athletic Banquet. Just when you think you've seen it all and you couldn't be surprised anymore...BAM!

Next to prom and graduation, the third most important event of the school year was the Spring Athletic Banquet. This was a special night when athletes, male and female alike, from every sport, dressed in their Sunday best and came together to celebrate the year's athletic achievements, both as a team and individually.

Red, white and blue balloons covered the gym, while ribbons and crepe paper hung from the ceiling. Banquet tables covered in red, white and blue filled the gym floor, each decorated with eye-catching centerpieces carrying out the athletic theme. Energetic music pumped through the sound system as teenage athletes, parents, coaches and faculty filled the large room. The stage served as a platform for the tables of shiny trophies and plaques soon to be awarded to the athletes.

"Man, barbeque is my favorite," Hamm said, sniffing the air while waiting in the food line.

"All food is your favorite, Hamm," Marcus joked.

"I don't eat any more than you do, bro," Hamm said. "You just have a faster metabolism than I do."

Drew burst out laughing. "Hamm, man, your metabolism has come to a screeching halt."

Jake wheeled up to the line. "What's so funny?" he asked.

"Aw, nothing," Marcus said. "We just talking about Hamm's metabolism."

"Or lack thereof," Drew remarked.

Jake looked at Hamm. "Well, the girls must like zero metabolism," he said.

"Why you say that?" Marcus asked.

Hamm also wondered where he was going with that comment.

"Based on what I've been seeing on Instagram and Twitter, the chicks can't get enough of that," Jake said, pointing to Hamm's 300-pound physique.

Hamm stood up straight, flexed his arm muscles and said, "Hey, who wouldn't want some of this?"

The guys laughed. They loaded their plates and sat down with their families.

When the crowd had almost finished eating, Coach Scott, who was also the Athletic Director, stepped behind the podium to begin the evening's award ceremony.

"Good evening, everyone. Welcome to the 2015 Spring Athletic Banquet. We have a lot to look forward to tonight. There are a lot of talented athletes among us, and I'm excited to have this time to acknowledge their accomplishments."

They applauded.

"Before we begin this evening, I'd like to ask our keynote speaker, Fellowship of Christian Athletes director for this area, Joseph Borden, to pray for us."

Joseph walked to the podium. "Would you bow your heads with me, please, as we pray?

"Daddy, bless this night. Bless the coaches, athletes and parents who have sown time, sweat and money into athletics with a supernatural return. Be with them and guide them as they go on to the next step of their journey in life and athletics. May all they do be for Your glory. Amen."

Coach Scott returned to the podium to begin passing out the awards. They were presented by sport and in seasonal order, which meant football was first.

"Tonight, our Most Improved Player award goes to a young man who has certainly earned it. I don't believe, in all my years of coaching, I've ever seen someone who deserves it more than this guy. When tragedy struck our team, he stepped up and led like a boss. He's also the most humble soul I've ever met. He has pressed through incredible adversity due to a severe injury early in the season and has persevered. He was a key player in our state championship victory. Tonight's Most Improved Player Award goes to... Bartholomew Hamm!"

The crowd stood and cheered as Hamm walked to the stage to receive his award. Hamm accepted the award from Coach Scott, his jaw open in disbelief.

As the applause died down, Hamm looked at Coach Scott. "Could I say something, please?"

The coach was surprised, as Hamm was usually a quiet young man. "Sure, son. It's all yours."

Nervous, Hamm looked out across the audience. "I don't normally talk much, but I feel like there's something I need to say."

The audience sat straight in their seats, anxious to hear what Hamm had to say.

"Umm...I ain't never really won anything. I'm tickled to death to get this, but I just feel so unworthy."

His humble statement warmed the hearts of the audience.

"I'm so thankful the Lord allowed me to play out the season and be a part of a championship team. That's enough for me. My heart feels like the person who really deserves this award is the player who didn't get to finish out the season or play in the championship game. So, Coach Scott, if it's OK with you, I'd like to give my award to Jake Adams."

A hush fell across the gym. Jake was stunned and didn't know what to do. Neither did Coach Scott.

Moving close to the podium, Coach Scott said, "Well, son, it's your award. I guess you can do whatever you want to with it."

Hamm smiled. He spotted Jake in the audience and motioned for him to come forward. Feeling humbled and uncomfortable, Jake slowly wheeled toward the stage. Hamm stepped down and met him on the floor. The audience was mesmerized at the touching scene before them.

Hamm handed the trophy to his friend. "Here, Jake. I want you to have this. You are my hero."

Jake's eyes filled with tears as he recalled the many hurtful things he had done to Hamm, including the stunt in the cafeteria that injured him. "Hamm, I can't..."

"Please, Jake," Hamm insisted. "I've felt so helpless until now. Let me do this."

Jake was humbled beyond belief. Nodding his head in acceptance, he said, "Thank you, Hamm. You are one of a kind, you know that?"

The audience rose to its feet, applauding the incredible act of honor. It would take several minutes for the crowd to recover, including Coach Scott. His show of emotion would quickly turn to fodder for laughter. He received it well and continued with the presentations.

"Tonight's final presentation is for our Most Valuable Player. I know the winner of this award is obvious. There's not enough build-up I can create for this player. He has it all...talent, smarts, good work ethic, a strong faith. There are no limits for this young man. Tonight's winner of the Most Valuable Player Award goes to... Marcus Riley!"

Once again, the audience happily applauded.

As Marcus received his award, he, too, requested to speak. Coach Scott graciously turned over the podium.

Marcus looked out over the audience. He cleared his throat and began. "It's such an incredible honor to stand before you tonight and accept this award." He looked at Jake, who tensed. "Jake, you ain't gettin' this one, bro."

Laughter filled the room.

"Seriously, my dream has always been to play pro football. My D.A.R.E. mentor, Blambo, told me that if I worked hard and made good grades and showed kindness to others, I could be anything I wanted to be. He's absolutely correct on that. But, when tragedy struck a few months ago, my desires were challenged. I had to ask myself, 'Why do I want to do what I want to do?' And more importantly, 'Who am I doing it for and for what greater good?' There's nothing wrong with playing pro football, if that's what the Lord has called me to do. But I had to face the fact that I never asked the Lord what He was calling me to do. So, a few weeks ago, I asked the Lord what He wanted me to do. His response wasn't pro football. His response was to preach."

Whispers rippled through the crowd.

"So, come this fall, I will be enrolling in Bible college."

Marcus's fellow teammates led the cheers for his decision. Supporting their friend was easy because they knew what was inside Marcus, yet Jake struggled to understand.

Coach Scott returned to the podium once more to make a final presentation, one that could have happened through God's sovereignty alone.

"This is also a bittersweet evening for all of us. We ended this year's football season with a state championship, but without two very important members of our team, Jake Adams and Ross Kelly." He cleared his throat, trying to keep his voice from breaking. The crowd grew still and somber.

Coach Scott continued. "While we are thankful to have Jake here with us, he cheers from a wheelchair, without his best friend at his side." Motioning toward Lance and Kate Kelly, Coach Scott introduced them to the fans. Through tears, the audience applauded the Kellys as they joined Coach Scott on the stage.

"One of the finest young men I have ever coached was Ross Kelly," Coach Scott said, overcome with emotion. After a brief pause to fight back tears, he continued. "He worked hard in practice and gave all he had on the field to this team. To ensure that his memory is honored in the most upright way, we are retiring Ross's football number. Today, number '84' is being memorialized, never to be worn on the Eagle football field again. It will always be known as Ross Kelly's football number." The audience was silent in respect, but tears flowed as friends and family looked at each other in sorrow.

"We would like to present this shadowboxed Eagles jersey to the Kellys as a token of our love and support as they continue to grieve and heal." Once again, a very emotional body of supporters showed their love with applause. "We would also like to present them with a team football, signed by all of Ross's coaches and teammates. As you read each name, may you be reminded of how much we loved your son. We will always keep him and you close to our hearts."

Kate and Lance Kelly stepped forward to accept the gifts in Ross's honor.

"Thank you very much," Lance said sincerely. Holding the football close to his chest, he continued. "Ross loved this team and this school – understandably so. We will cherish these gifts. We covet your continued prayers. Thank you."

For Jake, it was more than he could take. He quickly wheeled out of the gym. Marcus knew he was struggling and followed him. His calls to Jake went ignored as Jake continued to wheel away from him.

"Jake, c'mon, man," Marcus shouted. "You gotta get to a point of acceptance!"

Marcus's statement enraged Jake. He stopped abruptly and wheeled his chair around to face Marcus. "Acceptance?" he shouted. "What do you know about acceptance? I got a lot I have to accept!"

"Jake, I didn't mean it like that," Marcus said apologetically.

"You know what really ticks me off?" Jake added. "My dream of playing pro football is gone! Granted, it's my fault. I do accept that, but you are choosing to give it up! It makes no sense to me!"

"Jake, man, I can't help it if you don't understand. I know it seems crazy, but for me, it's clear. I have peace about it. I never had peace before. I was always striving for something that ultimately left me feeling empty. I thought now that you're a believer, you would get that."

Jake paused. "I don't know. I don't have all the answers yet. I just know that if I had my legs, I'd never let go of that dream."

Marcus sat down beside Jake's wheelchair. "In Proverbs 16:9, it says 'A man's heart plans his way, but the Lord directs his steps.' Jake, I was plotting my own course. I saw football as a way out of poverty. I made that my goal. It wasn't a *bad* thing, but it wasn't the *right* thing. God knew it wasn't out of rebellion – just lack of direction. He used your accident and Ross's death to reveal that to me."

Jake sat quietly, taking Marcus's words to heart.

"Jake, as good as it feels being on that football field, there is no place that feels better than being in the center of God's will."

"And how do you know when you're there?" Jake asked.

"That peace that passes all understanding, bro," Marcus said. "You just know."

Chapter 29

The end of our senior year had arrived. I made it, thanks to Lauren. She worked diligently to make sure that I not only passed, but passed well. Lauren is brilliant. Her self-discipline and "over-achiever" mentality had her on target to be our class valedictorian, but her grades fell after Ross's death, making her grade point average the second highest of our senior class. I bore the guilt of this as well. Fortunately, it didn't hinder her scholarship offers in the least. Lauren was still headed to the university of her choice. I didn't know what to expect this day – graduation. Just like every other event of our senior year since the accident, the feeling was bittersweet. I certainly didn't expect to be as close as I was to Lauren on graduation day, but I was very thankful. Ironically, having each other made us feel close to Ross, especially for the remainder of our senior events. Although I couldn't imagine going through graduation without them, I dreaded watching the Kellys endure it. It would be piercing. But God had done an incredible thing for them – something to give them hope as they walked through these special days with us – and without Ross.

The morning of graduation had arrived. Lance and Kate Kelly sat at the breakfast table. The day brought tears, but joy as well. As the Lord would have it, on this difficult day, Kate was scheduled for a sonogram to find out the gender of the baby growing inside her. Mixed thoughts ran through their minds. What would they be doing this very moment if Ross were here on his graduation day? What will the baby be? What should we name it? What color should the nursery be?

Kate giggled.

"What's so funny?" Lance asked.

"Can you believe that at ages forty-three and forty-four, we are going to have a baby?"

"No, I can't," Lance chuckled.

"Yesterday, Pastor Glenn called to see how 'Abraham' and 'Sarah' are doing," Kate said.

"That's about right," Lance said.

The doorbell rang.

"Are you expecting anyone?" Kate asked.

"No. You?" Lance asked.

"Nope."

"Well, shouldn't we still answer the door?" Lance asked playfully.

"Yes, you should," Kate remarked.

"Alright," Lance said. "Guess I'd better get used to doing everything around here."

"Yep," Kate agreed as she sipped on her decaffeinated coffee.

Lance opened the door. "Uh, Kate, I think you need to come here."

Concerned, she rose quickly from her seat. She looked toward the front door and saw two figures at the threshold. "Oh, my! Lauren! Jake!" she exclaimed.

Lauren and Jake stood with flowers and a framed photo of themselves taken with Ross at the beginning of their senior year.

"How very thoughtful of you!" Kate said softly, overcome with emotion. "Please, come inside."

"I'll grab a vase," Lance said.

They gathered in the living room where they had visited so many times before.

"So, you guys ready for tonight?" Kate asked.

"I guess so," Jake replied.

"Well, guess where we are spending our afternoon?" Kate asked, grinning ear to ear.

Jake and Lauren looked at each other with furrowed brows.

Kate answered, "At the clinic to find out what we are having!"

"Oh, wow!" Lauren yelled. "You've got to call me ASAP and let me know, Mrs. Kate!"

"Well, I tell ya what...we will be at graduation tonight, so why don't we tell you then?"

Disappointed, Lauren said, "No! That's too long to wait!"

"Aw, Lauren, you'll be fine," Jake said.

"Yes," Kate said. "Besides, you've got plenty to keep you busy until tonight."

"Oh, I guess so," Lauren reluctantly agreed.

Kate looked at both of them. "Look at you two. So grown up. I never dreamed we would be celebrating this day without Ross, but I'm so glad we get to celebrate it with you," Kate said, caressing their faces.

"I never dreamed we'd walk without Ross, either," Lauren said. "But I'm so thankful we get to celebrate new life with you."

Jake sat quietly, unsure of what to say.

"You know what, Jake?" Lance asked, noticing his discomfort. "It still feels like I have a son graduating today."

Jake turned to him, stunned.

"You've always been like a second son to us, Jake," Lance said.

"That's right, Jake," Kate agreed.

Jake smiled. "I love you guys."

"Now, come on," Kate said. "We've all got a big day today! Let's not get all stuffy-nosed and swollen-eyed."

The four of them embraced each other and said their good-byes.

"Thank you for thinking about us," Kate said.

"We're always thinking about you, Mrs. Kate," Lauren said.

Lance and Kate stood in the doorway to see them off. They watched as Jake asked Lauren, "Swollen-eyed? Is that really a word?"

The Kellys laughed and closed the door.

Lauren glanced at the clock on her phone. It read 7:37 p.m. The room off the city arena was a sea of navy-blue caps and gowns. Phones clicked and cameras flashed as students posed with friends, parents and even a few teachers. Lauren and her girlfriends took more selfies than they had ever taken, packing in memories of their last big night.

The golden cords that hung around her neck stood out against the dark navy graduation gown. Her accomplishments during her school years were many. Her hard work had paid off. Still, she hurt not having Ross with them. Between photo shoots, she texted Jake to see where he was. They had met earlier at a designated spot but were separated by the tugs and pulls of others seeking their attention. After a series of messages, they found each other again.

"There you are," Lauren said.

"All you had to do was look down," Jake said sarcastically.

"Ha-ha. OK...remember, we are supposed to meet our parents and the Kellys on the west side of the stage right after the ceremony," Lauren reminded him.

"I know, I know," Jake said.

"I can't wait to find out what they're having," Lauren said. "The suspense is killing me!"

"Well, you've got to stay focused on what's going on right now," Jake said.

"I know, but I'm dying to find out!" Lauren exclaimed. "Oh, there's the rest of our gang! Hey, guys! Over here!" She motioned for some friends to join them.

Marcus, Drew, Lizzy, Morgan and Eric hurried to them for a group photo before time to get in line. It was amazing how the horrific events just months earlier had helped to create friendships that once seemed impossible.

"OK, y'all, we gotta make this quick," Lizzy said.

"How's my make-up look?" Morgan asked. "Do I have lipstick on my teeth?" She rubbed them with her index finger.

"Alright, let's do this like we usually do," Lauren reminded them. "First shot, serious. Second shot, silly."

Hamm struggled to hold all of their smartphones while he took their pictures.

"Look, just set the phones down and hold one at a time," Marcus suggested.

Hamm hesitated, thinking through what Marcus had suggested. Seeing the logic behind it, he nodded in agreement.

As soon as the last shot was taken, the class sponsor called out, "Let me have your attention, please!"

"Just in time," Jake said.

Within moments, the excited talking stopped.

Grateful for their immediate cooperation, the sponsor continued. "Thank you for heeding my call. It's time to line up for the processional. I will be calling your name in alphabetical order," she said. "As I call your name, please fall in line in that order."

After years of being first in line alphabetically, Jake was prepared to be called first. So were the other students. The sponsor opened her mouth but before she could get the name out, the seniors called out in unison, "Jake Adams."

Taken aback, the senior sponsor broke out in laughter. "I guess after twelve years, you saw that one coming, huh?"

The seniors laughed.

Just as he was about to leave, Jake looked up at Lauren, grabbed hold of the tassel that dangled from his cap and pretended to move it from one side to the other. "See you on the flip side."

His statement made the moment real. Lauren began to tear up. "See you on the flip side," she replied as she bent down and gave him one more pre-graduation hug. Thankful to have Jake there with them, his classmates applauded as he wheeled to the front of the line.

The Lee County Academy graduating class of 2015 excitedly marched into the arena. Camera flashes and cheers erupted from proud family members and friends. The night was emotional enough, and *Pomp and Circumstance* always brought tears, but perhaps the most touching symbol of the night was the empty chair on the sixth row adorned with the cap and gown that would have belonged to Ross Kelly.

Jake led his 89 classmates to the area where they would congregate for the last time as students of Lee County Academy. Jake caught a glimpse of Ross's chair. Momentary heartsickness set in. All day he had pushed back the thought of Ross, but coming face-to-face with it was proving very difficult. Jake fought his emotions and pressed on until he reached the empty space provided for his wheelchair.

The graduates slowly filled the rows of chairs. Alphabetically, there were only three seats separating Lauren from where Ross would have been. Lauren was glad the students to her right obstructed the view. As the others took their places behind her, Lauren slowly leaned forward for a glimpse of Ross's chair. For a fleeting moment, Lauren saw an image of Ross standing in front of his seat, dressed in cap and gown. His big, brown eyes smiled at her, then he winked. Ross faded quickly, and now there was simply an empty chair. A sharp pain passed through her stomach. She faced forward, trying to focus on the ceremony and enjoy it as much as possible.

All 89 students were now in place. In unison, they sat down, and the ceremony began. Marcus Riley gave the invocation. His prayer was like poetry, and there was no doubt in anyone's mind about his decision to enter the ministry.

Lauren's best friend, Lizzy, welcomed the audience. Next was Lauren's turn. As salutatorian, she was to give an address, and she was led to share about Ross. As Lauren made her way to the stage, her heart felt as if it were going to beat out of her chest. She walked with her head down, taking in long, deep breaths to calm herself. She reached the podium and spread out the speech she had typed. Her heart continued to beat like a drum. She closed her eyes and took one more deep breath. Finally, she began.

"Fellow classmates, distinguished guests, family and friends: Tonight we come to the end of the preliminary trek of our lives, which has included years of building a foundation, creating a good work ethic and establishing good life skills by which we will govern our lives. At this point, we usually share about looking forward to the future. But tonight, I feel compelled to look back for a moment and focus on what it takes in order to move forward from this place.

"In my eighteen years on this earth, I have experienced great joy, fun and accomplishments. Some I earned through hard work and self-discipline, others from God's favor, unmerited by my own right. I've also suffered great tragedy. Five years ago, I lost my daddy. He was my hero. It was a freak accident that had no logical explanation. In God's sovereignty, it just happened. I was able to deal with it quite well, even though it caused great heartache, and it is on days like this that I miss him most.

"The second tragedy happened shortly after our senior year began. The kindest, most gentle guy I knew was tragically killed. This young man, I thought I might possibly marry at some point. It wasn't a freak accident. It was an accident that occurred after I begged him over and over again to avoid the circumstances that led to it. This angered me and shook my faith to its core. Why did God not answer my prayers and intervene? It brought out the ugly in me – ugliness I never dreamed was inside me. For a while, I didn't care. And during the time that I didn't care, I became a stumbling block to many. Finally, after my behavior had gotten out of control, one of the godliest women I know came to me and confronted me…in love, of course. It enraged me. But the truth was, until I dealt with it, I was holding myself back, and I was holding others back as well.

"I would like to share with you a prayer I wrote shortly after Ross died. At the time, it was written more from will than emotion, although there is clearly plenty of emotion. When I was writing it, I didn't necessarily feel what I was writing, although I knew what I was writing to be true. I can now testify that when I do things out of heartfelt obedience and listen to – instead of grieve – the Holy Spirit, the emotion does follow in His time. I now feel everything I wrote.

"Initially, when I read this, it tasted bitter and made me very angry. I can now read this with hands raised, tears of joy flowing and a sincere smile on my face because of God's mercy and grace. Sometimes, I feel like a hypocrite because of this process. Who am I to proclaim truth before I feel it to be true? Well, I don't have to feel the rain to know it's wet. The evidence is all around me. I once was blind, but now I see! I praise God because my best is filthy rags! He alone is worthy of praise! This process of obedience and faith reminds me who is really in control of the changing of my heart. Not by might, not by power, but by His Spirit alone. Thank you, Father."

Lauren paused for a moment and took a deep breath before she spoke again. When she did, it was with a peace that was almost tangible:

"Create in me a clean heart, O God, and renew a steadfast spirit within me.

Do not cast me away from Your presence, and do not take Your Holy Spirit from me.

Restore to me the joy of Your salvation, and uphold me by Your generous Spirit." [Psalm 51:10-12]

"I'm a fool. Forgive me, Father, for I have sinned…the most abhorrent sin in Your sight, I'm sure it to be. Praise be to God and His unfailing love! Give thanks and rejoice for His love endures forever! Face to the ground with open hands shaking. Who am I to question Your sovereignty? Surely, I spoke of things much too wonderful. You have delivered me and Your grace has set me free. I have sinned against Thee for I denied thanksgiving. Your sovereignty and infinite wisdom! Majesty! Your endless mercy. Your unfathomable grace! Who am I, Father? I am Your child despite my indecency. I do not know what is appropriate. You lift me up for Your Name's sake. And I will praise Your name, the Author. What authority do I have to demand life? Demand reason? The Lord gives and the Lord takes away. Blessed be the Name of the Lord! Where can I hide from Your Spirit? It follows me in depths of darkness to shine Your glory! I repent of usurping Your role. With a desire to control, I am filthy rags. It's never about me. It's always about You and what You've done for us. I've been ungrateful, bitter and unsatisfied. Thank You for Your grace. Thank You for a precious friend's untimely death and my pain and grief. These sufferings are a prized possession, a beautiful treasure and the most wonderful of gifts. I share Your sufferings, Lord. Do not let me waste my sorrows and be put to shame. In Jesus' holy name bring reconciliation! I wait expectantly. Lead me not into temptation. Deliver me from evil. You are the Deliverer, Prince of Peace. Amen.

"Ross Asher Kelly...we love you and miss you. You will remain in our hearts forever."

Not one eye remained dry. There was a mighty shift in perspective among those who listened. Hearing this after witnessing the change in Lauren's life over the past few months gave it great integrity. Jake was amazed at her speech. He thought about how so many times words come, but action fails to follow. Although the words came first here, they were kept in a secret place until after they had manifested themselves. Such power was displayed through Lauren's transparency and humility. If she added up all of her Christian duties and works she had done for the Lord, the total would still fall way short of this incredible act of courage. It was monumental, and Jake had a feeling it wouldn't stop here.

The valedictorian's speech fell under the shadow of Lauren's inspiring delivery. Each senior had his or her moment on the stage as they accepted that simple diploma that summed up twelve years of their lives. After the last students returned to their seats, the students, in unison, moved their mortarboard tassels from the right side to the left. With great pride, Dr. Sharp pronounced them as a graduated class. Cheers burst forth as the group tossed their caps into the air in celebration of their tremendous accomplishment. The audience rose to its feet in celebration with them.

Jake and Lauren met their families, along with the Kellys, on the west side of the stage, just as they had planned. Margaret couldn't get to her daughter fast enough. Enveloping Lauren in her arms, she wept.

"Lauren, I have never been more proud of you. I know your daddy is looking down right now applauding your bravery."

"Thank you, Mom," Lauren said as she cried with her.

Kate was next in line. "I don't know what to say," she cried.

"I hope it didn't hurt your feelings," Lauren said.

"No, honey," Kate said. "It was incredible!"

"I agree," Lance interjected. "I believe your speech brought healing today for so many."

"I hope so," Lauren said. As she hugged Kate closely, she felt Kate's stomach.

"So what did you find out at the doctor?" Lauren asked anxiously. "Are we having a boy or a girl?"

"We?" Jake asked.

"Yes, we," Lauren sharply replied.

Lance and Kate glanced at each other, grinning ear to ear, and simultaneously replied, "Yes."

Confused, Lauren stared at them. Jake looked at his mom, Grace, for clarity. Grace winked at him. After a few seconds of silence, Lauren understood.

"Twins?" she asked.

Smiling, Kate replied, "Twins!"

"No way!" Jake said in disbelief.

Lauren took Kate in her arms. Tears began to flow once again among the close-knit group. As Lauren hugged Kate, a thought occurred to her. "Oh my goodness, Mrs. Kate! In eighteen years, I'll be attending your kids' graduation!"

Chapter 30

As I prepared to speak tonight, I thought back to the day of my incredible salvation. How appropriate. There, in that cemetery, I died to self. I can't explain the relief and strength I felt at the point of surrender. But getting there was a battle like no other: the voices... the resistance... It was impossible to fight with my own strength, and I did not yet have the Holy Spirit living within me; so the prayers that were going up were vital to my rescue. But the turning point in my release was the moment Lauren humbled herself and asked for my forgiveness. Humility and forgiveness are the keys to unleashing God's supernatural power in our lives.

A year had passed since the tragic events that turned this community upside-down. The third annual Youth Explosion was tonight. Lauren had outdone herself in getting the guests for the event. The opportunities she and Jake had been given to share their testimonies on big platforms over the past several months had given her incredible connections in the Christian world. While Lauren knew the night's lineup was sure to knock the crowd's socks off, she was confident their favorite would certainly be hometown boy Jake Adams.

The number in attendance tonight exceeded the number of the first two years combined. The air was electric as the Christian rock band energized the primarily teen audience, setting a joyful mood that permeated the room. It was a worship experience that seemed to have the potential to mimic Heaven.

As the worship came to a close, Dr. Sharp prepared to make his annual appearance in introducing the guest speaker.

Backstage, while the night transitioned from singing to speaking, Jake and Lauren waited with their parents. Dr. Sharp walked onstage to introduce Jake, who looked at Mitch and Grace. "Thank you, guys...for everything."

Grace hugged him. "Oh, son. We are so proud of you!"

"Yes, we are," Mitch reiterated, patting Jake on the arm.

"I'm proud of you, too, Dad. We've all come a long way."

"I told you there would be good to come from this...somehow," Grace reminded him.

Lauren interrupted. "OK, Jake, you're up next."

"Yes, ma'am," Jake replied. "Where do you want me?"

"Just follow me," Lauren said, leading the way.

Jake looked back at his parents. "She's so bossy," he whispered.

"I heard that!" Lauren exclaimed.

Mitch and Grace laughed, and Margaret laughed even harder.

"So now," Dr. Sharp announced enthusiastically, "please welcome Lee County Academy's very own...Jake Adams!"

"Jake, that's your cue! Go, go, go!" Lauren ordered.

Jake walked onstage, dressed in khaki cargo shorts and a polo-style shirt. His new titanium prostheses shone as they caught the spotlights. The audience rose to its feet. While the sea of people cheered and chanted, Jake scanned over them. So many special faces stood out among the crowd. On the front row stood Dr. King, Nurse Velle, and Jake's personal nurse and dear friend, Joe Bill. And to his right, Coach Scott and his teammates Marcus, Drew and Hamm. On the row in front sat Eric, with Morgan at his side. Jake was humbled and honored that these classmates came home from college for the weekend to be a part of tonight's epic event.

In another section were Lance and Kate Kelly, each holding a newborn, and sitting next to them were the officers from the sheriff's department – Sheriff Howell, Mayhew, Daniels, Juicy and Blambo.

Bright television lights and camera flashes from the local media caught Jake off guard. He was overwhelmed. He struggled through emotions and nerves to gather his thoughts and focus on what was on his heart. Although he had traveled the country the past few months sharing his testimony on large platforms, doing it in front of the home crowd was the most challenging.

Finally, the crowd quieted and settled in their seats. Lauren stood backstage with nerves jumping and joy trickling in her heart. The Lord had done an incredible thing in her. Her humility and obedience had brought her to a place she never thought she would get.

Jake began to speak.

"As most of you know, this time last year I sat in this gym at this very event, against my will, with my best friend, Ross Kelly. For me, it was my last opportunity to change my mind about a terrible decision I was about to make. Sadly, I walked away, taking my best friend with me. As most of you know, that night ended in tragedy and was followed by incomprehensible consequences. In a matter of moments, I lost my best friend, my legs, and my future in football that I had worked so hard for. But…in the end…I gained my soul."

The Altar Call

Hi...I'm Jake Adams. I'm so pumped that you've made your way to the end of this God-breathed book. I hope you have been blessed and inspired by our story. Although it is filled with incredible life lessons and admonishment, I know I would be remiss if I failed to clearly communicate the gospel of Jesus Christ to you. Although He is visible throughout this story, I want to share with you from my heart not only the fact that He is the only way to Heaven, but how much He loves you and desires to have a personal relationship with you. I pray that you will take my next words very seriously and to heart.

Thus far, this story has been Christian fiction, inspired by true events. My prayer for you, the reader, is that you have seen a clear picture of the person of Jesus Christ through the pages of this book. If you read this book and were confronted by the realization that you do not have a relationship with Jesus, then you have arrived at a divine appointment. You must choose whether you will believe and put your trust in Jesus Christ – or not. The good news...you get to decide.

God's word says that today is the day of salvation. I pray that you will not do as Ross did in the story and reject the incredible gift being offered to you. You do not know if it will be your last opportunity. But if you have come to the point of belief after reading our story, and you desire to accept Jesus' free gift of salvation, Praise

God! All you need to do is tell Him. Not sure how? Then check this out…The next paragraph you are about to read is complete truth, and your willingness to believe it and surrender to it will assure you of an eternity in Heaven.

Please pray this prayer with me:

"Dear Jesus, I know that I am a sinner. I believe that You are the Son of the one true God. I believe that You were born of a virgin and lived a sinless life on this earth. I believe You were beaten beyond recognition, chose to die on a cruel cross for my sin, and were buried in a borrowed tomb. I believe You took the keys of Hell, death and the grave, that You rose again on the third day and are now seated on the right-hand side of God, waiting for Him to tell You when it's time for You to return for His children. Please forgive me of my sin. I accept Your free gift of salvation. I believe on Your holy name. I confess You as my Lord and Savior. Make me new, Jesus. I want to live for You."

If you prayed that prayer, my friend, you are a new creature in Christ! The old has gone and the new has come. Find a local Bible-believing church, and surround yourself with other believers who will help you grow in your walk with the Lord. If you so desire, contact us at HyperNike37@gmail.com, and we will be glad to help guide you in your new relationship with Christ. God bless you and keep you…in Jesus' name!

Armor of God –
has no covering for the Back
cause God does not expect us to
run. – Let go what lies behind –
and press forward.
The word of God is our weapon
Larry

CPSIA information can be obtained at www.ICGtesting.com
Printed in the USA
LVOW10s0111270816
502049LV00009B/21/P